A PEOPLE AND A NATION

FOURTH EDITION

VOLUME II: SINCE 1865

STUDY GUIDE

A People and A Nation

Fourth Edition
Volume II: Since 1865

STUDY GUIDE

George C. Warren
Central Piedmont Community College

Cynthia L. Ricketson
Central Piedmont Community College

Mary Beth Norton
Cornell University

David M. Katzman
University of Kansas

Paul D. Escott
Wake Forest University

Howard P. Chudacoff
Brown University

Thomas G. Paterson
University of Connecticut

William M. Tuttle, Jr.
University of Kansas

HOUGHTON MIFFLIN COMPANY BOSTON TORONTO
GENEVA, ILLINOIS PALO ALTO PRINCETON, NEW JERSEY

Copyright © 1994 by Houghton Mifflin Company. All rights reserved.

No part of this work may be reproduced or transmitted in any form or by any means, electronic or mechanical, including photocopying and recording, or by any information storage or retrieval system without the prior written permission of Houghton Mifflin Company unless such copying is expressly permitted by federal copyright law. Address inquiries to College Permissions, Houghton Mifflin Company, 222 Berkeley Street, Boston, MA 02116-3764.

Printed in the U.S.A.

ISBN: 0-395-67821-8

123456789-BW-97 96 95 94 93

Contents

To the Student		vii
To the Instructor		ix
Introduction: Taking the Mystery Out of Becoming "Good" at History		xi
16	Reconstruction: A Partial Revolution, 1865–1877	1
17	The Transformation of the West and South, 1877–1892	28
18	The Machine Age, 1877–1920	50
19	The Vitality and Turmoil of Urban Life, 1877–1920	83
20	Gilded Age Politics, 1877–1900	105
21	The Progressive Era, 1895–1920	127
22	The Quest for Empire, 1865–1914	153
23	Americans at War, 1914–1920	177
24	The New Era of the 1920s	200
25	The Great Depression and the New Deal, 1929–1941	222
26	Foreign Relations in a Broken World, 1920–1941	251
27	The Second World War at Home and Abroad, 1941–1945	274
28	Cold War Politics, McCarthyism, and Civil Rights, 1945–1961	297
29	The Cold War Era, 1945–1991	322
30	American Society During the Postwar Boom, 1945–1970	365
31	Contesting Nationalism and Revolution: The Third World and the Vietnam War, 1945–1989	382
32	Reform and Conflict: A Turbulent Era, 1961–1974	412
33	A Turn to the Right, 1974–1989	443
34	A New Century Beckons: America and the World in the 1990s	469
Answers		489
Duplicate Maps		561

To the Student

This study guide will help you master the themes and information in the second volume of *A People and a Nation*. It won't give you a short cut—there are no shortcuts—but it will give you direction and strategy, and if you use it conscientiously you will do well in your history course.

To get the most benefit from your study guide, you should read the introduction entitled "Taking the Mystery Out of Becoming 'Good' at History" before you do anything else. The introduction explains some of the ways of thinking about people and events that are particularly useful to history students, and it reviews the basics of good study habits applicable to a reading and writing course like history. Of course, it also tells you about how the book is arranged and what the standard chapter sections are for. You should read it carefully even before the course gets under way and you begin reading the first chapter of the textbook.

Once you get into an individual chapter in the study guide, you should do all the exercises and do them in order. It may be tempting to skip to the multiple-choice questions before you do the more time-consuming exercises or to omit the vocabulary exercise altogether. Don't yield to temptations. The less time-consuming exercises like the multiple-choice questions test the effectiveness of the work you have done on the more time-consuming exercises, such as the "Identification and Significance" and "Evaluating and Using Information" sections.

Remember as you use this book that it is working with the material that will make you understand and remember ideas and evidence. To do well requires a lot of hard work, but the right kind of hard work will make you do well. This study guide directs you toward the right kind of hard work.

To the Instructor

Looking over other study guides with all their fill-in-the-blanks, true-falses, and multiple-choices may have made you feel as though you were rifling through the files of some sorority or fraternity house on campus. But that's not how you are going to feel if you look closely at this one.

This study guide puts the objective question in its place. It does offer plenty of multiple-choice practice questions, but it places them near the ends of chapters where students can use them as culminating quizzes to find out how much they have learned. The multiple-choice section follows a series of exercises that have led students through the kind of active, mind-stretching studying you know they have to do to master the material. The answers to the multiple-choice questions in this book (at the back) are instructive, too—they explain why the right answers are right and the wrong answers are wrong. This same kind of approach to the answers section is seen in the instructive answer to the "Evaluating and Using Information" exercise for each of the first three chapters. Students are given a partial answer that helps them see whether they are on the right track without simply providing a whole essay written out for them to memorize.

And there's more.

Instead of the skeletal outline of each chapter that you see elsewhere, in this study guide you will see "Thematic Guides"—overviews in essay form presenting the major themes of the chapter in the textbook. These Thematic Guides help students see the proverbial forest and distinguish the leaves from the trees.

You will also find exercises that help students to work with and work through the material in the textbook. The key word is *work*. Look at some of the "Identification and Significance," "Organizing Information," and "Evaluating and Using Information" exercises, for example. These call upon the student to collect and synthesize information, to organize it, and to write out answers to potential essay questions using the information they have collected.

The almost all-new "Evaluating and Using Information" exercises tackle the problem of getting students, especially freshmen, to understand what's expected of them on essay tests, what your injunction to "be concrete and specific" means. In the first several chapters, these exercises lead students through the process of creating working drafts of answers to very broad essay questions. In later chapters, the "Evaluating and Using Information" exercises offer students the kind of essay questions that will force them to cover a lot of useful ground and some help in organizing information they collect, but for the most part by then they are expected to have learned to determine the kind of information they need and how to collect it.

This study guide should help both you and your students. The exercises should awaken a lot of your students to the depth of information mastery that you expect. For many students those expectations come as a shock, and perhaps the study guide will help them to see that you are not alone in holding out such lofty expectations. In addition, if you are involved in a writing-across-the-curriculum movement, in developing a writing-intensive course on your campus, or in the renewed interest across the nation in helping students develop their critical thinking skills, you may get some ideas or even assignments from these pages.

Introduction
Taking the Mystery Out of Becoming "Good" at History

A funny short story set hundreds of years after a late twentieth-century nuclear war nearly wiped out humanity describes archeologists excitedly explaining some highly polished ceramic and metallic relics from a religious shrine they have just discovered. As they describe the holy water receptacles and the fascinating devices for collecting coins for the gods, just what they have found suddenly becomes clear to the reader: a pay toilet in New York City.

For history students, the moral of this story is that it is not just collecting some facts that is important. It's what you do with the facts that counts. History uses clues or facts to explain or interpret a society's events, personalities, and places; to explain why a society is as it is, why its events happened as they happened, and why its people decided as they decided and acted as they acted. But, to come up with wise interpretations, history students have to make sure both that they have collected enough useful information and that they do not let their or others' blind spots cause them to go astray.

Some Factors a "Good" History Student Takes into Account

Among the most common causes of the kinds of blind spots that can get people off track are frames of reference, socialization, and, as *Star Trek*'s Mr. Spock would say, "insufficient data."

Frames of Reference

A real understanding of history will enable us to appreciate the past and apply what we learn to the problems we face today. But it will come only to those of us who can take people's *frames of reference* and *socialization* into account in judging their attitudes and behavior. Frames of reference and socialization are the emotional software that virtually forces people to think, feel, act, and react in particular, sometimes irrational, ways until they are somehow reprogrammed. Frames of reference and socialization are the input; the historical events are the output.

You can think of frames of reference as constantly growing "encyclopedias" that people carry around in their heads, encyclopedias in which all their personal impressions and experiences have been and are being recorded. People refer constantly to these "encyclopedias" to make sense of what happens around them.

If you have ever smelled a particular aroma and immediately experienced a flood of memories, you have felt the power of your own frame of reference. Cooking aromas or the smells of the street can release a nostalgic flood that represents your own unique way of relating to or interpreting the particular smell. Your nostalgia derives from your frame of reference, your unique experiences associated with the smell. Thus the way you perceive yourself and your surroundings comes from your frame of reference. Occupation, socio-economic status, sex, race, environment, political beliefs, religious beliefs, age, and nationality all go into people's frames of reference, which determine how they interpret what goes on in their world. The people we study in history are subjected to the force of their frames of reference and socialization just as we are, and their behavior must be interpreted in light of the influence these powerful forces exert. People's frames of reference, therefore, must be taken into account.

Socialization

A major part of people's frames of reference comes to them through *socialization,* the sum-total of all the teaching done by the members of a society, in whatever way, to make sure its culture survives. In any culture youngsters are taught to believe that some ideas are right and others wrong, some proper and others improper. That is socialization. You can see its results in the confrontation between the western Native Americans, who were socialized to see their relationship with nature as spiritual and sacred, and the white settlers, who, in viewing the West's abundance of minerals, timber, and oil, saw opportunities to exploit nature for monetary gain. Differences in the two peoples' belief systems gave them different frames of reference.

Just as the attitudes and behaviors of the individuals who people the pages of history books like *A People and a Nation* result from input in the form of frames of reference and socialization, history books themselves result from input. What you see in your history textbook is the output produced by the analysis of millions of bits of raw data (or *primary sources*) collected over many years by thousands of people. Often writers of a history textbook study the data and analyses of earlier historians and accept their interpretations. But when they think the earlier interpretations are erroneous, or when primary sources become available to them that were not available to earlier historians, they provide their own original interpretations or modifications of earlier interpretations. Always, though, primary sources are the raw material of history.

The Kind and Nature of Sources

Primary sources may be contradictory or incomplete or vague. Many primary sources are simply traces of the past, mere clues or hints that historians have to analyze to make sense of them. People in the past left the same kinds of clues that you leave as you go through your daily activities. If you carried around some carbon paper between the pages of a notepad for a few days, traces of your handling would remain on the sheets you did not use. People from the past have left similar traces, consciously or unconsciously in the form of footprints or written documents or farm implements or musical compositions. To the historian, these are like eyewitness accounts; but just as the eyewitnesses of this morning's accident do, historic eyewitnesses give conflicting accounts of what took place. Contradictory and conflicting facts make interpreting events difficult, and once historians start straightening out and interpreting the jumble of facts they have before them, they inevitably give one fact more weight than another. That is when their own socialization and frames of reference begin influencing the output.

Clearly, then, if we are to understand historical events and derive meaning from them, we must recognize the importance of the kind and amount of information with which we are working, and we must attempt to be as objective as possible. We must try to prevent the biases and prejudices that emanate from our own frames of reference and socialization from blinding us to those limitations that people of earlier times and other places had imposed upon themselves by their own frames of reference and socialization.

Making Interpretations Acceptable to Others

As long as you are a student rather than a professional historian, it is on tests that you will be presenting most of your interpretations of historical information. For your interpretations to be accepted as valid, you will have to show that they are based on solid information that you have studied and understood.

© 1994 Houghton Mifflin Company. All rights reserved.

Your explanations of how you came up with or derived your interpretations must have two qualities of effective composition: concreteness and specificity.

The Need for Concreteness

The real building blocks of the kind of interpretation that lies at the heart of history as an academic discipline are *facts*. Historians and history students must have something to interpret, and that something is a body of historical facts. So, as a history student who is expected to develop an ability to analyze and interpret data, your starting point is to master the facts themselves, facts that can be used to make an interpretation concrete and specific.

A *fact* is a bit of information that is perceived by the physical senses. It is facts that make an effective, concrete answer to an essay question. Facts are seen, heard, felt, tasted, or smelled. Facts used by history students are often actions and sounds, including the act of speaking and the sounds of speech; measurable characteristics, including dimensions, weights, distances, costs, counts; and the results of experimentation, including the raw data from polling. A fact is verifiable, confirmable either by qualified witnesses or, in the case of scientific experimentation or polling, by repetition ending in the same results. The information that the *Mayflower* landed at Plymouth could have been verified by any Indian who was around to meet the pilgrims at the shore or by any Pilgrim who climbed off the ship. The truth or falsehood of the information could have been established by the visual perception of those present.

Once perceivable, a bit of information is a fact; once perceived it is a known fact that can be reported as fact over and over again—handed down, for example, from an eyewitness to a historian and then handed on to other historians. And that brings up the problem of reliability.

To decide whether a bit of information that you have gotten second- or third-hand is a fact, you have to consider its source. If the witnesses are incapable of the kind of perceiving called for or if they are dishonest, the information they call fact may not be fact, and you will need other witnesses or other forms of corroboration. Witnesses or reporters also can color facts through their interpretations and wording. Like lying, coloring does not really change facts, but it can certainly blur them. For example, if you and your classmates are present when your history teacher comes in the classroom and crosses from the door to the lectern, everyone in the room can perceive the movement, but some will call it *striding*, some *ambling*, some *sidling*, and some *walking*. The only thing on which you will all agree is that movement has occurred. The movement is measurable. Your phrasing will affect how the fact is interpreted, but it does not affect the fact itself. The fact is the movement, not the style of movement.

The Need for Specificity

Facts are important to you as a student of history for at least two reasons. First, they are the material that you analyze to arrive at an interpretation. Second, they are essential ingredients in your presentation of the interpretation to others. The validity of your interpretation is going to be convincing only to the degree that it is perceived as having been derived logically from facts. That means that you, the interpreter, must cite the facts on which the interpretation is based (unless you are a widely known and established authority in the field). If you cite enough facts to make your interpretations clear and convincing, you have been "concrete." However, concreteness is not enough. To be convincing, you must also be specific. "A Hershey bar" is specific; "candy" is not. The difference between "An amendment to the Constitution passed about this time contained the reasons a state could use to keep a person from voting" and "The Fifteenth Amendment, passed in 1870, said no state could keep a person from voting solely because he was of a particular race, he was of a particular color, or he was at one time a slave" is the degree of specificity. Usually, the more specific evidence is, the better it is. Therefore, be specific.

The Need to Create Logical Ideas Out of the Facts

Historians' and history students' interpretations are not factual, but they are arguable assertions or interpretative conclusions based on facts. They are what are called *inferences*. When you look at a series of photographs of someone in a magazine and conclude that in the first picture the individual is angry, in the second sad, and in the third embarrassed, you are making inferences. Using clues or facts found in the pictures—facts such as the contortions of facial muscles, for example—you infer what the individual's emotional state is. *Inferences,* then, are ideas *created* from facts and must account for all the available facts on the topic.

An historian's total or final interpretation is an inference based on several narrow inferences. Facts are the building blocks of narrow inferences, and narrow inferences are the building blocks of a total interpretation, which is simply a broad inference.

An inference is not the same thing as an opinion. An inference can be thought of as a kind of educated guess—educated because it is clearly based on and derived from facts. An *opinion,* which is just as likely to be an uneducated guess as it is to be an educated guess, is a strong belief or conviction that may or may not be based on the facts. The person who offers a "mere" opinion simply does not cite the evidence that makes the basis of the opinion clear. On the other hand, a person who presents an inference is not expressing a "mere opinion."

Speculation is still another matter. A speculation is a cross between an opinion and an inference. It is a guess about the future, or about a matter we can explain only with guesses, either because we have inherited a shortage of facts or because the issue is such that facts alone cannot provide a clear-cut answer. Chapter 16 of your textbook, for example, offers the speculation that President Johnson's vanity and desire to be accepted as a political insider may explain why he pardoned large numbers of Confederate leaders early in the Reconstruction period.

Key to your success as a history student is your willingness to interpret, along with your willingness to master the facts on which to base your interpretations. It will be important not only in the way you read your history book and listen in class, but also in the way you share your thoughts with others and evaluate the thinking that others share with you. As you develop your interpretative approach to history, you will become more critical of your own ideas and learn to anticipate other people's objections to your ideas or to the way you support them. Your anticipation of possible objections will force you into refining both your thinking and your interpretations.

How to Study to Gain the Information Needed

To master the facts you will need to develop convincing interpretations of historical data, and you must study effectively. To study effectively, you have to interact deeply with the important components of the course—the textbook, the lectures, the students, and the professor. Merely attending class is not enough. Passively reading just to get to the end of each chapter is not enough. Answering questions only when you are directly asked to is not enough.

Previewing the Text

The component of your history course with which you will have to deal most independently is your textbook. Before you do anything else, you should get a feel for the course by previewing your text. To familiarize yourself with the textbook, you need to open it and:

1. Read the title of the text and ask what it says about the material inside. Doesn't the title *A People and a Nation* tell you that the book presents a social-cultural as well as a political history of the United States?
2. Read the preface to find out what the authors' purpose and approach are.

© 1994 Houghton Mifflin Company. All rights reserved.

3. Read the biographical data about the authors to see how much authority they have and what their special interests and areas of expertise are.
4. Read the table of contents to see where the course is going to take you; compare the dates given in the titles of chapters in your book with those listed in the title of your course and determine which chapters your class will be covering.

Once you have previewed the text, you are ready to study your first chapter systematically, using both your textbook and your study guide.

Studying the Chapter Systematically

To use your textbook effectively, it is a good idea to adopt the "SQ3R" system of studying developed some forty years ago by F. P. Robinson and to utilize the learning aids and exercises in this study guide. Research confirms the effectiveness of the system's five processes: (1) Surveying, (2) Questioning, (3) Reading, (4) Reciting, and (5) Reviewing—SQ3R.

Surveying and Questioning. The first two steps in the system, surveying and questioning, are intimately linked. As you survey each chapter, jot down questions about the material in it. For that purpose, you need a reading notebook. Then, when you begin your close reading of the chapter, you will find that your reading is purposeful. You will be looking for answers to your questions.

The surveying process itself begins with your actively reading the chapter title, making sure you understand the meaning of each word. Consider the word *transformation* in the title of Chapter 17, "Transformation of the West and South, 1877–1892," for instance. It implies a major change, leading to the questions: What kinds of major changes occurred between 1877 and 1892 in the West and South? What were the consequences of those changes?

The surveying and questioning process also includes reading the headings and the chapter's introductory vignette as well as studying the pictures and diagrams and framing the questions that they suggest. The introductory vignette, which personalizes and illustrates themes covered in the chapter; headings, which provide a road map of the chapter, and the illustrations (pictures, maps, diagrams, tables) all suggest questions, questions that you should ask yourself and record in your reading notebook.

Special learning aids in this study guide will help you go through the surveying and questioning process. In the chapter in the Study Guide that corresponds to the chapter in your textbook you are studying, the list of Learning Objectives tells you what you are supposed to accomplish. Then, the Thematic Guide helps put the facts and ideas found in the textbook into perspective by pointing out the chapter's major themes. You can derive questions from the Learning Objectives just as you derive questions from the title, headings, vignette, and illustrations.

The Learning Objectives are useful in another way. If you get bogged down in the details and "lose your way," you can refer to the Learning Objectives to find out where what you are reading fits into the chapter's total picture.

The Thematic Guide is designed to help you in much the same way. Chapter themes and the details in the chapter are like a long row of coat hooks and the coats hanging from them. The themes give you "hooks" on which to hang the facts. Without those hooks, you might be buried under a pile of "coats." You can refer to the Thematic Guide for help in ordering the facts in an understandable and meaningful way. The Thematic Guide can help you see whether the material you are presently reading relates to one of the major themes of the chapter. To what theme does it relate? Is the material factual information supporting one of the chapter's themes? Is it a statement of one of those themes? Is it a subtopic or an offshoot of one of the major themes?

The Building Vocabulary section for each chapter is still another feature of this study guide that is particularly useful in the surveying and questioning steps of the SQ3R system. Each Building Vocabulary section lists words and terms whose meanings you really need in order to understand the chapter in your textbook. When you open your dictionary and look up any words on the list that are unfamiliar to you, jot down their definitions in the space provided in your Study Guide, and you will have all the definitions you'll need when you study the chapter. Gaps in your vocabulary will neither keep you from understanding what you are reading nor make you interrupt your reading to look up words that are new to you.

One learning aid in the Study Guide, the Finding the Main Idea exercise, appears only in its first chapter and offers you a special kind of help related to the survey process. It is a helpful bridge between surveying the chapter and actually beginning to read the material in the chapter. If you have ever had trouble figuring out what information is really important for you to get from your textbooks, doing the Finding the Main Idea exercise in the study guide's first chapter should help you solve the problem. It will help you study all of the chapters in *A People and a Nation* more efficiently. This exercise is closely related to the explanations of how to mark your text and find main ideas that come later in this introduction (pages xvii–xix) and to a simple but important technique you can use to survey each chapter in your textbook. This technique is simply to identify each of the chapter's segments—groups of usually between two and five consecutive paragraphs (although occasionally a single paragraph is a segment)—devoted to a single topic or idea. Just take a pencil and draw a line between the last paragraph of one segment and the first paragraph of the next segment. Then, when you begin "looking for the main ideas," you will be looking for the main ideas of these segments or series of paragraphs.

The number of activities involved in surveying the chapter should tell you just how important surveying is. Only after you have done all of them, which sounds more time consuming than it really is, are you ready to dive into the chapter itself.

Reading. The next step is to begin reading the body of the chapter and looking for answers to your questions. Two features of the study guide will help you with the reading part of SQ3R system: the Learning Objectives and Identification and Significance sections. However, three other features are also helpful: the Thematic Guide, Essay Questions, and, in some chapters, the Organizing Information sections.

As you begin this step in the SQ3R system, it is more important than ever to remember that the verb *to study* is an active verb. Staring at a textbook an arm's length away, counting pages as you mentally trudge to the last page of the chapter, flipping pages with the end of a pencil—none of that is active studying. Studying is successful and rewarding only when you actively, physically involve yourself in the material you are studying. That's why it is so important for you to read with a pen in your hand and to use it to mark your textbook (page xix), record questions and notes in a reading notebook, and write definitions and answers to exercises in the pages of your study guide. The act of doing these things, the physical act of writing, is what makes the verb *to study* an active verb.

When you actually begin your close reading of a chapter, you should read manageable blocks of material rather than reading straight through to the end of the chapter. If in your surveying of the chapter you have drawn lines dividing the chapter into its segments, then each segment is what constitutes a manageable block.

Read a block of material and stop. Analyze the material you have read in that block and draw a box around the main idea in each paragraph—unless the paragraph does no more than simply connect other paragraphs. (Such paragraphs, especially if they come at the very beginning or end of the block, often state the whole point of the block. You might want to draw a box around such statements and mark them with asterisks.) Once you have marked the main ideas, jot them down in the margin of the textbook or in your reading notebook. Then underline the supporting details and number them in the margin of the textbook. Figure 1 on page xviii shows a paragraph that has been marked in this way.

It is in this reading step that you should be on the lookout for information that you need to compose the responses to items in the Identification and Significance section in the Study Guide. Once you find the information you need to identify and indicate the significance of an item on the list, write out your response to the item in your own words. (Merely copying from the textbook won't do. Copying is a rote, no-thinking-required activity as any skilled typist will tell you who routinely types long documents without having any idea what they say.) As you read the material, pay close attention to the questions you should answer to identify the item and those you need to answer to explain the item's significance. For some items, the significance section will be longer than it will be for others, because some items have more consequences (significance) than others.

Relating what you are reading to the Learning Objectives listed in the Study Guide is still another important part of the reading step. If the material relates to Learning Objective 1, write in the textbook margin "OBJ. 1." That will help you find specific material later in your studying process.

Reciting. The reciting part of studying should be both mental and physical. After you find the answer to a question, STOP. Look away from your book and recite both the question and the answer to yourself. It is best to keep working on formulating the answer until you can do it without looking at the text. You can do the same thing physically by putting your answer in writing. After you can recite it mentally, then write the question and compose your answer to it without looking at the text. If your answers are long—several pages or more—you should narrow them to keep your work manageable and the learning in bite-sized pieces.

Many of the Evaluating and Using Information exercises in this study guide will help you with the reciting step. Some of these exercises lead you through the process of gathering information from scattered parts of chapters and using the information to compose working drafts for responses to essay questions. Others simply call upon you to go through the gathering and composing process on your own. They all give you practice in using information from the textbook to create your own ideas about historical events, personalities, and concepts.

Reviewing. In the last stage of the SQ3R method, you review. Each day, before you begin the process of studying and learning new material, review the material you have studied and learned to that point. Go back and recite answers to questions listed in your reading notebook; go over your underlining and reading notes, and review the Identification and Significance items to make sure you remember major ideas and main supporting details. The Ideas and Details section and the Essay Questions section at the end of each chapter of the study guide are also useful as part of the review process.

Improving Your Reading and Recall

No matter how systematically you work, for your studying to pay off in a history course, you have to read effectively and develop techniques that will help you remember what you read. Many students find that once they learn to pick out main ideas, to insert simple and clearly written reminders in their textbook as they read, and to use outlining or other, less formal forms of note taking, the SQ3R method is a sure path to academic success. Why not adopt some of these techniques yourself?

Finding Main Ideas

Understanding some basic kinds of writing that you are likely to encounter will help you when you set about the task of separating main ideas and then finding the inferences and factual details that support them. Such understanding will also help you to see relationships among ideas and between a piece of evidence and the idea it supports. And having a strong sense of how all the information and ideas relate to one another is a tremendous help in remembering information. Therefore, let's stop and consider these basic kinds of writing.

Virtually all of the paragraphs that you encounter in a book like *A People and a Nation* fall into two categories: *developmental paragraphs* that announce ideas and then both clarify those ideas and provide evidence to support them; and *functional paragraphs* that introduce or conclude sections of chapters or shift the focus from one section or idea to another.

© 1994 Houghton Mifflin Company. All rights reserved.

Each *developmental paragraph* presents one central idea and supports it either with clarifying information, such as details, definitions, and sometimes "expert" testimony, too. These paragraphs can be arranged inductively—with listed evidence followed by an interpretation of the evidence—or deductively—with the interpretive statement followed by the list of evidence. *Functional paragraphs* merely announce ideas and shifts of focus. They offer no support themselves.

What you look for when you seek main ideas may be the main idea of a single, self-contained paragraph, but it could be the one main idea of a whole group or block of paragraphs, called a *paragraph series*. Ideally, a paragraph series is introduced by a functional paragraph that announces the central idea of the whole series, very much as the introductions to most essays do. Ideally, too, another functional paragraph, a transitional-concluding paragraph, will appear at the end of the series. The appearance of functional paragraphs, then, should help you identify paragraph series, which are important, bite-sized segments of the chapter. And you look for the main ideas of those bite-sized pieces. Knowledge of the two basic patterns, inductive and deductive, will tell you to expect the main idea to appear near the beginning or at the end of the paragraph or paragraph series.

Because the difference between a developmental paragraph and a developmental paragraph series is primarily a matter of scale, the procedure for determining their main ideas is pretty much the same. To see how the procedure works out in practice, take a look at Figure 1 below. It shows a paragraph reprinted from Chapter 1 of the textbook that has been marked as a student might have marked it.

The passage illustrates a particular and common problem in identifying main ideas; nowhere in this passage is there a single sentence that states its main idea. Look at the opening sentence, which calls the sharecropping system "a desirable compromise"; it has the kind of authoritative ring you might associate with a clear statement of a main idea. But then look at the fourth sentence. It calls that same system "a disaster, both for blacks and for the South as a whole." Because the main idea of any passage is the sum of *all* of its supporting ideas and details, the main idea of this passage must cover both the idea that sharecropping at first appeared desirable and the idea that sharecropping turned out to be a disaster. But how do we combine two such contradictory ideas? Which is more important? Notice that the first three sentences express and explain Sub-point 1 and the remaining four sentences express and explain Sub-point 2. Because the concluding part of any passage is its position of emphasis, and because a bit more space is devoted to the disaster idea, we can assume that the disastrousness of sharecropping should be given more weight than its original potential benefits. The main idea, then, is: **Sharecropping, a system that promised to benefit both whites and blacks, turned out to be disastrous.**

Marking Your Text

As our earlier discussion of the reading step in the SQ3R system suggests, marking the text is a very useful technique that makes it easier to remember what you have read. Not only does this help you concentrate on what you are reading, but it will also help you take notes on your reading. You should underline important concepts and ideas and write relevant, concise notes in the margin.

To emphasize the main idea of each paragraph or paragraph series, you can, for example, draw a box around it if the author has succinctly stated it for you. If the author takes more than one sentence to express the main idea or merely implies it, you can write it in your own words in the margin. And, finally, you can underline the supporting details in the passage and number them in the margin. What you want to avoid is over-marking or under-marking. Whether you underline just about everything or do virtually no marking at all, nothing is going to stand out when you review your chapter or look through it for specific information you need.

Figure 1 on page xviii illustrates this simple system as it might be applied to the paragraph we discussed in the previous section. Notice that in Figure 1, the student has written the main idea in the margin, has underlined and numbered the two sub-points, and has listed and labeled (1a, 1b and 2a, 2b) the supporting details of the sub-points.

Introduction   **xix**

Outlining Chapters

With your reading done and passages marked, you can outline the chapter to help yourself separate the important from the unimportant and to produce a guide for your practice recitations before examinations. Whether you choose to outline the whole chapter probably should depend on how effectively you can outline. You may prefer to outline key subsections of the chapter instead of outlining the whole chapter or, if you really just cannot outline very well, to replace outlining with other forms of note-taking.

The actual outlining process is one of dividing and redividing. You start with a "whole," and you divide it. The "whole" is the overall point of the chapter, what all the evidence supports and adds up to. Once you have read and marked the whole chapter—and, as the logic of outlining makes clear, you absolutely must do that first—you see that what you start out with is a whole idea. You have to think of that idea as a whole "thing" just as you would think of a pie as a whole thing. You then find the largest

---

| The sharecropping system originated as a desirable compromise. It eased landowners' problems with cash and credit; blacks accepted it because it gave them more freedom from daily supervision. Instead of working under a white overseer as in slavery, they farmed a plot of land on their own in family groups. But sharecropping later proved to be a disaster, both for blacks and for the South as a whole. When Democrats returned to power, they often changed the lien laws to favor landlords; when crop prices were low, landlords received their payment first, even if there was no money left over for the laborer. And in a discriminatory society whites had many opportunities to cheat sharecroppers. Owners and merchants frequently underpaid or overcharged blacks, and manipulated records so that the sharecropper remained always in debt. | Sharecropping, a system that promised to benefit both blacks and whites, turned out to be disastrous.
1. It was expected to have two benefits.
  1a. It would cut whites' financing problems.
  1b. It would free blacks from white supervision.
2. It actually led to disastrous consequences.
  2a. When crop prices were low, lien laws protecting landlords left blacks with no money to buy necessities.
  2b. It opened ways for merchants and landlords to cheat black laborers. |

Figure 1.   Passage in Text Marked by Student

© 1994 Houghton Mifflin Company. All rights reserved.

parts into which you can cut your pie, usually between two and five parts. No matter how many of these largest subtopics you recognize, each is now to be considered an absolutely new, whole subject. You divide the first into what you recognize as its largest components and then do the same with the second and the others until you have subdivided all of your largest subtopics into their largest subtopics. You then go back and treat each of the sub-subtopics as a divisible whole subject.

How long you keep up the dividing and subdividing process depends on what you're using the outline for. If you are merely trying to identify the main themes to help you in both in-class and out-of-class notetaking, then the process does not go much past three levels of division. If you are reducing all of your out-of-class notes to outline form and inserting information from your class notes, then you need a very thorough outline, one whose lowest-rank headings either cannot be subdivided or are enough to trigger your memory of the unnamed subdivisions. Outlines whose headings are too broad are not very helpful, but forcing unnecessary specificity into an outline wastes precious time.

It's a good idea to follow conventional outlining style in most particulars. Good headings are specific and substantive headings. They reflect the subject matter clearly and trigger recall of details. That rules out useless status headings (*Introduction, Body,* and *Conclusion*), which indicate the locations of information rather than the information itself. Good outline design includes a number-letter heading designator system and an indention system that suggest the rank and relative importance of the headings. The conventional system that you can find illustrated in almost any freshman English composition handbook is helpful, but an outline's format should never take on more importance than its content possesses.

Anticipating and Preparing for Tests

Ideally, of course, you go to all this trouble because you want to learn about the history of the United States so that you can become a more cultured person and a better citizen or observer of American society and politics. But you probably are also interested in doing well in your American history course, because how well you are deemed to have succeeded in it will become a part of your academic record. This second interest explains your desire to do well on history tests this term. How well you do on your tests will depend on how well you anticipate questions and how well you prepare yourself to answer the questions you anticipate.

Guessing What's Going to Be Asked

Obviously you can figure out some of the questions you will have to be able to answer simply by doing the exercises in this study guide. But you will want to enlarge that list of possibilities with some suggestions of your own based on your class notes, on your supplementary reading assignments, and on your familiarity with your instructor's emphases. One important way you can come up with potential essay questions is to find subject matter in your class and textbook notes that suits some of the writing styles most commonly called for on essay tests.

Questions calling for answers written in several particular writing styles crop up on almost all essay tests. Therefore, thinking up questions that call for answers written in these styles pays off most of the time. As you are going to see, the process of developing questions to suit the particular styles is illustrated in several of the "Evaluating and Using Information" exercises in this study guide. Among the most commonly used types of questions are ones calling for exemplification, comparison, contrast, definition, causal analysis, and classification. We can add to this list a type almost peculiar to history courses, the analytical narration (or "trace the development of") question. In the exemplification type, you are to show that you can back up one of your opinions by citing examples; in the comparison type, that you can show how two or more persons, events, or concepts resemble each other; in the contrast type, that you can show how two or more persons, events, or concepts differ from each other; in the definition type, that you can explain what something is or means or who someone is; in the causal

© 1994 Houghton Mifflin Company. All rights reserved.

analysis type, that you can explain the causes or the effects of something; in the classification type, that you can identify the types or kinds of something; and, in the analytical narration type, that you can trace the development of something by citing and explaining the key changes it has gone through. To anticipate questions, you simply go through all of your notes and find subject matter that suits any of the particular writing styles. You might find as many as twenty or twenty-five potential matches. When you find a match, you state the question that arises from it. From the resulting list of questions, cull the most likely candidates, trying to create a set of questions that covers all of the material the test is to cover and providing the best style-to-subject matter matches you can produce.

Preparing Answers to Essay Questions

Once you have your list of potential essay questions, it is time to plan your answers to those questions. That's right: actual answers to the questions you have produced. Some of the early Evaluating and Using Information exercises in this study guide lead you step-by-step through the whole process.

Think of it as taking an open-book, take-home test. You pore through your notes, your textbook, and your study guide to find all the relevant examples and other evidence to which you have been exposed. For each of your questions, you frame a basic one-sentence response based on the sum of the evidence you collect. You then outline the material that supports your one-sentence answer or actually write out your whole answer in the form of the working draft of an essay. The one-sentence answer is the thesis of your response. The body of your response is the written-out evidence that you have gathered from the chapter and from your class notes and have now organized. Such gathering, synthesizing, and organizing is, of course, exactly what you are asked to do in many of the Organizing Information exercises as well as in some of the Evaluating and Using Information exercises in this study guide. Be warned, though: you cannot expect to be able to write out such a full answer under the time and psychological pressure of the testing situation. Such pressure will end up forcing you to select what you can hope is the best evidence from all the evidence you collected. What you really want to happen is what usually does happen. In putting together an answer, you bring together related but previously scattered material and thus make it more meaningful and more memorable.

A Final Bit of Encouragement

So you see, becoming good at history isn't such a mysterious process after all. Yes, it takes hard work, but hard work does pay off. All these techniques at which we've been looking—from adopting an interpretative approach to history to marking passages in the textbook, from evaluating information to outlining, from anticipating test questions to writing out mock answers to the questions anticipated—have helped generations of young people become more interested in and knowledgeable about America's history and, yes, better history students. But, if you think that will never happen to you, here's one more technique for you: find your own reason for being interested, not some reason your textbook's authors give you or your parents give you or your history professor gives you, but a personal reason of your own. Once you want to learn, you will learn, and your success as a history student will rise dramatically. That's a promise!

© 1994 Houghton Mifflin Company. All rights reserved.

CHAPTER 16

Reconstruction: A Partial Revolution, 1865–1877

Learning Objectives

After you have studied Chapter 16 in your textbook and worked through this study guide chapter, you should be able to:

1. Discuss white northern attitudes toward blacks and black equality, and examine the impact of these attitudes on the Reconstruction process.
2. Explain the divergence between the provisions of President Johnson's Reconstruction plan and its actual operation.
3. Examine the clash between the executive and legislative branches of government over the issue of Reconstruction, and discuss the events and forces that affected the development of the congressional Reconstruction plans.
4. Cite the major provisions of the Fourteenth and Fifteenth Amendments; indicate the reasons for their passage by Congress; and explain the compromises embodied in each.
5. Cite the major provisions of the Military Reconstruction Act of 1867; indicate the reasons for its enactment by Congress; and explain why it diverged from the proposals of the Radical Republicans.
6. Discuss the political, social, and economic impact of the Reconstruction governments on southern society.
7. Examine and evaluate the means by which white southern Conservatives attempted to regain control in the South, and indicate the outcome of their efforts.
8. Examine and evaluate the Reconstruction experience for blacks.
9. Examine the events and forces that brought a weakening of the northern commitment to Reconstruction and an end to the Reconstruction era.

Thematic Guide

Reconstruction refers to the process by which the nation was rebuilt after the destruction caused by the Civil War. This rebuilding was social, political, and economic. Because there were no guidelines as to how it would be accomplished, questions and disagreements arose. Given such disagreements, as well as the emotional aftermath of four years of war and the force of individual personalities, Reconstruction proceeded by trial and error.

On the social question concerning the position of blacks within American society, events in the British Caribbean suggested that achieving black equality would require determination, commitment, and dedication by the white power structure. These characteristics were not evident in the prelude to Reconstruction played out on the Sea Islands. Instead, white paternalism and self-interest seemed paramount. In fact, it would become clear during the process of Reconstruction that Republican congressmen and their northern constituents had a limited view of equality. Although most believed in the concept of equality under the law, few believed in political, social, and economic equality.

When Congress reconvened in December 1865, it was faced with a presidential Reconstruction policy that not only allowed former Confederate leaders to regain power at the state and national levels but obviously abandoned the freedmen to hostile southern whites. Northern congressmen and the constituents they represented were unwilling to accept this outcome of the long, bitter struggle against a rebellious South. Believing that it had a constitutional right to play a role in the Reconstruction process, Congress acted. This action led to clashes with an intransigent President Johnson and to the passage of two congressional Reconstruction plans.

The first of these plans, the Fourteenth Amendment, evolved when the wrangling between President Johnson and Congress produced compromises among the conservative, moderate, and radical factions of the Republican party. Although Congress passed the Freedmen's Bureau bill and the Civil Rights Act of 1866 over the president's veto, there was concern that the Supreme Court would declare the basic provisions of the Civil Rights Act unconstitutional. Therefore, those provisions were incorporated into a constitutional amendment that was presented to the states for ratification in April 1866. The Fourteenth Amendment demonstrated that Congress wanted to guarantee equality under the law to the freedmen, but its provisions make it clear that the moderate and conservative Republicans who controlled Congress were not willing to accept the more progressive concept of equality advanced by the Radical Republicans.

When, at the urging of the president, every former Confederate state except Tennessee refused to ratify the Fourteenth Amendment, Congress passed its second Reconstruction plan—the Reconstruction Act of 1867. Although this act demonstrated some movement in the Radical direction by extending to blacks the right to vote in state elections, congressmen were still limited by the prejudices of the age. They labeled as extremist the suggestion that southern land be redistributed and so rejected the idea of giving blacks economic independence. They naively assumed that blacks would need only the ballot in their fight for a better life.

The same kinds of limitations worked within Reconstruction governments, preventing fundamental reform of southern society. Concurrently, southern Republicans adopted a policy that returned voting rights to former Confederates. These former Confederates, or Conservatives, ultimately led a campaign designed to return political and economic power to their hands by discrediting the Reconstruction governments. Adopting tactics ranging from racist charges and intimidation to organized violence, the Conservatives were able to achieve their objectives, as events in Alamance and Caswell counties in North Carolina demonstrated.

As the failures of Reconstruction revealed themselves, blacks renewed their determination to struggle for survival and true equality within American society. On one level they placed faith in education and participation in the political process as means of attaining equality, but they also turned to family and religion for strength and support. Denied the possibility of owning land, they sought economic independence through new economic arrangements such as sharecropping. However, sharecropping ultimately "proved to be a disaster, both for blacks and for the South."

These setbacks indicated that northern commitment to equality had never been total. The federal government even began to retreat from partial commitment—a retreat made obvious by the policies of President Grant, by the gradual erosion of congressional resolve on Reconstruction issues, by the conservative decisions of the Supreme Court, and by the emergence of other issues that captured the minds of white Americans. Finally, with the resolution of the disputed Hayes–Tilden election in 1876, Reconstruction ended. The promise of equality for black Americans remained unfulfilled.

Building Vocabulary

Listed below are important words and terms that you need to know to get the most out of Chapter 16. They are listed in the order in which they occur in the chapter. After carefully looking through the list, refer to a dictionary and jot down the definition of words that you do not know or of which you are unsure.

intransigence

enfranchise

antipathy

repertoire

imminent

compensation

travail

venerated

tenaciously

tentative

amnesty

resilient

repudiate

vagrancy

servility

intransigent

titular

abridge

ambivalence

infuse

impasse

impeachment

indictment

suffrage

exhort

disfranchise

enmity

vindictive

futile

exemption

derisive

filch

hapless

ostracism

intimidation

reprisals

subjection

harassment

fiscal

philanthropy

odyssey

lien

vacillate

paramilitary

ominous

disparate

purport

polygamy

contraction

deference

acquiesce

emasculate

filibuster

exigencies

Identification and Significance

After studying Chapter 16 of *A People and a Nation,* you should be able to identify fully *and* explain the historical significance of each item listed below.

1. Identify each item in the space provided. Give an explanation or description of the item. Answer the questions *who, what, where,* and *when.*
2. Explain the historical significance of each item in the space provided. Establish the historical context in which the item exists. Establish the item as the result of or as the cause of other factors existing in the society under study. Answer this question: *what were the political, social, economic, and/or cultural consequences of this item?*

Robert Smalls

    Identification

    Significance

Wade Hampton

    Identification

    Significance

emancipation in the British Caribbean

    Identification

    Significance

the experience of freedmen in the Sea Islands

    Identification

    Significance

Lincoln's "10 percent" plan

    Identification

    Significance

the Wade-Davis Bill

    Identification

    Significance

Johnson's Reconstruction plan

    Identification

    Significance

the oaths of amnesty

    Identification

    Significance

the black codes

    Identification

    Significance

the legal suicide theory

    Identification

    Significance

Radical Republicans

    Identification

    Significance

the Freedmen's Bureau

    Identification

    Significance

the Civil Rights Act of 1866

    Identification

    Significance

the Memphis and New Orleans riots

    Identification

    Significance

the Fourteenth Amendment

    Identification

    Significance

Johnson's "swing around the circle"

    Identification

    Significance

the congressional elections of 1866

    Identification

    Significance

Thaddeus Stevens

    Identification

    Significance

the Reconstruction Act of 1867

    Identification

    Significance

the Tenure of Office Act

    Identification

    Significance

Johnson's impeachment trial

    Identification

    Significance

Chapter 16

the Fifteenth Amendment

    Identification

    Significance

the constitutional conventions in the former Confederate states

    Identification

    Significance

Republican governments in the former Confederate states

    Identification

    Significance

the southern Republican party

    Identification

    Significance

the southern Conservatives

    Identification

    Significance

public schools in the former Confederate states

    Identification

    Significance

the charge of "Negro rule"

> Identification

> Significance

carpetbagger

> Identification

> Significance

Republican tax policies in the former Confederate states

> Identification

> Significance

the Ku Klux Klan

> Identification

> Significance

Klan violence in Alamance and Caswell counties of North Carolina

> Identification

> Significance

Freedmen's Bureau schools

> Identification

> Significance

the founding of black colleges

    Identification

    Significance

Francis Cardozo, P. B. S. Pinchback, Blanche K. Bruce, and Hiram Revels

    Identification

    Significance

reunification of black families

    Identification

    Significance

the founding of black churches

    Identification

    Significance

the sharecropping system

    Identification

    Significance

cotton and the southern economy

    Identification

    Significance

the presidential election of 1868

    Identification

    Significance

Ulysses S. Grant

    Identification

    Significance

the Enforcement Acts and the anti-Klan law

    Identification

    Significance

the Liberal Republican revolt

    Identification

    Significance

the Amnesty Act

    Identification

    Significance

the Civil Rights Act of 1875

    Identification

    Significance

14 *Chapter 16*

the Panic of 1873

    Identification

    Significance

greenbacks vs. sound money

    Identification

    Significance

William H. Seward

    Identification

    Significance

Ex parte Milligan

    Identification

    Significance

Bradwell v. *Illinois*

    Identification

    Significance

the *Slaughter-House* cases

    Identification

    Significance

United States v. *Cruikshank*

    Identification

    Significance

United States v. *Reese*

    Identification

    Significance

grandfather clauses

    Identification

    Significance

the presidential election of 1876

    Identification

    Significance

the Exodusters

    Identification

    Significance

Evaluating And Using Information

Using the questions in each of the four **Evidence Sets** on pages 16–22 as your guide, collect the evidence from Chapter 16 of your textbook that relates to changes in voting rights from 1865–1877. Such evidence will help you to identify the causes of change, to identify the changes themselves and the people and governmental bodies affected by them, and to point out the short- and long-term results of those changes. It will also help you to evaluate the significance of one of the questions that dominated this period of history: who should have the right to vote?

At the end of each Evidence Set is a **Conclusion** section. Answer the questions in each Conclusion section by stating the significance of the pieces of evidence compiled in that Evidence Set.

At the end of the four evidence sets is a **Thesis Question.** Answer the Thesis Question by stating the significance of the conclusions reached at the end of the four Evidence Sets.

Finally, boil down what you have said to create a working draft for an essay that has the kind of specificity and concreteness that will make it suitable as a response to an essay examination question.

In writing your essay, some reordering of material is needed. Begin the whole essay with the thesis statement—your one-sentence answer to the Thesis Question, which is also your answer to the essay question. Use each Evidence Set and its conclusion as the basis for a single section or long paragraph of your essay. Use the conclusion statement to *begin* the section. The four sections are your concrete, specific support for your answer.

Notice that in doing this exercise, you have, in fact, collected and organized material that may be used to answer several different essay questions that might appear on a test on Chapter 16. You have also prepared yourself to respond correctly to dozens of objective questions.

Evidence Set 1

Upon his succession to the presidency in 1865, what led people to expect Andrew Johnson to pursue Reconstruction policies that would promote changes in voting and other political rights, and, by so doing, would attempt to alter the pre-Civil War distribution of political power in the South?

_____

_____

What feature of the "pardon" rules proposed by Andrew Johnson suggested that some southerners would be kept from regaining political power in the Reconstruction South? Looking at the pardon rules as a whole, what specific group in the South could be expected to lose power as a result of the rules?

_____

_____

According to President Johnson himself, what was his attitude toward African-American suffrage? What limitation did he put on how far he would be willing to go with this attitude?

_____

_____

What impact did President Johnson believe the Civil War had on the Union? How did this belief affect Johnson's interpretation of his power as president to issue pardons to Confederate officers and government leaders?

_____

_____

© 1994 Houghton Mifflin Company. All rights reserved.

Reconstruction: A Partial Revolution, 1865–1877

How long after taking office did Andrew Johnson control Reconstruction policy without having to deal with Congress?

_____

_____

How were the voting rights of southern whites and blacks affected by Andrew Johnson's rules about one's eligibility to serve as a delegate to a state constitutional convention and one's eligibility to vote in the election of delegates to such a convention?

_____

_____

How was the makeup of the southern state constitutional conventions affected by the way President Johnson actually used the presidential power he thought he had to grant pardons? How did his use of this power affect the choice of representatives the southern states sent to Congress?

_____

_____

How did Johnson react to Congress's effort to oppose the Black Codes and to extend the Freedman's Bureau?

_____

_____

How did Johnson react to efforts to gain passage of the Fourteenth Amendment?

_____

_____

What steps did President Johnson take regarding enforcement of provisions of the Reconstruction Act of 1867 affecting who in the South could or could not vote?

_____

_____

What step did presidential candidate Ulysses S. Grant take that indicated his attitude on the question of suffrage for African-Americans?

_____

_____

In what way did President Grant's approach to Reconstruction affect the power of the Enforcement Acts of 1870 and 1871 to stop groups such as the Ku Klux Klan from stifling citizens' rights to vote and to participate freely in politics? What was the impact of Grant's approach, and how was it felt?

_____

_____

© 1994 Houghton Mifflin Company. All rights reserved.

Conclusion for Evidence Set 1

In what direction did the attitudes and policies of Presidents Lincoln, Johnson, and Grant (in combination) push voting and related political rights and the protection of those rights between 1865 and 1877?

_____

_____

Evidence Set 2

In what ways was the Civil Rights Bill of 1866 designed to affect the legal position of freedmen? What was the fate of this bill and its key provisions?

_____

_____

In what way were the Fourteenth and Fifteenth Amendments (especially the Fourteenth) affect Congress' plan for Reconstruction?

_____

_____

What did the Fourteenth Amendment say about the responsibilities of states to protect the rights of citizens? the rights of blacks to vote? the rights of women to vote?

Protection of citizens' rights _____

_____

Voting rights of blacks _____

_____

Voting rights of women _____

_____

How did what the Fifteenth Amendment *did prohibit* and what it *did not prohibit* influence the development of voting and related political rights?

_____

_____

What the Fifteenth Amendment *did* prohibit _____

_____

What the Fifteenth Amendment *did not* prohibit _____

_____

What impact did Congress believe the Civil War had on the Union? How did this belief affect Congress's interpretation of its right to inject itself into policymaking regarding Reconstruction?

_____

_____

How did the Reconstruction Act of 1867 affect the voting rights of Confederate leaders and freedmen?

Confederate leaders _____

_____

Freedmen _____

_____

Which provisions of the two Enforcement Acts and the anti-Klan law passed by Congress in the early 1870s were designed to combat the Ku Klux Klan's use of violence to intimidate potential voters? How effective were these measures?

_____

_____

What effect did the Amnesty Act of 1872 have on the voting or related political rights of former Confederate officers and leaders?

_____

_____

Conclusion for Evidence Set 2

How did the actions of Congress affect voting and related political rights and the protection of those rights between 1865 and 1877?

_____

_____

Evidence Set 3

What effects on voting and related political rights did the Supreme Court's decisions in the *Slaughter-House Cases, United States* v. *Cruikshank,* and *United States* v. *Reese* have?

Slaughter-House Cases _____

_____

United States v. *Cruikshank* _____

_____

© 1994 Houghton Mifflin Company. All rights reserved.

United States v. *Reese* _____
_____

Conclusion for Evidence Set 3

What kind of influence did the Supreme Court of the Reconstruction period exert on the outcome of the issue of who should have the right to vote and related political rights?

_____
_____

Evidence Set 4

What do President Johnson's cabinet's reaction to the idea of granting voting rights to freedmen, to the degree of success Radical Republicans had in gaining support for African-American suffrage from outside their own ranks, to the voting rights of groups in the North other than native-born white males, and to the results of votes and other indicators of public opinion on black suffrage in the North suggest about the North's interest in expanding voting rights in the nation as a whole?

_____
_____

Johnson's cabinet's reaction to the idea of black suffrage

_____
_____

Radical Republicans' success in enlisting support for black suffrage

_____
_____

Votes on black suffrage in the North (1865)

_____
_____

Other indicators of public opinion in the North on black suffrage

_____
_____

Groups in the North besides blacks without voting rights

_____
_____

Reconstruction: A Partial Revolution, 1865–1877

In the period when President Johnson controlled Reconstruction, what happened concerning southern elections and appointments of office holders to influence Congress to take an active role in making Reconstruction policy? How?

_____

_____

How did the Fourteenth Amendment fare in the South when it was first presented by Congress?

_____

_____

What effects did the Fourteenth Amendment, passed because of the strong encouragement of Congress, have on the makeup of the state constitutional conventions across the South? What racial group dominated the state conventions?

_____

_____

How widespread was participation by freedmen in voting after the ratification of the Fourteenth Amendment? What kinds of leaders did the newly enfranchised blacks vote for?

_____

_____

After the state constitutional conventions revised the southern state constitutions and restructured southern state governments, how well represented were blacks in state legislatures, appointive offices, Congress, governorships, and other high elective offices?

_____

_____

What provisions made the new state constitutions more democratic than the constitutions they replaced? How did they change qualifications for voting? Which offices would now be filled through elections? How did the provisions affect women's rights?

Qualifications to vote _____

_____

Elective/appointive offices _____

_____

Women's rights _____

_____

© 1994 Houghton Mifflin Company. All rights reserved.

Chapter 16

How did the South's new republican governments approach the question of voting rights for former Confederate leaders?

What group of white voters began cooperating with black voters in the South during Reconstruction? What was the basis of the cooperation between the two groups?

How common was intimidation by the Ku Klux Klan and similar groups of black, scalawag, and carpet-bagger participants in political activities? How vigorously and consistently were the perpetrators prosecuted?

How significant was political corruption in the new, Republican-dominated governments of the South? Was it more significant in the South than in the nation as a whole?

Conclusion for Evidence Set 4

What lasting change in voting and related political rights and attitudes toward extending them emerged from the turmoil of the Reconstruction period?

Thesis (Whole Point)

How was the cause of making the United States more democratic through extension of voting and related political rights served between 1865 and 1877?

Essay

Working Draft for Response to an Essay Question

Respond to the question:

Discuss how and how well the cause of making the United States more democratic through extension of voting and related political rights was served between 1865 and 1877.

Ideas and Details

Objective 1

_____ 1. Which of the following conclusions may be drawn from the actions of northern states concerning blacks in 1864 and 1865?
   a. The federal government demonstrated more commitment to equal rights than northern state governments did.
   b. The Democratic party was more committed to the ideal of equality than the Republican party was.
   c. The participation of blacks in the Union war effort caused northerners to reject racist attitudes.
   d. The mixed racial attitudes of white northerners would make it difficult for blacks to gain equality.

Objectives 2 and 3

_____ 2. Congress questioned President Johnson's Reconstruction plan because
   a. it promised federal aid to help the South rebuild.
   b. in actual operation, it returned power to the prewar southern elite.
   c. the plan required repudiation of the Confederate war debt.
   d. it did not extend the vote to the yeoman class.

Objective 3

_____ 3. Which of the following is true of the black codes?
   a. They required the freedmen to pay "freedom dues" to their former masters.
   b. They extended the right to vote to property-owning blacks.
   c. They were an attempt to relegate blacks to a position of servitude.
   d. They extended to the freedmen equal protection under the law.

Objective 3

____ 4. Congress believed that it had a right to a voice in the Reconstruction process because the Constitution
   a. grants treaty-making powers to Congress.
   b. grants Congress the power to declare war.
   c. assigns Congress the duty of guaranteeing republican governments in the states.
   d. assigns Congress the responsibility of "providing for the general welfare."

Objective 3

____ 5. In order to develop a new Reconstruction program, conservative and moderate Republicans began to work with the Radical Republicans because
   a. events in the South convinced them that blacks should be given full political rights.
   b. the Radicals convinced them that black freedom depended on a redistribution of land in the South.
   c. President Johnson and the congressional Democrats refused to cooperate with them.
   d. the northern electorate clearly favored the goals of the Radical Republicans.

Objective 4

____ 6. The Fourteenth Amendment
   a. guaranteed blacks the right to vote.
   b. was strongly supported by President Johnson.
   c. extended civil and political rights to women.
   d. was the product of a compromise among the Republican factions in Congress.

Objective 5

____ 7. The Reconstruction Act of 1867
   a. required the southern states to ratify the Fourteenth Amendment.
   b. called for a redistribution of land in the South.
   c. guaranteed blacks the right to vote in federal elections.
   d. stipulated that the southern states would be "adjusted" back into the Union over a ten-year period.

Objective 3

____ 8. The Senate's failure to convict President Johnson of the charges brought against him
   a. enhanced Johnson's prestige and power.
   b. established that impeachment was not a political tool.
   c. is evidence that northern opinion toward Johnson and the South was softening.
   d. caused a serious rift between the House and Senate.

Objective 6

_____ 9. The new state constitutions of the former Confederate states
   a. eliminated property qualifications for voting.
   b. extended the right to vote to women.
   c. made public school attendance compulsory.
   d. made yearly reapportionment of legislative districts mandatory.

Objective 6

_____ 10. The decision of southern Republicans to restore the voting rights of former Confederates
   a. meant that southern Republicans had to gain white support or face defeat.
   b. led to the formation of a broad-based Republican party in the South.
   c. caused the freedmen to support the more liberal southern Democrats.
   d. was politically embarrassing to congressional Republicans.

Objectives 7 and 8

_____ 11. Blacks participating in Reconstruction governments
   a. had little interest in the political process.
   b. were subjected to a racist propaganda campaign against them undertaken by the white Conservatives.
   c. insisted on social equality for blacks.
   d. displayed a vindictive attitude toward their former masters.

Objective 7

_____ 12. Activities of the Ku Klux Klan in Alamance and Caswell counties in North Carolina
   a. were disorganized and sporadic.
   b. were organized by the impoverished classes in North Carolina society.
   c. were undertaken by the former elite for the purpose of regaining political power.
   d. had little success in areas where blacks and yeoman farmers allied.

Objective 8

_____ 13. In the final analysis, the Reconstruction governments of the South
   a. were able to alter the social structure of the South.
   b. effected a lasting alliance between blacks and whites of the yeoman class.
   c. gave blacks the means to achieve equality by giving them the right to vote.
   d. left blacks economically dependent on hostile whites.

© 1994 Houghton Mifflin Company. All rights reserved.

Objective 9

____ 14. In the *Slaughter-House* cases, the Supreme Court
   a. ruled that the Fourteenth Amendment did not guarantee the Bill of Rights against state action.
   b. protected a citizen of the United States against discrimination by an individual or a group.
   c. ruled that corporations were legal persons and were protected under the Fourteenth Amendment.
   d. ruled that national citizenship was more important than state citizenship.

Objective 9

____ 15. From the outcome of the 1876 presidential election, it is evident that the electorate
   a. supported an inflationary monetary policy.
   b. feared that the expansionist policies of Secretary of State Seward would lead to war.
   c. had lost interest in Reconstruction.
   d. rejected government aid to business interests.

Essay Questions

Objective 1

1. Explain how the history of emancipation in the British Caribbean foreshadowed the Reconstruction experience of African-Americans.

Objective 2

2. Discuss Johnson's Reconstruction plan, and explain its actual operation. How did Congress respond to the plan? Why?

Objectives 3, 4, and 5

3. Discuss the political, social, and economic views of the Radical Republicans, and examine the role they played in the development of Congress's plans for Reconstruction.

Objective 3

4. Examine the attitudes and events that led to the impeachment of President Andrew Johnson, and assess the outcome of his trial by the Senate.

Objective 6

5. Discuss the successes and failures of the Reconstruction governments in the South.

Objective 7

6. Discuss the goals of the Conservatives and the means they used to achieve those goals.

Map Exercise

1. Refer to the map on page 491 in the textbook. In the table below, list the eleven Confederate states, the date each was readmitted to the Union, the date Conservative rule was re-established in each, and the length of time the Reconstruction governments were in power in each.

Former Confederate State	Date Readmitted to Union	Date Conservative Rule Re-established	No. of Years Reconstruction Governments in Power

2. Why was Tennessee readmitted to the Union before passage of the Reconstruction Act of 1867?
3. What states were still under Reconstruction governments in 1876? What bearing did this have on the election of 1876? How was the problem resolved?

CHAPTER 17

The Transformation of the West and South, 1877–1892

Learning Objectives

After you have studied Chapter 17 in your textbook and worked through this study guide chapter, you should be able to:

1. Examine the impact of white settlers and of United States government policies on the life, culture, and economies of the western Indian tribes in the late nineteenth century, and discuss the varying responses of Indians to the pressures they experienced.
2. Discuss the characteristics of each of the frontier societies listed below, and explain the contributions of each to the economic, social, and cultural transformation of the West.
   a. The mineral, timber, and oil frontiers
   b. The ranching frontier
   c. The farming frontier
3. Discuss efforts in the West at land reclamation through irrigation; assess the role played by state and federal governments in these efforts; and explain the debate over water rights that accompanied reclamation efforts.
4. Examine the impact of the expansion of the railroad industry on the American economy, perceptions of time and space, standardization of time, technology, and business organization.
5. Examine and assess the role played by federal, state, and local governments in the expansion of the railroad industry.
6. Explain the responses of Plains' settlers to the living conditions and challenges they encountered, and discuss the impact of their experience on their lives.
7. Discuss the forces responsible for the transformation of American agriculture in the late nineteenth century, and explain the consequences of this agricultural revolution.
8. Discuss the various forces affecting the lives of southern farmers during the late nineteenth century, and explain the social, economic, and political impact of these forces.
9. Explain the social, economic, and political oppression of southern blacks during the late nineteenth century, and discuss the response of the Supreme Court to this oppression.
10. Discuss the emergence of new industries in the South, and assess their impact on southern society.

Thematic Guide

Chapter 17 begins a series of four chapters that analyze the transition of American society from an agrarian society to an urban, industrialized society. The expansion westward in the late nineteenth century closed the physical frontier that had been part of American society since its beginning. As in the past, American expansion was carried out at the expense of Indians. Americans were and are an ethnocentric people. They see their civilization, their society, and their value and belief systems as being better than those of other peoples. This ethnocentrism led Americans to believe that they had a right to expand and to impose their values and beliefs on the peoples and societies they encountered. It is this attitude that formed the basis of the failed Dawes Severalty Act.

As Americans sought opportunity in this vast western region, they discovered and developed the riches of the land, thus conquering the natural-resource frontier—a prerequisite for the subsequent development of an industrialized economy. Exploitation of the land and its resources for profit raised questions in several areas: (1) who owns the resources, private developers or the American people, (2) which takes precedence, the desire for progress and profit or the desire to protect the natural landscape, and (3) who has rights to the precious streams, rivers, and basins of the West—only those along their banks or all those who intend a beneficial use of river water.

The natural-resources frontiers, especially the mining and lumbering frontiers, produced personalities who enriched American folklore; but reality was far different from folk tales. Most westerners worked long hours as they attempted to provide basics for themselves and their families. Furthermore, although individual initiative was important in the development of the West, individuals usually gave way to corporate interests, which had the capital necessary to undertake the expensive extraction of minerals, timber, and oil. In addition, the federal government, as owner of the western lands, encouraged the development of the area by actively aiding individuals and corporations through measures such as the Timber and Stone Act and the Newlands Reclamation Act.

As frontiers of opportunity were conquered in the West, the expansion of regional and transcontinental railroad lines—made possible by generous government subsidies—helped create a vast national marketplace. Besides providing nationwide economic opportunities to farmers and industrialists, the railroad altered concepts of time and space, gave rise to new communities, and brought technological reforms as well as organizational reforms that affected modern business practices.

Railroad expansion and Indian removal made possible the successful settlement and development of the ranching and farming frontiers. These frontiers shared the characteristics of the natural-resource frontier: use of public land for private enrichment; the importance of technological innovations to successful development; government promotion of settlement and development; the bowing of the individual to corporate interests; the emergence of a frontier folk culture, especially in relation to the ranching frontier; and contributions to urbanization and to national economic growth and expansion.

The South, too, changed in the late nineteenth century. By the 1880s, land in the South was concentrated in the hands of fewer people than had been the case in 1860. Sharecropping and tenant farming dominated southern agriculture and, through the crop-lien system, trapped many white and black farmers in a perpetual state of debt peonage. The shift to commercialized farming and the closing of the southern range also adversely affected backcountry yeoman farmers.

Moreover, southern blacks, who lived under the constant threat of violence and who remained economically dependent on whites, had to endure new forms of social oppression in the form of disfranchisement and "Jim Crow" laws. This oppression was, in turn, upheld by the Supreme Court, which interpreted the Fourteenth Amendment narrowly. Talk of a "New South" and of an industrialized South produced few real changes, and the same kind of paternalism associated with the plantation system was now associated with the cotton textile industry. Although new industries dotted the southern landscape, the region continued to be predominantly rural and to rely economically on staple-crop agriculture.

Building Vocabulary

Listed below are important words and terms that you need to know to get the most out of Chapter 17. They are listed in the order in which they occur in the chapter. After carefully looking through the list, refer to a dictionary and jot down the definition of words that you do not know or of which you are unsure.

subsistence

coercive

ingenuity

exploit

infinity

impotent

reciprocity

ecological

acquiesce

humanitarian

inculcate

ethic

integrity

succumb

acculturate

assimilation

diligence

monogamy

servile

forswear

induce

dupe

eradicate

syndicate

extractive

public domain

coalesce

omnibus

polygamy

hedonism

notoriety

eccentric

carouse

arid

reclamation

eminent domain

subsidy

salutary

formidable

climatological

torrid

monotony

sparse

hinterland

drover

pilgrimage

extralegal

diversify

subsidiary

lien

evict

peonage

forage

induce

disaffection

enfranchise

subjugation

vagrant

retribution

demean

disfranchise

bias

proximity

squelch

innovator

permeate

Finding the Main Idea

When you begin to read material assigned to you in the textbook, it is important for you to look for (and mark) the main idea and supporting details in each paragraph or paragraph series. To see how to do so, reread "Finding Main Ideas" in the Introduction to this study guide. Then work the following two exercises, and check your answers.

Exercise A

Read the paragraph on page 508 of the textbook that begins with this sentence:

> Lumber production—another large-scale extractive industry—required vast amounts of forest land.

1. What is the topic of this paragraph?

2. What is its main idea?

3. What details support the main idea?

Exercise B

Read the five successive paragraphs on pages 524–525 of the textbook that begin with this sentence:

> Threatened by violence, pushed into sharecropping and burdened with crop liens, blacks also had to contend with new forms of social and political oppression.

1. What is the topic of this paragraph series?

2. What is its main idea?

3. What details support the main idea?

Identification and Significance

After studying Chapter 17 of *A People and a Nation,* you should be able to identify fully *and* explain the historical significance of each item listed below.

1. Identify each item in the space provided. Give an explanation or description of the item. Answer the questions *who, what, where,* and *when.*
2. Explain the historical significance of each item in the space provided. Establish the historical context in which the item exists. Establish the item as the result of or as the cause of other factors

existing in the society under study. Answer this question: *what were the political, social, economic, and/or cultural consequences of this item?*

Frederick Jackson Turner

    Identification

    Significance

Indian subsistence cultures

    Identification

    Significance

slaughter of the buffalo

    Identification

    Significance

Sand Creek massacre

    Identification

    Significance

the United States government's reservation policy

    Identification

    Significance

Chapter 17

the Battle of Little Big Horn

    Identification

    Significance

George Manypenny and Helen Hunt Jackson

    Identification

    Significance

Canada's Indian policy

    Identification

    Significance

the Women's National Indian Association and the Indian Rights Association

    Identification

    Significance

the Dawes Severalty Act

    Identification

    Significance

the Indian Bureau of the Interior Department

    Identification

    Significance

© 1994 Houghton Mifflin Company. All rights reserved.

the Ghost Dance movement

    Identification

    Significance

Wovoka

    Identification

    Significance

the Massacre at Wounded Knee

    Identification

    Significance

the Clapp rider to the Indian appropriations bill

    Identification

    Significance

mining syndicates

    Identification

    Significance

the Timber and Stone Act

    Identification

    Significance

mining and lumber communities

> Identification

> Significance

John Muir

> Identification

> Significance

the omnibus bill

> Identification

> Significance

Calamity Jane and Johnny Ringo

> Identification

> Significance

the Earp brothers, "Bat" Masterson, and "Doc" Holliday

> Identification

> Significance

the shootout at the OK Corral

> Identification

> Significance

riparian rights v. *prior appropriation*

    Identification

    Significance

California irrigation legislation of 1887

    Identification

    Significance

reclamation

    Identification

    Significance

the National (Newlands) Reclamation Act

    Identification

    Significance

Promontory Summit, Utah

    Identification

    Significance

standard time zones

    Identification

    Significance

westward migration, 1870–1890

    Identification

    Significance

life on the Plains

    Identification

    Significance

grasshopper plagues

    Identification

    Significance

the Homestead Act of 1862

    Identification

    Significance

mail-order houses and Rural Free Delivery

    Identification

    Significance

mechanization of agriculture

    Identification

    Significance

© 1994 Houghton Mifflin Company. All rights reserved.

the Morrill Land Grant Act of 1862 and 1890

>Identification

>Significance

the Hatch Act of 1887

>Identification

>Significance

dry farming

>Identification

>Significance

Luther Burbank and George Washington Carver

>Identification

>Significance

the ranching frontier

>Identification

>Significance

the long drive

>Identification

>Significance

open range ranching

>Identification

>Significance

barbed wire

>Identification

>Significance

the crop-lien system

>Identification

>Significance

southern backcountry farmers

>Identification

>Significance

lynching of African-Americans

>Identification

>Significance

the poll tax

>Identification

>Significance

the *Civil Rights Cases* (1883)

    Identification

    Significance

Plessy v. *Ferguson* and *Cummins* v. *County Board of Education*

    Identification

    Significance

Jim Crow laws

    Identification

    Significance

the southern textile industry

    Identification

    Significance

the southern tobacco industry

    Identification

    Significance

the New South

    Identification

    Significance

© 1994 Houghton Mifflin Company. All rights reserved.

Organizing Information

Learning Objective 12 indicates that you should be able to explain the impact of the United States government's policy on the western Indian tribes in the late nineteenth century.

Use the chart below to organize information concerning the United States government's reservation policy and the Dawes Severalty Act. Once you have compiled information, you may then use the chart to prepare yourself to discuss the reservation policy and the Dawes Severalty Act separately or to discuss the similarities and differences between the two policies.

For a study aid of this type to be of maximum benefit, it should fit your needs and purposes. Therefore, feel free to modify the format to suit your purposes.

Reservation Policy	Dawes Severalty Act
Ideology on Which Policy Was Based	Ideology on Which Policy Was Based
Features of Policy	Features of Policy
Impact of Policy on Western Indian Cultures	Impact of Policy on Western Indian Cultures

Evaluating and Using Information

Use the chart on the next page (or your own modification of it) to organize information about factors that determined the socio-economic predicament of the South's backcountry yeoman farmer in the period from 1877 to 1892. Then use the information gathered for this chart along with the information gathered for the "Organizing Information" exercise above to write a working draft for an essay on the following question:

Support the assertion that the economy of the backcountry yeoman farmer "resembled those of western Indians."

The Economy of the Backcountry Yeoman Farmer				
Condition of Equipment and Stock	**Control of Farmland; Farm Size**	**Access to Markets**	**Key Crops**	**State Laws**
Kind of Change and Features of Change	Kind of Change and Features of Change	Kind of Change and Features of Change	Kind of Change and Features of Change	Kind of Change and Features of Change
Cause(s) of Change	Cause(s) of Change	Cause(s) of Change	Cause(s) of Change	Cause(s) of Change
Impact on Farmer's Lifestyle and Economic Status	Impact on Farmer's Lifestyle and Economic Status	Impact on Farmer's Lifestyle and Economic Status	Impact on Farmer's Lifestyle and Economic Status	Impact on Farmer's Lifestyle and Economic Status

Ideas and Details

Objective 1

_____ 1. To achieve subsistence, most western Indian tribes
   a. relied solely on the buffalo.
   b. combined capitalistic trading practices with crop raising.
   c. sold clothing, shoes, and blankets to get the money necessary to buy food in the marketplace.
   d. relied on a balance among crop raising, livestock raising, hunting, and raiding.

Objective 1

_____ 2. Which of the following was a feature of the federal government's reservation policy?
   a. It did not allow Indians any say over their own affairs.
   b. It helped foster mutually beneficial trade relationships between Indians and whites.
   c. It forced Indians to concentrate on crop production.
   d. It protected Indians against white encroachment.

Objective 1

_____ 3. As a result of the Dawes Severalty Act,
   a. thousands of Indian children educated in white boarding schools rejected Indian culture.
   b. most western Indians were Christianized.
   c. the community-owned tribal lands of the western Indians were dissolved.
   d. the western Indians were encouraged to participate actively in decisions that would affect their lives and their culture.

Objective 2

_____ 4. The mining, timber, and ranching frontiers had which of the following characteristics in common?
   a. In the earliest stages of development, these frontiers required large capital outlays.
   b. Those associated with the development of these frontiers found ways of using the Timber and Stone Act to their advantage.
   c. Individuals were ultimately replaced by corporations in the development of these frontiers.
   d. Those involved in the development of these frontiers understood the need for careful and planned use of natural resources.

Objective 2

_____ 5. In the frontier communities, ethnic minorities
   a. were welcomed because of the skills they brought with them.
   b. usually had to endure white prejudice.
   c. found that opportunities abounded.
   d. were usually able to gain economic and political power.

Objective 4

_____ 6. To help solve scheduling problems, the railroads in 1883
   a. began to coordinate all their schedules through a central clearing-house.
   b. requested that the government establish daylight-saving time.
   c. asked that the government create the Interstate Commerce Commission.
   d. established four standard time zones.

Objectives 2 and 5

_____ 7. Both the cattle-ranching industry and the railroad industry
   a. profited from free use of public lands.
   b. developed a mutually beneficial relationship with farmers.
   c. were respectful of Indian rights and culture.
   d. welcomed government regulation of industry.

Objective 6

_____ 8. Which of the following is associated with the Great Plains?
   a. A temperate climate
   b. An abundance of timber for housing and fuel
   c. Grasshopper plagues
   d. Vast stretches of desert

Objective 6

_____ 9. Social isolation was a characteristic of life on the Plains because
   a. the competitive frontier spirit did not create an atmosphere conducive to social interaction.
   b. the rugged terrain made traveling difficult.
   c. the absence of farm machinery resulted in no time for socializing.
   d. farmhouses on the 160-acre tracts received by settlers under the Homestead Act were widely separated.

Objective 6

_____ 10. Which of the following helped lessen the sense of isolation experienced by farm families in the Plains in the late nineteenth century?
   a. Railroad expansion
   b. The radio
   c. The telegraph
   d. Rural Free Delivery

© 1994 Houghton Mifflin Company. All rights reserved.

Objective 7

_____ 11. The extension of the farming frontier, including the conquering of the Plains, would not have been possible without
   a. the expanded use of farm machinery.
   b. new pesticides.
   c. better fertilizers.
   d. extensive use of migrant labor.

Objective 7

_____ 12. The federal government encouraged the advancement of farming technology by
   a. subsidizing the research of George Washington Carver.
   b. passing the Hatch Act of 1887.
   c. appointing Luther Burbank to head the research division of the Department of Agriculture.
   d. funding a vast irrigation network in the Plains.

Objective 8

_____ 13. As a result of the crop-lien System, many southern farmers
   a. were able to increase the prices they received for their goods.
   b. sank deeper and deeper into debt.
   c. were given the opportunity to become landowners.
   d. began to diversify their crops.

Objective 9

_____ 14. In the case of *Plessy* v. *Ferguson*, the Supreme Court asserted that
   a. states had the authority to impose a poll tax on voters.
   b. the Fifteenth Amendment prohibited the establishment of literacy as a prerequisite for voting.
   c. states could constitutionally enact legislation by which separate-but-equal facilities were required for whites and blacks.
   d. separate schools for blacks were by their very nature unequal and therefore unconstitutional.

Objective 10

_____ 15. Which of the following is true of southern textile mills?
   a. They fostered the development of new technologies for the production of cotton cloth.
   b. They were usually located in small southern towns.
   c. They were usually financed by northern banking interests.
   d. They provided the means by which poor white southerners could move into the middle class.

Essay Questions

Objective 1

1. Discuss the federal government's reservation policy, and explain its impact on western Indian tribes.

Objective 2

2. Discuss the characteristics of the natural-resource frontier and the methods by which developers gained land and extraction rights. What role did the federal government play in the development of this frontier?

Objective 3

3. Discuss the controversy over water rights in the West and assess the importance of this debate and its outcome.

Objective 4

4. Discuss the impact of the expansion of the railroad industry on the American economy.

Objective 5

5. Explain the role of federal, state, and local governments in the expansion of the railroad industry, and discuss the effects of that role.

Objective 6

6. Describe the life of a farm family of the Plains.

Objective 9

7. Explain the process that led to the disfranchisement of southern blacks and to the segregation of southern society by law. How did the Supreme Court respond to this process?

Objective 10

8. Contrast the concept of the New South with the reality of the New South.

CHAPTER 18
The Machine Age, 1877–1920

Learning Objectives

After you have studied Chapter 18 in your textbook and worked through this study guide chapter, you should be able to:

1. Cite the factors related to and resulting from industrialization in the United States.
2. Identify the contributions of Thomas Alva Edison, Henry Ford, and the du Ponts to industrial development in the United States.
3. Explain and assess the late-nineteenth-century obsession with time studies and scientific management.
4. Discuss late-nineteenth-century changes in the nature of work, in working conditions, and in the workplace itself, and explain the impact of these changes on American workers.
5. Examine the rise of unionism and the emergence of worker activism in the late nineteenth century, and discuss the reaction of employers, government, and the public to these manifestations of worker discontent.
6. Examine the position of women, children, immigrants, and blacks in the work force and in the union movement in the late nineteenth century.
7. Explain the emergence of the consumer society, and discuss the factors that determined the extent to which working-class Americans were able to participate in this society.
8. Discuss the impact of scientific developments and education on living standards between 1900 and 1920.
9. Discuss the impact of each of the following on American attitudes and life styles:
    a. The indoor toilet
    b. Processed and preserved foods
    c. The sewing machine
    d. Department stores and chain stores
10. Explain the characteristics of modern advertising and popular journalism, and examine the role of mass communications in the spread of mass culture throughout American society.
11. Examine the corporate consolidation movement of the late nineteenth century, and discuss the consequences of this movement.
12. Explain and evaluate the ideologies of Social Darwinism, laissez-faire capitalism, and the Gospel of Wealth. Explain the impact of these ideas on workers and on the role of government in society.
13. Discuss and evaluate the ideas and suggested reforms of those who dissented from the ideologies of the Gospel of Wealth, Social Darwinism, and laissez-faire capitalism.

14. Discuss the response of all branches of government at the state and national levels to the corporate consolidation movement on the one hand and to the grievances of workers on the other hand.

Thematic Guide

The theme of Chapter 18 is industrialization as a major component of American expansion in the late nineteenth century. A list of the factors linked with industrialization appears in the chapter's introduction (see page 530 of the textbook). These factors may be identified in the subsequent sections of the chapter. For example, the discussion of Thomas Alva Edison and the electrical industry, Henry Ford and the automobile industry, and the du Ponts and the chemical industry relates to the following factors: (1) production concentrated in large, intricately organized factories; (2) accelerated technological innovation, emphasizing new inventions and applied science; (3) expanded markets, no longer merely local and regional in scope. Keep these characteristics of industrialization in mind as you study the chapter, and try to determine which characteristics apply to the various topics discussed in the chapter.

Industrialism changed the nature of work and in many respects caused an uneven distribution of power among interest groups in American society. Industrial workers were employees rather than producers, and repeating specialized tasks made them feel like appendages to machines. The emphasis on quantity rather than quality further dehumanized the workplace. These factors, in addition to the increased power of the employer, reduced the independence and self-respect of workers, but worker resistance only led employers to tighten restrictions.

Industrialism also brought more women and children into the labor force. Although job opportunities opened for women, most women went into low-paying clerical jobs, and sex discrimination continued in the workplace. Employers also attempted to cut wage costs by hiring more children. Although a few states passed child-labor laws, such laws were difficult to enforce and employers generally opposed state interference in their hiring practices. Effective child-labor legislation would not come until the twentieth century.

As the nature of work changed, workers began to protest low wages, the attitude of employers, the hazards of the workplace, and the absence of disability insurance and pensions. The effectiveness of legislation designed to redress these grievances was usually limited by conservative Supreme Court rulings. Out of frustration, some workers began to participate in unions and in organized resistance. Unionization efforts took various directions. The Knights of Labor tried to ally all workers by creating producer and consumer cooperatives; the American Federation of Labor strove to organize skilled workers to achieve pragmatic objectives; and the Industrial Workers of the World attempted to overthrow capitalist society. The railroad strikes of 1877, the Haymarket riot, and the Homestead and Pullman strikes were all marked by violence, and they exemplify labor's frustration as well as its active and organized resistance. Government intervention against the strikers convinced many workers of the imbalance of interest groups in American society, whereas the middle class began to connect organized working-class resistance with radicalism. Although this perception was by and large mistaken, middle-class fear of social upheaval became an additional force against organized labor.

Not only did industrialization affect the nature of work, it also produced a myriad of products that affected the everyday lives of Americans. As America became a consumer-oriented society, most of its citizens faced living costs that rose faster than wages. Consequently, many people could not take advantage of the new goods and services being offered. But, as has been seen, more women and children became part of the paid labor force. Although many did so out of necessity, others hoped that the additional income would allow the family to participate in the consumer society.

Increased availability of goods and services to a greater number of people was not the only reason for a general improvement in living standards. The era also witnessed advances in medical care, better diets, and improved living conditions. Furthermore, education, more than ever a means to upward mobility, became more readily available through the spread of public education.

© 1994 Houghton Mifflin Company. All rights reserved.

American habits and attitudes were further affected by the democratization of convenience that resulted from the indoor toilet and private bathtub. At the same time, the tin can and the icebox altered lifestyles and diet, the sewing machine created a clothing revolution, and department stores and chain stores emerged that both created and served the new consumerism.

As American society became more consumer oriented, brand names for products were created. Used by advertisers to sell products, these brand names in turn created "consumption communities" made up of individuals loyal to those brands. As producers tried to convince consumers of their need for particular products, advertising became more important than ever. And because the major vehicle for advertising in the late nineteenth century was the newspaper, advertising was transformed into news.

Although the American standard of living generally improved during the late nineteenth century, there were unsettling economic forces at work. Although rapid economic growth is a characteristic of the period, the period is also characterized by the economic instability and uncertainty produced by cycles of boom and bust. In an effort to create a sense of order and stability out of the competitive chaos, industrialists turned to economic concentration in the form of pools, trusts, and holding companies. Therefore, the search of order led to the merger movement and to larger and larger combinations that sought domination of their markets through vertical integration.

Defenders of business justified the merger movement and their pursuit of wealth and profits by advancing the "Gospel of Wealth," based on Social Darwinism and on the precepts of laissez-faire capitalism. The business elite also used this philosophy to justify both its paternalistic attitude toward the less fortunate in society and its advocacy of government aid to business. The paradoxes and inconsistencies associated with the Gospel of Wealth gave rise to dissent from sociologists, economists, and reformers. The general public also began to speak against economic concentration in the form of monopolies and trusts. The inability of state governments to resolve the problem led to passage of the Sherman Anti-Trust Act by Congress in 1890, but this legislation represented a vaguely worded political compromise, the interpretation of which was left to the courts. Narrow interpretation by a conservative Supreme Court and failure by government officials to fully support the act meant that it was used more successfully against organized labor than against business combinations, again illustrating the uneven distribution of power among interest groups in late nineteenth-century American society.

Building Vocabulary

Listed below are important words and terms that you need to know to get the most out of Chapter 18. They are listed in the order in which they occur in the chapter. After carefully looking through the list, refer to a dictionary and jot down the definition of words that you do not know or of which you are unsure.

candid

ominous

phenomena

brash

adaptation

filament

tedious

publicist

deftly

pervasive

integral

artisan

eschew

docile

temperance

debauchery

menial

catalyst

remonstrate

maim

liability

watershed

carnage

precedent

avert

portend

anarchist

federation

autonomy

paternalistic

arbitration

ostensibly

espouse

rhetoric

rationalize

ingenuity

myriad

skew

scourge

conglomerate

tentative

exemplify

merger

ideology

philanthropy

paradox

ardent

commonwealth

consign

vanguard

Identification and Significance

After studying Chapter 18 of *A People and a Nation*, you should be able to identify fully *and* explain the historical significance of each item listed on pages 56–66.

1. Identify each item in the space provided. Give an explanation or description of the item. Answer the questions *who, what, where,* and *when*.
2. Explain the historical significance of each item in the space provided. Establish the historical context in which the item exists. Establish the item as the result of or as the cause of other factors existing in the society under study. Answer this question: *what were the political, social, economic, and/or cultural consequences of this item?*

the characteristics of industrialization

    Identification

    Significance

Thomas A. Edison

    Identification

    Significance

Menlo Park

    Identification

    Significance

the patent system

    Identification

    Significance

the Edison Electric Light Company

    Identification

    Significance

George Westinghouse

    Identification

    Significance

Granville T. Woods

    Identification

    Significance

Henry Ford

    Identification

    Significance

mass production and the moving assembly line

    Identification

    Significance

the du Pont family

    Identification

    Significance

economies of scale

    Identification

    Significance

Frederick W. Taylor

    Identification

    Significance

© 1994 Houghton Mifflin Company. All rights reserved.

producer versus employee

    Identification

    Significance

the Five-Dollar-Day plan

    Identification

    Significance

the occupational patterns of employed women

    Identification

    Significance

child labor

    Identification

    Significance

the "iron law of wages"

    Identification

    Significance

industrial accidents

    Identification

    Significance

Holden v. *Hardy*

    Identification

    Significance

Lockner v. *New York*

    Identification

    Significance

Muller v. *Oregon*

    Identification

    Significance

the general railway strike of 1877

    Identification

    Significance

the Knights of Labor

    Identification

    Significance

Terence V. Powderly

    Identification

    Significance

© 1994 Houghton Mifflin Company. All rights reserved.

the Southwestern Railroad System strike of 1886

> Identification

> Significance

the Haymarket riot

> Identification

> Significance

John P. Altgeld

> Identification

> Significance

the American Federation of Labor

> Identification

> Significance

Samuel Gompers

> Identification

> Significance

the Homestead and Pullman strikes

> Identification

> Significance

Eugene V. Debs

> Identification

> Significance

the Industrial Workers of the World

> Identification

> Significance

"Mother" Jones, Elizabeth Gurley Flynn, and William D. (Big Bill) Haywood

> Identification

> Significance

the "Uprising of the 20,000"

> Identification

> Significance

the Telephone Operators' Department of the International Brotherhood of Electrical Workers

> Identification

> Significance

the Women's Trade Union League

> Identification

> Significance

Chapter 18

public high school enrollment

    Identification

    Significance

the indoor toilet

    Identification

    Significance

the tin can and the icebox

    Identification

    Significance

John H. Kellogg, William K. Kellogg, and Charles W. Post

    Identification

    Significance

the sewing machine

    Identification

    Significance

department stores and chain stores

    Identification

    Significance

the Great Atlantic and Pacific Tea Company

    Identification

    Significance

modern advertising

    Identification

    Significance

consumption communities

    Identification

    Significance

brand names

    Identification

    Significance

cycles of boom and bust

    Identification

    Significance

the pool

    Identification

    Significance

© 1994 Houghton Mifflin Company. All rights reserved.

John D. Rockefeller

    Identification

    Significance

the trust

    Identification

    Significance

horizontal integration

    Identification

    Significance

the holding company

    Identification

    Significance

vertical integration

    Identification

    Significance

the merger movement

    Identification

    Significance

the U.S. Steel Corporation

>Identification

>Significance

Social Darwinism

>Identification

>Significance

the principles of laissez faire

>Identification

>Significance

the Gospel of Wealth

>Identification

>Significance

protective tariffs

>Identification

>Significance

Lester Ward

>Identification

>Significance

Richard Ely, John R. Commons, and Edward Bemis

    Identification

    Significance

Henry George

    Identification

    Significance

Edward Bellamy

    Identification

    Significance

Henry Demarest Lloyd

    Identification

    Significance

the Sherman Anti-Trust Act

    Identification

    Significance

U.S. v. *E. C. Knight Co.*

    Identification

    Significance

Organizing Information

Chapter 18 deals in part with worker unrest in the late nineteenth century and the reasons for that unrest. Learning objectives 4 and 5 indicate that you should be able to explain the changes in the nature of work and to examine the unrest and activism that emerged among workers during this period.

Use this exercise to organize information about the nature of work and worker activism. First indicate the underlying causes of worker unrest—changes in the nature of work, the attitude of employers, and the like. Then answer the questions about specific instances of worker unrest; widespread railroad strikes in 1877, the strike of railroads in the Southwest in 1886, the Haymarket riot, the Homestead strike, and the Pullman strike. The questions are intended to help you focus on the relevant issues concerning worker activism.

Your professor may want to add additional items to this exercise or ask you to do more extensive research on these events. If you want to do additional research, look at the bibliography at the end of Chapter 18, especially the section entitled "Work and Labor Organization," to find a listing of excellent secondary sources that give detailed analyses of worker activism in the late nineteenth century. In any event, use this section as a guide and modify it to serve your study purposes.

Worker Activism In the Late Nineteenth Century

What were the underlying causes of worker unrest in the late nineteenth century?

Widespread Railroad Strikes in 1877

What were the immediate causes of the strikes?

What demands did the striking workers make?

What tactics did the striking workers use to seek redress of their grievances?

How did employers respond to the workers' demands? How did employers try to end the strikes?

Was there any government (state or federal) involvement in the strikes? Explain.

© 1994 Houghton Mifflin Company. All rights reserved.

How did the public respond to the strikes?

What was the strikes' outcome?

What were the political, social, and economic consequences of the strikes?

Strike of Railroads in the Southwest in 1886

What were the immediate causes of the strike?

What demands did the striking workers make?

What tactics did the striking workers use to seek redress of their grievances?

How did the employers respond to the workers' demands?

How did the employers try to end the strike?

Was there any government (state or federal) involvement in the strike? Explain.

How did the public respond to the strike?

What was the strike's outcome?

What were the political, social, and economic consequences of the strike?

The Haymarket Riot

Why was there a labor demonstration in Chicago on May 1, 1886?

What happened at the McCormick plant in Chicago on May 3, 1886?

Why was there a labor rally at Haymarket Square on May 4, 1886?

What happened at the labor rally on May 4, 1886?

What were the consequences (immediate and long-term) of this incident?

The Homestead Strike

What were the immediate causes of the strike?

What demands did the striking workers make?

What tactics did the striking workers use to seek redress of their grievances?

How did the employer respond to the workers' demands? How did the employer try to end the strike?

Was there any government (state or federal) involvement in the strike? Explain.

How did the public respond to the strike?

What was the strike's outcome?

What were the political, social, and economic consequences of the strike?

The Pullman Strike

What were the immediate causes of the strike?

What were the political, social, and economic consequences of the strike?

What demands did the striking workers make?

What tactics did the striking workers use to seek redress of their grievances?

How did the employer respond to the workers' demands?

How did the employer try to end the strike?

Was there any government (state or federal) involvement in the strike? Explain.

How did the public respond to the strike?

What was the strike's outcome?

Evaluating and Using Information

To a large extent, Chapter 18 of your textbook is about how economic developments were defining the status of the American factory worker. Does the evidence suggest that American workers of 1920 would see themselves as better off than workers of 1877, as worse off, or simply as about the same? In this exercise, you are to collect and use the relevant evidence available to you to discover a logical answer to that question, an answer that grows out of the evidence you collect, and then you are to turn around and use the evidence to show that your conclusion (answer) is logical.

Using the questions in each of the four **Evidence Sets** on pages 72–77 as your guide to the kind of specific, concrete evidence you should look for, collect evidence from Chapter 18 and your class notes that shows or helps to explain any change from 1877 to 1920 in how American workers might realistically picture themselves, how they were valued, and how much control they had over their economic position. List the evidence in the blanks provided. (You may want to record where you found the evidence—textbook pages, class dates—for later reference.)

At the end of each evidence set is a **Conclusion** section. Answer the question in each Conclusion section by stating, in a single statement, the significance of all the evidence you have compiled in the preceding evidence set.

At the end of the four evidence sets is a **Thesis** question. Answer the question in a single statement that expresses the total meaning or significance of all the conclusions of all the Evidence Sets combined.

Finally, use the notes and conclusions you have recorded in the blanks to create the working draft of an essay. Begin your essay with the thesis statement—a one-sentence answer to the essay question. Then work through the body of the essay one section at a time. Use the statement of the conclusion you have derived from each Evidence Set as the opening sentence of the section of your essay based on that

Evidence Set. For each section, use evidence in the evidence set to explain and back up the section's opening statement.

The resulting working draft of an essay should have the kind of logic and the concreteness and specificity your professor expects to see in a response to an essay examination question. And by gathering and organizing the information you will have studied for several potential essay questions as well as dozens of potential objective questions.

Evidence Set 1

What innovation in industrial production did Henry Ford introduce in 1903? How did this innovation affect the kind of tasks performed by American industrial workers during the Machine Age?

_____

_____

How specialized and skilled and mentally challenging was the labor performed by the industrial worker? How much variety of activity did the work involve?

_____

_____

Who was Frederick W. Taylor? How did changes in the organization of industrial work, influenced by people such as Taylor, affect the role of individual workers on the factory floor in deciding how and when to work and affect the quality of work as a measure of a worker's value?

_____

_____

How did time-motion research like Taylor's affect the number of people employed in a factory? Their wages? Their on-the-job stress?

_____

_____

How long was the workday? Did early unions reflect worker concern over the length of the workday?

_____

_____

What changed industrial workers into "employees"? What had American workers been before? How do the two roles differ?

_____

_____

How did employers influence what workers did off the job? How did workers react? What did Ford workers have to do to qualify for the profit-sharing part of the Five-Dollar-Day Plan?

_____

_____

How safe was the workplace? What effect did mechanization and automation have on worker safety? What happened to workers injured on the job? What happened to the families of workers who were killed on the job?

_____

_____

How effectively did legislation safeguard workers from harsh or dangerous working conditions? How strong was judicial support for such legislation, especially that of the Supreme Court?

_____

_____

Conclusion for Evidence Set 1

According to this evidence in Evidence Set 1, what impact did the advent of the Machine Age have on American industrial workers and the conditions under which they worked?

_____

_____

_____

_____

Evidence Set 2

What was the "Iron law of wages" and what did it mean to the American industrial worker between 1877 and 1920? What stance did the courts take toward the application of this "law"? What effect did this "law" have on the growth of unions and the loyalty of their members?

_____

_____

How significant was the issue of wages in protests by workers, unions or otherwise?

_____

_____

How much were workers paid? How much did skilled laborers get? Unskilled laborers? Female factory workers? Did factory workers' incomes rise? Did working class families have other sources of income besides the head-of-household's wages? Did the share of the national wealth in the hands of the working class reflect the proportion of the population in the working class?

_____
_____

What alternative to hourly wages did some employers of factory workers offer? What effect did this alternative basis for establishing workers' pay have on their income? Hours? Pressure on the job?

_____
_____

How secure were jobs? Could workers count on holding their jobs year-around? Were workers hurt by any significant "busts" in the boom-and-bust cycle of American business? When?

_____
_____

Conclusion for Evidence Set 2

According to the evidence in Evidence Set 2, what impact did changes in the workplace during the Machine Age have on American industrial workers' income and their ability to increase it?

_____
_____
_____
_____

Evidence Set 3

Did the cost of living increase or decrease during the Machine Age? How much? Did incomes change in the same direction? Did incomes change as fast and as much as the cost of living?

_____
_____

How did economic conditions affect the number and ages of persons in a working-class family who worked outside the home for pay?

_____
_____

How did the nature of working-class families' expenditures change during the Machine Age? What items formerly considered luxuries, if any, were becoming necessities; and what items formerly considered necessities, if any, were becoming luxuries?

_____

_____

What important technological innovations and scientific discoveries affected the healthfulness of and variety in the diet of American factory workers from 1877–1920? Did the diet of American workers and their families improve or decline? Were perishable foods and foods produced in other parts of the country more or less readily available to working class families? Why?

_____

_____

How did death rates and life expectancy change during the Machine Age? How did disease-caused deaths change? How did suicide, homicide, and vehicular death rates change?

_____

_____

What changes in technology affected sanitation in the American home and the privacy of individuals in the home during the Machine Age? Did sanitation and privacy increase or decrease?

_____

_____

What innovations affected the amount and kinds of clothing working class families had and who produced it? What was the effect of these innovations?

_____

_____

What, if any, opportunities opened up during the Machine Age that would make it reasonable for factory workers to think they or their children could move upward into the middle or upper economic classes? Were there any signs that people trapped on the lowest rungs of the economic ladder were taking advantage of whatever opportunities were available for their own or their children's advancement?

_____

_____

Conclusion for Evidence Set 3

How did the overall quality of life change for the factory worker during the Machine Age (1877–1920)? Would it be reasonable for large numbers of such workers to look to the future with hope and optimism?

_____

_____

_____

_____

Evidence Set 4

How much help or sympathy would it have been reasonable for factory workers to expect from employers? What did employers say should determine wages and working conditions? How did such big employers as George Pullman and Jay Gould respond to workers' attempts to negotiate for better wages and working conditions? What did the outcome of Terence V. Powderly's efforts to work with employers to improve working conditions suggest about the willingness of big business to compromise with workers on matters of working conditions and wages?

_____

_____

Which, if any, Machine Age people, govervment agencies, or organizations did anything about providing pensions, insurance, workmen's compensation, job training, and aid for families of striking workers? Did these people, agencies, or organizations represent employers, government or the public, or the workers themselves? Who decided what causes would get the philanthropic dollars of such magnates as Andrew Carnegie?

_____

_____

What did legislation passed by Congress indicate about the legislative branch of government's sympathies regarding domestic consumer prices? Was Congress concerned with protecting factory workers from having to pay high prices for consumer goods?

_____

_____

How did the public view factory workers who participated in protests of working conditions? Would public attitudes toward them and their efforts to get better wages and working conditions suggest that the public trusted, respected, and valued them? What responses from the public suggested the public sympathized or did not sympathize with worker complaints and protests? What did the Triangle Shirtwaist Company fire suggest about what it would take to arouse public concern about working conditions in American factories?

_____

_____

© 1994 Houghton Mifflin Company. All rights reserved.

What did the responses of Presidents Hayes and Cleveland suggest about government sympathies or tolerance of worker protests?

What court decisions indicated whether the courts were sympathetic or not sympathetic to worker complaints about working conditions? Was the court sympathetic to workers? Which segment of society did the Supreme Court's interpretation of the Fourteenth Amendment benefit? Which did it harm? What did the Supreme Court's decisions arising out of anti-trust cases suggest about the Court's view of workers' attempts to influence working conditions and wages through strikes and protests and big business's attempts to control competition and consumer prices through creation of monopolies, trusts, and pools?

Conclusion for Evidence Set 4

On what or whom could factories workers depend for sympathy or, more importantly, for help in improving their working and living conditions and, indeed, their general economic outlook?

Thesis (Whole Point)

Would developments and features of the American economy between 1877 and 1920 lead realistic American workers of 1920 to portray themselves as better off than workers of 1877, or worse off, or simply as about the same?

Essay

Working Draft for Response to an Essay Question

Using the notes you have produced in this exercise, write out your response to the following question in your Reading Notebook:

> Would developments and features of the American economy between 1877 and 1920 lead realistic American workers of 1920 to portray themselves as better off than workers of 1877, or worse off, or simply as about the same? Explain your answer and make your explanation concrete and specific.

Ideas and Details

Objective 2

_____ 1. Which of the following innovations by Henry Ford reduced the cost of his automobiles and made them more affordable?
   a. Interchangeable parts
   b. The machine-tool industry
   c. The moving assembly line
   d. Team production

Objective 3

_____ 2. The emphasis on efficient production had the effect of
   a. making skilled labor more valuable.
   b. lowering the wage scale for most workers.
   c. increasing the size of the work force.
   d. making time as important as quality in the measure of acceptable work.

Objectives 4 and 5

_____ 3. In relation to the wage system, most wage earners
   a. appreciated the freedom it gave them to negotiate with the employer for higher wages.
   b. recognized that job competition among workers caused the base pay of all workers to rise steadily.
   c. advocated that Congress establish a minimum wage for all workers.
   d. felt trapped and exploited in a system controlled by employers.

Objectives 5 and 14

_____ 4. In cases involving legislation that limited working hours, the Supreme Court
   a. declared that Congress, not the states, had the power to enact such legislation.
   b. declared that the Fourteenth Amendment did not apply to state actions.
   c. reduced the impact of such legislation by narrowly interpreting which jobs were dangerous and which workers needed protection.
   d. consistently upheld the regulatory powers of the states.

Objective 5

_____ 5. The Knights of Labor, unlike the American Federation of Labor,
   a. advocated the use of violence against corporate power.
   b. pressed for pragmatic objectives that would bring immediate benefits to workers.
   c. believed in using strikes as the primary weapon against employers.
   d. welcomed all workers, including women, blacks, and immigrants.

Objective 5

_____ 6. Which of the following was a consequence of the Haymarket riot?
   a. National legislation was passed mandating an eight-hour workday for industry in the United States.
   b. The military forces of the United States were put on alert because of fear of revolution.
   c. Revival of the middle-class fear of radicalism led to the strengthening of police forces and armories in many cities.
   d. The Knights of Labor was strengthened.

Objectives 5 and 6

_____ 7. Which of the following is true of the Women's Trade Union League?
   a. Although initially dominated by middle-class women, working-class leaders gained control in the 1910s.
   b. Although its members opposed the idea, its leaders actively worked for a constitutional amendment guaranteeing equal rights to women.
   c. Both its leaders and its members worked tirelessly against extension of the vote to women.
   d. As an anarchist organization, it advocated working-class unity and the waging of war against capitalist society.

© 1994 Houghton Mifflin Company. All rights reserved.

Objective 7

_____ 8. Data on wages and living costs in the late nineteenth and early twentieth centuries indicate which of the following?
   a. Most working-class wage earners suffered because of declining wages and increasing living costs.
   b. Whereas wages rose for farmers and factory workers, they declined for most members of the middle class.
   c. Whereas incomes rose for most workers, the cost of living usually rose at a higher rate.
   d. Professional workers suffered more from the rising cost of living than did industrial workers.

Objective 9

_____ 9. As a result of the indoor bathroom, Americans of the later nineteenth and early twentieth centuries
   a. became conscious of personal appearance for the first time.
   b. viewed bodily functions in a more unpleasant light.
   c. insisted on private facilities in hotels.
   d. were unconcerned about human pollution.

Objectives 7 and 10

_____ 10. The main task of advertisers in a society of abundance is to
   a. respond to an individual's particular need by offering a product that uniquely fills that need.
   b. persuade groups of consumers that they have a need for a particular product.
   c. display products in an attractive way.
   d. convince the consumer that a particular product is a quality product offered at a fair price.

Objective 11

_____ 11. Businessmen turned to devices like trusts and holding companies because
   a. they were a means by which to combat the uncertainty of the business cycle.
   b. such cooperative business arrangements were responsive to consumer needs.
   c. they allowed business owners to concentrate on quality production while financial specialists handled monetary matters.
   d. they encouraged an open market in which many people had economic opportunity.

Objective 12

_____ 12. Social Darwinists believed that in a free society run in accordance with natural law
   a. there would be no poverty.
   b. power would flow into the hands of the most capable people.
   c. wealth would be distributed equally.
   d. people would become less aggressive.

Objective 12

_____ 13. The philosophy accepted by most businessmen in the late nineteenth century included the idea that
   a. government could intervene if it were doing so to protect the disadvantaged.
   b. government power could rightly be used to protect consumers from unfair prices.
   c. government should extend a helping hand to workers by encouraging the development of labor organizations.
   d. government should extend a helping hand to business interests through tariff protection.

Objective 13

_____ 14. Lester Ward expressed the belief that
   a. cooperative action and government intervention could be useful in creating a better society.
   b. business forms, like life forms, evolved from the simple to the complex as part of the natural order of things.
   c. tampering with natural economic laws would lead to economic disaster.
   d. the government had no responsibility in society other than national defense.

Objective 14

_____ 15. In the case of *U.S.* v. *E. C. Knight Co.*, the Supreme Court
   a. held all trusts to be illegal.
   b. strengthened the powers of the Interstate Commerce Commission.
   c. reduced the government's power under the Sherman Anti-Trust Act to combat combinations in restraint of trade.
   d. held that workers had the right to organize and strike.

Essay Questions

Objectives 4 and 5

1. Discuss the grievances of workers in the late nineteenth century, the means by which they sought redress and the effectiveness of those means.

Objectives 4, 5, and 14

2. Discuss the Haymarket riot, the Homestead strike, and the Pullman strike. Explain the reaction of the government and the public to these instances of labor unrest.

Objective 6

3. Examine the changing position of women in the labor market in the late nineteenth century.

Objectives 8 and 9

4. Indicate the developments that made the indoor bathroom possible, and discuss its impact on American attitudes and life styles.

Objective 10

5. Explain changes that took place in advertising in American society in the late nineteenth and early twentieth centuries, and discuss the impact of these changes on American society.

Objective 10

6. Define what is meant by *mass society*, and analyze the emergence of such a society in the United States in the late nineteenth and early twentieth centuries.

Objective 12

7. Explain the concept of Social Darwinism and its use by business leaders to justify their position and wealth in society.

Objectives 12 and 14

8. Analyze the relationships among the three branches of the federal government and the business community in the period between 1877 and 1920.

CHAPTER 19
The Vitality and Turmoil of Urban Life, 1877–1920

Learning Objectives

After you have studied Chapter 19 in your textbook and worked through this study guide chapter, you should be able to:

1. Examine the role played by mass transportation and industrial growth on the transformation of the early-nineteenth-century American city into the modern American city.
2. Examine the factors responsible for urban growth during the late nineteenth century.
3. Discuss the similarities and differences between the immigrants of the period from 1880 to 1920 and previous immigrants.
4. Examine the interaction between immigrants of the late nineteenth century and American society, and discuss the changes brought about by this interaction.
5. Examine the problems associated with American cities of the late nineteenth century, and evaluate the responses to those problems.
6. Examine household, family, and individual life patterns in American society between 1877 and 1920.
7. Explain the emergence and characteristics of each of the following, and discuss their impact on American society:
   a. Sports
   b. Show business
   c. Moving pictures
   d. Still pictures and the phonograph
   e. Popular journalism
8. Examine the means by which upward socioeconomic mobility could be achieved in the late nineteenth century, and discuss the extent to which such mobility was possible.
9. Discuss the impact of prejudice and discrimination on nonwhite Americans of the late nineteenth century.
10. Examine and evaluate the urban political machines and political bosses of the late nineteenth century.
11. Discuss the ideological basis of the urban reform movement, and explain the successes and failures of the reformers associated with this movement.
12. Define *cultural pluralism,* and discuss its impact on American society.

Thematic Guide

In Chapter 19, we examine urban growth, the third major theme (along with natural resource development and industrialization) of American expansion in the late nineteenth century. Mass transportation combined with urban growth destroyed the old pedestrian city of the past. The physical expansion of the city attracted industry, capital, and people. By the early 1900s, the modern American city, with its urban sprawl and distinct districts, was clearly taking shape.

Cities grow in three ways: through physical expansion, by natural increase, and through migration and immigration. In the late nineteenth century, *in*-migration from domestic and foreign sources was the most important cause of urban growth. The section "Peopling the Cities" shows that native whites, foreigners, and African-Americans were the three major migrant groups of the period. We consider why these groups moved to the cities, how they differed from and resembled each other, and, in the case of immigrants, how they differed from and resembled earlier immigrants. In discussing the cultural interaction between foreign immigrants and American society, we find that the city of the late nineteenth century nurtured the cultural diversity that so strongly characterizes modern America.

Rapid urban growth created and then intensified such urban problems as inadequate housing, overcrowding, and intolerable living conditions. This situation led to reforms that strengthened the hand of local government in regulating the construction of housing, but American attitudes toward the profit motive and toward private enterprise placed limits on the reforms enacted.

Although scientific and technological breakthroughs improved urban life, the burden of urban poverty remained. Whereas some reformers began to look to environmental factors to explain poverty, traditional attitudes toward poverty—attitudes that blamed the victim—restricted what most Americans were willing to do to alleviate poverty. Even private agencies insisted on extending aid only to the "worthy poor" and on teaching the moral virtues of thrift and sobriety.

Urban areas also had to contend with crime and violence. Whether crime actually increased or was merely more conspicuous can be debated, but in many cases native whites blamed crime on those they considered to be "outsiders" in American society—foreigners and blacks. The ethnic diversity of the cities, combined with urban overcrowding and uncertain economic conditions, hardened antiforeign and white racist attitudes and increased the incidence of violence in urban areas. Uneven, sometimes prejudicial, application of laws by law enforcement officials raised questions about the nature of justice, equality, and individual freedom in American society.

In "Family Life" the focus of the chapter shifts to a discussion of the family in American society and American life. Once distinctions are made between the household and the family, we identify the factors responsible for the high percentage of nuclear families. We also note the varying ways in which households expanded and contracted to meet changing circumstances. Changes in society changed family, as well as individual, lifestyles. Reduction in family size freed adults at an earlier age from the responsibilities of parenthood. Longer life expectancy increased the number of older adults. Childhood and adolescence became more distinct stages of life. As the authors state, "Americans became more age- and peer-conscious. People's roles in school, in the family, on the job, and in the community came to be defined by age more than by any other characteristic."

The leisure-time revolution brought about by labor-saving devices and by a shortened workweek changed the American way of life. As the average workweek decreased to forty-seven hours by 1910, individuals turned to croquet, bicycling, tennis, and golf as favorite leisure activities. Entertaining the public through spectator sports, the circus, show business, and moving pictures became a profitable business endeavor. Moreover, the mass production of sound and images made possible by the phonograph and the still camera "dissolved the uniqueness of experience." Even news was transformed into big business and a mass commodity by the "yellow journalism" tactics of Joseph Pulitzer and William Randolph Hearst.

Mass entertainment and mass culture had a nationalizing effect; however, even though show business provided new opportunities for women, blacks, and immigrants, too often it reinforced

© 1994 Houghton Mifflin Company. All rights reserved.

prejudicial stereotypes—especially concerning black Americans. Furthermore, in an America that was becoming more culturally diverse, different groups pursued their own form of leisure. This often caused concern on the part of some reformers who tended to label individuals as un-American if their activities did not conform to the Puritan traditions of the nation's past. These reformers wanted to use government to impose their values and lifestyles on immigrant groups. These attempts to create a homogeneous society led to questions concerning the role of government in society and in the life of the individual, questions that are as relevant today as they were in the late nineteenth century.

In the section "Promises of Mobility," we discuss the three basic ways by which upward socioeconomic mobility was made possible within American society, concentrating on the importance of migration. Certain myths concerning the availability and extent of upward mobility are dispelled, and the limiting impact of white prejudice on certain ethnic groups is explained.

As America became a culturally pluralistic society, interest groups often competed for influence and opportunity in the political arena. This competition and the rapidity of change in the urban environment caused confusion. In the midst of this confusion, political machines and political bosses emerged to bring some order out of chaos. Eventually, however, a civic reform movement developed. Most reformers strove for efficiency and focused on structural reform in city government. Some concerned themselves with social reform and with city planning and city design. Whatever the goal, American attitudes limited and undermined these reforms. As noted in the textbook, "early urban reform merged idealism with naiveté and insensitivity."

Despite these limiting attitudes, there were technical accomplishments in solving problems such as sanitation, garbage disposal, streetlighting, and bridge and street building. In this respect city engineers, who applied their technical expertise to urban problems, became very important to city governments.

The cultural pluralism that resulted from the late nineteenth-century influx of immigrants, African-Americans, and native white Americans into expanding cities is one of the dominant characteristics of modern America. This heterogeneity is one of America's greatest strengths and has created the richness and the variety that is modern America. In large measure, this diversity is also a reason for the failure of attempts to enforce homogeneity, because the very presence of a number of competing cultural groups prevented any one group from becoming dominant. This has meant, overall, the continued protection of individual rights and the gradual inclusion of more and more groups under the protective umbrella of the Bill of Rights.

Building Vocabulary

Listed below are important words and terms that you need to know to get the most out of Chapter 19. They are listed in the order in which they occur in the chapter. After carefully looking through the list, refer to a dictionary and jot down the definition of words that you do not know or of which you are unsure.

staple

exuberant

centrifugal

centripetal

periphery

insatiable

burgeon

demographic

contingent

disparity

enclave

amulet

repertoire

assimilate

accommodate

orthodox

accede

vermin

tenement

destitution

disparate

admonish

infamous

foist

concomitant

median

quasi

stifle

resilient

enmesh

pneumatic

scruple

demure

pluck

pander

dandy

sordid

exposé

homogenize

disparate

nonsectarian

desecration

affluent

demeaning

transiency

maxim

homogeneous

facet

mire

vie

broker

freelance

largess

equitable

harbinger

nuisance

legacy

pluralism

polarization

Identification and Significance

After studying Chapter 19 of *A People and a Nation,* you should be able to identify fully *and* explain the historical significance of each item listed below.

1. Identify each item in the space provided. Give an explanation or description of the item. Answer the questions *who, what, where,* and *when.*
2. Explain the historical significance of each item in the space provided. Establish the historical context in which the item exists. Establish the item as the result of or as the cause of other factors existing in the society under study. Answer this question: *what were the political, social, economic, and/or cultural consequences of this item?*

the Providence "macaroni riot"

    Identification

    Significance

the electric trolley

    Identification

    Significance

the electric interurban railway

    Identification

    Significance

annexation

>Identification

>Significance

the "new" immigration

>Identification

>Significance

transplanted immigrant communities

>Identification

>Significance

Conservative Judaism

>Identification

>Significance

African-American migration

>Identification

>Significance

New York State tenement legislation

>Identification

>Significance

the germ theory of disease

    Identification

    Significance

steel-frame construction

    Identification

    Significance

Brooklyn Bridge

    Identification

    Significance

"the worthy poor"

    Identification

    Significance

Charity Organization Societies

    Identification

    Significance

Rufus Minor

    Identification

    Significance

© 1994 Houghton Mifflin Company. All rights reserved.

professional law enforcement

    Identification

    Significance

the household and the family

    Identification

    Significance

the nuclear family and the extended family

    Identification

    Significance

the practice of boarding

    Identification

    Significance

the stages of life

    Identification

    Significance

baseball, croquet, bicycling, tennis, golf, college football, and basketball

    Identification

    Significance

© 1994 Houghton Mifflin Company. All rights reserved.

Intercollegiate Athletic Association

    Identification

    Significance

the circus

    Identification

    Significance

popular drama

    Identification

    Significance

musical comedies

    Identification

    Significance

George M. Cohan, Lillian Russell, and Jerome Kern

    Identification

    Significance

vaudeville

    Identification

    Significance

Eva Tanguay

    Identification

    Significance

the minstrel show

    Identification

    Significance

Burt Williams

    Identification

    Significance

moving pictures

    Identification

    Significance

The Birth of a Nation

    Identification

    Significance

the still camera

    Identification

    Significance

the phonograph

> Identification
>
> Significance

Joseph Pulitzer and William Randolph Hearst

> Identification
>
> Significance

Nellie Bly

> Identification
>
> Significance

yellow journalism

> Identification
>
> Significance

mass-circulation magazines

> Identification
>
> Significance

"Acres of Diamonds"

> Identification
>
> Significance

the American Protective Association

    Identification

    Significance

the Chinese exclusion laws of 1882 and 1902

    Identification

    Significance

the ghetto

    Identification

    Significance

political machines

    Identification

    Significance

the political boss

    Identification

    Significance

the urban reform movement

    Identification

    Significance

Mayors Hazen Pingree, Samuel Jones, and Tom Johnson

    Identification

    Significance

campaigns for social betterment

    Identification

    Significance

the Social Gospel

    Identification

    Significance

the settlement house

    Identification

    Significance

Jane Hunter and Modjeska Simkins

    Identification

    Significance

city engineers

    Identification

    Significance

98 Chapter 19

cultural pluralism

   Identification

   Significance

Evaluating and Using Information

The crossword puzzle joined the "hit parade" of America's leisure activities on December 21, 1913. So says the *Philadelphia Enquirer*'s William Ecenbarger. In keeping with the lifestyles and leisure theme in Chapter 19, here is a puzzle designed to help you test how carefully you have studied the chapter. Answers may be any part of speech, including proper nouns, and they may be more than one word long. Each number of a clue identifies the box where the first letter of the answer belongs. Fill boxes downward one letter per box to respond to a "down" clue and from left to right to respond to an "across" clue.

© 1994 Houghton Mifflin Company. All rights reserved.

Across

2. A once-scandalous sport that started out as a sport of the rich—or of the educated, at any rate.
6. A like-aged "pressure" group that had increasing influence over young people much, one may assume, to their families' dismay.
7. Family members that children in 1880–1920 were less likely to know "up close and personal" than are children today.
9. The group that led a black protest against 3 Down (initials).
11. Down-to-earth key word in the name of Pulitzer's New York newspaper, the newspaper that printed the world's first crossword puzzle.
12. Where the country's birthrate was in 1900 compared with the birthrate in 1800.
15. City whose baseball team won the first World Series Championship.
16. Cleveland woman who founded a home for unmarried, black working women.
19. A "comical" item among a printer's supplies whose color gave a style of journalism its name.
20. The kind of tenement that 24 Across and Lawrence Veiller dreamed of seeing built.
21. What young singles were likely to be living as once they got their first job and settled into life away from home.
23. What you might call these three exceptional men: Detroit's Hazen S. Pingree, Cleveland's Tom Johnson, and Toledo's Samuel Jones.
24. A newspaperman who promoted better housing for low-income families.
25. A future president who had very few kind words for immigrants.
26. Common name for ordinances banning many commercial and recreational activities on Sunday.

Down

1. The first and most popular of America's organized sports.
3. D. W. Griffith's racist film epic about the Civil War and Reconstruction.
4. The most remembered trait of the style of journalism made famous by Joseph Pulitzer.
5. Lawn game popular partly because it provided an excuse for men and women to socialize together.
8. The kind of family one might call a nearly minimal family; a family of two—unless baby makes three or more babies make four or five or . . . .
10. What you might call an urban politician with an affinity for "machines."
13. The kind of family group that includes aunts, uncles, and cousins.
14. An activity that some people call a "customer crime" although others don't call it any kind of crime at all.
17. The first name of that crazy investigative reporter Ms. Bly.
18. A welfare center established in an underprivileged neighborhood by Jane Addams to provide social services for people in the area.
20. What the political organization headed by someone who qualifies for the title called for in 10 Down is usually called.
22. A picturesque form of entertainment that the inventive Mr. Edison helped make possible.

Ideas and Details

Objective 1

_____ 1. Which of the following was the primary agent in making suburban life practical and possible?
   a. Long-term mortgage financing
   b. The automobile
   c. Neighborhood shopping centers
   d. Mechanized mass transit

Objective 2

_____ 2. Which of the following was the major contributor to urban population growth in late-nineteenth- and early-twentieth-century America?
   a. Natural increase
   b. Mergers
   c. Migration and immigration
   d. Annexation of outlying areas

Objective 3

_____ 3. "New" immigrants differed from "old" immigrants in that they were
   a. more likely to be non-Protestants.
   b. less family-oriented.
   c. attracted to rural as opposed to urban areas.
   d. escaping from persecution rather than seeking opportunity.

Objective 4

_____ 4. Information about immigrant cultures in the United States supports the statement that most immigrants
   a. quickly shed Old World attitudes and behaviors.
   b. retained their native languages.
   c. found that religion was the one area not affected by American society.
   d. found that their habits and attitudes had to be modified as they interacted with American society.

Objective 9

_____ 5. Black migrants to urban areas differed from foreign immigrants in which of the following ways?
   a. Black migrants were more likely to be males.
   b. Blacks did not have the peasant background of most foreign immigrants.
   c. Blacks found it more difficult to get factory employment.
   d. Black migrants did not move for economic reasons.

Objective 5

_____ 6. As a result of concern about urban housing conditions in the late nineteenth and early twentieth centuries,
   a. private investors pooled their resources to build low-income housing.
   b. some states strengthened the power of local government to regulate landlords' property rights.
   c. federal legislation was enacted that established a standard housing code throughout the United States.
   d. state governments established subsidized housing for the disadvantaged.

Objective 5

_____ 7. In the face of urban poverty, most Americans accepted which of the following beliefs?
   a. One's socioeconomic position within society is based largely on luck.
   b. Poverty can be cured by improving the conditions in which people live and work.
   c. Poverty is a sign that a person is unfit, weak, and lazy.
   d. The government can be a force for good in alleviating the ills of poverty.

Objective 6

_____ 8. The practice of boarding was important in which of the following ways?
   a. It provided a means through which people could find employment.
   b. It provided a transitional stage for many young people between living with their parents and setting up their own households.
   c. It provided childcare facilities to working mothers.
   d. It contributed significantly to overcrowding.

Objective 7

_____ 9. As a result of the popularity of bicycling,
   a. the activities of men and women became more separated.
   b. groups began to demand lighted suburban streets.
   c. women's fashions began to change toward freer styles.
   d. stop and go lights were installed in most cities.

Objectives 7 and 9

_____ 10. Information concerning Burt Williams's career and *The Birth of a Nation* supports which of the following?
   a. Blacks were subjected to prejudicial stereotyping in popular entertainment in the United States.
   b. The ethnic humor in popular entertainment was gentle and sympathetic.
   c. Show business provided economic opportunities to immigrants.
   d. Vaudeville was the most popular form of entertainment in early-twentieth-century America.

Objective 8

____ 11. Studies of occupational mobility in the late nineteenth and early twentieth centuries indicate that
   a. American society had become a static society in which there was little chance for occupational advancement.
   b. at least 10 percent of the population could expect to travel the rags-to-riches path.
   c. major urban areas had approximately equal upward and downward occupational movement.
   d. advancement resulting from movement to a higher status job was relatively common among white males.

Objective 10

____ 12. Urban political machines successfully gained and retained their power because they
   a. were successful in winning and retaining popular support.
   b. brought honesty to city government.
   c. lowered taxes by making city government more efficient.
   d. distributed favors evenly to all groups and classes.

Objective 11

____ 13. Most civic reform leaders
   a. were among the biggest supporters of the accomplishments of political bosses.
   b. concentrated on structural changes rather than on dealing with social problems.
   c. were interested in making government responsive to the social ills of urban society.
   d. supported district representation in city government.

Objective 11

____ 14. Which of the following statements best describes the goals of settlement-house founders?
   a. They wanted to establish an agency through which immigrants could find housing and employment.
   b. They wanted to provide for the needs of street people.
   c. They wanted to establish city-run, tax-supported social welfare agencies.
   d. They wanted to offer a variety of activities through which the lives of working-class people could be improved.

Objective 12

____ 15. The "new" American society created by the urbanization of the late nineteenth century was
   a. a pluralistic society in which different groups competed for power, wealth, and status.
   b. a society in which various ethnic groups had blended into one, unified people.
   c. a smoothly functioning society.
   d. a society in which most people accepted government as an agent for moral reform.

© 1994 Houghton Mifflin Company. All rights reserved.

Essay Questions

Objective 1

1. Examine the impact of mass transportation on late-nineteenth-century American cities.

Objective 3

2. Discuss the similarities and differences between "old" immigrants and "new" immigrants, and examine the response of Americans to the latter.

Objective 4

3. Discuss the interaction between Old World culture and New World reality as experienced by immigrants to the United States in the late nineteenth and early twentieth centuries. What changes in immigrant culture resulted from these interactions?

Objective 5

4. Discuss the problem of urban poverty and the responses of Americans to this problem in the late nineteenth century.

Objective 5

5. Discuss the problem of urban crime and the responses of Americans to this problem in the late nineteenth century.

Objective 6

6. Explain the usefulness of the practice of boarding in American society during the late nineteenth and early twentieth centuries.

Objective 7

7. Discuss the emergence of mass entertainment as a commodity in American society.

Objective 7

8. Discuss the characteristics of popular journalism in late nineteenth-century America.

Objective 8

9. Discuss occupational mobility as a means to get ahead and improve one's status in American society between 1870 and 1920.

Objective 10

10. Analyze the emergence and evaluate the effectiveness of the urban political machines.

CHAPTER 20
Gilded Age Politics, 1877–1900

Learning Objectives

After you have studied Chapter 20 in your textbook and worked through this study guide chapter, you should be able to:

1. Discuss the characteristics of American politics at the national and state levels during the Gilded Age.
2. Discuss the major political and economic issues of the Gilded Age, and examine governmental action on these issues.
3. Examine the progress of the women's suffrage movement during the Gilded Age.
4. Explain the characteristics of American presidents during the Gilded Age, and discuss how each carried out the duties of his office.
5. Discuss the reasons for farm discontent during the late nineteenth century.
6. Explain the organizational and ideological development of rural activism from the Grange to the Populist party.
7. Explain the causes and consequences of the depression of the 1890s, and evaluate Grover Cleveland's response to the depression.
8. Discuss the nature and extent of working-class activism during the era of protest, and explain the reaction of government officials and the public to this activism.
9. Examine the actions taken by southern white Democrats to disfranchise southern blacks, and discuss the consequences of those actions.
10. Analyze the presidential campaign and election of 1896, and explain the political and economic significance of the outcome.

Thematic Guide

In Chapter 20, we focus on the interaction of the political, economic, and social forces within American society during the Gilded Age. This period is characterized by high public interest in local, state, and national elections, political balance between Democrats and Republicans at the national level, and factional and personal feuds within the two parties. Democrats and Republicans in Congress were split on the major national issues: sectional controversies, civil service reform, railroad regulation, tariff policy, monetary policy, and women's suffrage. Though Congress debated these issues, factionalism, interest-group politics, and political equilibrium resulted in the passage of vaguely worded, ineffective legislation such as the Pendleton Civil Service Act, the Interstate Commerce Act, and the Sherman

Anti-Trust Act. Combined with a conservative Supreme Court, weak presidential leadership, and political campaigns that focused on issues of personality rather than issues of substance, these factors caused the postponement of decisions on major issues affecting the nation and its citizens.

The political impasse built up frustration within aggrieved groups in the nation. Aggrieved workers turned to organized labor, to strikes, and, at times, to violence (discussed in Chapter 18). Aggrieved farmers also began to organize. In "Stirrings of Agrarian Unrest and Populism," we examine the reasons for agrarian discontent and trace the manifestation of that discontent from the Grange, through the Farmers' Alliances, to the formation of the Populist party and the drafting of the Omaha platform in 1892.

The depression of the 1890s added to the woes of the United States. President Grover Cleveland failed to deal with the crisis effectively, and an air of crisis settled over the nation. Workers' protests multiplied; the Socialist Party of America, under the leadership of Eugene V. Debs, reorganized; Coxey's Army, demanding a federal jobs program, marched on the nation's capital; and fear of social revolution led business owners and government officials to use brute force to control what they perceived to be radical protest.

As the crisis persisted, the Populist party gained ground, causing leaders of the Democratic party in the South to fear an alliance between southern blacks and poor whites. Such an alliance would have been politically disastrous for southern Democrats; therefore, between 1890 and the early 1900s, with Mississippi Democrats leading the way, the southern states disfranchised blacks. At the national level, Populists, convinced that the "money power" and its imposition of the gold standard on the nation was the root cause of farm distress and the nationwide depression, continued to call for a return of government to the people and crusaded for the "free and unlimited coinage of silver."

The frustrations that had built up in the Gilded Age—an age of transition from rural to urban, from agrarian to industrial society—came to a head in the emotionally charged presidential contest of 1896. An analysis of the issues, outcome, and legacy of this election, which ended the political equilibrium of the age, is offered in the last section of the chapter.

Building Vocabulary

Listed below are important words and terms that you need to know to get the most out of Chapter 20. They are listed in the order in which they occur in the chapter. After carefully looking through the list, refer to a dictionary and jot down the definition of words that you do not know or of which you are unsure.

venality

patronage

redress

alignment

avid

flamboyant

mesmerize

pompous

roguish

potency

fervently

suffrage

rebuff

propriety

assiduously

potentate

temperate

banality

sordid

chide

obstinate

inequity

rhetoric

egalitarian

reprisal

amalgamation

canny

apocalyptic

ideologue

reactionary

ominous

contraction

sabotage

injunction

commonweal

revivify

vestige

pragmatism

founder (*verb*)

Gilded Age Politics, 1877–1900 **109**

Identification and Significance

After studying Chapter 20 of *A People and a Nation*, you should be able to identify fully *and* explain the historical significance of each item listed below.

1. Identify each item in the space provided. Give an explanation or description of the item. Answer the questions *who, what, where,* and *when.*
2. Explain the historical significance of each item in the space provided. Establish the historical context in which the item exists. Establish the item as the result of or as the cause of other factors existing in the society under study. Answer this question: *what were the political, social, economic, and/or cultural consequences of this item?*

James G. Blaine

    Identification

    Significance

the Stalwarts, the Half Breeds, and the Mugwumps

    Identification

    Significance

"waving the bloody shirt"

    Identification

    Significance

the Grand Army of the Republic

    Identification

    Significance

© 1994 Houghton Mifflin Company. All rights reserved.

Chapter 20

the Pendleton Civil Service Act

    Identification

    Significance

Munn v. *Illinois*

    Identification

    Significance

the *Wabash* case

    Identification

    Significance

the Interstate Commerce Act

    Identification

    Significance

the *Maximum Freight Rate* case

    Identification

    Significance

the *Alabama Midlands* case

    Identification

    Significance

© 1994 Houghton Mifflin Company. All rights reserved.

the McKinley Tariff of 1890

    Identification

    Significance

the Wilson-Gorman Tariff of 1894

    Identification

    Significance

the Dingley Tariff of 1897

    Identification

    Significance

reciprocity

    Identification

    Significance

the currency controversy

    Identification

    Significance

"the Crime of '73"

    Identification

    Significance

© 1994 Houghton Mifflin Company. All rights reserved.

the Bland-Allison Act of 1878

    Identification

    Significance

the Sherman Silver Purchase Act of 1890

    Identification

    Significance

the National Woman Suffrage Association

    Identification

    Significance

the American Woman Suffrage Association

    Identification

    Significance

Susan B. Anthony

    Identification

    Significance

Rutherford B. Hayes

    Identification

    Significance

James A. Garfield

> Identification

> Significance

Chester A. Arthur

> Identification

> Significance

the presidential campaign and election of 1884

> Identification

> Significance

Grover Cleveland

> Identification

> Significance

"rum, Romanism, and rebellion"

> Identification

> Significance

the Mills tariff bill of 1888

> Identification

> Significance

Benjamin Harrison

>Identification

>Significance

the Dependents' Pension Act

>Identification

>Significance

the "Billion Dollar Congress"

>Identification

>Significance

the Grange

>Identification

>Significance

the Farmers' Alliances

>Identification

>Significance

the subtreasury plan

>Identification

>Significance

the Populist (People's) party

> Identification

> Significance

the Omaha platform

> Identification

> Significance

the depression of the 1890s

> Identification

> Significance

the Cleveland-Morgan deal

> Identification

> Significance

the Coeur d'Alene strike

> Identification

> Significance

Karl Marx

> Identification

> Significance

Daniel DeLeon

    Identification

    Significance

Eugene V. Debs

    Identification

    Significance

Jacob S. Coxey

    Identification

    Significance

U.S. v. *Reese*

    Identification

    Significance

"the Mississippi Plan"

    Identification

    Significance

the grandfather clause

    Identification

    Significance

free coinage of silver

>Identification

>Significance

the presidential campaign and election of 1896

>Identification

>Significance

William McKinley

>Identification

>Significance

William Jennings Bryan

>Identification

>Significance

the Gold Standard Act

>Identification

>Significance

Organizing Information

Two of the major issues of the Gilded Age concerned tariff policy and monetary policy. Compile and organize information concerning these two issues.

The Tariff

Statement of the Issue:

Position of the Republicans:

Position of the Democrats:

Position of the Populists:

Tariff Legislation				
Proposed Legislation and Date	**Passed**	**Failed**	**Provisions**	**Consequences**

The Currency

Statement of the Issue:

Position of the Republicans:

Position of the Democrats:

Position of the Populists:

Currency Legislation				
Proposed Legislation and Date	**Passed**	**Failed**	**Provisions**	**Consequences**

Evaluating and Using Information

Nowhere can the dashed hopes of the Populist movement and its predecessors in the Agrarian Revolt be seen more clearly than in the movement's dismal showing in the election of 1896. To succeed, the movement would have had to unite a number of groups, enlist both governmental sympathy and help, and kindle the enthusiasm of the electorate. Why couldn't it? Was the movement's failure primarily internal—insufficient drawing power of the leaders and issues—or was it primarily external—a brick wall raised by a powerful and unsympathetic government?

Your goal in this exercise is to produce an essay that answers those questions and provides the information needed to make your answer convincing.

On your own, collect information from the chapter and your class notes and use it to create a description, in working-draft form, of the economic conditions between 1877 and 1900 that gave rise to Populism. You may want to design your own chart to help you find and organize the information you need.

After you have done that, use the two charts on pages 121 and 122 as guides to help you identify and organize the information you need to consider in arriving at a reasonable explanation of why, in such an economic climate, Populism did not enjoy more success.

Begin this phase of the exercise with the charts themselves. In the blanks, list—in chronological order as far as possible—the specifics called for, whether they are actions, attitudes, decisions, groups or regions. Be concise; all you are doing in this step is listing.

Next, expand the lists into full notes and then into the working draft of two discussions, one of the internal problems and another of the external problems. Combine your discussions of the economic conditions, the Populist movement's internal problems, and the Populist movement's external problems. The entire working draft should explain the failure of Populism. Feel free to add information not included in the charts if you think it is needed to support your essay's point (thesis).

Enter your essay in your Reader's Notebook.

From the Agrarian Revolt to the Populists (1877–1900)

Difficulties on the Road to Forming a Coalition with Clout

Natural Constituencies of the Grange, Farmers' Alliances, Populists	Which Definable Groups or Regions Had the Potential To Create an Alliance?	What Aims, Attitudes, or Economic Factors Made These Groups Natural Allies?	What Aims, Attitudes, or Economic Factors Divided These Groups?	Outcome (in the Campaign and Election of 1895–1896)
Sections of the Country				
Economic Have-Nots in the Work force				
Political Power Have-Nots				
Organized Politically Disaffected Groups				
Other—Race, Gender, National Origin, etc.				
Comment, Outcome, or Summary				

© 1994 Houghton Mifflin Company. All rights reserved.

From the Agrarian Revolt to the Populists (1877–1900)
Difficulties on the Road to Finding Support in Government

Where in the Government the Populists and Their Predecessors Might Have Found Support	Actions and Attitudes on Tariff Issues of Concern to the Populists and Their Predecessors	Actions and Attitudes on Currency Questions of Concern to the Populists and Their Predecessors	Actions and Attitudes on Price/Rate and Regulation Issues of Concern to the Populists and Their Predecessors	Actions and Attitudes on the Distribution of Political Power (Voting Rights) Affecting the Success of Populists and Their Predecessors
Congress				
President				
Supreme Court				
State Governments				
Comment, Outcome, or Summary				

Ideas and Details

Objective 1

_____ 1. Which of the following characterized politics during the Gilded Age?
   a. Party allegiance among the voters was so evenly distributed that no one party predominated for very long.
   b. Americans insisted that the government actively pursue solutions to social problems.
   c. There was little public interest in national elections.
   d. Political contests were very impersonal.

Objective 2

_____ 2. In cases arising from the Interstate Commerce Act, the Supreme Court
   a. broadly interpreted the regulatory powers of Congress.
   b. established that government aid to private industry was unconstitutional.
   c. reduced the regulatory powers of the Interstate Commerce Commission.
   d. completely rejected the principle of government regulation of industry.

Objective 5

_____ 3. The "Crime of '73" refers to
   a. passage of the Dingley Act.
   b. the decision by Congress to stop coining silver dollars.
   c. passage of the Sherman Silver Purchase Act.
   d. passage of the Pendleton Act.

Objective 3

_____ 4. Which of the following was the most common argument used by senators voting against the Women's Suffrage amendment?
   a. If women are given the right to vote, they will demand that the nation disarm.
   b. Giving women the right to vote will interfere with their family responsibilities.
   c. Women are not well enough educated to vote.
   d. Women are too emotional to be given the privilege of voting.

Objective 1 and 2

_____ 5. The action taken by Congress on the issue of veterans' pensions demonstrates that
   a. Congress was determined to give equal treatment to Union and Confederate veterans.
   b. memories of the Civil War no longer had an impact on national politics.
   c. Congress was opposed to all forms of welfare legislation.
   d. Congress responded to interest-group pressure.

© 1994 Houghton Mifflin Company. All rights reserved.

Objective 4

_____ 6. Which of the following words best describes the presidents of the Gilded Age?
   a. Inspiring
   b. Lazy
   c. Honorable
   d. Forceful

Objective 1

_____ 7. Which of the following was an important factor in Grover Cleveland's defeat in the presidential election of 1888?
   a. The Republicans successfully engaged in vote fraud in Indiana and New York.
   b. The British minister in Washington publicly supported Benjamin Harrison.
   c. Cleveland's ethnic jokes offended Irish Catholics.
   d. Cleveland offended consumers by suddenly calling for higher tariffs.

Objective 6

_____ 8. The Grange was important because
   a. it successfully increased farm income by eliminating the middle man between farmer and consumer.
   b. it mounted a successful campaign against the political power of corporations.
   c. its promotion of thrift and hard work led to solutions to farm problems.
   d. its activism served as a precedent for future action by farmers.

Objective 6

_____ 9. Farmers hoped that implementation of the subtreasury plan would
   a. lower the cost of farm machinery.
   b. make second mortgages available to farmers facing bankruptcy.
   c. provide higher prices for farm products and low-interest loans to farmers.
   d. lower transportation costs for farm goods.

Objective 6

_____ 10. The Omaha platform called for
   a. the establishment of national agricultural colleges in all states.
   b. a comprehensive welfare program for destitute farmers.
   c. a two-year moratorium on all debts.
   d. government ownership of railroad lines.

Objective 7

_____ 11. The broad-based nature of the 1890s depression was the result of
   a. an interdependent economy.
   b. overspeculation in the stock market.
   c. the Sherman Silver Purchase Act.
   d. the withdrawal of foreign investments.

Objective 8

_____ 12. Which of the following became the leading spokesperson for American socialism in the late 1890s?
   a. Jacob Riis
   b. Eugene V. Debs
   c. Ignatius Donnelly
   d. Leonidas Polk

Objective 8

_____ 13. To end the depression, Jacob Coxey advocated
   a. government aid to business.
   b. a return to the gold standard.
   c. tax cuts to encourage spending.
   d. the infusion of money into the economy through a federal jobs program.

Objective 9

_____ 14. Southern white Democrats decided that blacks should be disfranchised because
   a. they feared the emergence of a southern-based and black-led Socialist party.
   b. black legislators were demanding integrated schools.
   c. they feared a black-white Populist coalition against them.
   d. blacks were winning local elections in predominantly black districts throughout the South.

Objective 10

_____ 15. Which of the following best explains Bryan's defeat in the 1896 election?
   a. The silver issue prevented Bryan from building an urban-rural coalition.
   b. Bryan could not match McKinley's spirited campaign style.
   c. The Populists refused to endorse Bryan.
   d. Endorsement of Bryan by the Socialist party caused people to believe that he was a radical.

Essay Questions

Objective 1

1. Discuss the nature of politics, political parties, and political campaigns during the Gilded Age.

Objective 2

2. Discuss the problems that led to passage of the Interstate Commerce Act, and assess the act's effectiveness.

Objective 2

3. Explain the tariff issue, and trace tariff legislation from passage of the McKinley Tariff in 1890 through passage of the Dingley Tariff of 1897. What were the consequences of the tariff policies of the United States during this period?

Objectives 5 and 6

4. Explain the emergence of the farm protest movement, and examine its development through the 1896 election.

Objective 7

5. Discuss the causes and consequences of the depression of the 1890s.

Objective 10

6. Examine the personalities and issues of the 1896 presidential campaign, and explain the election's outcome.

CHAPTER 21
The Progressive Era, 1895–1920

Learning Objectives

After you have studied Chapter 21 in your textbook and worked through this study guide chapter, you should be able to:

1. Explain the emergence of progressivism and discuss the movement's basic themes.
2. Discuss the similarities and differences among the ideologies, goals, and tactics of the various groups that constituted the Progressive movement, and analyze the successes and failures of these groups in achieving political, social, and moral reform.
3. Explain the emergence of the Socialist movement, and indicate how it differed from progressivism in ideology, goals, and tactics.
4. Discuss and evaluate the impact of progressive ideas in education, law, and the social sciences.
5. Explain and evaluate the approaches of blacks, American Indians, and women to the problems they faced during the Progressive era, and discuss the extent to which they were successful in achieving their goals.
6. Explain the relationship between Theodore Roosevelt's political, social, and economic beliefs and his approach toward the major issues of the day.
7. Indicate the reasons for the break between William Howard Taft and Theodore Roosevelt, and explain the impact of this break on the 1912 election.
8. Examine the similarities and differences between Roosevelt and Woodrow Wilson.
9. Explain and evaluate the reform legislation of the Wilson presidency.
10. Assess the political, social, and economic impact of the Progressive era on American society.

Thematic Guide

In Chapter 21, we focus on the Progressive era and progressivism: a series of movements that brought together reform-minded individuals and groups with differing solutions to the nation's problems in the years 1895 to 1920. The progressives were members of nationwide organizations that attempted to affect government policy. They were people interested in urban issues and urban political and social reform. Although progressives came from all levels of society, new middle-class professionals formed the vanguard of the movement and found expression for their ideas in muckraking journalism.

Revolted by corruption and injustice, the new urban middle class called for political reform to make government more efficient, less corrupt, and more accountable. Such government, they believed, could be a force for good in American society. Some business executives argued for a society organized along the lines of the corporate model; women of the elite classes formed the YWCA and the Women's Christian Temperance Union. Working-class reformers pressed for government legislation to aid labor and improve social welfare. Although some reformers turned to the Socialist party, they were a decided minority and cannot be considered progressives. Progressives generally had far too great a stake in the capitalist system to advocate its destruction and, as a result, were political moderates rather than radicals.

The many facets of progressivism can be seen in the section "Governmental and Legislative Reform." Progressives generally agreed that government power should be used to check the abuses associated with the industrial age, but they did not always agree on the nature of the problem. At the city and state levels, progressives were initially interested in attacking the party system and in effecting political reform designed to make government more honest, more professional, and more responsive to the people. These aims can be seen through the accomplishments of Robert M. La Follette, one of the most effective progressive governors, and in the Seventeenth Amendment, one of the major political reforms achieved by progressives at the national level. Some progressives also worked for social reform at the state level, to protect the well-being of citizens from exploitative corporate power. Still other progressives believed in using the power of government to purify society by effecting moral reform. Such efforts were behind the Eighteenth Amendment and the Mann Act (White Slave Traffic Act).

The Progressive era also witnessed an assault on traditional ideas in education, law, and the social sciences. In the section "New Ideas in Education, Law, and the Social Sciences," we examine the new ideas, resistance to them, and the changes they brought, and we evaluate those changes. This section also outlines progressive reforms in public health. The following section, "Challenges to Racial and Sexual Discrimination," describes the dilemma faced by blacks, American Indians, and women seeking equality in American society. After contrasting the approaches of Booker T. Washington and W. E. B. Du Bois toward white racism, we look at attempts by American Indians to advance their interests through the formation of the Society of American Indians. We then turn to the various aspects of "the woman movement," contrasting the aims and goals of women involved in the women's club movement with those involved in the feminist movement and discussing the contrasting viewpoints of elite women and feminists involved in the suffrage movement.

The Progressive era reached the national level of government when Theodore Roosevelt became president in 1901. We examine Roosevelt's political, economic, and social frame of reference and evaluate the progressive legislation passed during his administration. The contrast between the Taft administration that followed and the Roosevelt years spurred progressives to found the Progressive party under Roosevelt's leadership. We also discuss the similarities and differences between Roosevelt's New Nationalism and Woodrow Wilson's New Freedom, and we examine the reasons for Wilson's election in 1912.

In "Woodrow Wilson and the Extension of Reform," we analyze Wilson's frame of reference and evaluate the legislation passed during his two administrations. The chapter ends with a summary and evaluation of the Progressive era.

Building Vocabulary

Listed below are important words and terms that you need to know to get the most out of Chapter 21. They are listed in the order in which they occur in the chapter. After carefully looking through the list, refer to a dictionary and jot down the definition of words that you do not know or of which you are unsure.

odyssey

ardent

cornucopia

amenity

arbitration

allegory

recoil

humanitarian

rebuke

charismatic

induce

connive

homily

rote

ingenuity

epitomize

impetus

vigilante

assimilation

accommodation

condescension

criterion

implicit

pariah

infuse

unbridle

unscrupulous

malefactor

insurgent

impetuous

Armageddon

exhort

evangelical

mandate

pince-nez

bellicose

Identification and Significance

After studying Chapter 21 of *A People and a Nation,* you should be able to identify fully *and* explain the historical significance of each item listed below.

1. Identify each item in the space provided. Give an explanation or description of the item. Answer the questions *who, what, where,* and *when.*
2. Explain the historical significance of each item in the space provided. Establish the historical context in which the item exists. Establish the item as the result of or as the cause of other factors existing in the society under study. Answer this question: *what were the political, social, economic, and/or cultural consequences of this item?*

Florence Kelley

    Identification

    Significance

interest-group politics

    Identification

    Significance

the National Municipal League and the National Civic Federation

    Identification

    Significance

muckrakers

    Identification

    Significance

© 1994 Houghton Mifflin Company. All rights reserved.

direct primaries and nonpartisan elections

> Identification

> Significance

the initiative, the referendum, and the recall

> Identification

> Significance

the Municipal Voters League and the U.S. Chamber of Commerce

> Identification

> Significance

the YWCA and the Woman's Christian Temperance Union

> Identification

> Significance

Alfred E. Smith, Robert F. Wagner, David I. Walsh, and Edward F. Dunne

> Identification

> Significance

Eugene V. Debs

> Identification

> Significance

"old guard" Republicans

    Identification

    Significance

Robert M. La Follette

    Identification

    Significance

the Seventeenth Amendment

    Identification

    Significance

state factory inspection laws

    Identification

    Significance

the National Child Labor Committee

    Identification

    Significance

the American Association for Old Age Security

    Identification

    Significance

National Association of Manufacturers

    Identification

    Significance

the Anti-Saloon League

    Identification

    Significance

the Eighteenth Amendment

    Identification

    Significance

white slavery

    Identification

    Significance

The Social Evil in Chicago

    Identification

    Significance

the Mann Act

    Identification

    Significance

G. Stanley Hall and John Dewey

    Identification

    Significance

land-grant colleges

    Identification

    Significance

Oliver Wendell Holmes, Jr.

    Identification

    Significance

Louis D. Brandeis

    Identification

    Significance

Mueller v. *Oregon*, *Lochner* v. *New York*, and *Holden* v. *Hardy*

    Identification

    Significance

Tenth Amendment

    Identification

    Significance

Richard T. Ely

    Identification

    Significance

Lester Ward, Albion Small, and Edward Ross

    Identification

    Significance

Charles A. Beard

    Identification

    Significance

the National Consumers League

    Identification

    Significance

W. E. B. Du Bois

    Identification

    Significance

Booker T. Washington

    Identification

    Significance

the Atlanta Compromise

    Identification

    Significance

the Niagara movement

    Identification

    Significance

the "Talented Tenth"

    Identification

    Significance

the National Association for the Advancement of Colored People

    Identification

    Significance

the Society of American Indians

    Identification

    Significance

"the woman movement"

    Identification

    Significance

© 1994 Houghton Mifflin Company. All rights reserved.

the women's club movement

    Identification

    Significance

the National Association of Colored Women

    Identification

    Significance

the feminist movement

    Identification

    Significance

Charlotte Perkins Gilman

    Identification

    Significance

Margaret Sanger

    Identification

    Significance

the suffrage movement

    Identification

    Significance

Harriott Stanton Blatch

    Identification

    Significance

Carrie Chapman Catt and Alice Paul

    Identification

    Significance

Theodore Roosevelt

    Identification

    Significance

the Northern Securities Company

    Identification

    Significance

the Hepburn Act

    Identification

    Significance

The Jungle

    Identification

    Significance

the Meat Inspection Act

    Identification

    Significance

the Pure Food and Drug Act

    Identification

    Significance

the coal strike of 1902

    Identification

    Significance

the National Reclamation Act

    Identification

    Significance

the national Conservation Congress

    Identification

    Significance

the Panic of 1907

    Identification

    Significance

William Howard Taft

    Identification

    Significance

the Payne-Aldrich Tariff

    Identification

    Significance

the revolt against "Cannonism"

    Identification

    Significance

Richard A. Ballinger-Gifford Pinchot dispute

    Identification

    Significance

the Mann-Elkins Act of 1910

    Identification

    Significance

the Sixteenth Amendment

    Identification

    Significance

Chapter 21

the National Progressive Republican League

    Identification

    Significance

the Progressive party

    Identification

    Significance

Woodrow Wilson

    Identification

    Significance

the presidential election of 1912

    Identification

    Significance

New Nationalism

    Identification

    Significance

New Freedom

    Identification

    Significance

the Clayton Anti-Trust Act

    Identification

    Significance

the Federal Trade Commission

    Identification

    Significance

the Federal Reserve Act of 1913

    Identification

    Significance

the discount rate

    Identification

    Significance

the Underwood Tariff

    Identification

    Significance

the income tax

    Identification

    Significance

the Federal Farm Loan Act of 1916

>Identification

>Significance

the Adamson Act of 1916

>Identification

>Significance

the presidential election of 1916

>Identification

>Significance

the War Industries Board

>Identification

>Significance

Organizing Information

Use the chart below to compile and organize information concerning Progressive reforms at the city, state, and national levels of government into three categories that correspond to the three major Progressive themes identified in the text.

Progressive Themes and Accomplishments			
	Opposition to Abuse of Power	**Reform of Social Institutions**	**Quest for Cooperation and Scientific Efficiency**
Action at City Level			
Action at State Level			
Presidential Action			
Congressional Action			
Supreme Court Decisions			

Evaluating and Using Information

During the Progressive Era, there were groups in American society that lacked economic, political, and social power. Because of this lack of power, they had few choices about the opportunities available to them, little control over their own health and safety, and little or no input into the decision-making process within the society of which they were a part. Review the discussions of these groups in Chapter 21 and use the significant information you discover to develop your own theory to answer the following question.

> Why did some groups have more difficulty than others in gaining greater recognition of their social, economic, and civil rights during the Progressive era?

Compose the working draft of an essay presenting and supporting your theory. Enter your essay in your Reading Notebook.

In reviewing the chapter and gathering the information you need, you might want to focus on such basic areas as these:

1. Strategies that leaders within the groups recommended and who those leaders were. Were the strategies at fault? Was there a lack of agreement on strategies?
2. What individual non-leaders in the groups were doing that affected their status and opportunities. Were members of the less successful groups behaving in ways that fostered antagonism? What made individuals of the group so satisfied with their lives—or so busy—that they lost interest in helping the group? Were members of the more successful groups doing anything special to gain support?
3. How factors and the power elite in Washington promoted or hindered the groups' efforts to achieve greater recognition and power. Were there factors that made civil and human rights issues unimportant outside the affected groups? Did powerful individuals think the groups' aspirations were inappropriate?

And you may want to use the chart on pages 147 and 148 as an aid in organizing the information you will need to make your answer specific and concrete. If so, first select the proposals, individuals, attitudes, behaviors, and events that you think are most significant, and then list them in the appropriate blocks. Use the items and brief notes you enter in the chart as reminders of what to mention and discuss in your essay.

The Progressive Era, 1895–1920

Approaches to Achieving Human and Civil Rights and Protection for Those Without Economic and Political Power

Groups Being Denied Key Human Rights, or Civil Rights, or Protection from Health Hazards or Other Abuses	Prominent Figures or Leaders within the Group, or Advocates Outside the Group Favoring Special Strategies	Strategies for Gaining Rights, Recognition, or Protection Recommended by These Figures, Leaders, or Advocates	Actions of Unorganized Individuals within the Group that Changed Their Lot or Influenced Attitudes Toward Their Group	Specific Factors, or Policies and Attitudes of National Leaders Outside the Group that Helped or Hindered the Group in Achieving Its Human and Civil-Rights Goals	Additional Comment Successes? Failures? Progress?
Women					
Blacks					
Indians					

Groups Being Denied Key Human Rights, or Civil Rights, or Protection from Health Hazards or Other Abuses	Prominent Figures or Leaders within the Group, or Advocates Outside the Group Favoring Special Strategies	Strategies for Gaining Rights, Recognition, or Protection Recommended by These Figures, Leaders, or Advocates	Actions of Unorganized Individuals within the Group that Changed Their Lot or Influenced Attitudes Toward Their Group	Specific Factors, or Policies and Attitudes of National Leaders Outside the Group that Helped or Hindered the Group in Achieving Its Human and Civil-Rights Goals	Additional Comment Successes? Failures? Progress?
Immigrants					
Children					
Laborers					
Radicals					

Ideas and Details

Objective 1

_____ 1. Organizations such as the American Bar Association, the National Consumers League, and the National Municipal League
   a. increased the loyalty of the electorate to political parties.
   b. introduced charismatic personalities to political campaigns.
   c. stifled debate on major urban issues.
   d. made politics more issue oriented than in previous eras.

Objective 2

_____ 2. In calling for direct primaries, middle-class progressives demonstrated which of the following beliefs?
   a. Government should be placed in the hands of professional politicians.
   b. All citizens should be allowed to participate in the decision-making process.
   c. Government can be improved by reducing the power of political parties.
   d. Government should respect the rights of the individual.

Objectives 1 and 2

_____ 3. With regard to governmental reform, progressives wanted to
   a. bargain with different interest groups to accomplish needed reforms.
   b. use the techniques of scientific management to bring efficiency to government.
   c. require literacy tests for voting to ensure that the electorate was educated and responsible.
   d. require full financial disclosure by all political candidates to ensure their independence from special-interest groups.

Objective 2

_____ 4. Unlike middle-class progressives, working-class progressives
   a. were interested more in political reform than in social reform.
   b. rejected the idea that the government should regulate the workplace.
   c. usually supported moral reform movements such as prohibition.
   d. often realized that urban political bosses could aid their reform efforts.

Objective 3

_____ 5. Most progressives did not ally with the socialists because
   a. progressives were offended by the abrasive personality of Eugene Debs.
   b. progressives had a stake in the capitalist system and did not want to overthrow it.
   c. progressives rejected the nationalist appeals of the socialists.
   d. progressives accepted the basic tenets of the laissez-faire philosophy.

© 1994 Houghton Mifflin Company. All rights reserved.

Objective 2

_____ 6. Governor Robert M. La Follette believed that
   a. corporations should be driven out of politics.
   b. the working classes could never gain social justice in a capitalist society.
   c. regulatory commissions represented a threat to the free enterprise system.
   d. the federal government should nationalize the railroads.

Objective 4

_____ 7. John Dewey believed that
   a. public education should concentrate on the teaching of basic moral principles.
   b. public school teachers should be accredited by a national accreditation agency.
   c. mastery by students of a given body of knowledge should be the primary aim of public education.
   d. public school curricula should be relevant to the lives of students.

Objective 5

_____ 8. Which of the following best expresses the beliefs of Booker T. Washington?
   a. Blacks should passively accept their inferior position in a white-dominated society.
   b. Blacks should prove themselves worthy of equal rights by working hard and acquiring property.
   c. Blacks should demand political and social equality in American society.
   d. Blacks should challenge discriminatory legislation in the courts.

Objective 5

_____ 9. The most decisive factor in the decision to extend the right to vote to women was
   a. acceptance of the argument that all Americans are equal and deserve the same rights.
   b. acceptance of the idea that women would humanize politics.
   c. the contributions made by women on the home front during the First World War.
   d. the militant tactics of women like Carrie Chapman Catt.

Objective 6

_____ 10. President Roosevelt's handling of trusts suggests that he accepted which of the following beliefs?
   a. Businesses must be allowed to operate and organize without government interference.
   b. Antitrust laws should be used to prosecute unscrupulous corporations that exploit the public and refuse to regulate themselves.
   c. Bigness is bad in and of itself.
   d. The tax power of the government should be used to punish irresponsible corporations.

Objective 7

_____ 11. Theodore Roosevelt and William Howard Taft differed in which of the following ways?
   a. Roosevelt acted assertively to expand presidential power; Taft was cautious in his use of power.
   b. Roosevelt took care not to offend business leaders; Taft was tactless and abrasive.
   c. Roosevelt insisted on operating within the letter of the law; Taft was willing to bend the law to his purposes.
   d. Roosevelt was sympathetic to reform; Taft found reform dangerous and unnecessary.

Objective 8

_____ 12. Roosevelt's New Nationalism, unlike Wilson's New Freedom, called for
   a. the destruction of big business.
   b. a restoration of laissez faire.
   c. cooperation between big business and big government through the establishment of regulatory commissions.
   d. equality of economic opportunity.

Objective 8

_____ 13. By advocating passage of the Clayton Anti-Trust Act and the creation of the Federal Trade Commission, President Wilson
   a. demonstrated his belief that restoration of free competition was possible.
   b. indicated his determination to challenge rulings of the Supreme Court.
   c. stubbornly challenged the probusiness Democratic leadership in Congress.
   d. acknowledged that government regulatory powers had to be expanded to deal with the reality of economic concentration.

Objective 8

_____ 14. The Underwood Tariff
   a. fostered competition by lowering tariff rates.
   b. was rejected by President Wilson because it levied a tax on personal income.
   c. established a 50-percent tax on incomes over $100,000.
   d. led to a trade war among the major trading nations.

Objective 9

_____ 15. In the final analysis, the progressives were able to
   a. bring about a redistribution of power in the United States.
   b. remove state and national government from the influence of business and industrial interests.
   c. force business and industrial interests to pay more attention to public opinion.
   d. unite behind a comprehensive reform program for American society.

Essay Questions

Objectives 1 and 2

1. Explain the social, political, and economic ideas of middle-class progressives, and evaluate their accomplishments at the local level of American society.

Objective 5

2. Discuss the similarities and differences between the approaches of Booker T. Washington and W. E. B. Du Bois to the problems faced by black Americans.

Objective 5

3. Discuss and evaluate the varying approaches of women to the problems they faced in early twentieth century America.

Objective 6

4. Explain Theodore Roosevelt's approach to big business and the philosophy behind that approach.

Objective 8

5. Defend the following statement: "As president, Wilson had to blend his New Freedom ideals with New Nationalism precepts, and in so doing he set the direction of federal economic policy for much of the twentieth century."

CHAPTER 22
The Quest for Empire, 1865–1914

Learning Objectives

After you have studied Chapter 22 in your textbook and worked through this study guide chapter, you should be able to:

1. Examine the late-nineteenth-century sources of American expansionism and imperialism.
2. Describe the expansionist vision of William H. Seward, and indicate the extent to which this vision was realized by the late 1880s.
3. Discuss the causes and consequences of the Hawaiian and Venezuelan crises.
4. Examine the causes (both underlying and immediate) and discuss the conduct of the Spanish-American-Cuban-Filipino War, and indicate the provisions of the Treaty of Paris.
5. Outline the arguments presented by both the anti-imperialists and the imperialists in the debate over acquisition of an empire, and explain why the imperialists prevailed.
6. Examine and evaluate late-nineteenth- and early-twentieth-century American policy toward Asia in general and toward China, the Philippines, and Japan specifically.
7. Examine and evaluate United States policy toward the countries of Latin America in the early twentieth century.

Thematic Guide

The expansionist and eventually imperialistic orientation of United States foreign policy after 1865 stemmed from the country's domestic situation. Those who led the internal expansion of the United States after the Civil War were architects of the nation's foreign policy. These national leaders, known collectively as the foreign policy elite, believed that extending American influence abroad would foster American prosperity, and they sought to use American foreign policy to open and safeguard foreign markets. The domestic roots of the nation's foreign policy are seen in the resurgence of nationalism in the United States after the Civil War. There was increased talk of Americans as a special people favored by God, Social Darwinism was used to support the idea of American superiority, and American missionaries went forth to convert the "heathen." This combination of political, economic, and cultural factors in the 1890s, prompted the foreign policy elite to move beyond support of mere economic expansion toward advocacy of an imperialistic course for the United States. American imperialism was characterized by a belief in the rightness of American society and American solutions. These characteristics produced what some historians have called the "tragedy of American diplomacy."

The section "Factory, Farm, and Foreign Affairs" shows in greater detail the relationship between internal economic expansion and economic expansion abroad. We examine further the connection between foreign economic expansion and increased American political, social, and cultural influence on foreign nations. We also begin to set the stage for the distinction drawn by some leaders between economic expansion and imperialism—a distinction that would ultimately lead to a national debate between anti-imperialists and imperialists.

The analysis of American expansionism serves as a backdrop for scrutiny of the American empire from the end of the Civil War to 1914. William H. Seward, as secretary of state from 1861 to 1869 and as a member of the foreign policy elite, was one of the chief architects of this empire. In examining Seward's expansionist vision and the extent to which it was realized by the late 1880s, we again see the relationship between domestic and foreign policy.

Acquisition of territories and markets abroad led the United States to heed the urgings of Captain Alfred T. Mahan and to embark on the building of the New Navy. The fleet gave the nation the means to protect America's international interests and to become more assertive, as in the Hawaiian, Venezuelan, and Cuban crises of the 1890s. The varied motives that led the United States into the Spanish-American-Cuban-Filipino War offer another striking example of the complex links between domestic and foreign policy. In these crises of the 1890s, the American frame of reference toward peoples of other nations became more noticeable in the shaping of foreign policy. In the Cuban crisis, as in the Venezuelan crisis, Americans insisted that the United States would establish the rules for nations in the Western Hemisphere.

The Treaty of Paris, which ended the Spanish-American-Cuban-Filipino War, sparked a debate between imperialists and anti-imperialists over the course of American foreign policy. In "The Taste of Empire: Imperialists vs. Anti-Imperialists," we examine the arguments of the two groups and the reasons for the defeat of the anti-imperialists.

In the last two sections of the chapter, we turn to the American empire in Asia and Latin America. The American frame of reference with regard to other ethnic groups, along with American political, economic, and social interests, shaped the Open Door policy as well as relations with Japan and caused the oppression of the Filipinos. The same factors determined American relations with Latin America, where the American search for order became dominant.

Building Vocabulary

Listed below are important words and terms that you need to know to get the most out of Chapter 22. They are listed in the order in which they occur in the chapter. After carefully looking through the list, refer to a dictionary and jot down the definition of words that you do not know or of which you are unsure.

archipelago

oligarchy

rectitude

lucrative

disparage

cosmopolitan

clannish

luminaries

exceptionalism

paternalism

hypocritical

coercive

entrepreneur

articulate

aggrandizement

fruition

persevere

rapprochement

bemoan

brash

parlance

© 1994 Houghton Mifflin Company. All rights reserved.

fiat

hegemony

interposition

jingoistic

autonomy

unilateral

inveterate

motley

usurp

retort

subvert

hierarchy

foray

tenet

imperious

uncowed

taut

stymie

subjugate

chafe

tutelage

despoil

bombastic

embroilment

Identification and Significance

After studying Chapter 22 of *A People and a Nation,* you should be able to identify fully *and* explain the historical significance of each item listed below.

1. Identify each item in the space provided. Give an explanation or description of the item. Answer the questions *who, what, where,* and *when.*
2. Explain the historical significance of each item in the space provided. Establish the historical context in which the item exists. Establish the item as the result of or as the cause of other factors existing in the society under study. Answer this question: *what were the political, social, economic, and/or cultural consequences of this item?*

the "Bayonet Constitution"

    Identification

    Significance

the McKinley Tariff of 1890

    Identification

    Significance

the Hawaiian revolution

    Identification

    Significance

expansionism versus imperialism

    Identification

    Significance

the foreign policy elite

    Identification

    Significance

Our Country

    Identification

    Significance

Grace Roberts

    Identification

    Significance

Turner's frontier thesis

    Identification

    Significance

"the tragedy of American diplomacy"

    Identification

    Significance

United Fruit Company

    Identification

    Significance

William H. Seward

    Identification

    Significance

the purchase of Alaska

    Identification

    Significance

Archduke Ferdinand Maximilian

    Identification

    Significance

the Burlingame Treaty

    Identification

    Significance

© 1994 Houghton Mifflin Company. All rights reserved.

160 *Chapter 22*

the transatlantic cable

    Identification

    Significance

the *Virginius* affair

    Identification

    Significance

Hamilton Fish

    Identification

    Significance

the Washington Treaty

    Identification

    Significance

Dominican Republic treaty of annexation

    Identification

    Significance

the Samoan Islands

    Identification

    Significance

the Pan-American Conference of 1889

> Identification

> Significance

Captain Alfred T. Mahan

> Identification

> Significance

the New Navy

> Identification

> Significance

the Hawaiian-annexation question

> Identification

> Significance

the Venezuelan crisis of 1895

> Identification

> Significance

the Cuban revolution

> Identification

> Significance

José Martí

    Identification

    Significance

the Wilson-Gorman Tariff

    Identification

    Significance

General Valeriano Weyler

    Identification

    Significance

the *Maine*

    Identification

    Significance

the de Lôme letter

    Identification

    Significance

McKinley's war message

    Identification

    Significance

the Teller Amendment

> Identification

> Significance

the Spanish-American-Cuban-Filipino War

> Identification

> Significance

wartime racial prejudice

> Identification

> Significance

George Dewey

> Identification

> Significance

the Treaty of Paris

> Identification

> Significance

anti-imperialist arguments

> Identification

> Significance

164 *Chapter 22*

imperialist arguments

    Identification

    Significance

the Open Door policy

    Identification

    Significance

the Boxer Rebellion

    Identification

    Significance

Emilio Aguinaldo

    Identification

    Significance

the Philippine Insurrection

    Identification

    Significance

the Moros

    Identification

    Significance

© 1994 Houghton Mifflin Company. All rights reserved.

the Jones Act

> Identification

> Significance

the Portsmouth Conference

> Identification

> Significance

the Taft-Katsura Agreement

> Identification

> Significance

the Root-Takahira Agreement

> Identification

> Significance

the Great White Fleet

> Identification

> Significance

"dollar diplomacy"

> Identification

> Significance

the San Francisco School Board segregation order

    Identification

    Significance

the Platt Amendment

    Identification

    Significance

Walter Reed

    Identification

    Significance

Puerto Rican-U. S. relations

    Identification

    Significance

the Foraker Act

    Identification

    Significance

the Hay-Pauncefote Treaty of 1901

    Identification

    Significance

the Panamanian revolution

    Identification

    Significance

the Panama Canal

    Identification

    Significance

the Roosevelt Corollary to the Monroe Doctrine

    Identification

    Significance

Anglo-American rapprochement

    Identification

    Significance

Organizing Information

In the years since the Spanish-American-Cuban-Filipino War, United States political, economic, and military involvement in Latin America has increased. Using information contained in this and subsequent chapters and information gained from independent research, chart United States involvement in Cuba and Central America over the years.

Cuba		Guatemala		Honduras	
Year	Nature of U.S. Involvement	Year	Nature of U.S. Involvement	Year	Nature of U.S. Involvement
1898	Spanish-American War. U.S. troops remain until 1902.	1899			
1903					

Panama		El Salvador		Nicaragua	
Year	Nature of U.S. Involvement	Year	Nature of U.S. Involvement	Year	Nature of U.S. Involvement

Evaluating and Using Information

A major focus of Chapter 22 is, of course, the *-isms* that drove the policies of the United States in its dealings with countries in both the Far East and the Americas—nationalism, evangelism, racism, expansionism, imperialism.

In this exercise you are to gather and organize specific information about American imperialism from the chapter and from your class notes and to compose the working draft of an essay to answer this question:

> What in America's attempts to extend its influence and control overseas between 1865 and 1914 explains why many people overseas call the United States imperialistic and fear what it might do next?

Review what Chapter 22 tells you about the meaning of *imperialism*. After having done that, use the following chart to help you analyze the methods the nation used from 1865 to 1914 to pursue the goals of those among its political and business elite who advocated imperialism.

The first column of the chart names some basic goals related to American foreign policy during the period from 1865 to 1914. Columns two through seven list methods used to accomplish these foreign-policy goals. Use columns two through seven to categorize examples of American actions that accomplished or were intended to accomplish the foreign-policy goals named in column one.

(In some cases you may need to list the same example under more than one method.) Make each entry specific, but enter only enough information to serve as reminders that can be expanded when you write out the working draft of your essay and that can be used in reviewing the material.

Expand the notes you enter in the chart and use the results to create the working draft of an essay responding to the question. Enter your essay in your Reading Notebook.

Purpose or consequence of the use of power or of influence derived from power	Methods of Influencing Asian and American Countries					Effect on or response of other countries
	Diplomatic pressure	Military actions or threats	Economic action or pressure	Covert action, conspiracies	Other (altruism, etc.)	
American Use of Its Power Abroad, 1865–1914							
To protect the property of citizens living in other countries or of companies doing business in other countries						
To taking over territory of or to change the boundaries of countries for the purpose of controlling assets or facilities of military or economic value						

Purpose or consequence of the use of power or of influence derived from power	Methods of Influencing Asian and American Countries					Effect on or response of other countries
	Diplomatic pressure	Military actions or threats	Economic action or pressure	Covert action, conspiracies	Other (altruism, etc.)	
To install leaders who would support American interests or to remove leaders who would oppose American interests						
To establish trade and tariff policies designed to protect domestic business interests without regard to the consequences in other nations or to influence the policies of other nations						
To control the outcome of civil wars or insurrections in other countries or the attempts of provinces within other countries to secede						
To control the forms of government, constitutions or legal institutions, or the trade agreements or treaties of other countries or territories						
To affect the class structure, the relative power of social and economic classes, or the racial and religious divisions within another country						
To influence the cultural development (language, dress, education, etc.) or to alter the religious makeup or the value system of another country						

© 1994 Houghton Mifflin Company. All rights reserved.

Ideas and Details

Objective 1

_____ 1. Foreign policy decisions in the late nineteenth century were shaped largely by
   a. the opinions of the American people.
   b. the business community.
   c. the foreign policy elite.
   d. generals and admirals.

Objectives 1, 6 and 7

_____ 2. The "tragedy of American diplomacy" was the
   a. inability of the United States to act decisively in matters of foreign policy.
   b. American disregard for the principle of self-rule when that idea was applied to other nations.
   c. willingness of the United States to use military force.
   d. unprofessional nature of the American diplomatic corps.

Objective 1

_____ 3. One of the sources of the expansionist sentiment of the late nineteenth century was the
   a. desire of American farmers to learn new agricultural techniques from foreign agricultural specialists.
   b. belief that foreign economic expansion would relieve the problem of overproduction at home.
   c. belief that more immigrants would solve domestic labor problems.
   d. desire of Latin American countries for the United States to exert political control over them.

Objective 2

_____ 4. William H. Seward's vision of an American empire
   a. was confined to the Americas.
   b. included the building of a Central American canal.
   c. involved acquisition of territory by military conquest.
   d. took a giant step forward with the purchase of the Danish West Indies in 1867.

Objective 2

_____ 5. The person largely responsible for popularizing the New Navy was
   a. Andrew Carnegie.
   b. Ulysses Grant.
   c. Hamilton Fish.
   d. Alfred T. Mahan.

Objective 3

_____ 6. President Grover Cleveland opposed the annexation of Hawaii because he
   a. saw no economic advantages to it.
   b. wanted no close ties with people of another race.
   c. did not believe in forced annexation.
   d. was afraid it would lead to war.

Objective 3

_____ 7. In the settlement of the Venezuelan crisis of 1895,
   a. the United States showed a disregard for the rights of Venezuela.
   b. the United States insisted that Venezuela adopt a democratic form of government.
   c. Great Britain was able to bully the United States into submission.
   d. the United States Navy showed its inability to operate in a crisis.

Objective 4

_____ 8. The Teller Amendment
   a. announced that the United States would annex Cuba.
   b. led to the declaration of war against Spain.
   c. expanded the theater of war to the South Pacific.
   d. renounced any American intentions to annex Cuba.

Objective 4

_____ 9. In the final analysis, the United States went to war with Spain because
   a. of a humanitarian desire to help the Cuban people.
   b. of a desire to carry the Christian message to other people.
   c. of the multifaceted spirit of expansionism, which had been building for some time.
   d. war offered an opportunity to fulfill the "large policy."

Objective 4

_____ 10. Most American casualties in the Spanish-American-Cuban-Filipino War were incurred
   a. through diseases contracted during the war.
   b. in the Santiago campaign.
   c. in Admiral Dewey's battle with the Spanish fleet in Manila Bay.
   d. by the Rough Riders in the charge up San Juan Hill.

Objective 5

_____ 11. The anti-imperialist campaign against the Treaty of Paris was
   a. based on purely constitutional arguments.
   b. hindered by the inconsistency of the anti-imperialist arguments.
   c. successful because of the influence of people like Mark Twain and Andrew Carnegie.
   d. successful because of Bryan's decision to support the treaty.

© 1994 Houghton Mifflin Company. All rights reserved.

Objective 6

_____ 12. Which of the following best expresses the ideology behind the Open Door policy?
   a. The self-determination of other nations must be preserved.
   b. The closing of any area to American trade is a threat to the survival of the United States.
   c. Freedom of the seas will lead to the economic expansion of the world community of nations.
   d. All nations of the world should be considered equals.

Objective 6

_____ 13. In the Philippines, the United States
   a. fought to suppress an insurrection against American rule.
   b. quickly lived up to its promise to give the country its independence.
   c. held a referendum to determine the wishes of the Filipino people.
   d. established a democratic government that guaranteed the same basic rights enjoyed by Americans.

Objective 6

_____ 14. Relations between the United States and Japan were negatively affected by
   a. the extension of American aid to French colonies in Indochina.
   b. American refusal to recognize Japanese hegemony in Korea.
   c. President Roosevelt's extension of military aid to Russia during the Russo-Japanese war.
   d. the involvement of American bankers in an international consortium to build a Chinese railway.

Objective 7

_____ 15. Which of the following best explains the rationale behind the Roosevelt Corollary to the Monroe Doctrine and the imperialistic behavior of the United States in Latin America?
   a. The United States believed it had the duty to help Latin Americans find the government best suited to their culture.
   b. The United States believed it should share its wealth and resources with the people of Latin America.
   c. The United States believed that order was essential in Latin America to preserve American security and prosperity.
   d. The United States believed that it had the right to colonize Latin America to exploit the resources of the region.

Essay Questions

Objectives 4 and 7

1. Defend or refute the following statement in the context of American policy toward Central America and the Caribbean in the late nineteenth and early twentieth centuries: "The persistent American belief that other people cannot solve their own problems and that only the American model of government will work produced what historian William Appleman Williams has called 'the tragedy of American diplomacy.'"

Objective 1

2. Explain the relationship between domestic affairs and foreign affairs. How did domestic affairs during the late nineteenth century lead to an expansionist foreign policy?

Objective 5

3. Discuss the debate between the imperialists and the anti-imperialists, and explain why the former prevailed.

Objective 6

4. Explain American foreign policy toward China in the late nineteenth and early twentieth centuries.

Map Exercise

1. Label the southernmost states of the United States shown on the outline map on page 176.
2. Locate and mark the following Latin American countries on the outline map (use the map in the textbook, on page 679, as a guide when necessary):

Countries

Mexico
Guatemala
British Honduras (now Belize)
Honduras
El Salvador
Nicaragua
Costa Rica
Panama
Colombia
Venezuela
Cuba
Jamaica
Haiti
Dominican Republic
Puerto Rico

Cities

Miami
New Orleans
Columbus, New Mexico
Mexico City
Tampico
Veracruz

© 1994 Houghton Mifflin Company. All rights reserved.

176 *Chapter 22*

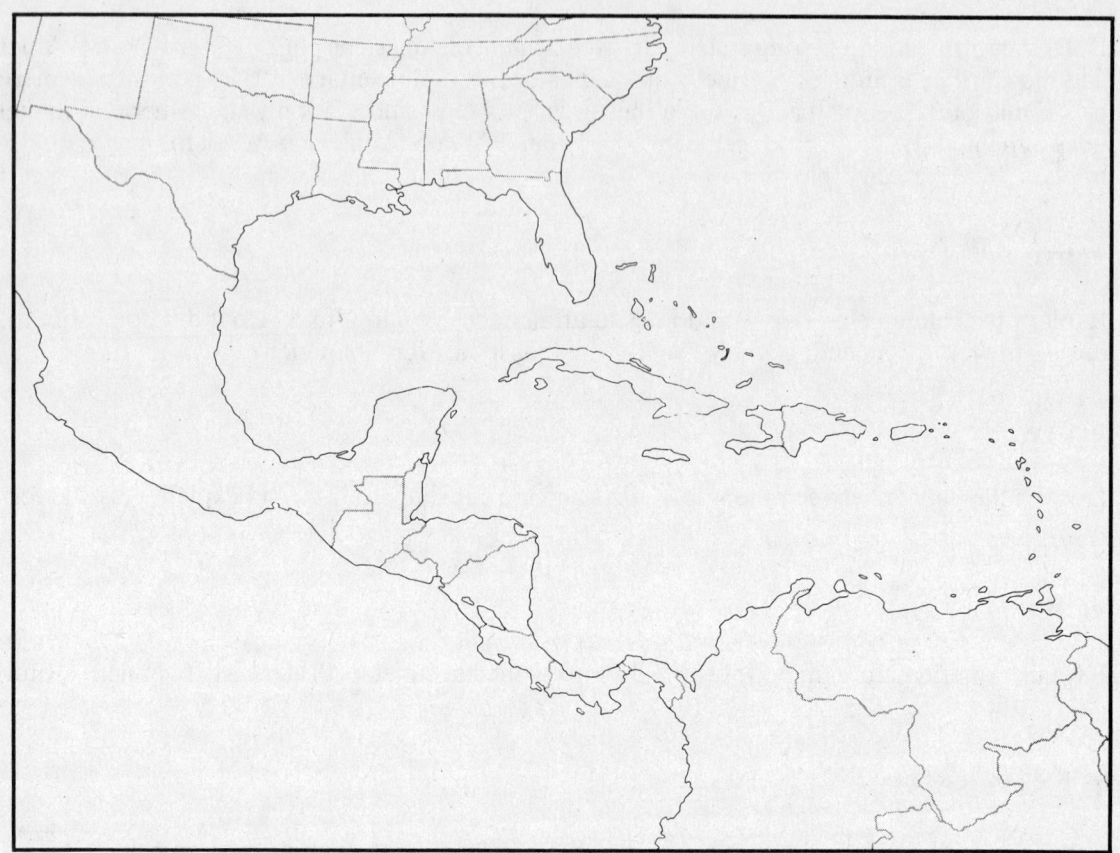

3. Using an atlas, mark the locations of the capitals of the Latin American countries that are shown on the outline map.
4. The United States has long been interested in and involved in Latin American affairs. Why?

CHAPTER 23
Americans at War, 1914–1920

Learning Objectives

After you have studied Chapter 23 in your textbook and worked through this study guide chapter, you should be able to:

1. Discuss Europe's descent into the First World War.
2. Discuss both President Woodrow Wilson's attempts and the attempts of antiwar activists to keep the United States out of the First World War, and explain the ultimate failure of those efforts.
3. Discuss the response of Americans to the First World War and to American entry into the war, and indicate the extent to which United States participation influenced the outcome of the conflict.
4. Describe the characteristics of draftees and volunteers in the American armed forces during the First World War and discuss their lives as soldiers.
5. Examine the impact of the First World War on the American home front, including its impact on the federal government, business, labor, women, and African-Americans.
6. Explain and evaluate the record of government at the local, state, and national levels on civil-liberties questions during and after the war.
7. Explain the differences and similarities between Wilsonianism and the provisions of the Treaty of Paris.
8. Examine the debate over ratification of the Treaty of Paris and American entry into the League of Nations, and explain the Senate's rejection of the treaty.
9. Examine the impact of the First World War on America's role in world affairs.

Thematic Guide

In Chapter 23, we deal with the causes of the First World War, American entry into the war, and the political, social, and economic impact of the war on the United States and its people. The nation's entry into the war is discussed in "Struggling with Neutrality" and "Wilson, the Submarine, and the Decision for War." Although President Wilson proclaimed the United States to be a neutral in the European conflict, three realities made neutrality practically impossible. Those realities confirm the interrelation of domestic and foreign policy (a dominant theme in Chapter 22). Furthermore, the discussion of the tenets of Wilsonianism and Wilson's strict interpretation of international law reinforces the concept that a nation's foreign policy is based on its perception of the world community of nations and of its relationship to those nations.

Besides the underlying reasons for American entry into the war, there were obvious and immediate reasons for that decision: the naval warfare between Great Britain and Germany, the use of the submarine by the Germans, and Wilson's interpretation of international law as he attempted to protect the rights of the United States as a neutral nation. The authors' inference that Americans got caught in the crossfire between the Allies and the Central Powers is supported through the tracing of United States policy from the sinking of the *Lusitania* to the adoption of unrestricted submarine warfare by the Germans. Therefore, the Zimmermann telegram, perceived as a direct threat to American security by American officials, the arming of American commercial ships, and additional sinkings of American ships by German submarines brought a declaration of war by Congress. Finally, America went to war because of a special sense of mission. The country went to war to reform world politics, war being the only means that guaranteed Wilson a seat and an insider's voice at the peace table.

In spite of antiwar sentiment in the United States, the country began to prepare for war before the actual declaration, as can be seen in the passage of the National Defense Act, the Navy Act, and the Revenue Act. Once war was declared, the country turned to the draft (the Selective Service Act) to raise the necessary army. Even though American military and political leaders believed that American virtue could reshape the world, they feared that the world would reshape the virtue of American soldiers. To protect that virtue, the government created the Commission on Training Camp Activities. In spite of this, venereal disease became a serious problem within the army. Furthermore, American soldiers could not be shielded from the graver threat of influenza and pneumonia, and more soldiers died from disease than on the battlefield. Another serious problem in the American army—one that government and army officials did little to combat—was racism. Not only were African-Americans segregated within the army, but they were also subjected to various forms of racial discrimination.

Mobilization of the nation for the war effort altered American life. Government power increased, especially in the economic sphere. Government-business cooperation became part of official government policy. Centralized governmental control and planning of the nation's economy were largely successful, but there were mistakes and problems. Government policy caused inflation; government tax policies meant that only one-third of the war was financed through taxes; and, although organized labor made some gains, it usually took a back seat to the needs of corporations.

The war intensified the divisions within the pluralistic American society. Entry of more women into previously "male" jobs brought negative reactions by male workers. Increased northward migration of African-Americans intensified racist fears and animosities in factories and neighborhoods. The government's fear of dissent and of foreigners led to the trampling of civil liberties at the national, state, and local levels. In the immediate aftermath of the war, events both within and outside the country heightened these fears, culminating in the Red Scare and the Palmer Raids. The American effort to "make the world safe for democracy" brought actions on the home front that seemed to indicate a basic distrust of democracy.

Divisions also intensified on the political front, as the debate over the Treaty of Paris indicates. In "The Peace Conference, League Fight, and Postwar World" Wilson's Fourteen Points are contrasted with the actual terms of the treaty. The divergence was an issue used in the arguments of those opposed to the treaty and to American entry into the League of Nations. But the core of the problem lay in Article 10 of the League covenant. Critics charged that the collective-security provisions of this article would allow League members to call out the United States Army without congressional approval. The *belief* of many that this was true was at the heart of the debate against the League. Fear that the United States would be forced to forgo its traditional unilateralism in foreign affairs led the Senate to reject the treaty and American entry into the League of Nations.

The American experience in the First World War influenced every aspect of American life, producing consequences for the future. The war changed America's place in world affairs to one of world prominence, and it continued to shape America's institutions and decisions both at home and abroad long after 1920.

© 1994 Houghton Mifflin Company. All rights reserved.

Building Vocabulary

Listed below are important words and terms that you need to know to get the most out of Chapter 23. They are listed in the order in which they occur in the chapter. After carefully looking through the list, refer to a dictionary and jot down the definition of words that you do not know or of which you are unsure.

virile

belligerent

heterogeneous

fractious

nativists

civil liberties

status quo

recoil

chide

unilateralism

goad

conflagration

ethnic

archetype

espouse

intone

unsavory

harass

flout

deftly

besmirch

maraud

decadent

futile

impede

avenge

ploy

breach

pantheon

maelstrom

prudent

imbibe

exhort

menial

pandemic

parochialism

conciliate

forage

conscripted

blatant

abate

extol

vigilantism

sanction

ardent

exacerbate

stalwart

reparations

rectify

placate

oligopoly

millennium

Identification and Significance

After studying Chapter 23 of *A People and a Nation,* you should be able to identify fully *and* explain the historical significance of each item listed below.

1. Identify each item in the space provided. Give an explanation or description of the item. Answer the questions *who, what, where,* and *when.*
2. Explain the historical significance of each item in the space provided. Establish the historical context in which the item exists. Establish the item as the result of or as the cause of other factors existing in the society under study. Answer this question: *what were the political, social, economic, and/or cultural consequences of this item?*

the Balkans

    Identification

    Significance

June 1914 assassination at Sarajevo

    Identification

    Significance

President Wilson's Proclamation of Neutrality

    Identification

    Significance

Wilsonianism

    Identification

    Significance

American exceptionalism

    Identification

    Significance

British naval policy

    Identification

    Significance

neutral rights

    Identification

    Significance

the submarine and international law

    Identification

    Significance

the *Lusitania*

    Identification

    Significance

© 1994 Houghton Mifflin Company. All rights reserved.

184 *Chapter 23*

Secretary of State Bryan's resignation

    Identification

    Significance

the *Arabic*

    Identification

    Significance

the Gore-McLemore resolution

    Identification

    Significance

the *Sussex*

    Identification

    Significance

the peace movement

    Identification

    Significance

unrestricted submarine warfare

    Identification

    Significance

the Zimmermann telegram

> Identification

> Significance

the armed-ship bill

> Identification

> Significance

Wilson's war message

> Identification

> Significance

Jeannette Rankin

> Identification

> Significance

the National Defense Act of 1916, the Navy Act, and the Revenue Act of 1916

> Identification

> Significance

the Selective Service Act

> Identification

> Significance

"evaders," "deserters," and COs

    Identification

    Significance

the Commission on Training Camp Activities

    Identification

    Significance

General John J. Pershing

    Identification

    Significance

trench warfare

    Identification

    Significance

venereal disease among American soldiers

    Identification

    Significance

Wilson's Fourteen Points

    Identification

    Significance

the Food Administration, the Railroad Administration, and the Fuel Administration

    Identification

    Significance

the War Industries Board

    Identification

    Significance

war-time inflation

    Identification

    Significance

the War Revenue Act of 1917

    Identification

    Significance

the National War Labor Board

    Identification

    Significance

the Women's Committee of the Council of National Defense

    Identification

    Significance

© 1994 Houghton Mifflin Company. All rights reserved.

African-American migration

> Identification

> Significance

the East St. Louis riot of 1917

> Identification

> Significance

the "Red Summer" of 1919

> Identification

> Significance

the influenza pandemic

> Identification

> Significance

the Committee on Public Information

> Identification

> Significance

the Espionage and Sedition Acts

> Identification

> Significance

Eugene Debs

> Identification

> Significance

"Americanization" and "100% Americanism" supporters

> Identification

> Significance

the Civil Liberties Bureau

> Identification

> Significance

Schenck v. *U.S.* and *Abrams* v. *U.S.*

> Identification

> Significance

Victor Berger

> Identification

> Significance

Wilson's anti-Bolshevik actions

> Identification

> Significance

the Red Scare

> Identification
>
> Significance

mail bombs of May 1919

> Identification
>
> Significance

the Boston police strike

> Identification
>
> Significance

the steel strike of 1919

> Identification
>
> Significance

William Z. Foster

> Identification
>
> Significance

the American left

> Identification
>
> Significance

the American Legion

    Identification

    Significance

A. Mitchell Palmer

    Identification

    Significance

the Palmer Raids

    Identification

    Significance

the Paris Peace Conference

    Identification

    Significance

the principle of self-determination

    Identification

    Significance

the mandate system

    Identification

    Significance

© 1994 Houghton Mifflin Company. All rights reserved.

the League of Nations

    Identification

    Significance

Article 10 of the League Covenant

    Identification

    Significance

the Treaty of Paris

    Identification

    Significance

the Lodge reservations

    Identification

    Significance

the "Irreconcilables"

    Identification

    Significance

collective security vs. unilateralism

    Identification

    Significance

Evaluating and Using Information

In the appropriate blocks in the chart on pages 194 and 195, record evidence about the attitudes and personal style of Woodrow Wilson that affected his handling of people, issues, and events. Your goal in compiling this evidence is to determine how and to what degree Wilson's personal attitudes contributed to his successes or failures and to later generations' judgments of him and his administration.

Organize the evidence you find and use it to compose the working draft of an essay on the role of personal attitudes and style on the success or failure of the Woodrow Wilson presidency. Enter the working draft of your essay in your Reading Notebook.

© 1994 Houghton Mifflin Company. All rights reserved.

Character and Attitudes of Woodrow Wilson

Area in Which the Behavior or Comment Arose	Type of Evidence			
	Wilson's Own Statements	Wilson's Own Actions, Behaviors	Others' Comments About Wilson	Others' Behavior in Reaction to Wilson's Behavior	Impact of the Attitude or Character Traits Revealed on Wilson's Achievement
America's Historical and Moral Role in the World					
Racial and Ethnic Groups and Issues					
Britain and Germany Before America's Entry into World War I					

Radicalism and Criticism of His Administration from Among Private Citizenry	Imperialism, Colonialism, Interventionism, Sovereignty of Nations, etc.	Other

Ideas and Details

Objective 1

_____ 1. Great Britain entered the First World War in response to
   a. the Austro-Hungarian invasion of Russia.
   b. acts of Russian terrorism in the Balkans.
   c. the Serbian invasion of Austria-Hungary.
   d. the German invasion of Belgium.

Objective 2

_____ 2. American neutrality in response to the First World War was never a real possibility because
   a. Wilson wanted to enter the war and force Germany into submission.
   b. the American press had built broad-based sympathy for Serbian nationalism.
   c. the United States had stronger economic ties to the Allies than to the Central Powers.
   d. Secretary of State Bryan worked secretly to bring the United States into the war.

Objective 7

_____ 3. The body of ideas known as Wilsonianism and summarized in the Fourteen Points included the belief that
   a. secret military alliances were the best means by which to maintain world peace.
   b. democratic societies had an obligation to colonize and civilize underdeveloped areas.
   c. democratic nations should build more arms to demonstrate their resolve against autocracy.
   d. there should be free trade among the nations of the world.

Objective 2

_____ 4. William Jennings Bryan resigned his post as secretary of state because
   a. he disagreed with President Wilson's refusal to ban American travelers from sailing on belligerent ships.
   b. the American public responded negatively to his protests concerning Britain's illegal blockade of Germany.
   c. his pro-German sympathies became a liability to the Wilson administration.
   d. President Wilson publicly reprimanded him for advocating American entry into the First World War.

Objective 2

_____ 5. Which of the following helped finance peace groups in the United States before American entry in the First World War?
   a. Jay Gould
   b. Andrew Carnegie
   c. John Pershing
   d. Bernard Baruch

Objective 2

_____ 6. As a result of the Zimmermann telegram, Wilson
   a. broke diplomatic relations with Germany.
   b. decided to rethink his position on international law in relation to the submarine.
   c. became more convinced that Germany was conspiring against the United States.
   d. decided that supporting the Mexican Revolution was in the best interest of the United States.

Objective 4

_____ 7. During the First World War, the Commission on Training Camp Activities
   a. was responsible for coordinating the military training of recruits in all of the services.
   b. coordinated the activities of groups that would help protect the virtue of American soldiers.
   c. recommended that military units be racially integrated.
   d. created a network of spies in order to find and prosecute army personnel who questioned the war effort.

Objectives 3 and 4

_____ 8. General Pershing refused to allow American soldiers to become part of Allied units because he
   a. would have to relinquish control over them.
   b. was afraid they would be corrupted by European ways.
   c. did not want to submit them to the horrors of trench warfare.
   d. did not believe they were as well trained as their Allied counterparts.

Objective 5

_____ 9. In mobilizing the economy for the war effort, the government
   a. rigidly enforced antitrust laws.
   b. protected consumers by instituting a wage and price freeze.
   c. established a partnership between government and business.
   d. insisted on annual cost of living wage increases for workers in war-related industries.

Objective 5

_____ 10. Some men reacted negatively to the movement of women into jobs previously reserved for males because women
   a. were more valued and received higher wages than men.
   b. had a higher productivity rate than men.
   c. began to receive more promotions.
   d. refused to join unions.

Objective 5

_____ 11. Which of the following statements accurately describes the experiences of blacks during the First World War?
   a. Military leaders attempted to combat racism by integrating their units.
   b. Southern whites welcomed the northward migration of blacks.
   c. The ideology used to justify the war was used to dismantle racial barriers within the United States.
   d. Some northern whites reacted with anger and violence to the northward migration of blacks.

Objective 6

_____ 12. In order to achieve its objective, the Committee on Public Information
   a. encouraged Americans to spy on each other and report evidence of suspicious behavior.
   b. encouraged a free and open debate of the American war effort.
   c. held daily briefings with reporters to ensure the dissemination of accurate war news.
   d. sponsored public question-and-answer forums to dispel rumors.

Objective 6

_____ 13. In the case of *Schenck* v. *U.S.*, the Supreme Court ruled that
   a. members of the Socialist party could be required to register with the government.
   b. freedom of speech could be restricted in time of war.
   c. the Sedition Act was unconstitutional.
   d. the teaching of foreign languages could be banned from public schools.

Objective 6

_____ 14. Which of the following statements is accurate in relation to the Palmer Raids?
   a. A well-organized Bolshevik conspiracy against the United States government was crushed.
   b. The attorney general, in dealing with supposed radicals, showed disregard for civil liberties.
   c. Wilson instructed several state legislatures to remove suspected Socialists from their ranks.
   d. Documents confiscated during the raids led the Wilson administration to declare labor unions illegal.

Objective 8

_____ 15. Opponents of the Treaty of Paris objected primarily to
   a. the collective-security provision of Article 10.
   b. Wilson's acceptance of the "mandate" system.
   c. the clause that blamed the war on Germany.
   d. Wilson's inability to secure reparations payments from Germany.

Essay Questions

Objective 2

1. Explain Wilson's attempts to keep the United States out of the Great War in Europe. Why was the country eventually drawn into the conflict?

Objective 5

2. Discuss the impact of the First World War on women and African-Americans.

Objective 6

3. Discuss the Wilson administration's record in the area of civil liberties during the First World War.

Objective 6

4. Discuss the fear of communism in American society in the early twentieth century, and explain how that fear manifested itself between 1917 and 1921.

Objective 8

5. Explain the foreign policy debate over ratification of the Treaty of Paris and entry into the League of Nations. Why did those opposed to ratification and to League membership carry the day?

CHAPTER 24
The New Era of the 1920s

Learning Objectives

After you have studied Chapter 24 in your textbook and worked through this study guide chapter, you should be able to:

1. Discuss the economic characteristics of the 1920s, and explain the reasons for the economic expansion and recovery that began in 1922.
2. Discuss the relationship between government and business during the 1920s, and indicate the factors responsible for the decline of organized labor.
3. Examine the political, social, and economic characteristics of the Harding and Coolidge administrations.
4. Discuss the nature and extent of reform legislation during the decade of the 1920s.
5. Examine the social, economic, and political changes in the position and attitudes of women and blacks in American society during the 1920s.
6. Examine the impact of the automobile and modern advertising on American society.
7. Explain both the trend toward urbanization and the growth of the suburbs during the 1920s, and discuss the consequences of both of these factors on American society.
8. Indicate the factors that caused an increase in immigration by Mexicans and Puerto Ricans during the 1920s, and discuss the characteristics of their lives in the United States.
9. Discuss the changes that took place in the way Americans used their time during the 1920s.
10. Discuss the causes and consequences of the 1920s trend toward longer life expectancy, and explain the responses of Americans to the needs of the elderly.
11. Examine the impact of change during the 1920s on Americans' values.
12. Examine the emergence of the Ku Klux Klan, nativists, and religious fundamentalists, and discuss their impact on American society in the 1920s.
13. Explain the characteristics of each of the following, and discuss the impact of each on American society during the 1920s:
    a. Games
    b. Movies
    c. Sports
    d. News
    e. Prohibition
14. Examine and evaluate the emergence of experimental movements in American literature, art, and music during the 1920s.

15. Discuss the issues and personalities in the 1928 presidential campaign, and explain the election's outcome.
16. Discuss the events that led to the 1929 stock market crash, and examine the causes of the crash and the Great Depression that followed.

Thematic Guide

The decade of the 1920s began with troubling economic signs but soon became an era of economic prosperity for many Americans. Prosperity was accompanied by probusiness attitudes and unparalleled consumerism. The federal government remained active in its support of business interests but became more passive in its regulation of those interests. While the Supreme Court handed down antiregulatory decisions and organized labor suffered setbacks, probusiness attitudes reminiscent of the Gilded Age marked the Harding, Coolidge, and Hoover administrations. Most reforms took place at the state and local levels. Interest in reform concerning Indian affairs led to the reorganization of the Bureau of Indian Affairs, but Indian policy matters continued to be characterized by paternalism. Furthermore, although newly enfranchised women lobbied and gained passage of some legislation helpful to them, women generally struggled to find their political voice.

The consumerism of the age was fueled by the growing purchasing power of many American families and the accompanying ability to acquire the goods associated with a consumer society. Both the automobile and the sophisticated techniques of modern advertising transformed the American lifestyle.

The urbanization of American society continued in the 1920s. Although movement to cities offered opportunities to many, black migrants found that white racism was as prevalent in urban areas as it had been in the rural South. However, blacks' urban ghetto experience aroused their class and ethnic consciousness, as seen both in Marcus Garvey's black nationalist movement and in the cultural outpouring known as the Harlem Renaissance. Racism also shaped the lives of Mexicans, Puerto Ricans, and other newcomers to American cities and contributed to white flight from the inner city and to suburban growth.

The way in which Americans spent their time changed. For instance, labor-saving devices lightened the tasks of women working in the home. But because women were still expected to clothe and feed the family and because few women produced clothes and preserved food at home, they spent their time shopping for these goods and became the primary consumers in society.

Altered attitudes and values brought about by societal changes found expression in new clothing and hair styles and in the increased incidence of premarital sex. Increased longevity resulting from improved diets and improved healthcare led to an increase in the number of older Americans and to limited attempts to respond to their needs. At the same time, compulsory-school-attendance laws increased the influence of the peer group in the socialization of children. Furthermore, a combination of consumerism and economic necessity caused more women, including married women, to work outside the home. The work they performed and the wages they earned were largely determined by the sex-segregated characteristics of the labor market. In spite of sexism, however, many women placed family needs above individual needs and questioned the ideas of economic feminism.

Many people felt threatened by change, and some, attempting to protect traditional attitudes and values, reacted defensively, sometimes with attempts to blame change on scapegoats. The emergence of the "new" Klan and the increase in nativism and fear of radicalism (evidenced in the Sacco and Vanzetti case) can be seen in this light. Religious fundamentalism also gained strength, as the Scopes trial revealed.

More leisure time and a search for entertainment meant that spectator sports and the movies became big business. As the conformist aspects of mass culture caused individuality to fade, Americans found heroes in sports figures, movie idols, and media-created personalities. Caught between two value systems, many Americans gave lip service to the old, as evidenced in their professed support of the Prohibition experiment, but chose the new, as the breakdown of Prohibition in the cities shows.

In literature, the 1920s saw the work of the Lost Generation and of the Harlem Renaissance. In music, it was the age of jazz, America's most distinctive art form, and of such talented composers as Aaron Copland and George Gershwin. In architecture, Frank Lloyd Wright predominated. Overall, the period stands as one of the most creative in American history.

In politics, the presidency remained in Republican hands in 1928 as most Americans affirmed their confidence in the building of a New Era of prosperity for all. But with the stock market crash of 1929, the optimism of 1928 gave way to concern and ultimately, with the onset of the Great Depression, to despair. The Jazz Age ended. The American economic system would have to be rebuilt.

Building Vocabulary

Listed below are important words and terms that you need to know to get the most out of Chapter 24. They are listed in the order in which they occur in the chapter. After carefully looking through the list, refer to a dictionary and jot down the definition of words that you do not know or of which you are unsure.

exonerate

rectitude

revere

entice

deviant

relegate

pervade

propagandist

exempt

disseminate

stifle

predatory

dour

fiscal

adversarial

perpetuate

paradox

homily

vanguard

whet

ecumenical

manipulate

burgeon

reminisce

prudent

abstain

agility

chaste

vamp

torrid

libertine

reactionary

mete

vigilante

wane

pervade

flout

notorious

irreverence

hedonistic

fundamentalism

pentecostal

comely

insatiable

poignant

satire

hyperbole

pomade

adulation

burly

crass

assail

lament

amalgamation

patronize

patron

motif

urbane

gregarious

formidable

edifice

Identification and Significance

After studying Chapter 24 of *A People and a Nation,* you should be able to identify fully *and* explain the historical significance of each item listed below.

1. Identify each item in the space provided. Give an explanation or description of the item. Answer the questions *who, what, where,* and *when.*
2. Explain the historical significance of each item in the space provided. Establish the historical context in which the item exists. Establish the item as the result of or as the cause of other factors existing in the society under study. Answer this question: *what were the political, social, economic, and/or cultural consequences of this item?*

Judge Kennesaw Mountain Landis

    Identification

    Significance

the installment plan

    Identification

    Significance

oligopolies

    Identification

    Significance

Fordney-McCumber Tariff Act

    Identification

    Significance

Chief Justice William Howard Taft

    Identification

    Significance

Bailey v. *Drexel Furniture Company and Adkins* v. *Children's Hospital*

    Identification

    Significance

welfare capitalism

    Identification

    Significance

Warren G. Harding

    Identification

    Significance

Charles Forbes, Thomas W. Miller, and Harry Daugherty

    Identification

    Significance

the Teapot Dome scandal

    Identification

    Significance

Calvin Coolidge

    Identification

    Significance

Andrew Mellon

    Identification

    Significance

the McNary-Haugen bills

    Identification

    Significance

the 1924 presidential election

    Identification

    Significance

the Indian Rights Association, the Indian Defense Association, and the General Federation of Women's Clubs

    Identification

    Significance

Indians' citizenship status

    Identification

    Significance

the Bureau of Indian Affairs

    Identification

    Significance

the Sheppard-Towner Act

    Identification

    Significance

the Cable Act

    Identification

    Significance

the National Women's Party

    Identification

    Significance

the League of Women Voters

    Identification

    Significance

the automobile

    Identification

    Significance

the Federal Highway Act

> Identification

> Significance

The Man Nobody Knows and *Moses, Persuader of Men*

> Identification

> Significance

the radio

> Identification

> Significance

urbanization

> Identification

> Significance

Marcus Garvey

> Identification

> Significance

Mexican immigrants

> Identification

> Significance

barrios

    Identification

    Significance

Puerto Rican immigrants

    Identification

    Significance

the growth of the suburbs

    Identification

    Significance

the eating-habits revolution

    Identification

    Significance

Isaac Max Rubinow and Abraham Epstein

    Identification

    Significance

compulsory-school-attendance laws

    Identification

    Significance

© 1994 Houghton Mifflin Company. All rights reserved.

economic feminism

> Identification

> Significance

Alice Paul

> Identification

> Significance

the flapper

> Identification

> Significance

Ku Klux Klan

> Identification

> Significance

Nicola Sacco and Bartolomeo Vanzetti

> Identification

> Significance

the Quota (Johnson) Act of 1921

> Identification

> Significance

the Immigration Act of 1924

    Identification

    Significance

the "national-origins" system

    Identification

    Significance

the Scopes trial

    Identification

    Significance

mahjongg, crossword puzzles, and miniature golf

    Identification

    Significance

motion pictures

    Identification

    Significance

baseball

    Identification

    Significance

© 1994 Houghton Mifflin Company. All rights reserved.

Jack Dempsey, Harold "Red" Grange, and George Herman "Babe" Ruth

    Identification

    Significance

Rudolph Valentino

    Identification

    Significance

Charles A. Lindbergh

    Identification

    Significance

Prohibition

    Identification

    Significance

Al Capone

    Identification

    Significance

the Lost Generation

    Identification

    Significance

the Harlem Renaissance

> Identification

> Significance

the Jazz Age

> Identification

> Significance

the 1928 presidential election

> Identification

> Significance

Herbert Hoover

> Identification

> Significance

Al Smith

> Identification

> Significance

Black Thursday

> Identification

> Significance

J. P. Morgan and Company

    Identification

    Significance

Black Tuesday

    Identification

    Significance

underconsumption

    Identification

    Significance

Evaluating and Using Information

The 1920s are often characterized as a probusiness era. Review Chapter 24 and your class notes to collect information on the specific factors that encouraged speculation, expansion, and optimism for the business sector during the 1920s. Once you have collected your data, organize it and compose the working draft of an essay presenting your response to the following question:

> How did the federal government, the public, and the marketing and financing developments of business itself fan the optimism and wild speculation characteristic of much of American business during the 1920s?

To begin organizing the information for possible use in your essay, make notations that relate to the pertinent data you collect in the appropriate blocks of the following chart on page 217. Then expand the notations you have made on the chart into more detailed (concrete, specific) passages in the working draft of your essay.

Enter your essay in your Reading Notebook.

Objective 11

_____ 6. As a consequence of child-labor laws and compulsory-school-attendance laws,
   a. daily newspaper circulation increased dramatically in the 1920s.
   b. consumption of consumer products began to decline in the 1920s.
   c. the role of the family in socializing children declined whereas that of the peer group increased.
   d. many industries faced a severe labor shortage.

Objectives 5 and 11

_____ 7. Which of the following statements concerning women in the work force during the 1920s is correct?
   a. The number of women in factories increased dramatically.
   b. Sex segregation in the workplace became less noticeable.
   c. The number of women in the work force declined.
   d. Married women joined the work force in increasing numbers.

Objective 5

_____ 8. Economic feminism did not appeal to many women in the 1920s because feminists
   a. did not address political issues.
   b. emphasized competitive rather than cooperative goals.
   c. seldom mentioned the issue of equal pay.
   d. avoided controversial issues.

Objective 12

_____ 9. During the early 1920s, the Ku Klux Klan
   a. had little power outside the South.
   b. lost most of its power in the South because of the new mood of militancy among blacks.
   c. gained power nationally as an antiblack, anti-immigrant, anti-Catholic movement.
   d. was outlawed by Congress as a terrorist organization.

Objective 12

_____ 10. Which of the following conclusions may be drawn from the Sacco and Vanzetti case?
   a. The fear of radicalism, which caused the Red Scare, had disappeared.
   b. In the future, immigration laws would be applied equally to all ethnic groups.
   c. Blacks could not be guaranteed a fair trial in the South.
   d. Justice was not necessarily blind to a person's political beliefs or ethnic background.

© 1994 Houghton Mifflin Company. All rights reserved.

Objective 13

_____ 11. Jack Dempsey, "Babe Ruth," and Rudolph Valentino demonstrate that the decade of the 1920s was an
   a. age of heroes.
   b. era of great actors.
   c. era of great baseball players.
   d. age of lawlessness.

Objective 13

_____ 12. Prohibition failed because
   a. Americans completely rejected the value system out of which it was born.
   b. illegal liquor was foisted on the public by organized crime.
   c. it hurt the nation economically.
   d. many people were willing to break the law in their quest for pleasure and their desire for personal freedom.

Objective 14

_____ 13. The writers of the Harlem Renaissance
   a. rejected the African past of black Americans.
   b. advocated that black Americans return to Africa.
   c. rejected the blending of black and white cultures.
   d. were mainly interested in economic issues.

Objective 15

_____ 14. The election of 1928 indicated that
   a. the Democrats were gaining strength in urban areas.
   b. the Democrats were losing their stronghold in the South.
   c. the Republicans were making gains in all sections of the country.
   d. the Republicans had become the minority party.

Objective 16

_____ 15. The government contributed to the stock market crash of 1929 and to the depression that followed in which of the following ways?
   a. Government regulations imposed on businesses reduced profits and investments.
   b. Tax policies before the crash took large sums of money out of circulation.
   c. The Federal Reserve Board followed an easy credit policy in the years prior to the crash.
   d. Government policies toward organized labor encouraged large wage increases and inflation.

Essay Questions

Objective 1

1. Discuss the factors responsible for the economic recovery that began in 1922. How long did this economic recovery last? Why is it said that this recovery was "uneven"?

Objective 2

2. Examine the relationship between government and business during the Republican era of the 1920s. What was the philosophy behind this relationship?

Objective 4

3. Examine the attitude toward reform during the 1920s, and discuss and assess the reforms that were achieved during the decade.

Objective 6

4. Discuss the impact of the automobile on American society, American values, and the American family.

Objective 5

5. Explain the emergence and the rise to power of Marcus Garvey.

Objectives 11 and 12

6. Defend the following statement, and explain how it also applies to the 1990s: "The emotional responses that Americans made to events during the 1920s were part of a larger attempt to sustain old, local values in a fast-moving, materialistic world."

Objective 16

7. Explain why the 1929 stock market crash led to the Great Depression.

CHAPTER 25

The Great Depression and the New Deal, 1929–1941

Learning Objectives

After you have studied Chapter 25 in your textbook and worked through this study guide chapter, you should be able to:

1. Discuss the impact of the Great Depression on the American economic system and on city dwellers, farmers, marriage patterns, and family life.
2. Examine how and why Americans responded to the Great Depression as they did.
3. Explain and evaluate the Hoover administration's attempts to deal with the economic and human crises posed by the Great Depression.
4. Examine the issues and personalities and explain the outcome of the 1932 presidential and congressional elections.
5. Discuss the impact of Franklin D. Roosevelt's personal and professional experiences before 1932 on his political, social, and economic views, and examine the relationship between his political, social, and economic views and his handling of the Great Depression.
6. Explain the practical and theoretical basis for the legislative enactments of the First New Deal (1933–1934), and evaluate the effectiveness of the First New Deal in solving the problems of the depression.
7. Examine the variety of criticisms leveled against the New Deal, and discuss the alternatives proposed.
8. Contrast the Supreme Court's reaction to New Deal legislation before and after 1937, and explain the reasons for the shift.
9. Explain the practical and theoretical basis for the legislative enactments of the Second New Deal (1935–1939), and evaluate the effectiveness of the Second New Deal in solving the problems of the depression.
10. Identify the components of the New Deal coalition, and examine the impact of this coalition on the 1936 presidential election.
11. Examine the problems encountered by President Roosevelt during his second term.
12. Examine the power struggle between craft unions and industrial unions during the New Deal era; discuss the victories and defeats of organized labor during this period; and assess the overall impact of the New Deal era on organized labor in the United States.
13. Examine the impact of the Great Depression and the New Deal era on African-Americans, American Indians, Mexican-Americans, and women, and explain the responses of these groups to the obstacles they faced.

14. Discuss the issues and personalities and explain the outcome of the 1940 presidential election.
15. Discuss the legacy of the New Deal.

Thematic Guide

Chapter 25 opens with a discussion of the Great Depression's impact on people's lives. The human story includes the increase in malnutrition and disease, the sufferings of drought- and debt-ridden farmers, descriptions of hobo towns, altered marital patterns, and changes to family life.

In the midst of the depression, few Americans thought in radical, revolutionary terms. Many accepted the traditional American belief in the self-made man and blamed themselves for the depression. The protests that emerged were relatively mild, the most spectacular being the Bonus March. Furthermore, in the case of the Bonus March, it was the government, not the people, that overreacted.

Hoover's response to appeals from the people that the government extend aid was at first defensive. Hoover was convinced that self-help was the solution, not government aid. As the depression deepened, Hoover reluctantly began to energize the government. But at the same time he pursued policies that caused further deterioration of the economic situation.

An understanding of Franklin Roosevelt's background, his perception of himself, his society, and American government is important to an understanding of his approach to the Great Depression. That background and Roosevelt's frame of reference are outlined as part of the discussion of the presidential election of 1932. Moreover, the authors explain the reasons for Roosevelt's victory and reveal that in spite of a deepening crisis, Americans did not adopt radical solutions. Instead, they continued to follow tradition by peacefully exchanging one government for another.

With the aid of a Brain Trust, Roosevelt adopted a theoretical basis for the New Deal he promised to the American people. Roosevelt believed that government could act as a positive force in American society; in deciding how it should act, he was a pragmatist and thus willing to experiment. At first he accepted the idea that government could and should effectively regulate big business. He accepted the idea that centralized planning by the federal government could solve some of the problems associated with the depression, and he was willing to have government engage in direct relief to alleviate the distress of the nation's citizens. Furthermore, the first New Deal was based on the assumption that overproduction was the underlying problem.

Roosevelt's initial actions, outlined in "Launching the New Deal and Restoring Confidence," demonstrate both the conservative nature of his approach and his realization that the psychology of pessimism within the country was as great an enemy as the depression itself. The legislation that was passed, as well as the fireside chats, provided a sense of movement that helped break the mood of pessimism.

An attempt to solve the problem of overproduction through centralized planning provided the theoretical framework for passage of the AAA, the NIRA, and the TVA. Belief in giving direct relief to states and to individuals may be seen in acts such as the Federal Emergency Relief Act and the CCC. The authors consider these and other measures passed during the Hundred Days, and they also discuss the concept of interest-group democracy, which is important for understanding the politics of the New Deal and the Democratic coalition that emerged.

The statistics provided show that the New Deal was not a cure-all and help explain the emergence of opposition to it. The range of criticism indicates that Roosevelt was a political moderate in the route that he chose. Furthermore, the kind of opposition from popular critics like Huey Long, as well as Supreme Court decisions against the AAA and the NIRA, help explain the launching of the Second New Deal.

The Second New Deal stemmed from the view that underconsumption was the nation's basic problem, that business and banking interests had to be regulated more closely, and that the government had a responsibility to the aged and the needy in American society. These assumptions were behind the

Emergency Relief Appropriation Act and five other major pieces of legislation passed during the Second Hundred Days.

The Second New Deal and the forging of the New Deal coalition carried Roosevelt to victory in the 1936 election. Mistakes and political reality meant that Roosevelt did not enjoy successes during his second term like those experienced in his first. He made a political and tactical mistake in his request for a restructuring of the Supreme Court. His dislike of deficit spending and desire for a balanced budget led to drastic cuts in federal spending, which in turn led to a new recession in 1937 and to a renewal of deficit spending. Such mistakes undercut some of Roosevelt's charisma, and with the passage of a new Agricultural Adjustment Act and the Fair Labor Standards Act, the last reforms of the New Deal were enacted.

Having discussed the reforms of the New Deal, the authors consider the impact of the New Deal era on organized labor, nonwhites, and women. Organized labor benefited from both Section 7(a) of the NIRA and the Wagner Act. Therefore, despite determined resistance by management and a division within the labor movement that led to the creation of the Congress of Industrial Organizations (CIO), the union movement made impressive gains during the 1930s.

Although passage of the Indian Reorganization Act indicates a more enlightened governmental approach to American Indians, the experience of African-Americans and Mexican-Americans demonstrates that racism continued as a force detrimental to the lives of nonwhites. The Scottsboro case serves as a symbol of the "ugliness of race relations in the depression era." Furthermore, despite the presence of the Black Cabinet, President Roosevelt was never fully committed to civil rights for blacks, and some New Deal measures functioned in a discriminatory way. However, there were some indications that change was on the horizon.

First, in relation to cases arising out of the Scottsboro trial, the Supreme Court ruled that the due process clause of the Fourteenth Amendment made the criminal protection procedures (the right to adequate defense counsel and the right to an impartial jury) of the Sixth Amendment applicable to the states. Second, Roosevelt created the Black Cabinet and had within his administration people committed to racial equality. Furthermore, African-Americans continued, as they had throughout their history, to work in their own behalf to overcome the injustices and abuses associated with white racism. The March on Washington Movement and Roosevelt's subsequent issuance of Executive Order No. 8802 can be seen in this light.

Like blacks, women continued to suffer discrimination during the depression era. Although their contributions to the family increased, their status within the family remained unchanged. As more women entered the work force, they continued to face hostility, wage discrimination, and limited employment choices because of sex-typed occupations. Women participated in the shaping and execution of the New Deal through the "women's network" and through formal appointment to governmental posts, but the fact remained that much New Deal legislation either discriminated against or excluded women.

The chapter ends with a discussion of the presidential election of 1940 and the way in which historians view the legacy of the New Deal.

Building Vocabulary

Listed below are important words and terms that you need to know to get the most out of Chapter 25. They are listed in the order in which they occur in the chapter. After carefully looking through the list, refer to a dictionary and jot down the definition of words that you do not know or of which you are unsure.

severance

severity

salvage

transient

beset

sordid

docile

moratorium

redemptive

ingratiating

penchant

plurality

solvent

status quo

queue (*verb*)

vehement

laissez faire

auspices

welter

subvert

scrutinize

ecological

demagogue

anti-Semitic

vitriolic

intrastate

innocuous

regressive

demise

ironic

personify

tenacious

pragmatic

privation

menial

specter

inducement

astute

dawdle

imminent

coherent

clout

bourgeoisie

ameliorate

Identification and Significance

After studying Chapter 25 of *A People and a Nation,* you should be able to identify fully *and* explain the historical significance of each item listed below.

1. Identify each item in the space provided. Give an explanation or description of the item. Answer the questions *who, what, where,* and *when.*
2. Explain the historical significance of each item in the space provided. Establish the historical context in which the item exists. Establish the item as the result of or as the cause of other factors existing in the society under study. Answer this question: *what were the political, social, economic, and/or cultural consequences of this item?*

Hoovervilles

    Identification

    Significance

© 1994 Houghton Mifflin Company. All rights reserved.

the Farmers' Holiday Association

>Identification

>Significance

Herbert Hoover

>Identification

>Significance

the Bonus Expeditionary Force

>Identification

>Significance

the Communist party

>Identification

>Significance

the Socialist party

>Identification

>Significance

Andrew Mellon

>Identification

>Significance

the President's Organization on Unemployment Relief

    Identification

    Significance

the Federal Farm Board

    Identification

    Significance

the Reconstruction Finance Corporation

    Identification

    Significance

the Hawley-Smoot Tariff

    Identification

    Significance

the Revenue Act of 1932

    Identification

    Significance

Franklin D. Roosevelt

    Identification

    Significance

Eleanor Roosevelt

>Identification

>Significance

the Brain Trust

>Identification

>Significance

the economics of scarcity

>Identification

>Significance

the Twentieth Amendment

>Identification

>Significance

Roosevelt's first inaugural address

>Identification

>Significance

national bank holiday

>Identification

>Significance

the First Hundred Days

    Identification

    Significance

the Emergency Banking Relief Bill (March 9, 1933)

    Identification

    Significance

Roosevelt's fireside chats

    Identification

    Significance

the Beer-Wine Revenue Act (March 22, 1933)

    Identification

    Significance

the Twenty-first Amendment

    Identification

    Significance

the Agricultural Adjustment Act (May 12, 1933)

    Identification

    Significance

parity

> Identification

> Significance

the Farm Credit Act (June 16, 1933)

> Identification

> Significance

the Civilian Conservation Corps (March 31, 1933)

> Identification

> Significance

the Federal Emergency Relief Act (May 12, 1933)

> Identification

> Significance

the National Industrial Recovery Act (June 16, 1933)

> Identification

> Significance

the Public Works Administration

> Identification

> Significance

the National Recovery Administration

    Identification

    Significance

Section 7(a) of NIRA

    Identification

    Significance

the Federal Securities Act (May 17, 1933)

    Identification

    Significance

the Banking Act of 1933 (June 16, 1933)

    Identification

    Significance

the Tennessee Valley Authority (May 18, 1933)

    Identification

    Significance

the Commodity Credit Corporation (October 18, 1933)

    Identification

    Significance

© 1994 Houghton Mifflin Company. All rights reserved.

the Taylor Grazing Act (June 28, 1934)

    Identification

    Significance

interest-group democracy

    Identification

    Significance

the American Liberty League

    Identification

    Significance

the "Okies" and "Arkies"

    Identification

    Significance

the Dust Bowl

    Identification

    Significance

Father Charles Coughlin

    Identification

    Significance

Dr. Francis E. Townsend

    Identification

    Significance

Huey Long

    Identification

    Significance

the Communist Party of the United States of America

    Identification

    Significance

Panama Refining Co. v. *Ryan* and *Schechter* v. *U.S.*

    Identification

    Significance

U.S. v. *Butler*

    Identification

    Significance

the Second New Deal

    Identification

    Significance

the Emergency Relief Appropriation Act (April 8, 1935)

    Identification

    Significance

the Works Progress Administration

    Identification

    Significance

the Federal Theater and Federal Writers' Projects

    Identification

    Significance

the Resettlement Administration

    Identification

    Significance

the Rural Electrification Administration

    Identification

    Significance

the National Youth Administration

    Identification

    Significance

the Second Hundred Days

    Identification

    Significance

the National Labor Relations (Wagner) Act (July 5, 1935)

    Identification

    Significance

the Social Security Act (August 15, 1935)

    Identification

    Significance

the Revenue (Wealth Tax) Act (August 30, 1935)

    Identification

    Significance

the 1936 presidential election

    Identification

    Significance

the New Deal coalition

    Identification

    Significance

© 1994 Houghton Mifflin Company. All rights reserved.

Roosevelt's Court-packing plan

> Identification

> Significance

NLRB v. *Jones* and *Laughlin Steel Corp.*

> Identification

> Significance

the recession of 1937–1939

> Identification

> Significance

the National Housing Act (September 1, 1937)

> Identification

> Significance

the Fair Labor Standards Act (June 25, 1938)

> Identification

> Significance

craft unions vs. industrial unions

> Identification

> Significance

John L. Lewis

    Identification

    Significance

the Congress of Industrial Organizations

    Identification

    Significance

the United Auto Workers' strike of 1936

    Identification

    Significance

the Memorial Day Massacre

    Identification

    Significance

Judge John J. Parker

    Identification

    Significance

the Scottsboro trials

    Identification

    Significance

A. Philip Randolph

> Identification

> Significance

the Black Cabinet

> Identification

> Significance

Marian Anderson

> Identification

> Significance

the March on Washington Movement

> Identification

> Significance

Executive Order No. 8802 (June 25, 1941)

> Identification

> Significance

John Collier

> Identification

> Significance

the Indian Reorganization Act (June 18, 1934)

    Identification

    Significance

the Farm Security Administration

    Identification

    Significance

It's Up to the Women

    Identification

    Significance

the "women's network"

    Identification

    Significance

Frances Perkins

    Identification

    Significance

the 1940 presidential election

    Identification

    Significance

Organizing Information

The charts on pages 243 and 244 include the major achievements of the First and Second New Deals discussed in Chapter 25. They are arranged in the same manner as in the chart on page 766 in the textbook. Use the charts to compile and organize information about New Deal achievements and categorize those achievements.

First New Deal Achievements

Labor	Agriculture	Business and Industrial Recovery	Relief
1933 Section 7A of NIRA Identification Significance	Agricultural Adjustment Act Identification Significance Farm Credit Act Identification Significance	Emergency Banking Act Identification Significance Beer and Wine Revenue Act Identification Significance Banking Act of 1933 Identification Significance National Industrial Recovery Act Identification Significance	Civilian Conservation Corps Identification Significance Federal Emergency Relief Act Identification Significance Home Owners Refinancing Act Identification Significance Public Works Administration Identification Significance Civil Works Administration Identification Significance
1934 National Labor Relations Board Identification Significance	Taylor Grazing Act Identification Significance		

Second New Deal Achievements

Labor	Agriculture	Business and Industry Recovery	Relief
1935 National Labor Relations Act Identification Significance	Resettlement Administration Identification Significance Rural Electrification Administration Identification Significance		Works Progress Administration Identification Significance National Youth Administration Identification Significance
1937	Farm Security Administration Identification Significance		
1938 Fair Labor Standards Act Identification Significance	Agricultural Adjustment Act Identification Significance		

Evaluating and Using Information

In Chapter 25, the authors of your textbook quote historian William Leuchtenburg: "For the first time for many Americans the federal government became an institution that was directly experienced. More than state and local governments, it came to be *the* government."

Review the chapter and your completed Organizing Information exercise to see (1) how the Roosevelt years reflected and shaped that new attitude on the part of the population toward the federal government and (2) how the behaviors and attitudes of President and Mrs. Roosevelt and the federal government during the Roosevelt years created new expectations concerning what the national government could and should do for the people.

Use either the chart on page 246 or a similar means of organizing the material to list behaviors or actions of the Roosevelts and the federal government during the Roosevelt years that you think best show the activism of the federal government and the strengthening of the role of the executive branch of the government in areas such as those appearing in the chart's column headings. When the behavior takes the form of enactment of legislation, select those that you believe are the best examples from the pieces of legislation on which you have taken notes in the Organizing Information exercise; you will not be able to cite all of the legislation nor should you. However, keep in mind that leadership in the Roosevelt years also rested on public relations, appointments, brokering, and the like.

After you have collected and organized your information, compose the working draft of an essay in response to this question:

> How did examples set during the Roosevelt years transform the federal government into *the* government in the United States and change Americans' perception of its role in protecting citizens from economic catastrophe and social unfairness?

Ideas and Details

Objective 1

_____ 1. As a result of the Great Depression,
   a. the Communist party became a major political force at the national level.
   b. the divorce rate soared.
   c. the number of marriages declined and the birthrate fell.
   d. shortages of basic agricultural commodities caused famine.

Objective 2

_____ 2. The reactions of Americans to the Great Depression indicate which of the following?
   a. Most Americans blamed the depression on the policies of the federal government.
   b. Anger at the capitalist system placed society on the verge of anarchy.
   c. Disillusionment with the American system caused the masses to think seriously of revolution.
   d. Many Americans blamed themselves for the depression.

© 1994 Houghton Mifflin Company. All rights reserved.

\multicolumn{5}{c}{Roles the Federal Government Assumed or Expanded To Turn Itself Into "The" Government}
Booster of Morale and Morality	**Regulator of Production, Consumption, Marketplace**	**Provider of Economic Safety Net for Individuals**	**Guardian of National Economic/ Financial Stability**	**Redistributor of Wealth, Resources, Power, and Status**
Public Confidence	Money Supply and Credit	Dependent Children	Regulator, Protector of Financial Institutions	Wealth
				Power/ Treatment of Minorities
Racism/Sexism	Business Competition	Elderly		African-Americans
	Farm Production, Prices	Disabled	Balanced Budget/Deficit Spending	Indians
Sale/Consumption of Alcoholic Beverages		Unemployed		Mexican-Americans
	Imports/Exports			Women

© 1994 Houghton Mifflin Company. All rights reserved.

Objective 3

_____ 3. Hoover responded to the Bonus March by
   a. calling out troops to disperse the marchers.
   b. establishing a comprehensive pension plan for future army veterans.
   c. encouraging Congress to authorize the immediate payment of veterans' benefits.
   d. meeting with the marchers and negotiating a settlement.

Objective 3

_____ 4. The Reconstruction Finance Corporation was based on the theory that
   a. an increase in supply leads to a corresponding increase in demand.
   b. the government must not interfere in the natural economic laws governing society.
   c. aid made available at the top of the economic ladder will trickle down to those at the bottom.
   d. taxes are a disincentive to economic recovery.

Objectives 4 and 5

_____ 5. Franklin Roosevelt's actions as governor of New York demonstrate that he
   a. accepted the theory that government should engage in deficit spending to combat an economic depression.
   b. was willing to experiment to find ways to combat the depression.
   c. believed that government should embark on a new trustbusting program to end bigness in industry.
   d. rejected the extension of direct government aid to the poor.

Objective 6

_____ 6. Both the Agricultural Adjustment Act and the National Industrial Recovery Act were based on the belief that
   a. the problems of the depression could best be solved by dealing with the problem of overproduction.
   b. prices of industrial and agricultural goods had to be lowered.
   c. deficit spending would result in an economic rebound.
   d. the depression could best be dealt with by state and local authorities.

Objectives 6 and 12

_____ 7. As a result of Section 7(a) of the National Industrial Recovery Act,
   a. unemployment insurance was provided to workers.
   b. federally guaranteed pension plans were required by all major corporations.
   c. workers were guaranteed the right to unionize and bargain collectively.
   d. workers were required to join company-sponsored unions.

© 1994 Houghton Mifflin Company. All rights reserved.

Objective 7

_____ 8. Conservative critics charged that the New Deal
   a. cooperated too closely with business interests.
   b. extended too little aid to the lower classes.
   c. exercised too little control over economic forces.
   d. destroyed individual initiative.

Objective 7

_____ 9. Through the Share Our Wealth program, Huey Long advocated that the government should
   a. nationalize all major industry in the United States.
   b. distribute free land to all families requesting it.
   c. provide a guaranteed annual income to all American families.
   d. create a national health insurance program.

Objective 8

_____ 10. The Supreme Court ruled part of the NIRA unconstitutional because it
   a. violated the First Amendment.
   b. delegated excessive legislative power to the executive branch.
   c. discriminated against small businesses.
   d. violated the due process clause of the Fourteenth Amendment.

Objective 9

_____ 11. The Second New Deal differed from the First in that it
   a. adopted a more aggressive, less cooperative approach toward big business.
   b. returned to the concept of laissez faire.
   c. rejected the concept of deficit spending.
   d. emphasized the importance of state action.

Objective 9

_____ 12. Which of the following is true of the Social Security Act?
   a. It established an old-age insurance plan for all workers in the United States.
   b. Through its enactment, the government acknowledged some responsibility toward the aged, the dependent, and the disabled.
   c. It established a national health insurance program for all Americans.
   d. All benefits were paid by employers and the government.

Objective 11

____ 13. Roosevelt's 1937 decision to cut federal spending resulted in
   a. a balanced budget.
   b. a lowering of interest rates.
   c. renewed spending by business on capital improvements.
   d. a new recession.

Objective 12

____ 14. During the 1930s the growth of organized labor was most impressive among
   a. skilled workers.
   b. industrial workers.
   c. farm workers.
   d. white-collar workers.

Objective 13

____ 15. Analysis of the AAA, the FHA, the CCC, and TVA indicates which of the following?
   a. These measures were quite effective in bringing about a redistribution of wealth in the United States.
   b. Money spent on such programs went mainly to the wealthy.
   c. All of these programs extended benefits to people in the city but not to the people in rural areas.
   d. Some New Deal measures functioned in ways that were discriminatory toward black Americans.

Essay Questions

Objective 1

1. Discuss the impact of the Great Depression on the lives of Americans. What was the response of the American people to the Depression? Why did they respond as they did?

Objective 3

2. Explain President Hoover's response to the depression.

Objectives 3 and 5

3. Discuss the similarities and differences between Herbert Hoover and Franklin Roosevelt in terms of personality, governing style, and view of the role of government.

Objectives 6 and 9

4. Discuss the similarities and differences between the theoretical basis of the First New Deal and that of the Second New Deal, and explain in both cases how the legislation enacted reflected this theory.

Objective 12

5. Discuss the impact of the New Deal on organized labor.

Objective 13

6. Examine the impact of the depression and New Deal on African-Americans.

CHAPTER 26
Foreign Relations in a Broken World, 1920–1941

Learning Objectives

After you have studied Chapter 26 in your textbook and worked through this study guide chapter, you should be able to:

1. Explain the ideas of independent internationalism and isolationism, and discuss how these ideas were manifested in the various attempts by American citizens and the American government to create a stable international order during the interwar years.
2. Examine and discuss the objectives and consequences of the foreign economic policy of the United States from 1918 to 1941.
3. Discuss the impact of the Great Depression on international relations, and explain Secretary of State Cordell Hull's response to intensified economic nationalism.
4. Examine and evaluate the interests, methods, and results of United States policy toward Latin America during the 1920s and 1930s.
5. Explain Europe's descent into the Second World War.
6. Explain the nature and growth of isolationist sentiment in the United States, and discuss the Neutrality Acts as an expression of such sentiment.
7. Discuss the foreign-policy ideas and diplomatic leadership of President Franklin Roosevelt from 1933 to United States entry into the Second World War.
8. Examine the erosion of American neutrality toward the war in Europe between September 1939 and December 7, 1941.
9. Examine the deterioration of Japanese-American relations from the 1920s to the Japanese attack against Pearl Harbor, and discuss American entry into the Pacific theater of the Second World War.

Thematic Guide

In this chapter, the authors seek to explain the instability of the world order in the 1920s and the coming of world war in the 1930s. Involvement in disarmament talks and arms limitation treaties, acceptance of the Kellogg-Briand Pact outlawing war, and international economic expansion by the United States serve as examples of the independent internationalist approach to foreign policy undertaken by the United States during the 1920s. These examples also illustrate the drawbacks of such an approach. United States acceptance of arms limitations treaties that did not include some of the most dangerous weapons of the age—submarines, destroyers, and cruisers—meant the continuation of rearmament. Acceptance of a treaty that outlawed war but had no enforcement provisions served a useful educational purpose but did not prevent war. International economic expansion, high United States tariff rates, United States policies concerning war debts and reparations, and the onset of the Great Depression caused an upsurge of economic nationalism and destabilized the international economy. Although Secretary of State Cordell Hull's attempts to move in the direction of economic internationalism were positive, they did not have a dramatic short-term impact.

In the 1920s, the United States altered its policy toward Latin America. Blatant military intervention no longer seemed to preserve American interests and maintain the order and stability so important to those interests. A new approach favored support for strong native leaders, training of the national guard in Latin American countries, continued economic expansion, Export-Import Bank loans, and political subversion. The discussion of American policy toward the Dominican Republic, Nicaragua, Haiti, Cuba, and Puerto Rico during the 1920s and early 1930s provides evidence of this change of approach. The Good Neighbor policy enhanced American power throughout the region but did not bring to Latin America the stable, democratic governments that the United States professed to desire. Mexico was a special case. In response to the expropriation controversy, President Roosevelt decided compromise was the best course of action. The general success of Roosevelt's policy can be seen in the 1936 Pan American Conference in Buenos Aires and the Declaration of Panama in 1939.

As the depression, economic nationalism, and aggressive fascist states began slowly to carry Europe into the abyss of war, the United States continued to follow the policy of independent internationalism, as evidenced in American economic ties with the Soviet Union and diplomatic recognition of that country in 1933. At the same time, isolationist sentiment (the desire to remain aloof from European power struggles and war) increased. Such sentiment found expression in the investigations of the Nye Committee, which attempted to prove that business interests had selfishly pulled the United States into the First World War. Although it failed to prove this assertion, the Nye Committee did find evidence of discreditable business practices during the 1920s and 1930s designed to increase arms sales. Furthermore, the chapter includes evidence of American business ties to Nazi Germany and fascist Italy. The publicity generated by the Nye Committee was in part responsible for passage of the Neutrality Acts of 1935, 1936, and 1937. Although Roosevelt supported these acts, events in Europe gradually convinced him that they should be revised and finally repealed.

In "Japan, China, and a New Order in Asia," the authors discuss American interests in Asia and trace the deterioration of United States-Japanese relations during the 1920s and 1930s. This discussion leads to the final section, Collision Course, 1939–1941, where the authors focus on events in Europe and explain President Roosevelt's policies, which carried the United States from neutrality to undeclared war. At the end of the chapter, the authors attempt to answer questions such as: could the United States have avoided going to war and why did the United States enter the war?

Building Vocabulary

Listed below are important words and terms that you need to know to get the most out of Chapter 26. They are listed in the order in which they occur in the chapter. After carefully looking through the list, refer to a dictionary and jot down the definition of words that you do not know or of which you are unsure.

clemency

disenchanted

bedevil

pinnacle

emasculate

arbitration

carnage

opportune

cartel

flounder (*verb*)

ingenious

ameliorate

vengeful

indemnity

permeate

usurp

blatant

abrogate

chafe

tutelage

disparage

hegemonic

expropriate

punitive

appease

apex

undaunted

covet

malcontent

imbibe

elicit

mongrel

abyss

contraband

minuscule

subjugate

affront

vestige

harry

ignoble

sanctions

retort

futile

analogy

deference

manipulate

embargo

precipitate

fortuitous

infamy

archaic

Identification and Significance

After studying Chapter 26 of *A People and a Nation*, you should be able to identify fully *and* explain the historical significance of each item listed on pages 256–266.

1. Identify each item in the space provided. Give an explanation or description of the item. Answer the questions *who, what, where,* and *when.*

2. Explain the historical significance of each item in the space provided. Establish the historical context in which the item exists. Establish the item as the result of or as the cause of other factors existing in the society under study. Answer this question: *what were the political, social, economic, and/or cultural consequences of this item?*

independent internationalism

    Identification

    Significance

isolationist

    Identification

    Significance

the Washington Conference

    Identification

    Significance

the Five-Power Treaty, the Nine-Power Treaty, and the Four-Power Treaty

    Identification

    Significance

the Locarno Pact of 1925 and the Kellogg-Briand Pact of 1928

    Identification

    Significance

the Webb-Pomerene Act and the Edge Act

    Identification

    Significance

the war debts and reparations issue

    Identification

    Significance

the Dawes Plan of 1924

    Identification

    Significance

the Young Plan of 1929

    Identification

    Significance

economic nationalism

    Identification

    Significance

Cordell Hull

    Identification

    Significance

the Reciprocal Trade Agreements Act

    Identification

    Significance

the most-favored-nation principle

    Identification

    Significance

the Export-Import Bank

    Identification

    Significance

the Good Neighbor policy

    Identification

    Significance

Rafael Leonidas Trujillo

    Identification

    Significance

César Augusto Sandino

    Identification

    Significance

General Anastasio Somoza

> Identification

> Significance

the occupation of Haiti

> Identification

> Significance

the Cuban Revolution of 1933

> Identification

> Significance

Ramon Grau San Martín

> Identification

> Significance

Fulgencio Batista

> Identification

> Significance

Puerto Rico

> Identification

> Significance

Pedro Albizo Campos

> Identification

> Significance

Luis Munoz Marin

> Identification

> Significance

Operation Bootstrap

> Identification

> Significance

the Mexican expropriation controversy

> Identification

> Significance

the 1936 Pan American Conference in Buenos Aires

> Identification

> Significance

the Declaration of Panama

> Identification

> Significance

fascism

>Identification

>Significance

the Rome-Berlin Axis and the Anti-Comintern Pact

>Identification

>Significance

the policy of appeasement

>Identification

>Significance

the Lincoln Battalion

>Identification

>Significance

the Munich Conference

>Identification

>Significance

the Nazi-Soviet Pact

>Identification

>Significance

the German invasion of Poland

> Identification

> Significance

diplomatic recognition of the Soviet Union

> Identification

> Significance

American isolationist sentiment

> Identification

> Significance

the Nye Committee

> Identification

> Significance

the Neutrality Acts of 1935, 1936, and 1937

> Identification

> Significance

Roosevelt's Chautauqua speech

> Identification

> Significance

repeal of the arms embargo (the Neutrality Act of 1939)

    Identification

    Significance

The Good Earth

    Identification

    Significance

Jiang Jieshi

    Identification

    Significance

Japanese seizure of Manchuria

    Identification

    Significance

the Stimson Doctrine

    Identification

    Significance

the Sino-Japanese War

    Identification

    Significance

Roosevelt's quarantine speech

    Identification

    Significance

the *Panay* incident

    Identification

    Significance

Japan's "New Order"

    Identification

    Significance

the fall of France

    Identification

    Significance

the destroyers-for-bases agreement

    Identification

    Significance

the Selective Training and Service Act

    Identification

    Significance

the Lend-Lease Act

    Identification

    Significance

the Atlantic Charter

    Identification

    Significance

the *Greer,* the *Kearny,* and the *Reuben James*

    Identification

    Significance

the Tripartite Pact

    Identification

    Significance

Japanese occupation of French Indochina

    Identification

    Significance

Operation MAGIC

    Identification

    Significance

the Japanese attack on Pearl Harbor

Identification

Significance

Evaluating and Using Information

Compose the working draft of an essay in which you compare or contrast the way Presidents Woodrow Wilson and Franklin D. Roosevelt led the country into participation in world war. Enter your essay in your Reading Notebook.

The first column in the chart on pages 267–269 will help you recall and find significant events in the earlier period and Wilson's response to them as he led the nation into World War I (Chapters 21 and 23). In the appropriate blocks in the second column, list similar situations from the World War II period and Roosevelt's responses to them as he led the nation into participation in World War II. Add other parallels or differences you think are significant in the three blank rows.

Ideas and Details

Objective 2

_____ 1. Secretary of State Charles Evans Hughes encouraged United States economic expansion abroad because he believed such expansion
   a. would lead to world stability.
   b. would foster healthy competition and rivalry.
   c. would bring power and glory to the United States at the expense of the less virtuous European nations.
   d. would promote economic nationalism.

Objective 1

_____ 2. As a result of the Five-Power Treaty,
   a. Britain, the United States, Japan, France, and Italy agreed to limits on the number of submarines that each nation could build.
   b. Britain, the United States, and Japan dismantled some capital ships to meet the tonnage ratio agreed to.
   c. provisions for the enforcement of the Open Door policy were accepted by Britain, the United States, Japan, France, and Italy.
   d. Britain, the United States, France, Italy, and the Soviet Union agreed to impose economic sanctions against Nazi Germany.

© 1994 Houghton Mifflin Company. All rights reserved.

Going to War—World War I and World War II	
Wilson	**Roosevelt**
Wilson kept America out of war for three years. During that time he tried to protect American trading interests, tried to improve the country's military posture, and lectured the belligerents.	
At first, in an attempt to keep America distanced from the war, President Wilson issued a proclamation of neutrality and asked Americans to refrain from taking sides. Privately, also, he said that the nation definitely had to remain neutral.	
When 128 Americans lost their lives in the sinking of the *Lusitania* by a German U-Boat and when the Germans attacked other Allied ships with Americans aboard, Wilson ruled out a military response. But he argued against the Gore-McLemore Resolution whose passage would have banned American travel on ships likely to be attacked.	

© 1994 Houghton Mifflin Company. All rights reserved.

Going to War—World War I and World War II	
Wilson	**Roosevelt**
As early as 1915, Wilson began planning a military build-up, and then in 1916 he got the legislation passed to launch and pay for it.	
Wilson's campaign slogan for the 1916 election was "He kept us out of war."	
Wilson responded to the direct threat to U.S. security posed by Germany's seeking an alliance with Mexico against the United States (the Zimmermann telegram) by asking Congress for "armed neutrality" to defend American lives and commerce.	

Going to War—World War I and World War II	
Wilson	**Roosevelt**
Under Wilson, the military draft came only after the United States declared war.	

Objective 1

_____ 3. The Kellogg-Briand Pact
   a. placed limits on the number of submarines and destroyers to be built by the world's five major powers.
   b. called for an end to international arms sales.
   c. made the United States an official observer at the League of Nations.
   d. renounced war as an instrument of national policy.

Objective 2

_____ 4. Which of the following conclusions may be drawn from an examination of the war debts and reparations issue?
   a. The United States handled the issue in a selfless manner.
   b. The triangular arrangement that emerged was economically destabilizing in the long run.
   c. The European nations demonstrated a willingness to forgive Germany in the aftermath of the First World War.
   d. The German government used the issue to create tensions between the United States and Great Britain.

Objectives 2 and 3

_____ 5. In response to the Hawley-Smoot Tariff,
   a. European states raised tariffs against American imports, causing economic nationalism to gain momentum.
   b. European nations exported inexpensive goods to the United States in record numbers.
   c. European states pledged to support the Open Door policy.
   d. Japan imposed an embargo against all American-made goods.

Objectives 2 and 3

_____ 6. The central feature of the Reciprocal Trade Agreements Act of 1934 was
   a. the adoption of free trade by the United States.
   b. low-interest loans to foreign countries agreeing to buy American goods.
   c. the most-favored-nation principle.
   d. the establishment of a free trade zone in the Western Hemisphere.

Objective 4

_____ 7. The Good Neighbor policy meant that
   a. the United States would strictly adhere to the doctrine of nonintervention in Latin America.
   b. the United States would be less blatant in dominating Latin America.
   c. American businesses in Latin America would invest their profits there rather than in the United States.
   d. the United States would practice isolationism in Latin America.

Objective 4

_____ 8. Both the Trujillo regime in the Dominican Republic and the Somoza regime in Nicaragua are evidence that
   a. American concepts of government were planted in fertile soil in Latin America.
   b. the United States was careful to support Latin American rulers who were strongly supported by the masses.
   c. Latin American dictators often rose through the ranks of a United States trained national guard.
   d. the United States continued to live up to its own revolutionary tradition by supporting liberation movements in Latin America.

Objective 5

_____ 9. As a result of the Munich Conference,
   a. Britain and France accepted Hitler's seizure of the Sudeten region of Czechoslovakia.
   b. Britain agreed to extend financial and military aid to France in the event of German aggression.
   c. Britain, France, and the Soviet Union entered into a defensive alliance against Nazi Germany.
   d. Germany and France agreed to withdraw their troops from Austria and the Rhineland respectively.

Objectives 2 and 6

_____ 10. Records from the 1920s and 1930s concerning American business practices abroad indicate that
   a. all major American corporations strongly supported arms control in the belief that fewer armaments would generate peace and prosperity.
   b. American petroleum exports to Italy increased after that country's attack on Ethiopia.
   c. all major American corporations severed their business ties with Germany when the Nazis gained power.
   d. all American firms severed economic ties with Germany after learning about the persecution of Jews.

Objective 6

_____ 11. The Neutrality Acts of 1935 and 1936
   a. were attempts to provide aid to the Allies while avoiding war with Hitler.
   b. imposed a unilateral freeze on further deployment of destroyer-class vessels.
   c. allowed the president to intervene in the Spanish Civil War.
   d. prohibited arms shipments and loans to nations declared by the president to be in a state of war.

Objective 8

_____ 12. As a result of the outbreak of war in Europe in September 1939,
   a. Roosevelt promised that the United States would involve itself in the conflict if British defeat seemed imminent.
   b. Congress, at Roosevelt's urging, approved arms exports on a cash-and-carry basis.
   c. the United States broke diplomatic relations with the Soviet Union.
   d. Roosevelt asked Congress for a declaration of war against Germany.

Objective 9

_____ 13. In response to the Japanese invasion of Manchuria, the United States
   a. issued the Stimson Doctrine by which it refused to recognize any impairment of Chinese sovereignty.
   b. froze Japanese assets in this country.
   c. called for economic sanctions against Japan through the League of Nations.
   d. signed a defensive treaty of alliance with China.

Objective 8

_____ 14. By the Lend-Lease Act,
   a. the United States traded fifty old destroyers to the British for leases to four British bases.
   b. the provisions of the Neutrality Acts were revoked.
   c. Roosevelt was authorized to ship war material to the British.
   d. the United States canceled Allied debts from the First World War.

Objective 9

_____ 15. The Roosevelt administration
   a. plotted to start a war with Japan.
   b. was completely surprised by the Japanese decision in favor of war.
   c. was aware of Japanese war plans but did not conspire to leave Pearl Harbor vulnerable.
   d. expected a Japanese attack against the American mainland.

Essay Questions

Objective 1

1. Discuss the Washington Conference's treaty agreements and the Kellogg-Briand Pact as examples of the United States independent-internationalist approach to foreign policy during the 1920s, and explain the strengths and weaknesses of that approach.

Objectives 1 and 2

2. Explain and evaluate American handling of the war debts and reparations issue.

Objective 4

3. Discuss the dominant themes suggested by American policy toward the Dominican Republic, Nicaragua, Haiti, Cuba, and Puerto Rico during the 1920s and 1930s.

Objective 6

4. Explain the sources of isolationist thought in the United States in the 1920s and 1930s, and discuss the actions taken by Congress to prevent United States involvement in European power struggles.

Objective 8

5. Explain the process by which the United States moved from neutrality in 1939 to undeclared war with Germany in 1941.

Objective 9

6. Trace relations between the United States and Japan during the 1920s and 1930s, and explain the Japanese decision to bomb Pearl Harbor.

CHAPTER 27

The Second World War at Home and Abroad, 1941–1945

Learning Objectives

After you have studied Chapter 27 in your textbook and worked through this study guide chapter, you should be able to:

1. Describe the military strategy and the major military operations undertaken by the Allies in the European theater; discuss the disagreements that arose concerning strategy; and explain the resolution of these disagreements.
2. Discuss United States military strategy and the major military operations in the Pacific theater that brought America to the verge of victory by 1945.
3. Explain and evaluate President Truman's decision to use the atomic bomb.
4. Examine the impact of the Second World War on America's economic institutions, organized labor, agriculture, and the federal government, and discuss and assess the role played by the federal government in the war effort.
5. Discuss the impact of military life and wartime experiences on the men and women in the United States armed forces during the Second World War.
6. Examine and evaluate the civil liberties record of the United States government during the Second World War, and discuss the government's response to the Holocaust and to the plight of Jewish refugees.
7. Discuss the impact of the Second World War on African-Americans, Mexican-Americans, women, and the family.
8. Discuss the decline of political liberalism during the early 1940s; examine the issues and personalities of the 1944 presidential election and explain its outcome.
9. Examine the relations, the issues debated, and the agreements reached among the Allies from the second-front controversy through the Yalta and Potsdam conferences, and discuss the issues left unresolved after Yalta and Potsdam.
10. Assess the impact of the Second World War on the world community of nations and on the world balance of power.

Thematic Guide

The first two sections of Chapter 27, "Winning the Second World War in Europe" and "Winning the Second World War in the Pacific," trace the European and Pacific theater campaigns that led to Allied victory in World War II. The undercurrent of suspicion among the Allies, obvious in the second-front controversy, provides the theme for discussion of the European campaigns. Discussion of the war in the Pacific focuses on America's wartime perception of Japan as the major enemy. The authors also consider the "island-hopping strategy" adopted by American forces after breaking the momentum of Japan's offensive at the Battle of Midway, and the American goal of crippling Japan's merchant marine. The success of these strategies led to the conventional bombing of Japan's cities and ultimately to the use of atomic bombs on Hiroshima and Nagasaki. Truman's rejection of suggested alternatives to the atomic bomb and the strategic, emotional, psychological, and diplomatic reasons for his decision to use it are explained at the end of the section on the war in the Pacific.

The focus of the chapter then shifts to a discussion of the impact of World War II on the home front. In the economic sphere the war brought (1) renewed government-business cooperation and an acceleration of corporate growth, (2) the growth of scientific research facilities through government incentives, (3) the growth of labor unions, and (4) increased mechanization of agriculture as part of a transition from family-owned farms to mechanized agribusiness. The Second World War, to an even greater extent than the First World War, was a total war, requiring not only military mobilization but mobilization of the home front as well. The responsibility for coordinating total mobilization fell on the federal government. As a result, the federal bureaucracy mushroomed in size.

Life in the military, life away from family, and the experience of war profoundly affected the men and women who served in the armed forces during the course of the Second World War. The frame of reference of many GIs was broadened by associations with fellow soldiers from backgrounds and cultures different from their own. Some men and women homosexuals found the freedom within the service to act upon their sexual feelings. As a consequence of the military's technical schools, many soldiers returned home with new skills and ambitions. But as GIs returned to civilian life, they quickly realized that life at home had continued without them; thus, many felt a sense of loss and alienation.

The war had a special impact on Japanese-Americans, nonwhites, and women. The authors note that the treatment of Japanese-Americans was "the one enormous exception to the nation's generally creditable wartime civil liberties record"; Japanese-Americans were interned chiefly because of their ethnic origin. For African-Americans, the war did provide some opportunities in the military and at home, but the Detroit riot of 1943 made clear that racism remained a shaping force in blacks' lives. The zoot-suit riot in Los Angeles in 1943 demonstrated that the same was true for Mexican-Americans.

For women, the war became a turning point. More women, including more married women and mothers, entered the labor force than ever before. As some of the negative attitudes toward women working in heavy industry began to change, women experienced more geographic and occupational mobility. Although they continued to receive lower pay than men and were still concentrated in sex-segregated occupations, more women than ever were deciding to remain in the labor market. But even with those changes, home and family responsibilities continued to fall on their shoulders. In many cases, the wartime absence of husbands and fathers made women fully responsible for the family. The combination of these factors and experiences meant that many women gained a new sense of independence.

The political impact of the war is the theme of "The Decline of Liberalism and the Election of 1944." Then, in the last two sections of the chapter, the authors examine wartime foreign policy. The goals of the United States, embodied in the Atlantic Charter, were based to some extent on the memory of the post-First World War period. Continued suspicions among the Allies made cooperation to achieve these objectives difficult. Despite these suspicions and continued disagreement over Poland, Stalin and Churchill reached some agreements about Eastern Europe; and, though China's role was not determined, the Allies agreed in most other respects on the charter for a United Nations Organization.

After a brief discussion of American policy toward Jewish refugees—a policy characterized by anti-Semitism and fear of economic competition—the authors turn to the Yalta and Potsdam conferences. The Yalta Conference was "the high point of the Grand Alliance." The agreements reached there are explained in the context of the suspicions among the Allies, the goals of each of the Allies, and the positions of each of the Allied armies. The Potsdam Conference, on the other hand, revealed a crumbling alliance in which any sense of cooperation had given way to suspicions among competitive nation states. These suspicions, so obvious at Potsdam, were a portent concerning the post-war world.

Building Vocabulary

Listed below are important words and terms that you need to know to get the most out of Chapter 27. They are listed in the order in which they occur in the chapter. After carefully looking through the list, refer to a dictionary and jot down the definition of words that you do not know or of which you are unsure.

capitulate

advent

watershed

unsavory

mollify

amphibious

clandestine

saboteurs

tenacious

deterrent

ominous

mandatory

elicit

lament

internment

plausible

wantonly

articulate

perpetuate

formidable

moot

futile

lax

lament

novice

Identification and Significance

After studying Chapter 27 of *A People and a Nation,* you should be able to identify fully *and* explain the historical significance of each item listed below.

1. Identify each item in the space provided. Give an explanation or description of the item. Answer the questions *who, what, where,* and *when*.
2. Explain the historical significance of each item in the space provided. Establish the historical context in which the item exists. Establish the item as the result of or as the cause of other factors existing in the society under study. Answer this question: *what were the political, social, economic, and/or cultural consequences of this item?*

Why We Fight

      Identification

      Significance

Winston Churchill

      Identification

      Significance

Josef Stalin

      Identification

      Significance

the second-front controversy

      Identification

      Significance

© 1994 Houghton Mifflin Company. All rights reserved.

the battle for Stalingrad

    Identification

    Significance

the Teheran Conference

    Identification

    Significance

D-Day

    Identification

    Significance

the Battle of the Bulge

    Identification

    Significance

the "Europe first" formula

    Identification

    Significance

the Bataan Death March

    Identification

    Significance

the Battle of the Coral Sea and the Battle of Midway

    Identification

    Significance

Operation Magic

    Identification

    Significance

the "island-hop" strategy

    Identification

    Significance

the Philippines campaign

    Identification

    Significance

the Battles of Iwo Jima and Okinawa

    Identification

    Significance

kamikaze attacks

    Identification

    Significance

the bombing of Tokyo

> Identification

> Significance

the Manhattan Project

> Identification

> Significance

Hiroshima and Nagasaki

> Identification

> Significance

the War Production Board

> Identification

> Significance

the synthetic-rubber industry

> Identification

> Significance

government-business interdependence

> Identification

> Significance

© 1994 Houghton Mifflin Company. All rights reserved.

National Defense Research Committee and the Office of Scientific Research and Development

    Identification

    Significance

the no strike-no lockout pledge

    Identification

    Significance

the National War Labor Board

    Identification

    Significance

the War Labor Disputes (Smith-Connally) Act

    Identification

    Significance

agribusiness

    Identification

    Significance

the War Manpower Commission

    Identification

    Significance

the Office of Price Administration

    Identification

    Significance

the Office of War Information

    Identification

    Significance

Post-traumatic Stress Disorder

    Identification

    Significance

the internment of Japanese-Americans

    Identification

    Significance

the *Hirabayashi* ruling

    Identification

    Significance

the *Korematsu* case

    Identification

    Significance

the Commission on Wartime Relocation and Internment of Civilians

    Identification

    Significance

Colonel Benjamin O. Davis

    Identification

    Significance

the "Double V" campaign

    Identification

    Significance

Executive Order No. 8802

    Identification

    Significance

the Detroit riot of 1943

    Identification

    Significance

the *bracero* program

    Identification

    Significance

the zoot-suit riot

    Identification

    Significance

women's war work

    Identification

    Significance

Rosie the Riveter

    Identification

    Significance

latchkey children

    Identification

    Significance

the Lanham Act

    Identification

    Significance

Extended School Services

    Identification

    Significance

© 1994 Houghton Mifflin Company. All rights reserved.

the 1942 congressional elections

    Identification

    Significance

the Economic Bill of Rights

    Identification

    Significance

Harry S Truman

    Identification

    Significance

the presidential election of 1944

    Identification

    Significance

the Polish question

    Identification

    Significance

the Katyn Forest massacre and the Warsaw Uprising

    Identification

    Significance

the Lublin regime

    Identification

    Significance

the Dumbarton Oaks Conference

    Identification

    Significance

Jewish refugees from the Holocaust

    Identification

    Significance

the voyage of the *St. Louis*

    Identification

    Significance

the War Refugee Board

    Identification

    Significance

the Yalta Conference

    Identification

    Significance

the Declaration of Liberated Europe

    Identification

    Significance

the Potsdam Conference

    Identification

    Significance

Organizing Information

During the Second World War the American government acted to mobilize, coordinate, and oversee America's war effort on the home front. Use the chart on page 289 to organize information concerning the government's role and to describe the social, political, and economic consequences of government actions.

	The Government as Coordinator and Overseer of America's War Effort			
What Task Must Be Accomplished? What Goal Must Be Met?	What Action Did the Government Take to Accomplish This Task (Allocation of Funds, Creation of Board, Issuance of Directives, Etc.)?	How Was This Action Designed to Accomplish the Task and Meet the Goal?	How Well Did This Action Work in Accomplishing the Task and Meeting the Goal?	What Were the Social, Political, and/or Economic Consequences of This Action?

Evaluating and Using Information

Throughout American history, women and minorities have been discriminated against politically, socially, and economically. Based on the information in Chapter 27, determine the extent to which the United States made progress during the course of the Second World War in eliminating discrimination against women and minorities.

Examine the wartime treatment of each of the groups identified in the chart on pages 291 and 292. Then weigh the progress toward equitable treatment of all groups in American society against any signs of regression and against signs of continued discrimination. Based on your examination of the record, compose an essay responding to the following question:

> Examine the extent to which the United States made progress in the extending full political, social, and economic rights to women and minorities during the course of the Second World War.

To use the following chart to help you organize the information you will need, list reminders of the useful evidence you find in Chapter 27 and your class notes in the appropriate blocks. (You will not find evidence to record in every block.) Expand your reminders to create your working-draft essay.

American Treatment of Minorities During World War II

Standard of Measurement	Women	African-Americans	Mexican-Americans	Japanese-Americans	Homosexuals	Jews and Other Refugees
Acceptance in Armed Forces						
Degree of Integration Into Activities of Dominant Group						
Job Opportunities and Wages/ Provision of Needed Job-Related Social Services						

American Treatment of Minorities During World War II

Standard of Measurement	Women	African-Americans	Mexican-Americans	Japanese-Americans	Homosexuals	Jews and Other Refugees
Victimization in Riots or Other Violence						
Kind of Support Given or Denied in Immigration Policies and Diplomatic Efforts						

Ideas and Details

Objective 1

_____ 1. Roosevelt initially wanted to open a second front in 1942 because
   a. he wanted to check Russian power on the European continent.
   b. the North African campaign had been highly successful.
   c. Churchill insisted it was the only way to save England.
   d. he was afraid Russia might be defeated, leaving Hitler free to invade England.

Objective 1

_____ 2. As a result of the Teheran Conference, the Allies
   a. reached agreement on launching Operation OVERLORD.
   b. agreed to launch an attack against North Africa.
   c. reluctantly decided to recognize the pro-Nazi Vichy French regime in North Africa.
   d. made plans for the battle for Stalingrad.

Objective 2

_____ 3. As a result of the Battle of Midway,
   a. the United States destroyed Japan's merchant marine.
   b. Japanese momentum in the Pacific was broken.
   c. American naval losses made Hawaii more vulnerable to attack.
   d. President Roosevelt began to harbor private fears of Japanese victory in the Pacific.

Objective 3

_____ 4. Truman decided to drop the atomic bomb on Japan because
   a. he believed it was the only way the United States could win the war in the Pacific.
   b. a quick American victory against Japan would allow the United States to concentrate on defeating Hitler.
   c. the Allies decided collectively at Potsdam that it was the quickest and most humane way to defeat Japan.
   d. he wanted to prevent the Soviet Union from having a role in the reconstruction of postwar Asia.

Objective 4

_____ 5. The first task of the War Production Board was to
   a. vigorously enforce the nation's antitrust laws.
   b. minimize the cost of the war by ensuring competitive bidding on government contracts.
   c. oversee the conversion of industry from civilian to military production.
   d. analyze the military situation in order to determine what weapons needed to be produced and in what quantity.

Objective 4

_____ 6. The Smith-Connally Act
   a. reduced the powers of the NWLB.
   b. prohibited strikes and lockouts.
   c. guaranteed cost of living increases to workers in defense-related industries.
   d. authorized the president to seize and operate any strike-bound plant deemed necessary to the national security.

Objective 4

_____ 7. The Second World War affected America's basic economic institutions in which of the following ways?
   a. Large economic units were broken up by the government to increase competition.
   b. The trend toward bigness in industry and agriculture accelerated as a result of the war.
   c. The withdrawal of government money from the economy brought a restructuring of industry and agriculture.
   d. The banking industry was virtually nationalized to ensure the availability of money for the war effort.

Objective 5

_____ 8. Those who served in the United States armed forces during the Second World War
   a. often found their horizons broadened because of associations with people of differing backgrounds.
   b. found that the technical training they received in the military was useless in civilian life.
   c. usually received no training before being sent into combat.
   d. were given no background information on the history and culture of the places to which they were sent.

Objective 6

_____ 9. Which of the following is the major reason for the internment of Japanese-Americans during the Second World War?
   a. Criminal behavior
   b. Evidence of disloyalty to the government of the United States
   c. Their ethnic origin
   d. Their economic challenge to white businesses

Objective 7

_____ 10. During the Second World War, African-Americans
   a. continued to move to northern cities, where they began to gain more political power.
   b. experienced equal opportunity in housing and employment.
   c. experienced a deterioration of their economic position.
   d. steadfastly refused to participate in the war effort.

Objective 8

_____ 11. Which of the following is true of the 1944 presidential election?
   a. Roosevelt was elected to a fourth term by a popular-vote landslide.
   b. Fear of a postwar depression led many people to vote for Roosevelt.
   c. Although Roosevelt won the election, the Republicans carried the South.
   d. Harry Truman won a narrow victory over Thomas Dewey in both the popular vote and the electoral vote.

Objective 6

_____ 12. In response to Nazi persecution of the Jews, the United States
   a. did not act in a decisive manner until the creation of the War Refugee Board in 1944.
   b. relaxed immigration requirements in the mid-1930s in order to allow Jewish refugees free entry into the United States.
   c. cooperated closely with the British in opening Palestine to Jewish refugees.
   d. bombed the gas chambers at Auschwitz toward the end of the war.

Objective 9

_____ 13. A major factor that influenced the agreements at Yalta was
   a. Roosevelt's ill health.
   b. dissension between Roosevelt and Churchill over German reparations.
   c. the military positions of the Allies.
   d. Stalin's insistence that China be recognized as a major power.

Objective 10

_____ 14. Which of the following countries suffered the most casualties as a result of the Second World War?
   a. Great Britain
   b. the United States
   c. Japan
   d. Russia

Objective 10

_____ 15. Which of the following countries emerged from the Second World War more powerful than it had been when it entered the war?
   a. Great Britain
   b. the United States
   c. Japan
   d. Russia

Essay Questions

Objective 9

1. Discuss the disagreements within the Grand Alliance over the opening of a second front, and explain how these disagreements were ultimately resolved.

Objective 3

2. Examine and assess President Truman's decision to use the atomic bomb.

Objective 4

3. Discuss the various responsibilities assumed by the federal government as coordinator and overseer of America's war effort, and evaluate its performance.

Objective 4

4. Discuss the trend toward bigness in American industry, organized labor, and agriculture during the course of the Second World War.

Objective 7

5. Discuss the impact of the Second World War on nonwhite Americans.

Objective 8

6. Examine the issues and explain the outcome of the 1944 presidential election.

Objective 9

7. Discuss the similarities and differences between the "spirit of Yalta" and the "brawl at Potsdam," and explain and assess the agreements reached at these conferences.

CHAPTER 28
Cold War Politics, McCarthyism, and Civil Rights, 1945–1961

Learning Objectives

After you have studied Chapter 28 in your textbook and worked through this study guide chapter, you should be able to:

1. Examine the domestic economic problems that faced the Truman administration during the immediate postwar period; explain Truman's actions concerning those problems; and discuss the consequences of those actions.
2. Discuss the outcome of the 1946 congressional election; explain the actions of the Eightieth Congress concerning major domestic issues; and discuss the consequences of those actions.
3. Examine the issues and personalities and explain the outcome of the 1948 congressional and presidential elections.
4. Discuss the gains of African-Americans during the late 1940s and early 1950s, and examine the factors responsible for those gains.
5. Discuss the combination of forces and incidents that caused the postwar wave of anti-Communist hysteria, and examine the various ways in which this hysteria manifested itself, especially in its manipulation by Senator Joseph McCarthy.
6. Explain Senator Joseph McCarthy's rise to power and his ultimate decline, and discuss the impact of the postwar wave of anti-Communist hysteria on American society.
7. Examine the issues and personalities and explain the outcome of the 1952 congressional and presidential elections.
8. Discuss the legacy of the Truman years, and assess the Truman presidency.
9. Discuss the 1950s as an age of consensus and conformity, and explain the beliefs associated with this consensus mood.
10. Discuss the domestic issues facing the Eisenhower administration; explain and evaluate the administration's handling of those issues; and discuss the consequences of those actions.
11. Examine the reinvigoration of the civil rights movement during the 1950s; discuss the response of white southerners and of the federal government to the demands and actions of African-Americans; and explain the extent to which African-Americans were successful in achieving their goals.
12. Examine the issues and personalities and explain the outcome of the 1960 presidential election.
13. Discuss the legacy of the Eisenhower years, and assess the Eisenhower presidency.

Thematic Guide

After the Second World War, the United States experienced an uneasy and troubled transition to peace. The Truman administration was plagued by postwar economic problems, and the administration's handling of those problems led to widespread public discontent which in turn led to Republican victory in the 1946 congressional elections. However, the actions of the conservative Eightieth Congress worked to Truman's political advantage; and, to the surprise of most analysts, he won the presidential election of 1948.

Under Truman, the federal government, for the first time since Reconstruction, accepted responsibility for guaranteeing equality under the law—civil rights—to African-Americans. Furthermore, work by the NAACP, aid by the Justice Department in the form of friend-of-the-court briefs, and decisions by the Supreme Court resulted in a slow erosion of the separate-but-equal doctrine and of black disfranchisement in the South. These factors, plus some changes in public attitudes and the pressure of world opinion, offered a ray of hope that the long struggle waged by African-Americans against racism was beginning to pay off.

The Truman years also witnessed a wave of anti-Communist hysteria. The tracing of events from the *Amerasia* case to Truman's loyalty probe, the Hiss trial, and the Klaus Fuchs case supports the view that (1) fear of communism, long present in American society, intensified during the postwar years; (2) the building of this fear in the late 1940s was in many ways a "top-down" phenomenon; (3) revelations gave people cause to be alarmed; and (4) McCarthy's name has been given to a state of mind that existed before he entered the scene. Further discussion supports the characterization of McCarthy as a demagogue, the idea that McCarthyism was sustained by events, and the contention that anti-Communist measures received widespread support.

As McCarthyism gained momentum, the American people also had to contend with the domestic consequences of the Korean War. Although the war brought prosperity, it also brought inflation and increased defense spending at the expense of the domestic programs of Truman's Fair Deal. Furthermore, both the nature and length of the Korean War led to disillusionment and discontent on the part of many Americans. These factors, coupled with reports of influence peddling in the Truman administration, led to a Republican triumph in the presidential and congressional elections of 1952.

After a discussion of the Truman legacy, the authors turn to a discussion of the "age of consensus"—a period in which Americans agreed on their stance against communism and their faith in economic progress. Believing in the rightness of the American system, many people viewed reform and reformers in a negative light and saw conflict as the product of psychologically disturbed individuals, not as the product of societal ills. President Dwight D. Eisenhower, sharing these beliefs, actively pursued policies designed to promote economic growth and to defeat communism at home and abroad.

In pursuit of economic growth, Eisenhower tried to reduce federal spending and the federal government's role in regulating the forces of the marketplace. Eisenhower's farm policies reflected these efforts, and his belief that government should actively promote economic development may be seen in the St. Lawrence Seaway project, the president's tax reform program, the Atomic Energy Act, and the Highway Act of 1956. Furthermore, Eisenhower's conservative fiscal policy, as well as his states' rights philosophy, may be seen in the Indian termination policy adopted during his administration. The authors relate these programs to Eisenhower's frame of reference and study their impact on American society.

Despite Eisenhower's fiscal conservatism, the administration's activist foreign policy and three domestic economic recessions caused increased federal expenditures, decreased tax revenues, and deficit spending. As a result, Eisenhower oversaw only three balanced budgets during his eight years in office.

The Sherman Adams scandal, large Democratic gains in the congressional elections of 1958, and Democratic charges that the United States had not kept pace with the Soviet Union in the arms race meant that a beleaguered Eisenhower was on the defensive during his last two years in office.

© 1994 Houghton Mifflin Company. All rights reserved.

Eisenhower's strong anti-Communist views are reflected in his broadening of the loyalty program, his actions in the Rosenberg and Oppenheimer cases, and his support for the Communist Control Act of 1954. Furthermore, Eisenhower chose to avoid a direct confrontation with Senator Joe McCarthy. As a result, McCarthy proceeded to add more victims to his list of alleged subversives and continued to jeopardize freedom of speech and expression. Ultimately, McCarthyism did decline, with McCarthy himself being largely responsible for his own demise.

One group that challenged the consensus mood of the age was African-Americans. The authors explain this challenge in "An Awakened Civil Rights Movement," where they examine the Supreme Court's decision in *Brown v. Board of Education of Topeka* and the hostile reaction of white southerners to that decision. Though believing in states' rights, Eisenhower felt compelled to use federal troops to prevent violence in the desegregation of public schools in Little Rock, Arkansas. In this section, the authors trace the emergence of the civil rights movement through a discussion of the Montgomery bus boycott and the formation of the Southern Christian Leadership Conference and the Student Nonviolent Coordinating Committee. The authors note that courageous actions by rank-and-file African-Americans, as much as by leaders, constituted the civil rights movement.

Within the context of mounting foreign problems and domestic economic recession, Richard M. Nixon and John F. Kennedy became the standard-bearers for the Republican and Democratic parties in the presidential election contest of 1960. The chapter ends with a discussion of this election and an evaluation of the Eisenhower years.

Building Vocabulary

Listed below are important words and terms that you need to know to get the most out of Chapter 28. They are listed in the order in which they occur in the chapter. After carefully looking through the list, refer to a dictionary and jot down the definition of words that you do not know or of which you are unsure.

espouse

volatile

consensus

articulate (*verb*)

effectuate

unscrupulous

quiescent

respite

impasse

spate

scapegoat

volatile

livid

mandate

vindicate

oblivious

exhort

disfranchisement

redbait

ardent

rampant

demagogue

founder (*verb*)

exacerbate

bona-fide

cerebral

deride

sporadic

coalesce

syntax

ideologue

schism

tenet

extricate

parity

entice

penal

vexing

transgress

sully

vicuna

punitive

apathetic

pragmatic

adroitly

daunting

placid

Identification and Significance

After studying Chapter 28 of *A People and a Nation,* you should be able to identify fully *and* explain the historical significance of each item listed below.

1. Identify each item in the space provided. Give an explanation or description of the item. Answer the questions *who, what, where,* and *when.*
2. Explain the historical significance of each item in the space provided. Establish the historical context in which the item exists. Establish the item as the result of or as the cause of other factors existing in the society under study. Answer this question: *what were the political, social, economic, and/or cultural consequences of this item?*

postwar unemployment

    Identification

    Significance

the Employment Act of 1946

    Identification

    Significance

the United Mine Workers' strike of 1946

    Identification

    Significance

the railroad strike of 1946

> Identification

> Significance

meat-price controls

> Identification

> Significance

Harold Ickes and Henry A. Wallace

> Identification

> Significance

the 1946 congressional elections

> Identification

> Significance

the Eightieth Congress

> Identification

> Significance

the Taft-Hartley Acts

> Identification

> Significance

the Progressive party

    Identification

    Significance

the Dixiecrats

    Identification

    Significance

the presidential and congressional elections of 1948

    Identification

    Significance

To Secure These Rights

    Identification

    Significance

The Employment Board of the Civil Service Commission

    Identification

    Significance

Committee on Equality of Treatment and Opportunity in the Armed Services

    Identification

    Significance

Thurgood Marshall

    Identification

    Significance

Smith v. *Allwright* and *Morgan* v. *Virginia*

    Identification

    Significance

Shelly v. *Kraemer* and *District of Columbia* v. *John R. Thompson Company*

    Identification

    Significance

An American Dilemma, Native Son, and *Black Boy*

    Identification

    Significance

the Alien Registration (Smith) Act

    Identification

    Significance

the *Amerasia* incident

    Identification

    Significance

Truman's loyalty program (Employee Loyalty Program)

    Identification

    Significance

redbaiting

    Identification

    Significance

the Alger Hiss trial

    Identification

    Significance

Klaus Fuchs

    Identification

    Significance

the hydrogen bomb

    Identification

    Significance

Senator Joseph McCarthy

    Identification

    Significance

the Rosenbergs

> Identification

> Significance

the Internal Security Act of 1950

> Identification

> Significance

Dennis et al. v. *U.S.*

> Identification

> Significance

"five-percenters"

> Identification

> Significance

Nixon's "Checkers" speech

> Identification

> Significance

Adlai Stevenson(p34)

> Identification

> Significance

the presidential and congressional elections of 1952

>Identification

>Significance

the age of consensus

>Identification

>Significance

"the vital center"

>Identification

>Significance

dynamic conservatism

>Identification

>Significance

"fifth-column Democrat"

>Identification

>Significance

the Agricultural Act of 1954, the Soil Bank Act of 1956, and the farm bill of 1958

>Identification

>Significance

the St. Lawrence Seaway project

    Identification

    Significance

the Housing Act of 1954

    Identification

    Significance

tax reform of 1954

    Identification

    Significance

the Atomic Energy Act

    Identification

    Significance

the termination policy

    Identification

    Significance

J. Robert Oppenheimer

    Identification

    Significance

the Communist Control Act of 1954

> Identification

> Significance

the Army-McCarthy hearings

> Identification

> Significance

the congressional elections of 1954

> Identification

> Significance

Lyndon B. Johnson

> Identification

> Significance

the Highway Act of 1956

> Identification

> Significance

the presidential and congressional elections of 1956

> Identification

> Significance

the congressional elections of 1958

> Identification

> Significance

Brown v. *Board of Education of Topeka*

> Identification

> Significance

White Citizens' Councils

> Identification

> Significance

Little Rock crisis

> Identification

> Significance

Rosa Parks

> Identification

> Significance

Martin Luther King, Jr.

> Identification

> Significance

the Montgomery bus boycott

    Identification

    Significance

the Southern Christian Leadership Conference

    Identification

    Significance

the Civil Rights Act of 1957

    Identification

    Significance

the sit-in movement

    Identification

    Significance

the Student Nonviolent Coordinating Committee

    Identification

    Significance

John F. Kennedy

    Identification

    Significance

© 1994 Houghton Mifflin Company. All rights reserved.

Richard M. Nixon

>   Identification

>   Significance

the 1960 presidential election

>   Identification

>   Significance

the military-industrial complex

>   Identification

>   Significance

Evaluating and Using Information

In Chapter 28, comments attributed to President Dwight D. Eisenhower suggest issues that were uppermost in Americans' minds during his two terms in office. In this exercise you are to focus on some of Eisenhower's comments that relate to the key issues of the 1950s. In your analysis of these comments, you are to determine:

1. how Eisenhower's personal attitude is reflected in his action or inaction on the issue to which the comment relates; and
2. how Eisenhower's action or inaction influenced the resolution of the issue and how long that resolution would take (or is taking)?

Specifically, your essay should be a response to this question:

> How did actions and refusals to act on the part of President Dwight D. Eisenhower and the federal government (executive, legislative, judicial branches) he led reflect the philosophy and leadership style of Eisenhower himself?

The chart on pages 314–316 should help you organize the information you need. In the first column you will find comments attributed to Eisenhower. In the blocks in the second and third columns, enter brief reminders of the context of the comments and the personalities, events, and issues that triggered them. In the fourth and fifth columns enter reminders of the conspicuous action or inaction of Eisenhower and his administration concerning those triggering events, personalities, events, and issues. In the last column, end each row of information with your own interpretation or conclusion about the information in the other blocks in the row.

Once you have completed the chart, compose the working draft of your essay and enter it in your Reading Notebook.

A Voice in the Age of Consensus:
Comments of President Dwight D. Eisenhower in the Context of His Times

Comment Attributed to Eisenhower	Context of the Comment	Important Issue to Which the Comment Refers	Action/Inaction of Eisenhower or Eisenhower Administration or Appointees in Keeping with the Comment	Action/Inaction of Eisenhower or Eisenhower Administration or Appointees NOT in Keeping with the Comment	Summary, Conclusion, or Interpretation
"...life-long professional soldiers should abstain from seeking high political office."					
"[I will not] get into the gutter with that guy."					

Comment Attributed to Eisenhower	Context of the Comment	Important Issue to Which the Comment Refers	Action/Inaction of Eisenhower or Eisenhower Administration or Appointees in Keeping with the Comment	Action/Inaction of Eisenhower or Eisenhower Administration or Appointees NOT in Keeping with the Comment	Summary, Conclusion, or Interpretation
[What are some significant decisions of Vice-President Richard Nixon?] "If you give me a week, I might think of one."					
"[My appointment of Earl Warren to the Supreme Court is] the biggest damn fool mistake I ever made."					

A Voice in the Age of Consensus
Comments of President Dwight D. Eisenhower in the Context of His Times

Comment Attributed to Eisenhower	Context of the Comment	Important Issue to Which the Comment Refers	Action/Inaction of Eisenhower or Eisenhower Administration or Appointees in Keeping with the Comment	Action/Inaction of Eisenhower or Eisenhower Administration or Appointees NOT in Keeping with the Comment	Summary, Conclusion, or Interpretation
"Punitive or compulsory federal law" will discourage improvement in race relations; improvement will come "only if it starts locally."					
"[My] advice to Americans is for them to guard against the military-industrial complex."					

Ideas and Details

Objective 1

_____ 1. Truman's popularity suffered in the period before the congressional elections of 1946 because
   a. his stance on the threatened railroad strike angered organized labor.
   b. his veto of the National Health Insurance Act angered liberals and the elderly.
   c. manufacturers and farmers were angered when he lifted OPA controls.
   d. his stand on civil rights angered black leaders.

Objectives 2 and 3

_____ 2. Truman won the presidency in 1948 because
   a. the Dixiecrat and Progressive parties threw their support to Truman in the final weeks of the campaign.
   b. the Republican party was seriously divided over domestic issues and could not conduct a unified campaign.
   c. the Eightieth Congress offended many interest groups, which in turn threw their support to Truman.
   d. the electorate believed that the Republican party platform was too liberal.

Objective 4

_____ 3. Black Americans made gains in American society in the postwar period because
   a. Congress passed a strong voting rights bill.
   b. racist practices at home made it more difficult to compete with the Soviet Union for the support of nonaligned nations.
   c. Truman persuaded southern congressmen to support federal laws against lynching and against the poll tax.
   d. Congress took a decisive stand against racist organizations by outlawing the Ku Klux Klan.

Objectives 5 and 6

_____ 4. Which of the following contributed to the emergence of McCarthyism?
   a. The use of redbaiting by politicians
   b. News of a treaty of alliance between Mexico and the Soviet Union
   c. The rapid increase in Communist party membership
   d. Discovery of a well-formed Communist conspiracy under the leadership of Henry Wallace

Objective 7

_____ 5. The Democrats' loss of the presidency in 1952 was due in part to
   a. Truman's failure to deal with double-digit inflation.
   b. displeasure over the funding of Fair Deal programs at the expense of the military.
   c. evidence of influence-peddling within the Truman administration.
   d. Adlai Stevenson's refusal to join with Eisenhower in a public condemnation of McCarthyism.

Objective 9

_____ 6. Which of the following was a characteristic of American thought in the 1950s?
   a. A belief that the faults of American society should be publicly debated
   b. A belief that reform was unnecessary
   c. An often-expressed fear that Americans could not withstand the pressures of the Cold War world
   d. A belief that people in positions of authority were to be questioned and forced to justify their decisions

Objective 10

_____ 7. The Housing Act of 1954
   a. provided low-interest home mortgage loans to middle- and low-income families wanting to buy their first home.
   b. established a national housing code to apply to all new residential construction.
   c. provided federal funds for the construction of low-rent housing for the elderly.
   d. provided federal funds for the construction of houses for low-income families displaced by urban renewal.

Objective 10

_____ 8. As a result of the termination policy supported by the Eisenhower administration,
   a. Indian reservations were expanded and Indian culture further protected.
   b. Native Americans were successfully relocated to urban areas and assimilated into American society.
   c. federal benefits to Indian tribes were withdrawn, causing the displacement and impoverishment of many Indians.
   d. the federal government agreed to aid Indian reservations in the extraction of natural resources from tribal lands.

Objectives 5, 6, and 10

_____ 9. Which of the following is true of the Communist Control Act of 1954?
   a. The liberal senators who opposed the act were labeled Communist sympathizers.
   b. Liberal Republicans who opposed the act were expelled from the Republican party.
   c. The act was supported by liberals and conservatives and made membership in the Communist party illegal.
   d. Debate over the act split the Democratic party causing heavy losses in the congressional elections of 1954.

Objective 6

_____ 10. Which of the following was responsible for the downfall of Senator Joseph McCarthy?
   a. McCarthy made wild and unsupported accusations against the U.S. Army before a national television audience.
   b. The Republican party ousted the senator from its ranks.
   c. McCarthy was expelled from the Senate.
   d. President Eisenhower chose to confront the senator directly.

Objective 11

_____ 11. In the *Brown* decision, the Supreme Court held that
   a. the poll tax was unconstitutional.
   b. segregation in public educational facilities was unconstitutional.
   c. black Americans had benefited from segregated public educational institutions.
   d. racial discrimination in public accommodations was unconstitutional.

Objective 11

_____ 12. The Montgomery bus boycott was organized and led by
   a. Martin Luther King, Jr.
   b. Medgar Evers.
   c. Mary McLeod Bethune.
   d. Rosa Parks.

Objective 11

_____ 13. Dr. Martin Luther King, Jr., urged his followers to adhere to the philosophy of
   a. accommodation.
   b. socialism.
   c. nonviolence.
   d. Black Power.

Objective 11

_____ 14. Which of the following organizations was founded as a result of the sit-in movement?
   a. The Southern Christian Leadership Conference
   b. The White Citizens' Council
   c. The Congress of Racial Equality
   d. The Student Nonviolent Coordinating Committee

Objective 12

_____ 15. Which of the following was an important factor in deciding the presidential race of 1960?
   a. Nixon's effective use of television
   b. Kennedy's contention that America had lost power and prestige under the Republicans
   c. Kennedy's Catholicism
   d. Eisenhower's strong endorsement of Nixon

Essay Questions

Objective 4

1. Discuss the Truman administration's record on civil rights.

Objectives 5 and 6

2. Defend the following statement: "The Cold War heightened anti-Communist fears at home, and by 1950 they reached hysterical proportions. McCarthy did not create this hysteria; he manipulated it to his own advantage."

Objective 9

3. Defend or refute the following statement: "During the 1950s, Americans were confident to the verge of complacency about the perfectibility of American society, anxious to the point of paranoia about the threat of communism."

Objectives 11

4. Discuss the reaction of the southern states and the Eisenhower administration to the *Brown* decision.

Objective 11

5. Discuss the emergence of Dr. Martin Luther King, Jr., as the leader of the civil rights movement that emerged in the aftermath of the *Brown* decision and explain Dr. King's philosophy.

Objective 11

6. Discuss the successes and failures of the civil rights movement from the Montgomery bus boycott through the 1960 presidential election.

Objective 13

5. Discuss Dwight D. Eisenhower as a leader and evaluate his tenure as president of the United States.

CHAPTER 29
The Cold War Era, 1945–1991

Learning Objectives

After you have studied Chapter 29 in your textbook and worked through this study guide chapter, you should be able to:

1. Examine and explain the sources of the Cold War.
2. Examine the reasons for the activist, expansionist, globalist diplomacy undertaken by the United States in the aftermath of the Second World War, and explain the exaggeration of the Soviet threat by United States officials during the course of the Cold War.
3. Discuss the similarities and differences between American and Soviet perceptions of major international problems and events from 1945 to 1991.
4. Explain the rationale behind the containment doctrine; examine the evolution of the doctrine from its inception in 1947 to the end of the Cold War in 1991; discuss the history, extent, and nature of criticisms of the doctrine; and evaluate the doctrine as the cornerstone of American foreign policy from 1947 to 1991.
5. Examine the nature and extent of the arms race between the United States and the Soviet Union during the course of the Cold War; explain and evaluate arms-control agreements reached between the two superpowers throughout the history of the Cold War; and discuss the consequences of the arms race for the world community of nations in general and for the two superpowers in particular.
6. Examine, evaluate, and discuss the consequences of the defense and foreign policy views, goals, and actions of the Truman administration.
7. Discuss the nature and outcome of the Chinese Civil War, and examine United States policy toward the People's Republic of China from 1949 to 1980.
8. Discuss the origins of the Korean War; explain its outcome; and examine its impact on domestic politics and United States foreign policy.
9. Examine, evaluate, and discuss the consequences of the defense and foreign policy views, goals, and actions of the Eisenhower administration.
10. Examine, evaluate, and discuss the consequences of the defense and foreign policy views, goals, and actions of the Kennedy and Johnson administrations.
11. Discuss Cuban-American relations from 1959 to October 1962; explain the causes, outcome, and consequences of the Cuban missile crisis; and evaluate President John Kennedy's handling of the crisis.
12. Explain the theories on which the Nixon-Kissinger "grand strategy" was based; examine and evaluate the policies and actions inspired by those theories; and examine the international crises and issues that placed the grand strategy in jeopardy.

13. Examine, evaluate, and discuss the consequences of the defense and foreign policy views, goals, and actions of the Carter administration.
14. Examine, evaluate, and discuss the consequences of the defense and foreign policy views, goals, and actions of the Reagan administration.
15. Discuss the multiplicity of factors that led to the collapse of the Soviet empire in Eastern Europe, the disintegration of the Soviet Union, and the reunification of Germany.
16. Explain the reasons for the end of the Cold War, and discuss the war's legacy for the United States, the former Soviet Union, and the world community of nations.

Thematic Guide

Chapter 29 surveys the history of the bipolar contest for international power between the United States and the Soviet Union that lasted more than forty years, a contest known as the Cold War, and discusses the impact of this struggle on the two major combatants and on the world community of nations.

We first examine the Cold War as the outgrowth of a complex set of factors. At the end of the Second World War, international relations remained unstable because of (1) world economic problems; (2) power vacuums caused by the defeat of Germany and Japan; (3) civil wars within nations; (4) the birth of nations resulting from the disintegration of empires; and (5) air power, which made all nations more vulnerable to attack. This unsettled environment encouraged competition between the United States and the Soviet Union, the two most powerful nations at the war's end.

Furthermore, both the United States and the Soviet Union believed in the rightness of their own political, economic, and social systems, and each feared the other's system. Their decisions and actions, based on the way each perceived the world, confirmed rather than alleviated these fears. For example, the American resolution to avoid appeasement and hold the line against communism, the American feeling of vulnerability in the air age, and American determination to prevent an economic depression led to an activist foreign policy characterized by economic expansionism and globalist diplomacy. These factors, together with Truman's anti-Soviet views and his brash personality, intensified Soviet fears of a hostile West. When the Soviets acted on the basis of this feeling, American worries that the Soviet Union was bent on world domination intensified.

Despite knowledge that the Soviet Union had emerged from the Second World War as a regional power rather than a global menace, United States officials exaggerated the Soviet threat. They did so because of (1) Truman's desire for simple answers; (2) the desire of military officers for larger military budgets; (3) some Americans' fixation on stated Soviet goals rather than on actual Soviet behavior; (4) fear that world conditions made United States interests vulnerable to Soviet subversion; and (5) the desire of the United States to use its postwar position of strength to its advantage. When the actions of the United States brought criticism, the United States perceived this as further proof that the Soviets were determined to dominate the world.

The interplay of these factors provides the thread running through the examination of American-Soviet relations during the course of the Cold War. The action-reaction theme is evident in the sections entitled "Confrontation and Containment in Europe" and "Confrontations in Asia." Furthermore, the events discussed in those two sections and the discussion of the origins of the Korean War serve as evidence to support the authors' interpretation of the sources of the Cold War. Although Truman acted out of the belief that the Russians started the war against South Korea, analysis of the situation shows the strong likelihood that North Korea started the war for its own nationalistic purposes. We examine the conduct of the war, Truman's problems with General Douglas MacArthur, America's use of atomic diplomacy, and the war's domestic political impact. The war also produced a debate over the globalist foreign policy used to justify it. This debate, characterized by an exaggeration of the Communist threat and won by the globalists, led to an increase in foreign commitments and military appropriations and solidified the idea of a worldwide Soviet threat.

© 1994 Houghton Mifflin Company. All rights reserved.

President Dwight D. Eisenhower and his secretary of state, John Foster Dulles, accepted this view of a worldwide Communist threat. During Eisenhower's administration, this belief and the fear of domestic subversives that accompanied it led to the removal of talented Asian specialists from the Foreign Service, an action that would have dire consequences later on. Meanwhile, a new jargon invigorated the containment doctrine; and despite Eisenhower's doubts about the arms race, as expressed in his 1953 "Chance for Peace" speech, the president continued the activist foreign policy furthered during the Truman years and oversaw the acceleration of the nuclear arms race. Therefore, during the Eisenhower-Dulles years, the action-reaction relationship between the superpowers continued. Each action by one side caused a corresponding defensive reaction by the other in a seemingly endless spiral of fear and distrust. As a result, problems continued in Eastern Europe, Berlin, and Asia.

Despite the strategic superiority of the United States over the Soviet Union in 1960, John F. Kennedy's presidential campaign was based, in part, on the false premise that the Eisenhower administration had allowed a "missile gap" to develop between the United States and its arch-rival. Once elected, President Kennedy oversaw a significant military build-up based on the principle of "flexible response," and his policies and actions in the field of foreign policy were shaped by his acceptance of the containment doctrine and his preference for a bold, interventionist foreign policy. His activist approach not only helped bring the world to the brink of nuclear disaster in the Cuban missile crisis but also led to a significant acceleration of the nuclear arms race—a trend that continued through the administration of Kennedy's successor, Lyndon B. Johnson.

Although a great deal of energy was expended on questions relating to the Vietnam War during the Richard M. Nixon's presidency, Nixon considered other foreign policy matters, especially the relationship between the United States and the Soviet Union, to be more important. In an attempt to create a global balance of power, Nixon and Henry Kissinger (Nixon's national security adviser and later his secretary of state) adopted a "grand strategy." By means of détente with the Soviet Union and the People's Republic of China, Nixon and Kissinger sought to achieve the same goals as those of the old containment doctrine, but through accommodation rather than confrontation. Despite détente, the United States still had to respond to crises rooted in instability in the Middle East and elsewhere.

When Jimmy Carter assumed the presidency in 1977, Americans were involved in an intense foreign-policy debate, somewhat reminiscent of the debates at the end of the Spanish-American-Cuban-Filipino War and at the end of the First World War. The 1970s debate stemmed from the Vietnam disaster, the continuing challenge of the Soviet Union, and the heightened animosity of Third World nations. Americans differed on how to interpret these events and on what they meant in relation to America's world leadership position.

Carter and Secretary of State Cyrus Vance at first pledged a new course for the United States. However, this course was challenged by Carter's national security adviser Zbigniew Brzezinski, by Democratic and Republican critics, and by the Soviet Union, which reacted in anger and fear to the human rights aspect of Carter's policies. The Cold War seemed to have its own momentum. Despite the Carter administration's successful negotiation of the SALT-II treaty and its achievements in the Middle East, Africa, and Latin America, it was overwhelmed by critics at home, the Iranian hostage crisis, and the Soviet invasion of Afghanistan. The grain embargo, the 1980 Olympics boycott, and the Carter Doctrine all seemed more reminiscent of the containment doctrine and the sources of the Cold War than of a new course in American foreign policy.

Ronald Reagan's election in 1980 marked a return to foreign-policy themes rooted in America's past and reminiscent of the early days of the Cold War. As a result, relations between the United States and the Soviet Union deteriorated and arms talks between the two nations broke down. Public concern over the administration's anti-Soviet stance and propensity toward confrontation led to international concern and to massive support for a freeze in the nuclear arms race. Public pressure, combined with other forces, led to a resumption of arms talks in 1985; the same year Mikhail Gorbachev assumed power in the Soviet Union. Under Gorbachev's leadership, the Soviet Union undertook an ambitious domestic reform program, and Soviet foreign policy underwent significant changes. These dramatic changes helped reduce international tensions and, in 1987, led to a Soviet-American agreement to eliminate intermediate-range nuclear missiles in Europe. Even more dramatic change came in 1989 and 1990 with the collapse of communism in Eastern Europe, the reunification of Germany, the disintegration of the Soviet Union, and Gorbachev's fall from power—all of which signaled the end of the Cold War.

The chapter ends with a discussion of four trends that led to the decline of the United States and the Soviet Union in the international system and caused the two superpowers ultimately to end the Cold War. Moreover, the authors discuss the legacy of the Cold War for the world community of nations in general and for the United States in particular.

Building Vocabulary

Listed below are important words and terms that you need to know to get the most out of Chapter 29. They are listed in the order in which they occur in the chapter. After carefully looking through the list, refer to a dictionary and jot down the definition of words that you do not know or of which you are unsure.

subjugation

bipolar

topography

consensus

infrastructure

volatile

appeasement

totalitarian

ingratiating

evasive

brash

ostracize

monolithic

nuance

ambiguity

penchant

subservient

succumb

clandestine

ostentatious

retort

coercion

enunciate

oust

cataclysm

hegemony

resurgent

thwart

bastion

ensnare

rankle

pell-mell

chasten

contentious

perpetuate

acrimony

rail (*verb*)

moratorium

sovereign

reproach

quarantine

expunge

impetuous

lard (*verb*)

trite

© 1994 Houghton Mifflin Company. All rights reserved.

metaphor

parity

quash

venerable

bedevil

olympian

malevolent

ignobly

wily

adept

volatile

tenacious

enshroud

bequeath

Identification and Significance

After studying Chapter 29 of *A People and a Nation,* you should be able to identify fully *and* explain the historical significance of each item listed below.

1. Identify each item in the space provided. Give an explanation or description of the item. Answer the questions *who, what, where,* and *when.*
2. Explain the historical significance of each item in the space provided. Establish the historical context in which the item exists. Establish the item as the result of or as the cause of other factors existing in the society under study. Answer this question: *what were the political, social, economic, and/or cultural consequences of this item?*

the Cold War

      Identification

      Significance

the Truman-Molotov encounter

      Identification

      Significance

Dean Acheson

      Identification

      Significance

Poland, Rumania, Hungary, and Czechoslovakia

      Identification

      Significance

© 1994 Houghton Mifflin Company. All rights reserved.

Josip Broz Tito

> Identification

> Significance

atomic diplomacy

> Identification

> Significance

the Baruch Plan

> Identification

> Significance

the World Bank and the International Monetary Fund

> Identification

> Significance

the "long telegram"

> Identification

> Significance

George F. Kennan

> Identification

> Significance

the "Iron Curtain" speech

    Identification

    Significance

Henry A. Wallace

    Identification

    Significance

the Truman Doctrine

    Identification

    Significance

the Greek civil war

    Identification

    Significance

the "Mr. X" article

    Identification

    Significance

the containment doctrine

    Identification

    Significance

Walter Lippmann

    Identification

    Significance

the Marshall Plan

    Identification

    Significance

the National Security Act of 1947

    Identification

    Significance

the Rio Pact and the Organization of American States

    Identification

    Significance

recognition of Israel

    Identification

    Significance

the Berlin blockade and airlift

    Identification

    Significance

the North Atlantic Treaty Organization

> Identification

> Significance

the hydrogen bomb

> Identification

> Significance

NSC-68

> Identification

> Significance

Japanese reconstruction

> Identification

> Significance

the Chinese civil war

> Identification

> Significance

Jiang Jieshi

> Identification

> Significance

Mao Zedong

    Identification

    Significance

the People's Republic of China

    Identification

    Significance

the China lobby

    Identification

    Significance

the Korean War

    Identification

    Significance

General Douglas MacArthur

    Identification

    Significance

the Inchon Landing

    Identification

    Significance

Chinese entry into the Korean War

    Identification

    Significance

General Omar Bradley

    Identification

    Significance

the POW question

    Identification

    Significance

the Korean armistice

    Identification

    Significance

the globalist policy

    Identification

    Significance

John Foster Dulles

    Identification

    Significance

© 1994 Houghton Mifflin Company. All rights reserved.

Scott McLeod

> Identification

> Significance

liberation

> Identification

> Significance

massive retaliation

> Identification

> Significance

John Foster Dulles

> Identification

> Significance

Scott McLeod

> Identification

> Significance

liberation

> Identification

> Significance

massive retaliation

    Identification

    Significance

deterrence

    Identification

    Significance

the *New Look* military

    Identification

    Significance

brinkmanship

    Identification

    Significance

the domino theory

    Identification

    Significance

the nuclear arms race

    Identification

    Significance

the *Lucky Dragon*

    Identification

    Significance

Sputnik and the missile race

    Identification

    Significance

the National Defense Education Act

    Identification

    Significance

the "missile gap"

    Identification

    Significance

the nuclear triad

    Identification

    Significance

Eisenhower's 1953 critique of the nuclear arms race

    Identification

    Significance

SANE

    Identification

    Significance

the "atoms for peace" and "open skies" proposals

    Identification

    Significance

the Geneva disarmament talks and the Geneva summit

    Identification

    Significance

"peaceful coexistence"

    Identification

    Significance

the Hungarian uprising

    Identification

    Significance

the Berlin crisis of 1958

    Identification

    Significance

the U-2 incident

> Identification

> Significance

the Quemoy-Matsu crisis

> Identification

> Significance

The Formosa Resolution

> Identification

> Significance

action intellectuals

> Identification

> Significance

flexible response

> Identification

> Significance

the 1961 Berlin crisis

> Identification

> Significance

Fidel Castro

>Identification

>Significance

the Bay of Pigs invasion

>Identification

>Significance

Operation Mongoose

>Identification

>Significance

the Cuban missile crisis

>Identification

>Significance

Robert S. McNamara

>Identification

>Significance

the credibility gap

>Identification

>Significance

Henry A. Kissinger

> Identification

> Significance

the Nixon-Kissinger grand strategy

> Identification

> Significance

détente

> Identification

> Significance

the SALT treaty

> Identification

> Significance

MIRVs

> Identification

> Significance

Nixon's China trip

> Identification

> Significance

Jimmy Carter

    Identification

    Significance

Carter's human rights policy

    Identification

    Significance

Zbigniew Brzezinski

    Identification

    Significance

Cyrus Vance

    Identification

    Significance

the SALT-II treaty

    Identification

    Significance

the Soviet invasion of Afghanistan

    Identification

    Significance

Chapter 29

the Carter Doctrine

    Identification

    Significance

Ronald Reagan

    Identification

    Significance

George P. Shultz

    Identification

    Significance

Reagan's "devil theory"

    Identification

    Significance

the Reagan defense build-up

    Identification

    Significance

the U. S.-Canada Free Trade Agreement of 1988

    Identification

    Significance

the Reagan Doctrine

>Identification

>Significance

Solidarity

>Identification

>Significance

the nuclear weapons debate

>Identification

>Significance

the nuclear freeze movement

>Identification

>Significance

the Catholic Bishops' Pastoral letter

>Identification

>Significance

"nuclear winter"

>Identification

>Significance

346 *Chapter 29*

the 1985 Geneva summit

    Identification

    Significance

Mikhail S. Gorbachev

    Identification

    Significance

perestroika and *glasnost*

    Identification

    Significance

the 1987 INF treaty

    Identification

    Significance

George Bush

    Identification

    Significance

James Baker

    Identification

    Significance

the collapse of Communism in Eastern Europe

    Identification

    Significance

the disintegration of the Soviet Union

    Identification

    Significance

Evaluating and Using Information

As Chapter 29 makes clear, for nearly fifty years the United States saw the U.S.S.R. as a major and terrifying adversary. America's fear of the U.S.S.R. throughout the Cold War period has affected the relationships the United States has forged with other nations as well as politics and public debate at home. Identify and sort out the evidence of fear exhibited by the United States, and then select the most significant evidence. Using the evidence you have selected to support and illustrate your points, compose the working draft of an essay responding to this question:

> What significant actions and postures did the United States adopt during the Cold War years from 1945 to 1992 that suggest it felt more than a reasonable fear of the USSR?

    The table on pages 348–350—or a blown up version of it that you create for yourself—should help you organize the information you will need. (By completing the entire table, you will have organized the information needed to compose an essay about the nation's Cold War mentality during any of the presidential administrations listed or to trace the reflections of the country's Cold War mentality in any of the ten areas listed in the first column.)

    After you have filled in the blocks on the table, compose your essay and enter it in your Reading Notebook.

© 1994 Houghton Mifflin Company. All rights reserved.

The United States and the Cold War

Evidence of American Fears of the USSR, 1945–1991

Area in Which the Evidence of Fear is Most Apparent	Truman Years	Eisenhower Years	Kennedy Years	Johnson Years	Nixon/Ford Years	Carter Years	Reagan Years	Bush Years	Conclusion
Arms Development and Buildup									
Signing "Entangling" Defense Alliances									
Attempts to Interfere in USSR's Sphere of Influence or Its Efforts to Maintain or Expand Its Sphere of Influence									

Use of Trade Policy and Dollar Diplomacy as Cold War Weapons	Adoption of Covert Operations and Morally Questionable Methods of Influencing or Overthrowing Foreign Regimes	Recognizing or Withholding Recognition of New Governments

The United States and the Cold War

Evidence of American Fears of the USSR, 1945–1991

Area in Which the Evidence of Fear is Most Apparent	Truman Years	Eisenhower Years	Kennedy Years	Johnson Years	Nixon/Ford Years	Carter Years	Reagan Years	Bush Years	Conclusion
Other									
Conclusion									

Ideas and Details

Objectives 1 and 2

_____ 1. The fact that United States exports constituted about 10 percent of the gross national product in 1947 is evidence in support of which of the following ideas?
   a. American officials believed that an activist foreign policy was necessary for the economic well-being of the United States.
   b. The economic crisis in postwar Europe had no impact on American exports.
   c. The United States decided to abandon its prewar policy of economic expansionism.
   d. Few American products depended on foreign markets.

Objective 2

_____ 2. In the immediate aftermath of the Second World War, the Soviet Union
   a. had the military power to overrun Western Europe.
   b. was economically powerful and had no reason to fear the West.
   c. was a regional power, not a global menace.
   d. had no territorial ambitions.

Objectives 1 and 2

_____ 3. In the aftermath of the Second World War, American officials
   a. attempted to satisfy Truman's desire for details by compiling volumes of information on Soviet government and society.
   b. failed to recognize that poverty and social unrest abroad could be detrimental to United States interests.
   c. concentrated on Soviet behavior in assessing the nature of the Soviet threat.
   d. often exaggerated the Soviet menace in order to persuade Congress to pass larger defense budgets.

Objective 4

_____ 4. The containment policy, expressed in the Truman Doctrine and George Kennan's "Mr. X" article, committed the United States to
   a. extend economic and medical aid to impoverished people throughout the world.
   b. help only those countries that showed a determination to help themselves.
   c. assist peoples throughout the world in resisting Communist expansion.
   d. create a more stable world through the use of diplomatic rather than military means.

Objectives 3, 6, and 7

_____ 5. Which of the following is true of United States policy toward China during the Chinese civil war?
   a. The United States attempted to open diplomatic relations with Mao's forces but was rebuffed.
   b. United States officials recognized the nationalist origins of the struggle.
   c. The United States decided not to take sides in the struggle.
   d. United States officials supported Jiang Jieshi (Chiang Kai-shek) largely out of the belief that Mao was subservient to the Soviet Union.

Objectives 3, 4, 6, and 8

_____ 6. Truman's belief that the Soviet Union was the mastermind behind North Korea's invasion of South Korea is questionable because
   a. the Soviet Union gave no aid to North Korea during the course of the war.
   b. the Soviet delegate was absent from the Security Council when the Security Council voted to aid South Korea.
   c. the Soviet Union was sending military aid to South Korea at the time of the invasion.
   d. North Korea was fiercely independent and had broken its ties with the Soviet Union.

Objective 8

_____ 7. President Truman fired General Douglas MacArthur because
   a. MacArthur publicly criticized Truman's war policies.
   b. MacArthur refused to obey Truman's order to attack China with massive bombing raids.
   c. the United Nations Security Council demanded MacArthur's removal.
   d. the failure of the Inchon operation destroyed MacArthur's credibility.

Objectives 4, 5, and 9

_____ 8. The *New Look* military of the Eisenhower-Dulles years emphasized
   a. nuclear weapons rather than conventional military forces.
   b. a United Nations police force.
   c. conventional military forces.
   d. Soviet-American cooperation in space.

Objectives 4, 5, and 10

_____ 9. Which of the following is true in relation to the "missile gap"?
   a. Revelation of the inferiority of United States forces led to Soviet invasion of Hungary in 1956.
   b. If such a gap existed, it was in favor of the United States.
   c. The superiority of Soviet ICBMs caused the United States to back down in the 1958 Berlin crisis.
   d. Eisenhower's reluctance to spend money on defense had allowed the Soviets dangerously to surpass the United States in missile technology.

Objectives 4, 5, and 9

_____ 10. As a result of the 1954 crisis concerning Quemoy and Matsu,
   a. the United States severed relations with Jiang Jieshi.
   b. the United States recognized the People's Republic of China.
   c. nuclear-capable missiles were installed on Formosa.
   d. Khrushchev called for "peaceful coexistence" with the United States.

Objectives 4, 5, and 10

_____ 11. Kennedy chose to adopt the policy of flexible response because
   a. he wanted to streamline the decision-making process in the executive branch.
   b. it would allow subtle shifts in domestic policy statements to match the changing mood of the electorate.
   c. he wanted the United States to be able to respond to any kind of warfare.
   d. the policy would enable the United States to reduce its nuclear arsenal.

Objectives 4, 10, and 11

_____ 12. In the aftermath of the Bay of Pigs invasion, the United States government
   a. attempted to overthrow the government of Fidel Castro.
   b. apologized to the Cuban people for infringing on their national sovereignty.
   c. re-established trade with the Castro regime.
   d. restored diplomatic relations with Cuba.

Objectives 4, 5, 10, and 11

_____ 13. As a result of the Cuban missile crisis,
   a. the Soviet Union made new demands in Berlin.
   b. the United States agreed to dismantle its missiles in Western Europe.
   c. the Soviet Union was publicly humiliated and embarked on a program to match the nuclear strength of the United States.
   d. the United States conducted air strikes against Cuba and destroyed the missile bases on the island.

Objectives 5 and 12

_____ 14. The 1972 SALT I treaty
   a. left the United States with a disadvantage in deliverable nuclear warheads.
   b. allowed each side to construct antiballistic missile systems.
   c. placed no restriction on the number of independently targetable warheads that could be placed on each missile.
   d. failed to freeze the number of offensive nuclear missiles each side could have.

Objectives 14 and 15

_____ 15. The improvement in Soviet-American relations during Reagan's second term may be attributed, in part, to
   a. Reagan's apology for his "Evil Empire" rhetoric.
   b. the Reagan administration's agreement to limit research on the Strategic Defense Initiative.
   c. cooperation between the United States and the Soviet Union to combat international terrorism.
   d. the withdrawal of Soviet troops from Afghanistan and Cuban troops from Angola.

Essay Questions

Objectives 1, 2, 3, and 5

1. Defend or refute the following statement: "Both the United States and the Soviet Union must share responsibility for the Cold War."

Objectives 3, 4, 6, 7, and 8

2. Explain and evaluate the American perception of events in Asia between the end of the Second World War and North Korea's invasion of South Korea. What bearing did these perceptions have on the Truman administration's response to North Korean aggression?

Objectives 4, 6, and 8

3. Explain the impact of the Korean War on United States foreign policy.

Objective 5

4. Examine and evaluate the nuclear arms race and attempts at arms control between the United States and the Soviet Union during the course of the Cold War.

Objective 4

5. Examine the containment doctrine as the cornerstone of American foreign policy during the course of the Cold War.

Objectives 9, 10, and 11

6. Discuss the causes and consequences of the Cuban missile crisis and evaluate President John Kennedy's handling of the crisis.

Objective 14

7. Explain the following statement: "Ronald Reagan's foreign policy was driven by beliefs rooted in America's past."

Objectives 15 and 16

8. Explain the improvement in Soviet-American relations from 1985 to the present, and discuss the tangible results of this improvement.

Objective 16

9. Discuss the factors that brought an end to the Cold War, and discuss the legacy of the war for the United States, the Soviet Union, and the world community of nations.

Map Exercise

Exercise A

As part of the containment doctrine, the United States in 1949 formed the North Atlantic Treaty Organization (NATO), consisting of the United States, Great Britain, Canada, France, Belgium, the Netherlands, Luxembourg, Italy, Denmark, Norway, Iceland, and Portugal. Greece and Turkey joined NATO in 1952, and West Germany joined in 1954.

To counter NATO, in May 1955 the Soviet Union formed the Warsaw Pact consisting of the Soviet Union, Albania,[1] Bulgaria, Czechoslovakia, East Germany, Hungary, Poland, and Romania. China did not sign but did pledge support.

In addition, the United States (1) entered into a military alliance with Latin American countries, the Rio Pact, in 1947; (2) sent military advisory missions to Latin America, Greece, Turkey, Iran, China, and Saudi Arabia; (3) activated an air base in Libya in 1948; (4) recognized the new state of Israel in May 1948; (5) entered into a mutual defense agreement, the ANZUS Treaty, with Australia and New Zealand in 1951; and (6) entered into a similar defense agreement in 1954, the Southeast Asia Treaty Organization (SEATO), that first included Britain, France, Australia, New Zealand, Pakistan, Thailand, and the Philippines, and was extended to include South Vietnam, Cambodia, and Laos.

Consider all such alliances, air bases, and military advisory missions in your answers to the following questions:

1. Using two markers of different colors, mark on the map on pages 362–363 the nations allied with or friendly toward the United States in or around 1973 with one color, and those allied with or friendly toward the Soviet Union with the other color.
2. How successful was the alliance aspect of the containment doctrine as of 1973?
3. The Soviet Union complained of encirclement in the early 1950s and after. Was there reason to complain?
4. As of 1973, would you feel more secure as a citizen of the Soviet Union or as a citizen of the United States? Why?

---

[1] Albania withdrew from the Warsaw Pact in 1968.

© 1994 Houghton Mifflin Company. All rights reserved.

The following exercises are concerned with events in Eastern Europe and the Soviet Union since 1989. Although some of the information required to complete these exercises is found in Chapter 29 of the textbook, additional information may be found in recent periodical literature and recent publications that deal with the events in question.

Exercise B

Since 1989, dramatic changes have taken place in the Soviet Union and in Eastern Europe. These changes signify the crumbling of the Soviet empire and the crumbling of the Warsaw Pact as a defensive military alliance. Moreover, these changes affect the world community of nations, Western Europe, the NATO alliance, and United States foreign policy.

Using Map 2 contained in this chapter, locate and mark the fifteen republics that constituted the Soviet Union.

Armenia	Lithuania
Azerbaijan	Moldova
Byelarus	Russia
Estonia	Tadzhikistan
Georgia	Turkmenistan
Kazakhstan	Ukraine
Kyrgyzstan	Uzbekistan
Latvia	

1. The fifteen republics that constituted the Soviet Union each proclaimed its independence in 1991. On the chart below or on a chart of your own making, indicate the present relationship of each of these republics to each other and to Russia.

Republics	Relationship to Other Republics	Relationship to Russia
Armenia		
Azerbaijan		
Byelarus		
Estonia		
Georgia		
Kazakhstan		
Kyrgyzstan		
Latvia		
Lithuania		
Moldova		
Russia		
Tadzhikistan		
Turkmenistan		
Ukraine		
Uzbekistan		

2. Ethnic Unrest in the republics of the former Soviet Union. Using backward slash marks (\\\\), mark the republics on the map in which there has been ethnic unrest. Indicate on the chart below the nature of the ethnic unrest in these republics and the present status of that unrest in each of them.

Republics	Nature of Ethnic Unrest	Present Status of Ethnic Unrest
Armenia		
Azerbaijan		
Byelarus		
Estonia		
Georgia		
Kazakhstan		
Kyrgyzstan		
Latvia		
Lithuania		
Moldova		
Russia		
Tadzhikistan		
Turkmenistan		
Ukraine		
Uzbekistan		

© 1994 Houghton Mifflin Company. All rights reserved.

Exercise C

Using the chart below:

1. Identify and list the nations in Europe and Asia that have experienced democracy movements since 1988.
2. Indicate with a mark in the proper column those nations on your list that were members of the Warsaw Pact.
   What is the present status of the Warsaw Pact?
3. Note in the proper column the present status of the democracy movement in each nation on your list.

European and Asian Nations Experiencing Democracy Movements, 1988–Present	Member of Warsaw Pact?	Present Status of Democracy Movement?

© 1994 Houghton Mifflin Company. All rights reserved.

Exercise D

1. The containment doctrine was the cornerstone of American foreign policy from the time of the Truman Doctrine and George Kennan's "Mr. X" article of 1947 to 1991. Have the recent changes in the former Soviet Union and in Eastern Europe and economic and political instability in Russia made the containment doctrine obsolete?

2. Consider the following three statements from Chapter 29.
   a. The Soviets emerged from the Second World War "with a weak military establishment, a hobbled economy, and obsolete technology.... The Soviet Union was a regional power in Eastern Europe, not a global menace."
   b. "Some Americans fixed their attention, as they had since [the Bolshevik Revolution of] 1917, on the utopian Communist goal of world revolution rather than on actual Soviet behavior...."
   c. President Reagan "believed in a devil theory: that a malevolent Soviet Union ... was the source of the world's troubles."

   How do these statements relate to the crumbling of the Soviet empire in Eastern Europe and the disintegration of the Soviet Union? To what extent was American policy during the Cold War based on reality? To what extent was it based on myth?

3. Another cornerstone of American foreign policy since the presidency of Woodrow Wilson is the concept of self-determination—the idea that a nation has the right to determine its own destiny without outside interference. Since the end of the Second World War, the United States and the NATO alliance have consistently chastised the Soviet Union for not allowing self-determination in the nations in Eastern Europe under Soviet domination. Under Gorbachev, the Soviet Union reversed its totalitarian policies and allowed self-determination. As a result, the Eastern European nations under Soviet domination during the course of the Cold War have undergone democratic revolutions and have begun to restructure their economic systems.

   What opportunities and problems do these changes in Eastern Europe pose for the world community of nations, the NATO alliance, and the United States?

   Problems:

   Opportunities:

4. Yugoslavia broke with the Soviet Union in 1948 and traveled an independent Communist path.
   a. What impact did the democracy movements and the collapse of Communism in the Soviet Union and Eastern Europe have on Yugoslavia?
   b. What problems do the changes in the former Yugoslavia pose for the world community of nations, the NATO alliance, and the United States?
5. Soon after Mikhail Gorbachev came to power, he said to the United States: "We will deny you an enemy." What did he mean by that statement? Did he fulfill that promise?
6. Redbaiting has been a dominant feature of American political campaigns since the Second World War. Did the absence of the Soviet Union as an enemy affect the way the 1992 presidential candidates ran their campaigns? Did it affect the outcome of the 1992 presidential campaign? Explain.

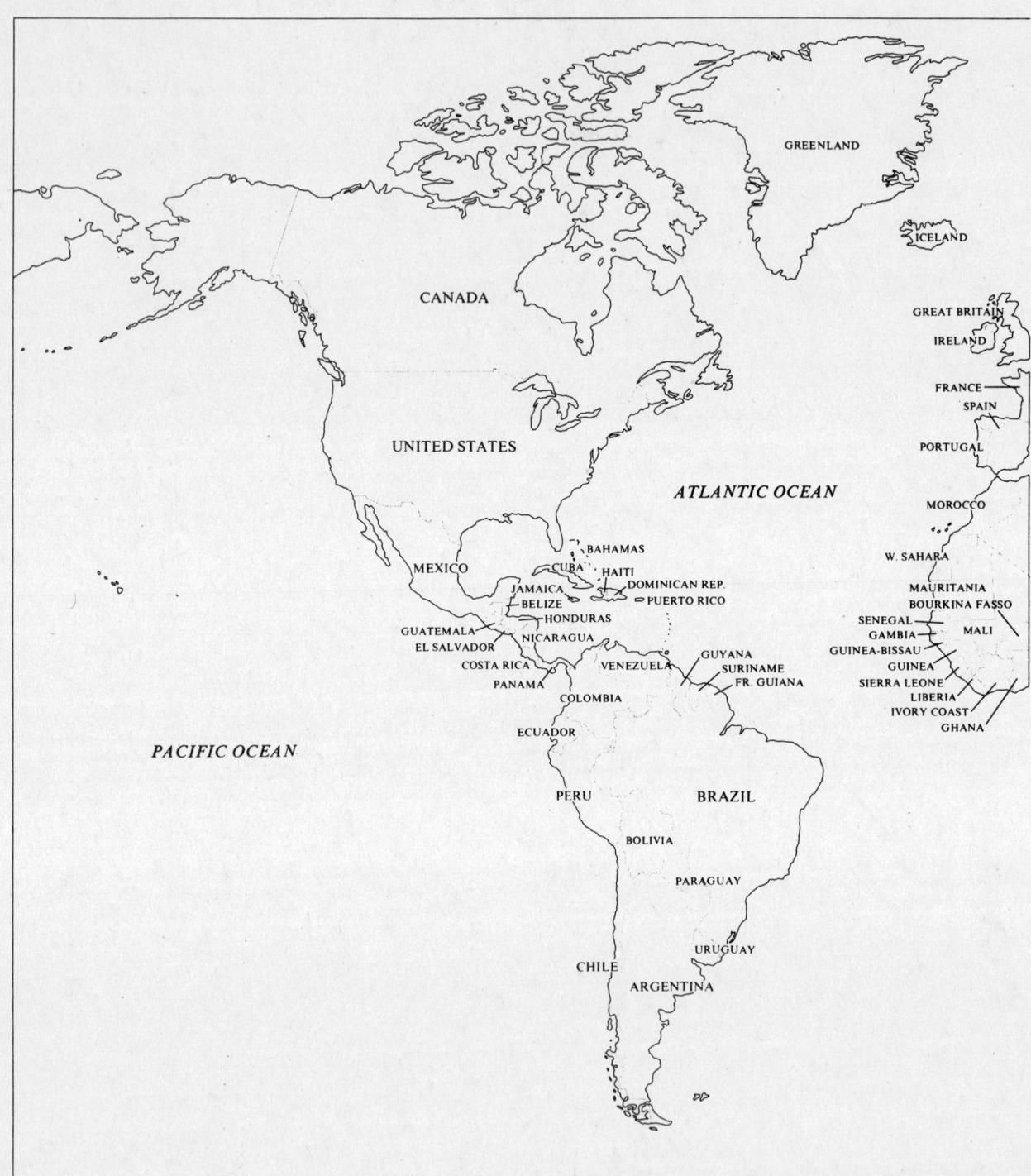

The Cold War Era, 1945–1991

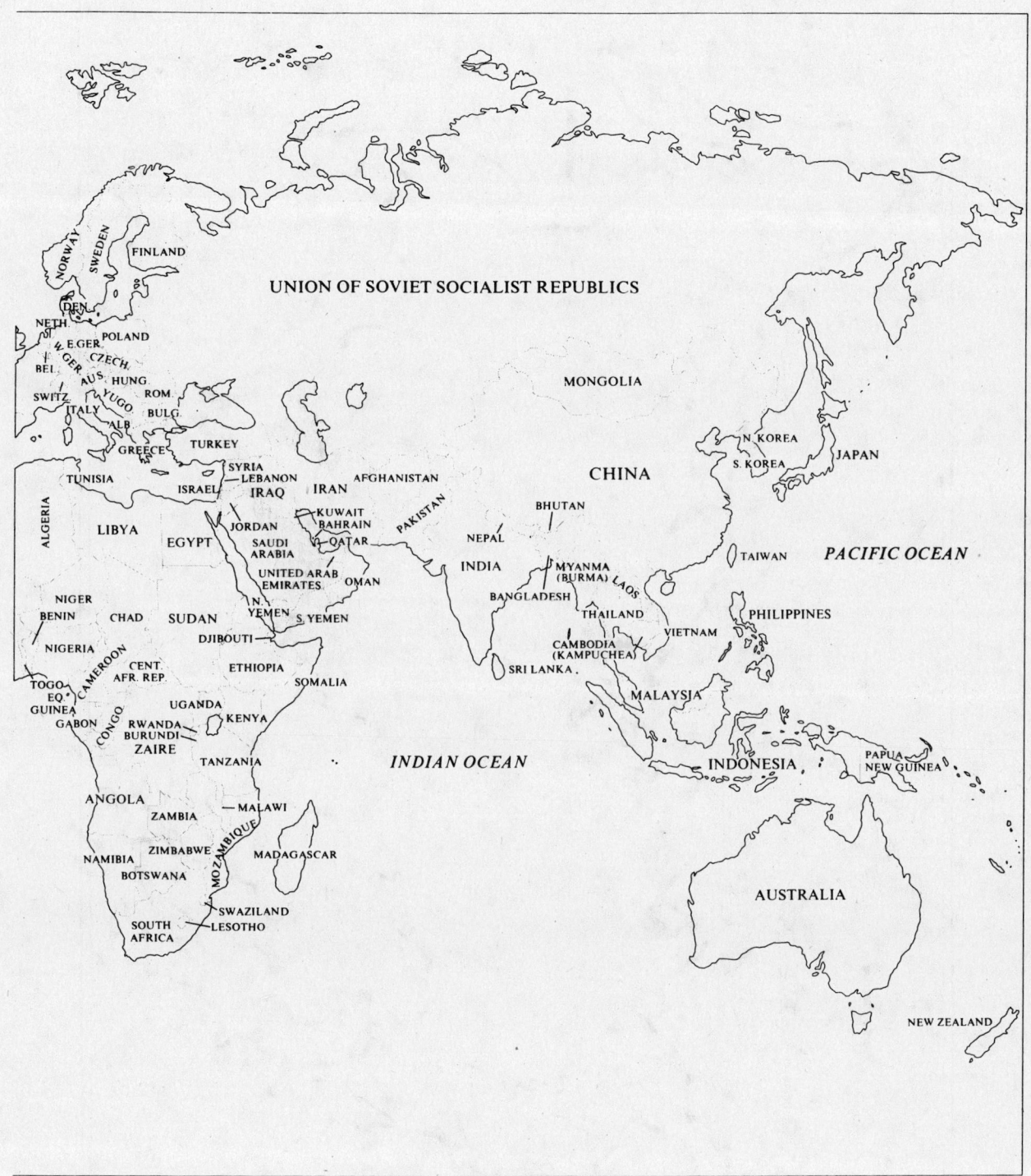

364 *Chapter 29*

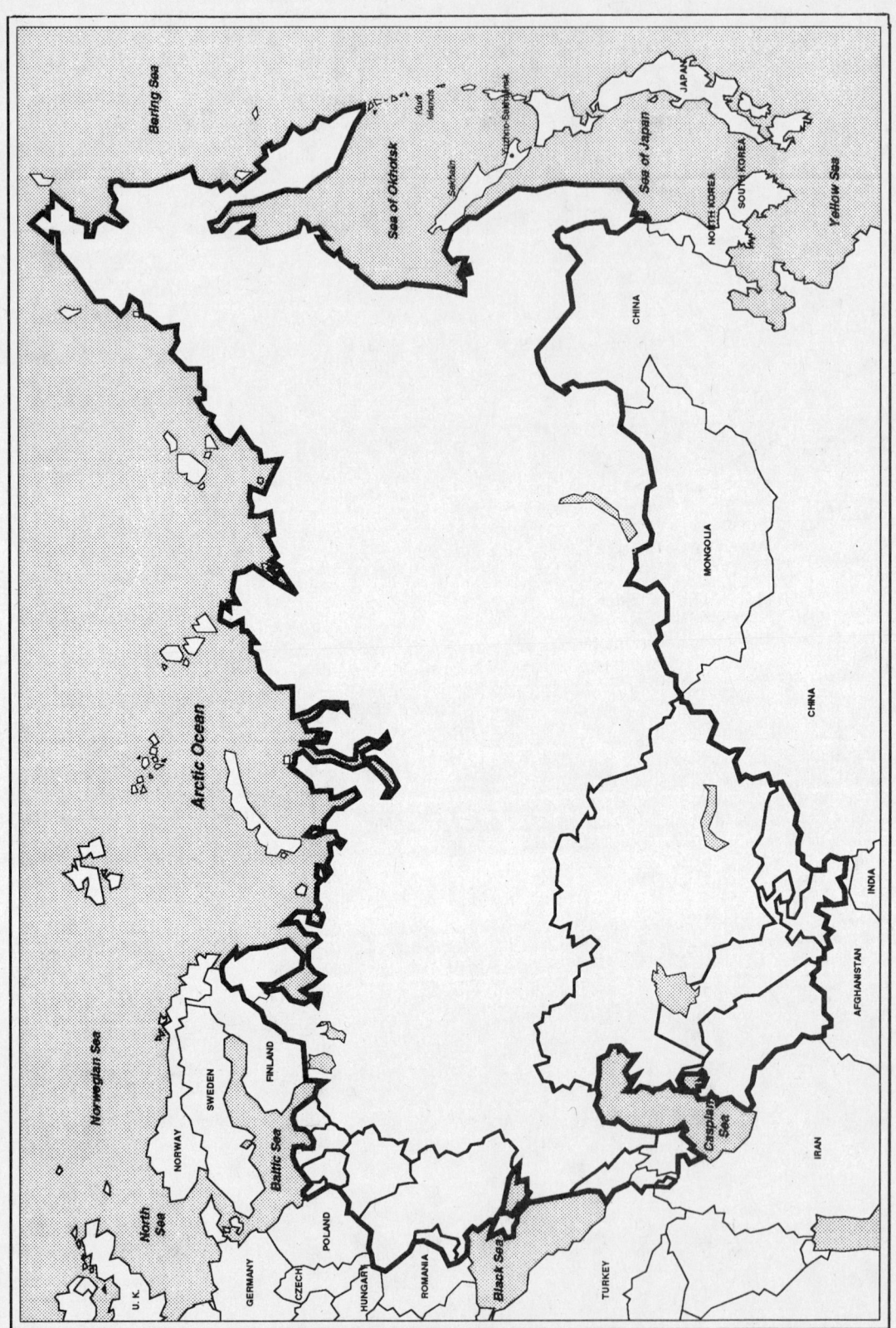

CHAPTER 30
American Society During the Postwar Boom, 1945–1970

Learning Objectives

After you have studied Chapter 30 in your textbook and worked through this study guide chapter, you should be able to:

1. Discuss the reasons for and indicate the extent of the postwar baby boom.
2. Examine the cornerstones of the postwar economic boom, and discuss the causes and consequences of the computer revolution.
3. Discuss the concentration of ownership in industry, and explain how the merger wave of the 1950s and 1960s differed from previous merger waves.
4. Discuss the characteristics of and the trends within the labor movement and agriculture from 1945 to 1970.
5. Discuss the impact of the postwar economic boom on the environment.
6. Examine the forces that contributed to the growth of the suburbs and the emergence of the megalopolis during the postwar period; indicate the characteristics associated with suburban life; and discuss the criticisms leveled against suburbia.
7. Discuss changes in the American family, the role of women, and the concept of motherhood during the 1950s and 1960s.
8. Discuss American concepts about education and American attitudes about religion and sex during the 1950s.
9. Discuss the impact of the postwar economic boom on Americans' buying and spending habits, resource consumption, and public health.
10. Explain the growth of the Sunbelt, and discuss the political and economic consequences of this growth.
11. Examine the reasons for, extent of, and effects of poverty in America during the postwar era, and discuss the characteristics of the poor.
12. Explain the characteristics of each of the following, and discuss their impact on American society in the 1940s, 1950s, and early 1960s:
    a. Television
    b. Advertising
    c. Paperbound books
    d. Motion pictures
    e. Popular music
    f. Fads
13. Explain the trends and themes in serious dance, art, and literature during the 1950s and early 1960s.

Thematic Guide

In Chapter 30, we focus on the social and cultural development of American society between 1945 and 1970. Sustained economic growth and prosperity made these years a period of optimism for many Americans. One result of this optimism was the "baby boom," which fueled more economic growth. This increase in population was especially important to the automobile and construction industries, two of the cornerstones of the economic expansion during the period. The third cornerstone, military spending, was sustained by the government.

As in the past, government aid played a role in developments that would have a momentous impact on American society. In the late nineteenth century, government aid to the railroad industry led to the development of a national marketplace and to pivotal economic changes within American society (see Chapter 17). In the late 1940s, government aid to weapons research led to the development of the transistor, which brought the computer and technological revolution to American society. This revolution affected employment patterns, led to the third great merger wave (characterized by conglomerate mergers), played a role in stabilizing union membership, and was a factor in the growth of the Sunbelt. Consolidation in industry was matched by consolidation in labor (the merging of the AFL and the CIO) and an acceleration of the trend toward bigness in American agriculture. As the cost of farm machinery, pesticides, fertilizer, and land soared, agribusiness presented more of a threat than ever to the family farm.

Economic growth inspired by government defense spending and by the growth of a more affluent population demanding more consumer goods and larger quantities of agricultural products had a negative impact on the environment. Automobiles and factories polluted the air. Human and industrial waste polluted rivers, lakes, and streams. Pesticides endangered wildlife and humans alike, as did the waste from nuclear processing plants. Disposable products marketed as conveniences made America a "throw-away society." As stated by the authors, "America was becoming a dumping-ground as never before."

As many white middle-class Americans made more money, bought more goods, and created more waste, they also sought the lifestyle offered by the suburbs. Drawn to the suburbs by many factors, including a desire to be with like-minded people and the desire for "family togetherness," life in suburbia was often made possible by government policies that extended economic aid to families making such a move. Federal, state, and local expenditures on highway construction also spurred the growth of suburbia and led to the development of the megalopolis. Although suburbia had its critics, most Americans seemed to prefer the lifestyle it offered.

As we see in the section "Ideals of Motherhood and the Family," the postwar economic boom also affected the family. The changes it brought included the influence of Dr. Benjamin Spock on the parent-child relationship, the conflicting and changing roles of women as more entered the labor market, and the enrollment in college of thousands of married veterans who decided to take advantage of the educational provisions of the GI Bill of Rights. Both education and religion gained importance in American life during the postwar years. At the same time, the pioneering work of Dr. Alfred Kinsey in the late 1940s and early 1950s influenced American attitudes toward sexual behavior.

Prosperity and access to credit further expanded the consumer culture. Prosperity made better medical care available to more people and made increased funding to medical research possible. In some measure, the rise in the average life span between 1945 and 1970 can be attributed to economic growth.

As in the late nineteenth century (see Chapter 19), Americans saw relocation as a means of economic and social mobility. In the earlier period, the cities of the Northeast had attracted those on the move, but in the 1960s the Sunbelt drew the migrants. The authors discuss the reasons for this movement pattern and its economic and political consequences.

Prosperity did not bring about a meaningful redistribution of income in American society during the period under study. Therefore, many Americans (about 25 percent in 1962) lived in poverty. In the section "The Other America," the authors provide a statistical picture of America's poor, who stood in decided contrast to the affluence around them. As before, the poor congregated in urban areas. Blacks, poor whites, Puerto Ricans, Chicanos, and Native Americans continued their movement to low-income inner-city housing, while the more affluent city residents—mostly whites—continued their exodus to the suburbs. Although low-interest government housing loans made life in suburbia possible for many middle-class whites, government programs such as "urban renewal" hurt the urban poor. The authors discuss the reasons for poverty, as well as the feminization of poverty and the psychological and emotional impact of poverty on its victims.

That most Americans dismissed poverty and were caught up in the materialistic values and pleasures of the era is further revealed in the last section, "Middle-Class America at Play." Here the authors describe the effects of television on American society during the postwar era and discuss the emergence of a youth subculture, the birth of rock 'n' roll, trends in art, and the fads of the era. The chapter ends with a brief discussion of the era's serious literature and of the critique of American society offered by the Beat Generation of the 1950s.

Building Vocabulary

Listed below are important words and terms that you need to know to get the most out of Chapter 30. They are listed in the order in which they occur in the chapter. After carefully looking through the list, refer to a dictionary and jot down the definition of words that you do not know or of which you are unsure.

aphorism

ensconce

squalid

hallmark

successive

piety

vindication

aspire

consolidation

oblivious

burgeoning

arid

obsolescence

proliferation

induce

blasé

exponent

homogenized

castigate

defer

perennial

obsolete

promulgate

prenatal

clout

abject

emulate

tantalize

sumptuous

boorish

flaunt

oblivious

Identification and Significance

After studying Chapter 30 of *A People and a Nation*, you should be able to identify fully *and* explain the historical significance of each item listed below.

1. Identify each item in the space provided. Give an explanation or description of the item. Answer the questions *who, what, where,* and *when.*
2. Explain the historical significance of each item in the space provided. Establish the historical context in which the item exists. Establish the item as the result of or as the cause of other factors existing in the society under study. Answer this question: *what were the political, social, economic, and/or cultural consequences of this item?*

the baby boom

    Identification

    Significance

the computer revolution

    Identification

    Significance

technological unemployment

> Identification

> Significance

conglomerate mergers

> Identification

> Significance

the postwar labor movement

> Identification

> Significance

farm mechanization

> Identification

> Significance

agricultural consolidation

> Identification

> Significance

DDT

> Identification

> Significance

"planned obsolescence"

    Identification

    Significance

growth of the suburbs

    Identification

    Significance

"family togetherness"

    Identification

    Significance

GI and FHA mortgages

    Identification

    Significance

Arthur Levitt and Sons

    Identification

    Significance

the interstate highway system

    Identification

    Significance

© 1994 Houghton Mifflin Company. All rights reserved.

the megalopolis

    Identification

    Significance

David Riesman, William H. Whyte, Sloan Wilson, and C. Wright Mills

    Identification

    Significance

Dr. Benjamin Spock

    Identification

    Significance

Momism

    Identification

    Significance

"anatomy is destiny"

    Identification

    Significance

the GI Bill of Rights

    Identification

    Significance

© 1994 Houghton Mifflin Company. All rights reserved.

the National Defense Education Act

>Identification

>Significance

Norman Vincent Peale and Billy Graham

>Identification

>Significance

the Kinsey reports

>Identification

>Significance

"sexual containment"

>Identification

>Significance

the affluent society

>Identification

>Significance

prenatal and pediatric care, penicillin, wonder drugs, and the Salk polio vaccine

>Identification

>Significance

the Sunbelt

    Identification

    Significance

Kevin Phillips

    Identification

    Significance

inner-city poverty

    Identification

    Significance

Operation Wetback

    Identification

    Significance

the National Housing Act of 1949

    Identification

    Significance

The Other America

    Identification

    Significance

television

> Identification
>
> Significance

paperbound books

> Identification
>
> Significance

the cult of youth

> Identification
>
> Significance

rock 'n' roll

> Identification
>
> Significance

Elvis Presley

> Identification
>
> Significance

"bebop"

> Identification
>
> Significance

Jackson Pollock

> Identification

> Significance

the Pop Art movement

> Identification

> Significance

Slinky, Silly Putty, and Hula-Hoops

> Identification

> Significance

Invisible Man

> Identification

> Significance

the Beat writers

> Identification

> Significance

The Affluent Society

> Identification

> Significance

Evaluating and Using Information

References to the special place of women in American society can be found throughout Chapter 30. Compile information from the chapter and from your class notes on women and women's issues in order to create a picture of the American woman's place in America during the 1950s. Use the information you collect to answer this question:

> Do the special roles they were expected to play and their responsibilities and opportunities suggest that the 1950s were as good for American women as they were for the population as a whole? Explain.

The following table should help you find and organize the information you will need. In the appropriate blanks in the table, enter reminders of the information you find. Sort that information into marital/parenthood status categories when appropriate.

When you have completed the table, expand the entries into notes and use those notes to compose the working draft of your essay. Enter your working draft in your Reader's Notebook.

America's Women in the 1950s						
Special Problems, Responsibilities, and Standards of Behavior						
	Standards Related to Sexual Behavior	Education	Jobs and Job Opportunities	Wages and Benefits	Special Responsibilities, Emotional Burdens Based on Gender	Support from Feminist Movement and Government
Women in General						
Single, Childless Women						
Female, Single Parents						

© 1994 Houghton Mifflin Company. All rights reserved.

Ideas and Details

Objective 1

_____ 1. Which of the following is true of the postwar baby boom?
   a. The boom did not lead to a corresponding increase in average family size.
   b. The boom was largely due to an increase in the birthrate among immigrants and poor Americans.
   c. Ignorance concerning birth control and family planning was probably the most important reason for the boom.
   d. The boom may be seen as an expression of postwar optimism.

Objectives 1 and 2

_____ 2. Which of the following was, as a cornerstone of the postwar economic boom, related to the baby boom?
   a. Automobile manufacturing
   b. Military spending
   c. Fast-food restaurant franchises
   d. Television production

Objectives 2 and 3

_____ 3. A major reason for the continued trend toward bigness in American industry during the 1950s and 1960s was
   a. vertical integration.
   b. the spread of computer technology.
   c. economic instability.
   d. a desire to increase competition.

Objective 4

_____ 4. The decline of the family farm during the 1950s and 1960s was due in large part to
   a. the absence of technological improvements to reduce the drudgery of farm life.
   b. a decline in the value of farm output.
   c. the expense of land, machinery, and fertilizers necessary for modern farming.
   d. the decrease in farm labor productivity.

© 1994 Houghton Mifflin Company. All rights reserved.

Objectives 6 and 7

_____ 5. The emphasis on family togetherness during the 1950s probably resulted from
   a. the Kinsey reports.
   b. the Great Depression and Second World War experiences of 1950s parents.
   c. television shows such as "Father Knows Best."
   d. the writings of David Riesman.

Objective 6

_____ 6. Which of the following contributed to the rise of the megalopolis?
   a. Keynesian economics
   b. Government defense spending
   c. The construction of interstate highways
   d. Government subsidies for low-income housing

Objective 7

_____ 7. As a result of the advice of Dr. Spock,
   a. permissiveness became the norm in child rearing.
   b. mothers felt free to work outside the home.
   c. many mothers felt guilty if they did not put their children's needs before their own.
   d. fathers began to assume a much larger role in child rearing.

Objective 9

_____ 8. The economic basis of the consumer culture of postwar America was
   a. the rising value of stocks and bonds.
   b. the rise in GNP.
   c. credit.
   d. the computer.

Objective 10

_____ 9. The migration of people to the Sunbelt
   a. was brought about by the movement of heavy industry to the South and West.
   b. greatly increased the national political power of the region.
   c. was largely due to the growth of organized labor in the South.
   d. led to a fundamental redistribution of wealth in the South and West.

Objective 11

_____ 10. Which of the following is true of the black population between 1940 and 1970?
   a. Most blacks moved from inner-city ghettos to the suburbs.
   b. The black population became increasingly urban.
   c. The south-to-north pattern of black movement was reversed during this period.
   d. Poverty among blacks decreased dramatically.

© 1994 Houghton Mifflin Company. All rights reserved.

Objective 11

____ 11. Which of the following was most likely to be poor in the America of the 1950s and 1960s?
   a. A retired white man
   b. A black American
   c. A Mexican-American
   d. A Native American

Objective 11

____ 12. As a result of the urban redevelopment features of the National Housing Act of 1949,
   a. the poor were displaced from slum-clearance areas.
   b. substandard housing in the nation's cities became the subject of national debate.
   c. public housing was built on the site of former slums.
   d. inner-city housing had to meet standards established by the federal government.

Objective 11

____ 13. In 1960, a woman was more likely than a man to be poor because
   a. occupational segregation limited the availability of well-paying jobs.
   b. the courts did not award child-support payments in divorce proceedings.
   c. women were generally overeducated for the 1960s job market.
   d. women were more likely to suffer from catastrophic illnesses.

Objective 12

____ 14. Rock 'n' roll music was derived from
   a. jazz.
   b. bluegrass music.
   c. black rhythm-and-blues.
   d. shape-note singing.

Objective 13

____ 15. The Beats were important because they
   a. introduced the "bebop" style.
   b. introduced the new, sophisticated advertising techniques associated with the television era.
   c. were the first group to perform rock 'n' roll publicly.
   d. produced some important literary works in which they challenged the materialism of the 1950s.

Essay Questions

Objectives 1 and 2

1. Discuss the baby boom, and explain its social and economic impact on American society.

Objective 4

2. Explain the trends in American agriculture from 1945 to 1970.

Objectives 6 and 7

3. Discuss the concept of the American family and American attitudes concerning gender roles during the 1950s and early 1960s.

Objective 7

4. Discuss the following statement: "A reason for woman's dilemma was the conflicting roles she was expected to fulfill."

Objective 10

5. Explain the movement to the Sunbelt, and discuss the impact of this movement on American society.

Objective 11

6. Examine the reasons for and the extent of poverty in American society during the 1950s and early 1960s.

CHAPTER 31

Contesting Nationalism and Revolution: The Third World and the Vietnam War, 1945–1989

Learning Objectives

After you have studied Chapter 31 in your textbook and worked through this study guide chapter, you should be able to:

1. Discuss the rise of the Third World and explain the role the developing nations played in the Cold War.
2. Explain the obstacles to United States influence in the Third World.
3. Examine the role of the CIA as an instrument of United States policy in the Third World throughout the course of the Cold War.
4. Examine, evaluate, and discuss the consequences of the Third World policies and actions of the Eisenhower and Kennedy administrations.
5. Examine and evaluate the events and decisions that led to deepening United States involvement in Vietnam from 1945 to 1968, and discuss the course of the war from 1950 to 1968.
6. Discuss the nature of the Vietnam War, the characteristics of American soldiers who served in the war, and the war's impact on those soldiers.
7. Explain the factors that contributed to the emergence of anti-Vietnam War sentiment and protests within the United States.
8. Discuss the course of the Vietnam War from 1968 to 1975; explain the war's impact on Southeast Asia and American society; and discuss the debate in the United States over the meaning of the American experience in Vietnam.
9. Examine, evaluate, and discuss the consequences of the Third World policies and actions of the Johnson and Nixon administrations, and explain how crises and issues in the Third World placed the Nixon-Kissinger grand strategy in jeopardy.
10. Examine the global economic issues separating the wealthier northern nations from the poorer southern nations of the world; explain the impact of these issues on international relations; and discuss United States policy concerning these issues.
11. Examine, evaluate, and discuss the consequences of the Third World policies and actions of the Carter and Reagan administrations.
12. Discuss the activities that constituted the Iran-contra scandal, and explain the scandal's impact on the presidency of Ronald Reagan.

Thematic Guide

The process of decolonization begun during the First World War accelerated in the aftermath of the Second World War. As scores of new nations were born, the Cold-War rivalry between the United States and the Soviet Union began. Both superpowers began to compete for friends among the newly emerging nations of the Third World; however, both the United States and the Soviet Union encountered obstacles in finding allies among the Third World nations. The factors that created obstacles for the United States in its search for Third World friends included:

1. America's negative view toward the nonaligned movement among Third World nations;
2. embarrassing incidents in the United States in which official representatives of the Third World were subjected to racist practices and prejudices;
3. America's intolerance of the disorder caused by revolutionary nationalism; and
4. America's great wealth.

To meet the perceived Soviet threat and protect its own economic interests, the United States during the Eisenhower administration began increasingly to rely on the covert actions of the Central Intelligence Agency, as demonstrated in the Guatemalan and Iranian examples. Moreover, the attitude of the United States toward neutralism and toward the disruptions caused by revolutionary nationalism may be seen in the Eisenhower administration's reaction to the events surrounding the 1956 Suez Crisis. In the aftermath of that crisis, fear of a weakened position in the Middle East led to the issuance of the Eisenhower Doctrine, which in turn was used to justify American military intervention in Lebanon in 1958, thus expanding the nation's "global watch" approach to the containment of Communism.

In its quest for friends in the Third World and ultimate victory in the Cold War, the Kennedy administration adopted the goal of nation building, to be accomplished, for example, through the Alliance for Progress and the Peace Corps as well as through the techniques of counterinsurgency. Such methods perpetuated an idea that had long been part of American foreign policy: that other people cannot solve their own problems and that the American economic and governmental model can be transferred intact to other societies. William Appleman Williams believed that such thinking led to "the tragedy of American diplomacy" (see Chapter 22), and historian Arthur M. Schlesinger, Jr., refers to it as "a ghastly illusion." The idea is further evidenced in the CIA's intervention in the Congo (Zaire) from 1960 to 1961 and in Brazil from 1962 to 1964.

The authors trace the course of American involvement in Vietnam from the collapse of French authority in Indochina during the Second World War to the collapse of South Vietnam in April 1975. This discussion is based on a restatement of the "tragedy" theme. In relation to Vietnam, the authors also introduce another theme: the belief by the United States that it had a right to influence the internal affairs of Third World countries led to disaster in Southeast Asia. This theme runs through the discussion of United States involvement in Vietnam in several variations: the United States decision to sabotage the Geneva accords, United States support of the overthrow of the Diem regime, Johnson's "welfare imperialism" and his view of Vietnam as a "raggedy-ass fourth-rate country," the arrogance of power on the part of the United States, and Nixon's "jugular diplomacy."

Several subthemes remind us of the sources of the Cold War, discussed in Chapter 29. It is within this context that the authors state: "Overlooking the native roots of the nationalist rebellion against France, and the long, tenacious Vietnamese resistance to foreign intruders, American presidents from Truman through Ford took a globalist view of Vietnam, interpreting events through a Cold War lens." And in a review of the material we find that the following sources of the Cold War from Chapter 29 fit the war in Vietnam:

1. The unsettled international environment at the end of World War II encouraged competition between the United States and the Soviet Union. Empires were disintegrating (France's attempt to reinstate its authority in Indochina ended in disaster at Dienbienphu); nations were being born (Ho

Chi Minh attempted to create an independent Vietnam); and civil wars were raging within nations (the National Liberation Front emerged against Ngo Dinh Diem's South Vietnamese regime).
2. United States fear of the Soviet system led to economic expansionism (the United States recognized Southeast Asia as an "economic asset") and globalist diplomacy (Southeast Asia seemed vital to the defense of Japan and the Philippines).
3. United States officials exaggerated the Soviet threat because of desires for simple answers and a fixation by some on stated Soviet goals rather than actual Soviet behavior. (American presidents from Truman through Nixon failed to recognize the nationalist roots of the problem in Vietnam. Instead, they saw Ho Chi Minh as a Communist and Vietnam as the "Berlin of Asia," and they accepted the tenets of the domino theory.)

In the aftermath of the Vietnam War, Americans began to debate its causes and consequences. Just as they had disagreed over the course and conduct of the war, they were now unable to reach any real consensus on its lessons for the nation.

While the Nixon administration saw Vietnam as an "historical footnote" and concentrated on its "grand strategy" to achieve world stability by following a policy of détente with the Soviet Union, it also had to respond to Third World crises rooted in instability. Nowhere was the fragility of world stability via the grand strategy more apparent than in the Middle East, where war again broke out between the Arab states and Israel in 1973. While the Soviet Union and the United States positioned themselves by putting their armed forces on alert, OPEC imposed an oil embargo against the United States. Kissinger was able to persuade the warring parties to agree to a cease fire; OPEC ended its embargo; and, through "shuttle diplomacy," Kissinger persuaded Egypt and Israel to agree to a United Nations peacekeeping force in the Sinai. But many problems remained, and the instability of the region continued to be a source of tension between the United States and the Soviet Union.

President Nixon believed, just as previous presidents had believed, in America's right to influence the internal affairs of Third World countries. It was out of this belief and the concomitant belief that the United States should curb revolution and radicalism in the Third World, that Nixon accepted the Johnson Doctrine in Latin America, as evidenced by the overthrow of the Allende government in Chile. However, in relation to the extension of covert aid to counterrevolutionary forces in Angola, Congress successfully reasserted its power in the making of foreign policy and, in the process, demonstrated that long-held Cold War assumptions were being questioned.

As Nixon and Kissinger sought world order through the grand strategy, global economic issues highlighted the differences between the rich and poor nations of the world and heightened the animosity of Third World nations (the South) toward what they perceived to be the exploitive industrialized nations of the world (the North). The United States, the richest nation on Earth, exports large quantities of goods to developing nations as well as importing raw materials from those nations. This important trade, along with America's worldwide investments, in part explains the interventionist nature of United States foreign policy, a policy accepted and continued by Presidents Nixon and Gerald Ford, and by their foreign-policy overseer, Henry Kissinger. Therefore, during the Nixon-Ford-Kissinger years America's global watch against forces that threatened its far-flung economic and strategic interests continued.

With the election of Jimmy Carter to the presidency in 1977, there were signs that United States policy toward the Third World would change. For example, U.N. Ambassador Andrew Young believed that the United States should assume a "hands-off" approach to local disputes in Third World nations. On the basis of that belief he persuaded the Carter administration not to intervene in the 1979 war between Zaire and Angola. Carter also markedly advanced the peace process in the Middle East through the Camp David accords and successfully diffused revolutionary nationalism in Panama by negotiating the Panama Canal treaties. On the other hand, Carter was unable to contain revolutionary nationalism and anti-American hostility in Nicaragua and ultimately cut off American aid to the Sandinista government in 1981. Furthermore, the excesses in which the United States had engaged in the past in its attempts to create stability, protect American economic interests, and contain the Communist threat

© 1994 Houghton Mifflin Company. All rights reserved.

rained down on the Carter administration in the form of the Iranian hostage crisis. In this crisis America's missiles, submarines, tanks, and bombers ultimately meant nothing if the lives of the hostages were to be saved. But many Americans wished for a return to the immediate post-war world, a world in which the United States had a monopoly on economic and military power. In this spirit of nostalgia, the electorate chose Ronald Reagan as its president in the 1980 election.

President Reagan was in many respects a return to a previous time and previous attitudes. The questioning of U.S. intervention in Third World nations, so apparent in the immediate aftermath of the Vietnam disaster, was absent in the Reagan administration. Fearing communism, Reagan simplistically blamed unrest in the world on the Soviets, failed to see the local roots of problems, and formed alliances with antirevolutionary regimes, which tended to be unrepresentative. American relations with the Third World during the 1980s evoke memories of the sources of the Cold War, of the containment policy, and of attempts to protect American economic interests against the force of revolutionary nationalism. Therefore, in the name of protecting private American companies, the Reagan administration rejected the Law of the Sea Treaty and voted against restrictions on the marketing of baby formula in developing nations. In the same vein, American policies toward El Salvador and Nicaragua recall phrases used to describe American policy in previous eras; and Reagan's desire for victory rather than negotiation, seen especially in his policies toward Central America, brings to mind the early years of the Kennedy administration. However, since the Kennedy years the American people had been through the traumas of Vietnam and Watergate, and the power of Congress, relative to that of the president, had increased. Therefore, Congress in the mid-1980s was much more willing to play an active role in foreign policy decisions than it had been in the 1960s. But Congress, reflecting the debate among the American people over the nation's policy toward Nicaragua, vacillated between ending aid to the contras in mid-1984 and again extending aid in 1986. During the period when aid was prohibited, the executive branch of the government, through the National Security Council and the Central Intelligence Agency, acted to circumvent the will of Congress. These actions came to light in 1986 in the Iran-contra scandal, a scandal that deeply wounded Ronald Reagan's ability to lead during his last two years in office.

From this discussion of the Iran-contra scandal, the authors turn their attention to continuing problems in the Middle East, the problem of terrorism against United States citizens and property, and to a discussion of America's ill-fated 1983 mission in Lebanon. Chapter 31 closes with a discussion of the Reagan administration's policy of "constructive engagement" toward South Africa, Congress' ability to force the administration to alter that policy, and an examination of the major problems facing the United States in the Third World at the close of the 1980s.

Building Vocabulary

Listed below are important words and terms that you need to know to get the most out of Chapter 31. They are listed in the order in which they occur in the chapter. After carefully looking through the list, refer to a dictionary and jot down the definition of words that you do not know or of which you are unsure.

protracted

indigenous

covet

pervasive

abstain

garner

covert

expropriate

volatile

stalwart

renege

tenacious

moot

charismatic

attrition

carnage

discernible

reciprocity

pusillanimous

languish

renegade

chide

visceral

nuance

foment

eschew

intransigence

collusion

divestment

exacerbate

Identification and Significance

After studying Chapter 31 of *A People and a Nation,* you should be able to identify fully *and* explain the historical significance of each item listed below.

1. Identify each item in the space provided. Give an explanation or description of the item. Answer the questions *who, what, where,* and *when.*
2. Explain the historical significance of each item in the space provided. Establish the historical context in which the item exists. Establish the item as the result of or as the cause of other factors existing in the society under study. Answer this question: *what were the political, social, economic, and/or cultural consequences of this item?*

the Third World

     Identification

     Significance

© 1994 Houghton Mifflin Company. All rights reserved.

Chapter 31

the process of decolonization

    Identification

    Significance

the Bandung Conference of 1955

    Identification

    Significance

the G. L. Mehta incident

    Identification

    Significance

The Ugly American

    Identification

    Significance

the Central Intelligence Agency

    Identification

    Significance

plausible deniability

    Identification

    Significance

Jacobo Arbenz Guzmán

    Identification

    Significance

Operation Poor Richard

    Identification

    Significance

Mohammed Mossadegh

    Identification

    Significance

Gamal Abdul Nasser

    Identification

    Significance

the Suez crisis

    Identification

    Significance

the Eisenhower Doctrine

    Identification

    Significance

the Lebanese crisis of 1958

    Identification

    Significance

the concept of nation building

    Identification

    Significance

the Alliance for Progress

    Identification

    Significance

the Peace Corps

    Identification

    Significance

the doctrine of counterinsurgency

    Identification

    Significance

Patrice Lumumba and João Goulart

    Identification

    Significance

Ho Chi Minh

    Identification

    Significance

the Vietminh

    Identification

    Significance

Bao Dai

    Identification

    Significance

Dienbienphu

    Identification

    Significance

the domino theory

    Identification

    Significance

the 1954 Geneva accords

    Identification

    Significance

SEATO

    Identification

    Significance

Ngo Dinh Diem

    Identification

    Significance

the National Liberation Front (the Vietcong)

    Identification

    Significance

Project Beef-up

    Identification

    Significance

the Strategic Hamlet Program

    Identification

    Significance

the Tonkin Gulf incident and the Tonkin Gulf Resolution

    Identification

    Significance

© 1994 Houghton Mifflin Company. All rights reserved.

Laos

> Identification
>
> Significance

Pleiku

> Identification
>
> Significance

Operation Rolling Thunder

> Identification
>
> Significance

Agent Orange

> Identification
>
> Significance

the My Lai massacre

> Identification
>
> Significance

fragging

> Identification
>
> Significance

draft resisters

> Identification

> Significance

the National Committee to End the War in Vietnam

> Identification

> Significance

George F. Kennan

> Identification

> Significance

the Tet offensive

> Identification

> Significance

the gold crisis

> Identification

> Significance

the Nixon Doctrine

> Identification

> Significance

Vietnamization

    Identification

    Significance

jugular diplomacy

    Identification

    Significance

the antiwar demonstrations of October and November 1969

    Identification

    Significance

the invasion of Cambodia

    Identification

    Significance

the Kent State incident

    Identification

    Significance

the *Pentagon Papers*

    Identification

    Significance

the Christmas bombing

>Identification

>Significance

the Vietnam cease-fire agreement

>Identification

>Significance

the War Powers Resolution

>Identification

>Significance

the fall of Saigon

>Identification

>Significance

"boat people"

>Identification

>Significance

"empire shock"

>Identification

>Significance

Vietnam syndrome

>Identification

>Significance

post-traumatic stress disorder

>Identification

>Significance

the Six-Day War

>Identification

>Significance

the Palestine Liberation Organization

>Identification

>Significance

the 1973 Middle East war

>Identification

>Significance

the OPEC oil embargo

>Identification

>Significance

shuttle diplomacy

    Identification

    Significance

Dominican Republic intervention

    Identification

    Significance

the Johnson Doctrine

    Identification

    Significance

Salvador Allende

    Identification

    Significance

the Angolan civil war

    Identification

    Significance

multinational corporations

    Identification

    Significance

the "New International Economic Order"

    Identification

    Significance

Andrew Young

    Identification

    Significance

the Camp David Agreements

    Identification

    Significance

the Panama Canal treaties of 1977

    Identification

    Significance

Anastasio Somoza

    Identification

    Significance

the Sandinistas

    Identification

    Significance

the Ayatollah Ruhollah Khomeini

    Identification

    Significance

the Iranian hostage crisis

    Identification

    Significance

the Iranian rescue mission

    Identification

    Significance

the Law of the Sea Treaty

    Identification

    Significance

the baby-formula debate

    Identification

    Significance

the Salvadoran civil war

    Identification

    Significance

the *contras*

>Identification

>Significance

the Iran-contra scandal

>Identification

>Significance

international terrorism

>Identification

>Significance

the Lebanese crisis of 1982–1983

>Identification

>Significance

Persian Gulf escorts

>Identification

>Significance

intifadah

>Identification

>Significance

apartheid

>Identification

>Significance

the policy of constructive engagement

>Identification

>Significance

African famine

>Identification

>Significance

the Third World debt crisis

>Identification

>Significance

Evaluating and Using Information

Using the charts on pages 403–405 to help you look for and organize the information you will need, analyze the methods and goals of United States intervention into the affairs and conflicts of Third World nations from 1945 through 1989. Use the information you gather to compose an essay responding to this question:

> Identify and evaluate the key methods and goals of the interventionist policies that the United States government pursued in the Third World between 1945 and 1990.

In the charts, record reminders of the relevant information that you find in Chapter 31 and in your class notes. Then expand the reminders first into full notes and then into the working draft of your essay.
  Enter the working draft of your essay in your Reader's Notebook.

United States Intervention in the Third World, 1945–1989				
Third World Nation	**Direct Military Action by U.S. Forces**	**Arms sales, Military aid, Support for Counter-insurgency**	**Diplomacy, Negotiation, Economic Sanctions, Non-Military Foreign aid**	**Covert Action, Destabilization, Support for coups or Assassinations**
Indochina				
Vietnam				
Laos				
Cambodia				
Central America				
Guatemala				
El Salvador				
Honduras				
Costa Rica				
Nicaragua				

United States Intervention in the Third World, 1945–1989				
Third World Nation	**Direct Military Action by U.S. Forces**	**Arms sales, Military aid, Support for Counter-insurgency**	**Diplomacy, Negotiation, Economic Sanctions, Non-Military Foreign aid**	**Covert Action, Destabilization, Support for coups or Assassinations**
Middle East				
Iran				
Lebanon				
Egypt				
Israel				
Africa				
Angola				
South Africa				
Congo (Zaire)				

Goals of United States Intervention, 1945–1989				
Third World Region	**Gain in Cold War Competition, Undermining of Neutralism**	**Protection of Private Enterprise, Investments, Raw Material Supplies**	**Support for Colonial Powers, Allies, Real or Perceived Commitments, Enemies of Foes of United States**	**Thwarting Feared Nationalism Radicalism**
Indochina				
Central America				
Latin America				
Africa				
Middle East				

© 1994 Houghton Mifflin Company. All rights reserved.

Ideas and Details

Objective 2

_____ 1. The United States found it difficult to make friends in the Third World because
   a. the United States usually supported the propertied, antirevolutionary elements in the Third World.
   b. diplomats from Third World countries disliked America's pluralistic society.
   c. American business interests refused to invest in Third World countries.
   d. the Soviets were more adept at doing so.

Objectives 3 and 4

_____ 2. What do Jacobo Arbenz Guzmán of Guatemala and Mohammed Mossadegh of Iran have in common?
   a. Both agreed to the deployment of Russian intermediate-range missiles in their respective countries.
   b. Both strongly supported United States interests in the Third World.
   c. Both were killed while observing the 1954 test of a 15-megaton H-bomb.
   d. Both threatened American investments in their respective countries and were overthrown in CIA-supported coups.

Objective 4

_____ 3. The concept of nation building was based on the idea that
   a. the industrialized nations of the world should pool their resources to aid Third World nations.
   b. the United States could win the friendship of Third World countries by helping them as they struggled through the infant stages of nationhood.
   c. the European states should demonstrate their acceptance of self-determination by allowing their colonies to become independent nations.
   d. a nation's social, political, and economic system must be based on its own unique historical experience.

Objective 5

_____ 4. For which of the following reasons did the United States refuse to recognize Vietnamese independence in 1945?
   a. The United States feared that such recognition would jeopardize negotiations with China.
   b. Ho Chi Minh had worked with the Japanese against the United States during World War II.
   c. FDR had guaranteed the return of French colonies at the end of the Second World War.
   d. Because Ho Chi Minh was a Communist and had lived in the Soviet Union, the United States chose to support the imperialist stance of its Cold War ally France.

Objective 5

_____ 5. In the Gulf of Tonkin Resolution, Congress
   a. publicly questioned President Johnson's escalation of the Vietnam War.
   b. gave virtually a free hand to President Johnson in conducting the war in Vietnam.
   c. condemned the My Lai massacre.
   d. declared war against North Vietnam.

Objective 7

_____ 6. In the late 1960s, growing numbers of Americans began to question United States involvement in the Vietnam War in large part because they
   a. were frightened by China's threat to launch a nuclear attack against the United States.
   b. accepted the Republican party's assessment that the United States should abandon the corrupt government of South Vietnam.
   c. recognized the democratic nature of Ho Chi Minh's regime in North Vietnam.
   d. saw the ugliness of the war each evening on the nightly news.

Objectives 5 and 6

_____ 7. Which of the following is the most plausible explanation for atrocities such as the My Lai massacre?
   a. Soldiers who engaged in such atrocities were drug addicts.
   b. Soldiers who engaged in such atrocities usually acted out of frustrations stemming from the nature of the war itself.
   c. High-ranking Pentagon officials ordered such atrocities.
   d. CIA operatives disguised as Vietcong engaged in such atrocities.

Objectives 7 and 8

_____ 8. As a result of the Tet offensive,
   a. the Soviet union sent troops to Vietnam.
   b. the Joint Chiefs of Staff advised American withdrawal from Vietnam.
   c. the North Vietnamese were driven to the north of the Demilitarized Zone and requested peace negotiations.
   d. President Johnson, realizing the Vietnam War was unwinnable, decided to open negotiations with the North.

Objective 8

_____ 9. Under the Nixon-Kissinger policy of "Vietnamization,"
   a. stability slowly returned to Indochina as the Vietnam War de-escalated.
   b. withdrawal of American troops was accompanied by increased bombing of the North and the invasion of Cambodia.
   c. the South Vietnamese army proved that it was an effective fighting force.
   d. a coalition government was established in Hanoi and the war quickly drew to a close.

Objective 8

_____ 10. In the aftermath of the Vietnam War, Americans
   a. disagreed over the lessons to be drawn from the experience.
   b. withdrew from the United Nations.
   c. vowed to support Third World revolutions.
   d. agreed to increase the powers of the president in foreign policy.

Objective 9

_____ 11. As a result of Kissinger's "shuttle diplomacy,"
   a. an autonomous Palestinian state under United Nations protection was created.
   b. the Palestine Liberation Organization recognized Israel's right to exist.
   c. OPEC agreed to reduce oil prices.
   d. Egypt and Israel agreed to a United Nations peacekeeping force in the Sinai.

Objectives 2 and 10

_____ 12. Because of extensive investments abroad, the United States
   a. became an interventionist power.
   b. suffered more than the Third World nations from the economic decline of the 1970s.
   c. enjoyed improved relations with developing nations in the 1970s.
   d. increased its commitment to and support for the United Nations.

Objective 10

_____ 13. Which of the following issues caused division between the industrialized and developing countries?
   a. Most industrialized nations refused to extend any aid to Third World nations.
   b. Third World nations complained about the exploitative nature of multinational corporations.
   c. Developing nations refused to sell their surplus food to industrialized nations.
   d. Industrialized nations insisted that seabed resources should be shared by all nations.

Objective 11

_____ 14. In defending its policies in El Salvador, the Reagan administration warned that
   a. the Soviets were installing nuclear missiles in El Salvador.
   b. the rebel forces in El Salvador would continue to grow if the United States ignored the plight of impoverished Salvadoran peasants.
   c. Communists would soon be at the Mexican-American border if they were not stopped in El Salvador.
   d. the United States should abandon right-wing governments that lacked mass popular support.

Objective 11

_____ 15. What was the Reagan administration's goal in Nicaragua?
   a. To persuade the Sandinista government to hold elections
   b. To remove the Sandinista government from power
   c. To reduce foreign military bases and advisers in that country
   d. To bring about a negotiated settlement between the Sandinista government and the contras

Essay Questions

Objective 4

1. Explain and evaluate the Eisenhower administration's perception of and response to nationalist movements in the Third World. Illustrate with examples from the Middle East and Latin America. Pay particular attention to the administration's response to Jacobo Arbenz Guzmán and Gamal Abdul Nasser.

Objectives 5 and 8

2. Debate the following statement: "The belief in the right of the United States to influence the internal affairs of other countries led to disaster in Southeast Asia."

Objective 6

3. Discuss the characteristics of soldiers who served in the Vietnam War; explain their war-related experiences; and discuss the impact of those experiences on their lives.

Objective 8

4. Discuss the domestic debate over the meaning of the American experience in Vietnam.

Objectives 1, 2, 8, 9, 10, and 11

5. Define *nationalism;* discuss its role in international affairs in the 1970s; and explain the response of the United States to revolutionary nationalism.

Objective 9

6. Explain how events in the Middle East placed the Nixon-Kissinger "grand strategy" in jeopardy.

Objective 11

7. Discuss and evaluate the Reagan administration's policy toward Third World nations, paying particular attention to its policy toward Central America.

© 1994 Houghton Mifflin Company. All rights reserved.

Map Exercise

Refer to the map on page 957 of the textbook to complete this exercise. You may also find it helpful to refer to an historical atlas. You will need three pens of different colors to complete this exercise. (Highlight pens may be used.)

Label each of the following on the map of the Middle East on page 411 of this Study Guide:

Countries	Bodies of Water	Territories	Capital Cities
Egypt	Gulf of Aqaba	Gaza Strip	Amman
Iran	Gulf of Suez	Golan Heights	Beirut
Iraq	Jordan River	Sinai Peninsula	Baghdad
Israel	Mediterranean Sea	West Bank	Cairo
Jordan	Persian Gulf		Damascas
Lebanon	Red Sea		Jerusalem
Saudi Arabia	Sea of Galilee		Riyadh
Syria	Suez Canal		Tehran

Color the map as follows:

- Use one color to denote the Jewish state after the partition of Palestine, 1947.
- Use a second color to denote the territory Israel gained as a result of the War of 1948–1949.
- Use a third color to denote the territory controlled by Israel after the Six-Day War, 1967.
- Place backward slashes (\\\\\) in the Sinai Peninsula to denote that by the Egyptian-Israeli Agreements of 1975 and 1979 Israel withdrew from the Sinai in 1982.
- Do not put backward slashes in the area known as the Gaza Strip. That area was not returned to Egypt when Israel withdrew from the Sinai.
- Place forward slashes (//////) in the Golan Heights to denote that Israel annexed this area in 1981.

Contesting Nationalism and Revolution: The Third World and the Vietnam War, 1945–1989

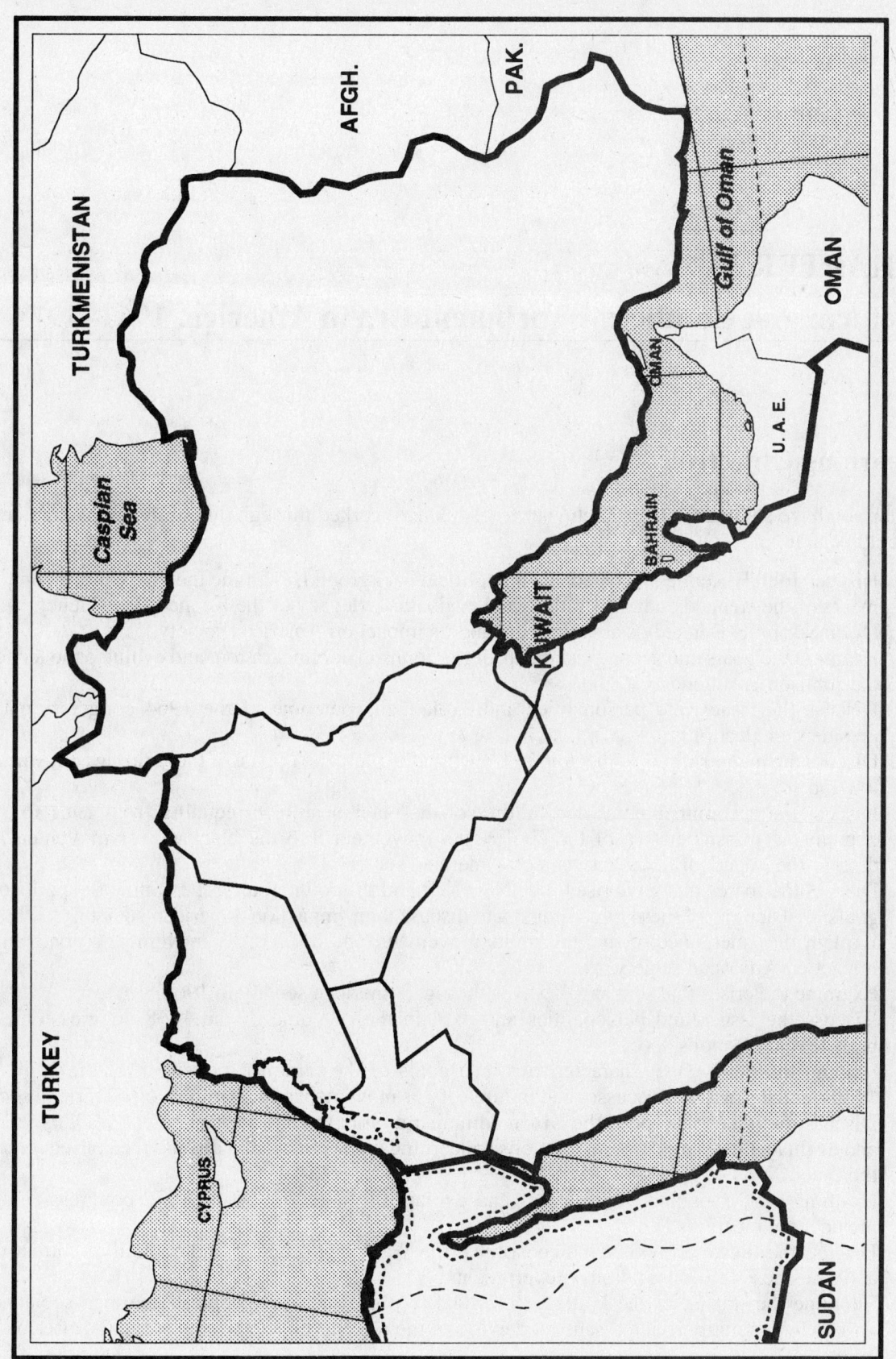

CHAPTER 32

Reform and Conflict: A Turbulent Era in America, 1961–1974

Learning Objectives

After you have studied Chapter 32 in your textbook and worked through this study guide chapter, you should be able to:

1. Discuss John F. Kennedy's personal and political background; examine the goals and accomplishments of the Kennedy administration, and evaluate the legacy of the Kennedy presidency.
2. Discuss John F. Kennedy's assassination and its impact on American society.
3. Examine the goals and accomplishments of the Johnson administration, and evaluate the legacy of the Johnson presidency.
4. Discuss the issues and personalities and explain the outcome of the 1964 congressional and presidential elections.
5. Discuss the major rulings of the Warren Court, and explain the impact of these rulings on American life and society.
6. Discuss the accomplishments and failures of the black search for equality from 1961 to 1973; explain the transformation of the civil rights movement into the black power movement; and discuss the impact of black activism on American society.
7. Discuss the forces that gave rise to the New Left and the counterculture; examine the philosophy, goals, and actions of these two groups; and discuss their impact on American society.
8. Explain the emergence of the gay rights movement, and discuss the movement's goals and its impact on American society.
9. Examine the crises that sent shock waves through American society in 1968.
10. Discuss the issues and personalities and explain the outcome of the 1968 congressional and presidential elections.
11. Explain the emergence, characteristics, and goals of the feminist movement of the 1960s and 1970s, and discuss the successes and failures of this movement and its impact on American society.
12. Discuss the issues that faced the Nixon administration in the late 1960s and early 1970s; explain and evaluate the administration's actions concerning those issues; and discuss the consequences of those actions.
13. Examine the issues and personalities and explain the outcome of the 1972 congressional and presidential elections.
14. Discuss the illegal activities that constituted the Watergate scandal, and explain the threat these activities posed to constitutional government.
15. Examine the impact of the Watergate scandal on the American people, American society, and American institutions, and discuss and evaluate the reforms enacted in the scandal's aftermath.

Thematic Guide

In Chapter 32, we examine the crises that engulfed American society during the 1960s and early 1970s. As we learn from the first section, "The Civil Rights Movement and Kennedy's New Frontier," the New Frontier was overly ambitious in light of the political distance between the new president's liberal agenda and a Congress dominated by a conservative coalition. When he attempted to deal with this conservative coalition, Kennedy at first failed to press forward on civil rights issues. At this point, violence began to have an impact on developments. In the face of violent challenges from southern segregationists to an expanding black civil-rights movement, the Kennedy administration gradually committed itself to a decisive stand in favor of black equality. But only because of continuing racial violence and Kennedy's assassination did Congress finally pass civil rights legislation.

The section "The Great Society and the Triumph of Liberalism" covers the legislative accomplishments of the Johnson administration—the most sweeping reform legislation since 1935. This legislation comprised the Civil Rights Act of 1964, the Economic Opportunity Act of 1964, and the tax cuts of the same year. The authors look closely at the legislation that constituted the War on Poverty and discuss the problems and successes of this program.

The liberal decisions rendered by the Supreme Court during the 1960s and early 1970s matched the liberalism reflected in the progressive legislation of the Johnson years. The authors examine these rulings, the aspects of American life and American society they affected, and the praise and criticisms they evoked.

As the three branches of the federal government slowly began to deal with such long-standing American problems as poverty and minority rights, frustrations that had built up over generations of inaction manifested themselves. Events convinced civil-rights activists in the South that the "power structure" in American society was not to be trusted. Northern blacks began to reach the same conclusions. Both the civil-rights movement and Johnson's antipoverty programs had offered African-Americans hope for a better day in American society. However, as discussion of the social, economic, and political plight of urban blacks reveals, that hope had not been fulfilled. Among other factors, unfulfilled expectations and the continued display of wealth and possessions in the consumer-oriented American society led to the urban riots of the 1960s. Militant black leaders gained prominence and questioned Martin Luther King's philosophy of nonviolence as well as his goal of integration. Malcolm X, Stokely Carmichael, and the Black Panther party called for "black power" within the context of black nationalism.

Along with this revolution of rising expectations among blacks, some whites involved in the civil rights movement began to become disillusioned with American society. Although their disillusionment stemmed from different sources than that of blacks, it led to the political and social activism associated with the New Left and the counterculture. The authors discuss the emergence, characteristics, and goals of both of these groups as well as the reaction of the middle class to their attacks on traditional values. In addition, the activism of blacks, the New Left and counterculture, and women gave rise to gay activism and to the gay rights movement. As the Vietnam War escalated and the New Left and the counterculture found common cause in their antiwar stance, the middle class became more and more convinced that traditional society was under siege.

The forces of frustration, rage, and anger born of racism, sexism, poverty, disillusionment, materialism, and the revolution of rising expectations practically ripped America apart in the tumult of 1968. After explaining the events of that year, the authors discuss the emergence, characteristics, and goals of both moderate and radical feminists. They also examine the problems encountered by many working women in the 1960s and note gains made by women against sexism in the late 1960s and early 1970s.

Continuation of chaos into the 1970s convinced President Nixon and many Americans that society was on the verge of anarchy. Nixon attempted to use the perceived danger to his political advantage by portraying critics, including the Democratic opposition, as Communist pawns and enemies of American society. These tactics gained Nixon little in the 1970 congressional elections, and publication of the *Pentagon Papers* fostered more distrust of government. As Nixon prepared for the 1972 presidential election, he turned to Keynesian economics to deal with the country's economic problems and opened relations with the People's Republic of China.

In "The Southern Strategy and the Election of 1972," the authors examine the factors that contributed to Nixon's landslide victory in the 1972 election. These factors include the "southern strategy," Nixon's success in associating the Democratic party with groups and movements that threatened traditional values, the nature of George McGovern's campaign, division within the Democratic party, and Nixon's announcement that peace was at hand in Vietnam. Even though the voters overwhelmingly chose to return Nixon to the White House in 1972, they also chose to leave both houses of Congress in the hands of the Democrats.

Unfortunately, Nixon's landslide victory did not guarantee an end to the crisis atmosphere that had plagued the nation since the late 1960s. The Watergate scandal caused more disillusionment with government and increased the somber mood of the people, for it involved a series of illegal activities approved at the highest level of American government. Some of these activities, such as the break-in at Daniel Ellsberg's psychiatrist's office, had been undertaken to discredit political opponents; others, such as the paying of hush money to witnesses, were part of an elaborate cover-up.

Beyond the illegal actions, the Watergate scandal was a constitutional crisis; the "imperial presidency" threatened the balance-of-power concept embodied in the Constitution and the guarantees of individual rights embodied in the Bill of Rights. We see the constitutional nature of the crisis in the clash between the executive and judicial branches of government, the impeachment hearings undertaken by the House Judiciary Committee, and ultimately the resignation of the president. Unlike the scandals of previous administrations, the activities linked to Watergate were aimed not at financial gain but at monopolizing political power. After citing the events associated with Watergate, the authors outline and briefly evaluate congressional attempts to correct the abuses associated with the scandal.

Building Vocabulary

Listed below are important words and terms that you need to know to get the most out of Chapter 32. They are listed in the order in which they occur in the chapter. After carefully looking through the list, refer to a dictionary and jot down the definition of words that you do not know or of which you are unsure.

oblivious

polarize

staid

verve

parochial

vigilante

filibuster

traumatize

aura

ponderous

solicitous

enunciate

salvo

milestone

ire

tandem

debilitating

resurgence

impropriety

espouse

furtive

rueful

debacle

anarchy

espouse

fiscal

benign

moratorium

solicit

expunge

feign

tenuous

replete

mandate (*verb*)

capricious

Identification and Significance

After studying Chapter 32 of *A People and a Nation,* you should be able to identify fully *and* explain the historical significance of each item listed below.

1. Identify each item in the space provided. Give an explanation or description of the item. Answer the questions *who, what, where,* and *when.*
2. Explain the historical significance of each item in the space provided. Establish the historical context in which the item exists. Establish the item as the result of or as the cause of other factors existing in the society under study. Answer this question: what were the political, social, economic, and/or cultural consequences of this item?

© 1994 Houghton Mifflin Company. All rights reserved.

John F. Kennedy

    Identification

    Significance

Profiles In Courage

    Identification

    Significance

"the best and the brightest"

    Identification

    Significance

the New Frontier

    Identification

    Significance

Martin Luther King, Jr.

    Identification

    Significance

Freedom Riders

    Identification

    Significance

Student Nonviolent Coordinating Committee

    Identification

    Significance

James Meredith

    Identification

    Significance

the March on Washington

    Identification

    Significance

Medgar Evers

    Identification

    Significance

Sheriff "Bull" Connor

    Identification

    Significance

Sixteenth Street Baptist Church bombing

    Identification

    Significance

the assassination of John Kennedy

> Identification
>
> Significance

Lee Harvey Oswald

> Identification
>
> Significance

Jack Ruby

> Identification
>
> Significance

the space program

> Identification
>
> Significance

the Kennedy aura

> Identification
>
> Significance

Lyndon B. Johnson

> Identification
>
> Significance

the Great Society

    Identification

    Significance

the Civil Rights Act of 1964

    Identification

    Significance

the Equal Employment Opportunity Commission

    Identification

    Significance

the Economic Opportunity Act of 1964

    Identification

    Significance

Barry Goldwater

    Identification

    Significance

the presidential and congressional elections of 1964

    Identification

    Significance

the Medicare program

> Identification

> Significance

the Elementary and Secondary Education Act

> Identification

> Significance

the Voting Rights Act of 1965

> Identification

> Significance

the Civil Rights Act of 1968

> Identification

> Significance

the Indian bill of Rights

> Identification

> Significance

the War on Poverty

> Identification

> Significance

© 1994 Houghton Mifflin Company. All rights reserved.

Earl Warren

    Identification

    Significance

Baker v. *Carr*

    Identification

    Significance

the Supreme Court's school-prayer decision

    Identification

    Significance

Griswold v. *Connecticut*

    Identification

    Significance

Jones v. *Mayer*

    Identification

    Significance

Gideon v. *Wainwright*, *Escobedo* v. *Illinois*, and *Miranda* v. *Arizona*

    Identification

    Significance

© 1994 Houghton Mifflin Company. All rights reserved.

the Mississippi Summer Project of 1964

    Identification

    Significance

J. Edgar Hoover

    Identification

    Significance

the Mississippi Freedom Democratic party

    Identification

    Significance

race riots of 1964

    Identification

    Significance

Aid to Families with Dependent Children

    Identification

    Significance

Watts race riot

    Identification

    Significance

Malcolm X

    Identification

    Significance

the Black Muslims

    Identification

    Significance

Stokely Carmichael

    Identification

    Significance

black nationalism

    Identification

    Significance

the Black Panther party

    Identification

    Significance

the Free Speech Movement

    Identification

    Significance

The Uses of the University

    Identification

    Significance

the SDS

    Identification

    Significance

the Port Huron Statement

    Identification

    Significance

the New Left

    Identification

    Significance

the counterculture

    Identification

    Significance

Timothy Leary

    Identification

    Significance

the Beatles

    Identification

    Significance

Bob Dylan, Jimi Hendrix, and Janis Joplin

    Identification

    Significance

Woodstock

    Identification

    Significance

hippies

    Identification

    Significance

the birth-control pill

    Identification

    Significance

Stonewall Inn riot

    Identification

    Significance

antiwar protests

>Identification

>Significance

the *U.S.S. Pueblo*

>Identification

>Significance

the assassination of Martin Luther King

>Identification

>Significance

the assassination of Robert Kennedy

>Identification

>Significance

the 1968 Democratic convention

>Identification

>Significance

the presidential and congressional elections of 1968

>Identification

>Significance

George C. Wallace

    Identification

    Significance

The Feminine Mystique

    Identification

    Significance

American Women

    Identification

    Significance

the National Organization for Women (NOW)

    Identification

    Significance

radical feminism

    Identification

    Significance

occupational segregation

    Identification

    Significance

Title IX of the Educational Amendments of 1972

    Identification

    Significance

the Equal Rights Amendment

    Identification

    Significance

Roe v. *Wade*

    Identification

    Significance

Reed v. *Reed* and *Frontiero* v. *Richardson*

    Identification

    Significance

Kent State and Jackson State

    Identification

    Significance

"Fortress America"

    Identification

    Significance

© 1994 Houghton Mifflin Company. All rights reserved.

the Attica prison revolt

    Identification

    Significance

stagflation

    Identification

    Significance

wage, price, and rent controls

    Identification

    Significance

the Twenty-sixth Amendment

    Identification

    Significance

the modern environmental movement

    Identification

    Significance

revenue sharing

    Identification

    Significance

the Family Assistance Plan

    Identification

    Significance

Nixon's "southern strategy"

    Identification

    Significance

Warren Burger

    Identification

    Significance

Swann v. *Charlotte-Mecklenburg*

    Identification

    Significance

the presidential and congressional elections of 1972

    Identification

    Significance

George McGovern

    Identification

    Significance

the Watergate scandal

> Identification

> Significance

CREEP and the Plumbers

> Identification

> Significance

John W. Dean III

> Identification

> Significance

the White House tapes

> Identification

> Significance

the Saturday Night Massacre

> Identification

> Significance

Spiro Agnew

> Identification

> Significance

Gerald R. Ford

    Identification

    Significance

Carl Bernstein and Bob Woodward

    Identification

    Significance

U.S. v. Nixon

    Identification

    Significance

the impeachment hearings of the House Judiciary Committee

    Identification

    Significance

the pardon of Richard Nixon

    Identification

    Significance

the imperial presidency

    Identification

    Significance

the War Powers Act

Identification

Significance

Evaluating and Using Information

Exercise A

This crossword puzzle tests how familiar you are with the specifics of the turbulent Sixties and Seventies—names, organizations, and issues. See how many answers you can get without looking them up.

When you finish, turn to the answers section of the Study Guide to see how well you did.

Puzzle answers may be any part of speech, including proper nouns, and may be more than one word (or name) long. Each clue number also identifies the box where the first letter of the answer belongs. Fill boxes downward one letter per box to respond to a "down" clue and from left to right to respond to an "across" clue.

Across

2. A principal in the 1962 court case in which the "one person, one vote" principle calling for widespread reapportionment of state legislatures was enunciated.
6. Director of the FBI who spread charges concerning Martin Luther King's sexual activities and bugged his hotel rooms, and who is said to have broken up a Nixon scheme to use illegal means to investigate people seen as possible "internal threats."
7. SNCC chairman who urged African-Americans to take control of their own businesses, political voice, and institutions—in other words, to exert Black Power.
12. Last name of the assassin of Martin Luther King, Jr.
13. Author of *The Feminine Mystique,* a book that expressed the dissatisfaction of American women with the role assigned to them in the American dream.
14. Murdered director of the Mississippi NAACP.
15. Black Muslim who advocated black pride, separation from white society, and the use of violence in self-defense and who was murdered in February 1965 for having softened his views.
17. Reform organization founded to encourage governmental enforcement of gender equality provisions of the Civil Rights Act of 1965 (acronym).
19. Proposed change in the Constitution, supported by feminist groups, that Congress approved and sent to the states for ratification in 1972.
20. Building that gave its name to a secret Defense Department report that the *New York Times* obtained and published in June 1971.
22. A principal in the 1966 case in which the Supreme Court ruled that the police are responsible for telling suspects what their rights are.
25. Number of women appointed to positions in the Kennedy administration.
26. What Martin Luther King told the 1963 March on Washington crowd at the Lincoln Memorial.
28. Loose, unofficial combination of all sorts of social protesters who were agreed in their opposition to racism and the Vietnam war but not necessarily in their acceptance of violence or negotiation as appropriate tools of protest.
30. Gay bar in New York's Greenwich Village that was the site of a police raid and riot that marked the beginning of the gay liberation movement.
31. Ohio university where on May 4, 1970, four students protesting American extension of the Vietnam war into neutral Cambodia were shot by national guardsmen.

Down

1. A New Deal liberal whose long association with the cause of civil rights for African-Americans and whose party's association with it cost him votes in the 1968 presidential election.
2. Armed black nationalist group whose aim to destroy capitalism met with some sympathy among young antiestablishment whites.
3. African-American civil-rights group known especially for organizing the "Freedom Riders" to promote the desegregation of interstate transportation.
4. The _____ Commission, the investigative panel that in 1968 pointed to white racism as the cause of summer race riots of the early- and mid-1960s.
5. Court case principal who is to the suspect's right to have a lawyer present during questioning what Miranda is to the suspect's right to be informed of his or her rights to see a lawyer and to remain silent.

© 1994 Houghton Mifflin Company. All rights reserved.

8. Chief Justice of the Supreme Court, called the "midwife" to the great social changes the United States experienced in the 1960s.
9. The kind of discrimination the Supreme Court ruled against in *Frontiero* v. *Richardson* and *Reed* v. *Reed*.
10. Initials used to refer to University of California student resistance to the impersonal atmosphere of huge college campuses and to university curbs on student political involvement.
11. Initials of the organization that directed Martin Luther King, Jr.'s nonviolent, civil disobedience protest strategy.
16. First African-American student to attend University of Mississippi.
18. Leader of the "free speech" movement started by University of California students frustrated by the university's impersonal bureaucracy and its attempts to control student political activity.
21. Attorney General whose contribution to Nixon's southern strategy was to try to slow African-American advances in school desegregation and participation in elections.
23. Organization of students whose primarily white middle-class members issued the Port Huron (Michigan) Statement.
24. Last name of the segregationist Alabama governor who made a numerically respectable run for the presidency as the candidate of the American Independent party in 1968 and was shot in the midst of making another run in 1972.
27. Los Angeles neighborhood gutted in August 1965 by blacks rioting in frustration over lack of jobs and opportunities.
29. Organization of southern African Americans that worked hard to get Mississippi and Georgia African-Americans registered to vote.

Exercise B

Using concrete details from the clues and answers for Exercise A and similar details from Chapter 32 that they suggest, plan a short essay answering this "thought" question:

What do the 1960s and early 1970s suggest about the impact of the activism of private citizens?

The table on pages 437–438 should help you identify suitable information on which to base your response and to organize your essay. Enter the working draft of your essay in your Reader's Notebook.

Activism of the Turbulent Era, 1961–1974

Activist Organizations	Key Leaders	Cause or Purpose	Techniques for Encouraging Change	Cost (Sacrifices)	Success in Producing Change	Conclusion

Activism of the Turbulent Era, 1961–1974

Activist Organizations	Key Leaders	Cause or Purpose	Techniques for Encouraging Change	Cost (Sacrifices)	Success in Producing Change	Conclusion

Ideas and Details

Objectives 1, 2, 3, and 6

_____ 1. Passage of the Civil Rights Act of 1964 was in large part due to
   a. the work of the Freedom Riders.
   b. Kennedy's ability to push legislation through Congress.
   c. two tragedies: murder by terrorist bombing at a black church in Birmingham, Alabama, and Kennedy's assassination.
   d. mobilization of nationwide support by the Student Nonviolent Coordinating Committee.

Objective 3

_____ 2. The 1965 Elementary and Secondary Education Act
   a. provided separate classes and increased funding for the teaching of the academically gifted.
   b. was the first general program of federal aid to education.
   c. required federal certification of all public school teachers.
   d. established a job placement service at the federal level for public school teachers in the United States.

Objectives 3 and 6

_____ 3. As a result of the Voting Rights Act of 1965,
   a. the right to vote was extended to eighteen-year-olds.
   b. the number of registered voters in the South dramatically increased.
   c. literacy tests were required of all voters in federal elections.
   d. eligible voters were legally required to register through federal registrars.

Objective 5

_____ 4. In the Supreme Court's 1962 ruling concerning school prayer, the Court held that
   a. public schools could require nondenominational prayer at the beginning of each school day.
   b. God had no place in the public schools of the United States.
   c. required prayers in public schools were unconstitutional.
   d. there could be no prayers in public schools.

Objective 5

_____ 5. Cases such as *Gideon* v. *Wainwright* and *Miranda* v. *Arizona* were controversial because they
   a. broadened the definition of religion.
   b. reinforced and expanded freedom of expression.
   c. transformed the criminal justice system by protecting the rights of criminal suspects.
   d. affected people's personal lives by dealing with sexual issues.

Objective 6

____ 6. The urban race riots of the 1960s and the emergence of black nationalism in the voices of Malcolm X and Stokely Carmichael were the result of
   a. the deterioration of the social and economic conditions of many northern blacks.
   b. communist infiltration of civil rights groups.
   c. denial of the right to vote to northern blacks.
   d. a shift in the tactics of the SCLC from passive resistance to violent confrontation.

Objective 7

____ 7. The counterculture differed from the New Left in which of the following ways?
   a. The counterculture completely condemned the use of drugs.
   b. The counterculture was more realistic in its goals than the New Left.
   c. The counterculture used music to attack the status quo.
   d. The counterculture was more supportive of the Vietnam War.

Objective 8

____ 8. The Stonewall riot
   a. marked the beginning of the gay rights movement.
   b. occurred in Atlantic City when radical feminists disrupted the 1968 Miss America contest.
   c. was the result of overreaction by the Chicago police to street demonstrations at the Democratic national convention.
   d. was an expression of black rage over the assassination of Martin Luther King.

Objectives 9 and 10

____ 9. The 1968 Democratic presidential candidate killed by an assassin's bullet was
   a. George Wallace.
   b. Robert Kennedy.
   c. Eugene McCarthy.
   d. Edmund Muskie.

Objective 11

____ 10. In the late 1960s, radical feminists differed from the members of the National Organization for Women in which of the following ways?
   a. Radical feminists opposed the gay rights movement.
   b. Radical feminists were concerned with political issues, not social and economic issues.
   c. The radical feminist movement repudiated the work of Betty Friedan.
   d. Radical feminists turned to the tactic of direct action to accomplish their goals.

Objective 12

_____ 11. In an effort to help Republican candidates in the 1970 congressional elections, the Nixon administration
   a. advocated the passage of a national health insurance program.
   b. pledged an immediate end to the Vietnam War.
   c. announced the imposition of wage and price controls.
   d. tried to associate the Democratic party with radicalism and violence.

Objective 13

_____ 12. Nixon's 1972 victory was in large part due to
   a. the campaign proposals of his opponent, George McGovern.
   b. his support for extension of the Voting Rights Act of 1966, which gained him the black vote.
   c. public support for his economic policies, which had reduced the federal deficit and lowered inflation.
   d. his support for environmental protection legislation.

Objective 14

_____ 13. Which of the following authorized the payment of hush money to E. Howard Hunt to prevent disclosures concerning the break-in at Democratic headquarters?
   a. James McCord
   b. John Mitchell
   c. Richard Nixon
   d. John Ehrlichman

Objectives 14 and 15

_____ 14. As a result of its impeachment hearings, the House Judiciary Committee
   a. voted in favor of President Nixon's impeachment on three of five counts.
   b. declared President Nixon to be guilty of tax fraud.
   c. chose to make no recommendation concerning the impeachment of the president.
   d. declared President Nixon to be innocent of all charges of wrongdoing.

Objectives 14 and 15

_____ 15. The War Powers Act required the president to
   a. consult with Congress "in every possible instance" before sending American troops into foreign wars.
   b. withdraw troops from any foreign assignment after ten days unless Congress specifically authorized otherwise.
   c. get approval from Congress before sending American troops to foreign territory.
   d. get a declaration of war from Congress before sending American soldiers into a foreign war.

Essay Questions

Objective 6

1. Explain the transformation of the civil rights movement in the mid-1960s and the impact of this transformation on blacks and on American society.

Objective 3

2. Discuss the successes and failures of the War on Poverty.

Objectives 3, 4, 5, and 6

3. Explain the erosion of the liberal consensus in the years after 1964.

Objective 7

4. Explain the similarities and differences between the New Left and the counterculture.

Objectives 10, 12, and 13

5. Explain the political strategy of Richard Nixon and the Republican party in the 1968, 1970, and 1972 elections.

Objective 11

6. Explain the emergence of radical feminism, and discuss its impact on American society in the late 1960s and early 1970s.

Objectives 14 and 15

7. Discuss the Watergate scandal as a constitutional crisis, examine President Richard Nixon's role in the scandal, and explain the House Judiciary Committee's decision concerning the articles of impeachment against the President.

CHAPTER 33
A Turn to the Right, 1974–1989

Learning Objectives

After you have studied Chapter 33 in your textbook and worked through this study guide chapter, you should be able to:

1. Discuss the causes, characteristics, and consequences of the economic and energy crises of the 1970s, and explain and evaluate the attempts by the Nixon, Ford, and Carter administrations to deal with these crises.
2. Examine the issues and personalities and explain the outcome of the 1976 presidential election.
3. Discuss Jimmy Carter's personal and political background; examine the domestic issues and political problems that faced the Carter administration; and explain and evaluate the administration's actions concerning those issues and problems.
4. Examine the emergence, characteristics, goals, and accomplishments of the new conservative coalition, and discuss the impact of this coalition on the election of 1980.
5. Discuss Ronald Reagan's personal and political background, and explain his political, social, and economic views.
6. Examine the issues and personalities and explain the outcome of the 1980 congressional and presidential elections.
7. Examine Ronald Reagan's economic policies in relation to federal spending, federal income taxes, and federal environmental, health, and safety regulations; explain Congress's reaction to these policies; and assess the impact of these policies on the United States.
8. Discuss the causes and consequences of the 1981–1983 economic recession.
9. Identify the groups that opposed the policies and actions of the Reagan administration, and explain the reasons for their opposition.
10. Examine the issues and personalities and explain the outcome of the 1984 presidential election.
11. Examine the domestic economic challenges that faced the Reagan administration during its second term; explain Reagan's actions concerning those challenges; and discuss the consequences of those actions.
12. Discuss the problems that nonwhites, immigrants, and women faced in American society during the 1970s and 1980s; explain their approaches to those problems; and discuss the extent to which they were successful in achieving their goals.
13. Discuss the emergence, characteristics, and goals of the antifeminist and antiabortion movements, and discuss their impact on American society during the 1970s and 1980s.
14. Examine the forces that caused increased polarization of American society during the 1980s.

© 1994 Houghton Mifflin Company. All rights reserved.

15. Examine the reasons for, the extent of, and the effects of poverty in America during the 1970s and 1980s, and discuss the characteristics of the poor.
16. Discuss the drug epidemic and the AIDS epidemic; explain their impact on the American people and American society; and assess the government's response to the threats posed by these epidemics.
17. Explain the reaction of the American people to the Iran-contra scandal and hearings; discuss the revelations concerning Reagan's management style; and examine the scandal's impact on President Reagan's ability to govern.
18. Discuss the political problems faced by Ronald Reagan during his last two years in office.
19. Examine the issues and personalities and explain the outcome of the 1988 presidential election.

Thematic Guide

The nation's disillusionment with its government—disillusionment produced by the crises of the 1960s and early 1970s—intensified further when governmental leaders could not deal successfully with the disruptive economic forces of the 1970s. In "The Energy Crisis and the End of the Postwar Economic Boom," we examine the nature of the economic crisis and its causes. This section also covers Nixon's and Ford's responses to the economic and energy crises, the nuclear power debate, and the fiscal crisis experienced by some of the nation's cities.

An apathetic electorate elected Jimmy Carter to the presidency in the 1976 election. Although Carter did score some notable domestic accomplishments, his unwillingness to compromise alienated congressional representatives of both parties, and his fiscal conservatism put him at odds with the liberal wing of the Democratic party. In addition, Carter was plagued by political and economic forces beyond his control; his popularity declined dramatically, and he became politically impotent.

As the American people became more deeply troubled and frightened by changes and forces over which they and their government seemed to have little control, they became more distrustful of government and of those groups that continued to advocate change within society. This conservative mood was buttressed by the uniting of conservative politicians of the "old right" with evangelical Christians of the "new right." The channeling of these forces into a new conservative coalition, plus a distrust of government born of a decade of chaos produced America's "turn to the right" in 1980 and led to Ronald Reagan's victory in the presidential election of that year.

With widespread support from the American people, President Ronald Reagan, the standard-bearer of a new conservative coalition and a strong advocate of supply-side economic theory, persuaded Congress to enact two major aspects of his conservative agenda: (1) deep spending cuts in social and health programs and (2) a five-year, $750 billion tax cut that primarily benefited the wealthy. In addition, out of the belief that government regulations reduced business profits and slowed economic growth, the Reagan administration launched an attack against federal environmental, health, and safety regulations.

Although inflation and interest rates declined during Reagan's first two years in office, these successes resulted from the Federal Reserve Board's policies, a decline in oil prices, which had a ripple effect throughout the economy, and a massive recession lasting from mid-1981 to late 1983. The recession affected both industrial and agricultural workers; and, in spite of an economic recovery that began in 1984, poverty increased to pre-Great Society levels. The one group that did not experience increased poverty levels was the elderly, a group that had more political power than ever before. Although Reagan promised to maintain a "safety net" for the most needy in American society, when faced with a mounting federal deficit, he reduced welfare and social programs, maintained his tax cuts, and increased defense spending for a major military build-up. Using these issues to their advantage, the Democrats picked up twenty-six seats in the House of Representative in the 1982 congressional elections but were unable to take control of the Senate.

However, issues that ordinarily would have posed severe political liabilities for an incumbent during a presidential election year had little impact on the voters' perceptions of President Reagan. Although in many cases the voters disagreed with the president's policies, they liked Reagan personally and seldom seemed to hold him responsible for the failures of his administration. These and other factors led to Reagan's landslide victory over his Democratic opponent in the 1984 presidential election. Despite the "feel-good" campaign conducted by Reagan in 1984, once re-elected he and Congress were forced to grapple with the economic problems posed by the spiraling federal deficit. Reagan also began to make his mark on the Supreme Court and oversaw enactment of a sweeping tax reform bill in 1986.

From this discussion of the attempts by successive administrations to deal with the nation's domestic problems during the 1970s and 1980s, the focus of the chapter shifts to an analysis of the impact of the economic and energy crises on various groups in American society. The increase in poverty accompanying the stagnant economy of the 1970s and the recession of the early 1980s occurred most often among nonwhites, children, and female heads of households. Although many Americans accepted traditional beliefs that blamed the victims of poverty for their distress, economic reality meant that occupational opportunities, especially for unskilled workers, were severely limited.

While poor unskilled blacks languished in poverty, the black middle class expanded. In spite of increased opportunities for some blacks, the resurgence of white racism, the problems encountered by Indians, and the struggle of Hispanics and other immigrants make clear that the divisive elements long present in pluralistic America were worsened by the political, social, and economic crises of the 1970s and 1980s.

Divisiveness also continued in the form of sexism. Although women had made gains in American society, they still faced barriers. In "Women and Children Last," the authors discuss the emergence, characteristics, and aims of the antifeminist forces that gained strength in the 1970s. Although, according to feminist scholar Barbara Ehrenreich, the appeal of the *Playboy* lifestyle was a major factor in the soaring divorce rate of the 1960s and 1970s, most antifeminists blamed the revolt against marriage on feminists. Arguing in favor of "traditional" American values in the midst of a rapidly changing society, antifeminists successfully stalled ratification of the Equal Rights Amendment and began to campaign actively against legalized abortion. The recession also affected women adversely. Occupational segregation continued, and many women found themselves caught in "the Superwoman Squeeze."

As the United States moved toward the presidential election of 1988, the domestic problems it faced continued to mount. The 1980s brought increased polarization and tension within pluralistic America. As the gap widened between rich and poor, a variety of factors increased the severity of poverty. Nonwhite minorities, immigrants, and women continued to face the discrimination accompanying racism, nativism, and sexism. The crack epidemic and the AIDS epidemic continued to plague, and divide, the American people. Within the context of these problems, the authors discuss the decline of Reagan's ability to lead during his last two years in office, the presidential and congressional elections of 1988, and the challenges facing President George Bush and the American people in the 1990s.

Building Vocabulary

Listed below are important words and terms that you need to know to get the most out of Chapter 33. They are listed in the order in which they occur in the chapter. After carefully looking through the list, refer to a dictionary and jot down the definition of words that you do not know or of which you are unsure.

symmetry

auspicious

flounder (*verb*)

fetter

lambaste

polarize

exacerbate

bequeath

grapple

reverberate

tenet

scapegoat

doldrums

credence

gibe

pragmatic

formidable

facet

epitaph

renege

genial

espouse

chastise

sully

bilingual

augur

jettison

pathology

disparity

burgeon

pernicious

concomitant

intravenous

promiscuous

monogamy

inane

insolvent

Identification and Significance

After studying Chapter 33 of *A People and a Nation,* you should be able to identify fully *and* explain the historical significance of each item listed below.

1. Identify each item in the space provided. Give an explanation or description of the item. Answer the questions *who, what, where,* and *when.*
2. Explain the historical significance of each item in the space provided. Establish the historical context in which the item exists. Establish the item as the result of or as the cause of other factors existing in the society under study. Answer this question: *what were the political, social, economic, and/or cultural consequences of this item?*

the Teflon-coated presidency

    Identification

    Significance

OPEC price increases of 1973

    Identification

    Significance

recession in the auto industry

    Identification

    Significance

neo-Keynesianism

    Identification

    Significance

© 1994 Houghton Mifflin Company. All rights reserved.

deindustrialization

> Identification
>
> Significance

annual productivity growth, 1966–1980

> Identification
>
> Significance

easy credit

> Identification
>
> Significance

WIN (Whip Inflation Now)

> Identification
>
> Significance

the 1974 congressional elections

> Identification
>
> Significance

monetarists

> Identification
>
> Significance

© 1994 Houghton Mifflin Company. All rights reserved.

the nuclear power debate

    Identification

    Significance

Brown's Ferry and Three Mile Island

    Identification

    Significance

the New York City financial crisis

    Identification

    Significance

the 1976 presidential election

    Identification

    Significance

the environmental "superfund"

    Identification

    Significance

the Chrysler bail-out

    Identification

    Significance

lobbyists from corporations and special interest groups

> Identification

> Significance

the Federal Reserve Board's policies, 1979–1980

> Identification

> Significance

the 1980 federal census

> Identification

> Significance

population shift to the Sunbelt

> Identification

> Significance

Proposition 13

> Identification

> Significance

the Moral Majority

> Identification

> Significance

Ronald Reagan

    Identification

    Significance

the 1980 congressional and presidential elections

    Identification

    Significance

Reaganomics

    Identification

    Significance

supply-side economics

    Identification

    Significance

the 1981 tax cuts

    Identification

    Significance

Reagan's policies toward regulatory agencies

    Identification

    Significance

the Federal Reserve Board's policies, 1981

>Identification

>Significance

the recession of the early 1980s

>Identification

>Significance

the "safety net" for the "truly needy"

>Identification

>Significance

John W. Hinkley, Jr.

>Identification

>Significance

the 1982 congressional elections

>Identification

>Significance

organized labor in the 1980s

>Identification

>Significance

Rita Lavelle

    Identification

    Significance

Walter Mondale

    Identification

    Significance

Geraldine Ferraro

    Identification

    Significance

the 1984 presidential election

    Identification

    Significance

the federal deficit

    Identification

    Significance

the Gramm-Rudman bill

    Identification

    Significance

William Rehnquist and Antonin Scalia

    Identification

    Significance

the Tax Reform Act of 1986

    Identification

    Significance

the 1981 Children's Defense Fund survey concerning black children

    Identification

    Significance

the black middle class in the 1980s

    Identification

    Significance

white backlash

    Identification

    Significance

Bakke v. *University of California,* *Richmond* v. *Croson,* and *Martin* v. *Wilks*

    Identification

    Significance

the Miami and Chattanooga race riots of 1980

    Identification

    Significance

Sandra Day O'Connor

    Identification

    Significance

the Indian seizure of Alcatraz Island

    Identification

    Significance

the seizure of the Pine Ridge Reservation trading post

    Identification

    Significance

the dual status of Indians

    Identification

    Significance

the Indian Claims Commission

    Identification

    Significance

Latino immigrants

    Identification

    Significance

"brown power"

    Identification

    Significance

the "new immigrants" of the 1970s and 1980s

    Identification

    Significance

the Immigration Reform and Control (Simpson-Rodino) Act

    Identification

    Significance

the Equal Credit Opportunity Act

    Identification

    Significance

the antifeminist ("profamily") movement

    Identification

    Significance

© 1994 Houghton Mifflin Company. All rights reserved.

Barbara Ehrenreich

    Identification

    Significance

the Equal Rights Amendment

    Identification

    Significance

the anti-abortion ("prolife") movement

    Identification

    Significance

the Hyde Amendment

    Identification

    Significance

the gender gap

    Identification

    Significance

the comparable-worth issue

    Identification

    Significance

"the Superwoman Squeeze"

    Identification

    Significance

"the working poor"

    Identification

    Significance

the homeless

    Identification

    Significance

the "crack" epidemic

    Identification

    Significance

the AIDS epidemic

    Identification

    Significance

"Safe Sex" campaigns

    Identification

    Significance

© 1994 Houghton Mifflin Company. All rights reserved.

Dr. C. Everett Koop

    Identification

    Significance

Robert Bork

    Identification

    Significance

the 1987 stock market crash

    Identification

    Significance

George Bush

    Identification

    Significance

Michael Dukakis

    Identification

    Significance

Jesse Jackson

    Identification

    Significance

the 1988 presidential election

Identification

Significance

Evaluating and Using Information

Exercise A

This crossword puzzle tests how many of the names, organizations, and issues that made the headlines in the 1970s and 1980s you recall. See how many answers you can get without looking them up. When you finish, turn to the answers section of this Study Guide to see how well you did.

Puzzle answers may be any part of speech, including proper nouns, and may be more than one word (or name) long and several may be hyphenated. (However, hyphens and spaces are ignored in the puzzle.) Each clue number also identifies the box where the first letter of the answer belongs. Fill boxes downward one letter per box to respond to a "down" clue and from left to right to respond to an "across" clue.

Across

1. An economic policy—sometimes referred to as "trickle-down economics"—calling for tax cuts for businesses with the expectation that they will put the money they no longer have to pay in taxes into capital investments.
3. Last name of an antifeminist leader of the successful campaign to prevent ratification of the Equal Rights Amendment.
4. Feminist movement concept that two jobs requiring about the same level of training and skill and involving about the same amount of responsibility deserve equal pay even if one is held by a man and the other by a woman.
8. The _____ amendment, a legislative amendment deleting abortions from the list of medical procedures covered by Medicare.
9. Air traffic controllers union that insisted on striking in 1981 and did not survive after President Reagan clipped its wings.
13. Simultaneous recession and rising unemployment.
14. The one group among those traditionally having large numbers falling below the poverty level that did not see an increase in the number of its members counted among the nation's poor at the end of the Reagan years.
15. Militant Indian group that took hostages at the site of an 1890 massacre of Sioux Indians to push and dramatize its demands that the United States government live up to its treaty obligations (acronym).
16. Politically conservative section of the country that attracted many of the jobless from the Frostbelt in the 1970s and 1980s.
18. People who hold jobs but do not get paid enough to keep them above the poverty level.
22. Legislation passed in 1986 designed to cut down on the number of illegal aliens entering the country but that did not work.
23. Scandal over the Reagan administration's passing on of profits from secret sales of weapons to Iran to the contras in Nicaragua so the latter could buy weapons during a period in which Congress had banned all military aid to the contras.
24. Last name of the leader of the United Farm Workers, the first Hispanic interest group to be well known across the country.
25. The national debt, an astronomical problem contributed to the most in the 1980s by the administration of the president who complained about it the loudest.
26. Last name of Reagan's conservative surgeon general who surprised the nation by overseeing a massive mailing of a booklet on AIDS in 1988.

Down

2. Special interest groups that so multiplied in the 1970s that by the 1980s they gave President Carter fits and led him to complain that the nation had been "Balkanized."
3. An expression first widely used in 1984 referring to the effect scandals might have on the outcome of an election.
5. A major health problem with emotional and political overtones because its early outbreaks were confined mainly to gays and drug users.
6. Pennsylvania power plant site of a 1979 nuclear accident.

7. Last name of the first woman appointed to the Supreme Court, a Reagan appointee.
10. Last name of a white man whose "reverse discrimination" suit against the University of California led the Supreme Court to outlaw admissions quotas in 1978.
11. Last name of the first African-American to win widespread support in a presidential election, forger of the "Rainbow Coalition."
12. Legislation passed in 1985 that called for a balanced budget by 1991.
17. Last name of the conservative named by President Reagan to be chief justice of the Supreme Court.
19. The "_____ Majority," that political-religious group of Americans to which the evangelist Jerry Falwell says he belongs.
20. A euphemism for "antiabortion."
21. Last name of the first woman nominated by a major political party (the Democrats) as its candidate for the vice presidency of the United States.
22. Last name of one of three Reagan appointees who made it to the Supreme Court.

Exercise B

1. In the reference section of your college library, look up the term *conservative* in the *Oxford English Dictionary* and in two general, recent American dictionaries, such as the *American Heritage Dictionary* and *Webster's Collegiate Dictionary*. As you read the definitions in these dictionaries, concentrate on those that apply to politics, but note other meanings, too. Take notes on what you find. Then study the statements printed below. Write *Yes* in the blanks preceding statements that can be inferred logically from the definitions and *No* in the other blanks.

   _____ a. Conservatives prefer sticking with traditional methods and policies.

   _____ b. In the United States, conservatism is almost synonymous with *Democrat*.

   _____ c. In the United States almost all conservatives belong to the same political party.

2. Study the following collections of information from several chapters in your textbook and then the statements printed beneath it. Write *Yes* in the blanks preceding statements that can be inferred logically from the information and *No* in the other blanks.

   - Conservative critics of globalism . . . suggested that America should reduce its overseas commitments. . . .
   - In 1954 the Communist Control Act demonstrated that both liberals and conservatives shared the consensus of anticommunism. In effect making membership in the Communist party illegal, the measure passed the Senate unanimously and the House 265 to 2. . . .
   - Reagan and the conservatives he selected to advise him believed that a malevolent Soviet Union was the source of the world's troubles.

   _____ a. Conservatives reject the Monroe Doctrine.

   _____ b. In the 1950s, conservatives opposed the spread of communism.

   _____ c. Conservatives are particularly distrustful of the Russians.

3. Study the following collection of information from several chapters in your textbook and then the statements printed beneath it. Write *Yes* in the blanks preceding statements that can be inferred logically from the information and *No* in the other blanks.

   - Truman had continued to be loyal to the welfare state fashioned in the 1930s. . . .

- Members of the Eightieth Congress . . . were committed conservatives. . . [who] perceived the Republican landslide in 1948 as a mandate to reverse the New Deal to curb the power of government and labor. . . .
- As a Democratic politician, John F. Kennedy inherited the New Deal commitment to the welfare state. He generally cast liberal votes in line with the prolabor sentiments of his low-income, blue-collar constituents. . . .
- By August 1961, eight months into his first year, it was evident that Kennedy lacked the ability to move Congress, which was largely ruled by a conservative coalition of Republicans and southern Democrats. . . .
- Jimmy Carter's conservative policies alienated Democrats who had grown up in the party's New Deal liberal tradition. His support of deregulation and his oppositon to wage and price controls and gasoline rationing ran counter to the liberal Democratic position.
- Seeing inflation as more of a threat to the nation's health than either recession or unemployment, Carter announced that his top priority would be to cut federal spending even though doing so would add to the jobless rolls. . . .
- In 1978 California voters approved a tax-cutting referendum called Proposition 13, which reduced property taxes and put stringent limits on state spending for social programs. On the national level conservatives lobbied for a constitutional amendment to prohibit federal budget deficits . . . .
- By 1980, the number of retired persons had increased by more than 50 percent since 1972. The census figures meant that the American population was becoming more conservative.

_____ a. Conservatives tend to give low priority to balancing the federal budget.

_____ b. Conservatism implies support for a powerful federal government.

_____ c. Conservatives are wary of welfare programs.

_____ d. American conservatism generally implies sympathy for the labor movement and labor positions.

_____ e. In the United States in recent years, conservatism is associated with the Republican Party.

_____ f. Conservatives typically do not press for tax cuts.

_____ g. Conservatives are more concerned about inflation than about unemployment.

Exercise C

Organize and compose a working draft of an essay in response to this question:

> How was the conservatism of the Reagan years simply traditonal American conservatism and how did it add to or change the traditional meaning of *American conservatism*?

Include plenty of details like those you find among the clues and answers for Exercise A and similar additional details from Chapter 33 to make your essay concrete and specific.
Enter the working draft of your essay in your Reader's Notebook.

Ideas and Details

Objective 1

_____ 1. As a result of the dramatic increase in energy prices in the early 1970s,
   a. the United States faced double-digit inflation in 1974.
   b. multinational oil companies prospered.
   c. automobile and related industries suffered a lingering recession.
   d. all of the above were true.

Objective 1

_____ 2. As a result of the slowing of growth in productivity during the 1970s,
   a. workers realized they could no longer expect the wage increases they had enjoyed during the 1960s.
   b. interest rates declined.
   c. American products became less competitive in the marketplace.
   d. business investments increased.

Objective 3

_____ 3. Which of the following created difficulties for the Carter administration?
   a. Carter alienated members of his own party as a result of his stand on deregulation of certain industries.
   b. The decrease in the number of political action committees made it difficult for Carter to raise campaign funds.
   c. Carter was not prepared to deal with the increase in the power of the president relative to the power of Congress.
   d. Carter's veto of legislation to impose a windfall-profits tax on the oil companies alienated the Republican-controlled Congress.

Objectives 4 and 6

_____ 4. The passage of Proposition 13 and the emergence of a powerful political network consisting of evangelical Christians and members of the Hoover Institute indicate that
   a. conservatism was the dominant political mood in the late 1970s.
   b. there was a resurgence of political power in the frostbelt in the late 1970s.
   c. economic issues dominated the political scene in the late 1970s.
   d. Americans were no longer concerned with the threat of Communist expansion.

Objective 5

_____ 5. As governor of California, Ronald Reagan
   a. dismantled the state's welfare system.
   b. signed one of the nation's most liberal abortion laws.
   c. proposed the legalization of marijuana.
   d. instituted a statewide healthcare program.

© 1994 Houghton Mifflin Company. All rights reserved.

Objective 7

_____ 6. Which of the following benefited the most from the 1981 tax reductions?
   a. The poor
   b. The wealthy
   c. The middle class
   d. Married couples

Objectives 7 and 8

_____ 7. A major reason for the dramatic decline in inflation from 1980 to 1982 was
   a. increasing productivity among American workers.
   b. the deepening recession during that period.
   c. increased spending by Americans.
   d. the rise in GNP from increased investment spending.

Objectives 7 and 9

_____ 8. President Reagan's appointees to the National Labor Relations Board
   a. actively encouraged companies to declare bankruptcy as a way of canceling union contracts.
   b. questioned the right of union members to strike.
   c. consistently voted in favor of management.
   d. campaigned in favor of the closed shop.

Objectives 7, 8, 10, and 11

_____ 9. An issue of growing public concern throughout the Reagan presidency concerned
   a. the nation's weakening defense posture.
   b. Reagan's opposition to abortion.
   c. the federal deficit.
   d. America's lack of influence over Israel.

Objectives 8 and 12

_____ 10. As a result of changes in the job market in the 1980s,
   a. occupational segregation by sex slowly disappeared.
   b. the number of blue-collar jobs increased dramatically.
   c. the unskilled and poorly educated found it increasingly difficult to find work.
   d. organized labor became more interested in unskilled laborers.

Objective 12

_____ 11. Which of the following was true of black Americans during the 1970s and 1980s?
   a. The number of blacks attending college decreased during the decade.
   b. The gap between poor blacks and middle-class blacks increased.
   c. The number of black families with a female head of household decreased.
   d. Increasing numbers of blacks fell out of the middle class into the ranks of the poor.

Objectives 9, 12, and 14

_____ 12. Black civil rights leaders denounced the Reagan administration because it
   a. encouraged local school districts to defy court-ordered busing.
   b. stood against renewing intact the Voting Rights Act of 1965.
   c. sought repeal of fair-housing laws.
   d. secured the passage of legislation outlawing affirmative action.

Objectives 4 and 13

_____ 13. Antifeminist forces were able to prevent ratification of the Equal Rights Amendment by
   a. successfully organizing a nationwide strike of working women.
   b. persuading the Senate to rescind its approval of the amendment.
   c. publishing a study that proved gender-based discrimination to be nonexistent in the United States.
   d. frightening people with false claims about what would happen if it were ratified.

Objective 16

_____ 14. The growth of the crack epidemic of the 1980s was especially alarming among
   a. the elderly.
   b. transportation workers.
   c. young women.
   d. Mexican immigrants.

Objective 17

_____ 15. Evidence presented in the Iran-contra hearings indicated that President Reagan
   a. clearly instructed his national security aid Robert McFarlane not to sell arms to Iran.
   b. had full knowledge of the diversion of profits from the sale of arms to Iran to the contras in Nicaragua.
   c. respected the role of Congress in the making and implementation of foreign policy.
   d. was an unengaged and uninformed leader.

Essay Questions

Objective 1

1. Discuss the economic problems of the United States in the 1970s, and evaluate the attempts by Nixon, Ford, and Carter to deal with those problems.

Objectives 1 and 3

2. Discuss the domestic successes and failures of the Carter presidency, and explain why it may be said that many of Carter's problems were not of his own making.

© 1994 Houghton Mifflin Company. All rights reserved.

Objectives 7, 8, 11, 14, and 15

3. Discuss the economic policies of the Reagan administration, and examine the impact of these policies on the United States.

Objectives 9, 10, 12, 14, and 15

4. Identify the major groups during the course of the 1980s that opposed Reagan administration policies and actions, and discuss the reasons for their opposition.

Objective 12

5. Discuss the economic, social, and political position of Latino-Americans during the 1970s and 1980s.

Objective 13

6. Explain the emergence and evaluate the goals of the antifeminist movement.

Objectives 14 and 15

7. Examine the reasons for and the extent of poverty in the United States in the 1980s. What groups were most affected? Why?

Objective 16

8. Discuss the extent of the AIDS epidemic, and explain the impact of the epidemic on the sexual behavior and attitudes of Americans.

Objectives 16, 17, and 18

9. Discuss the following statement: "The main challenge of Reagan's last two years in office was to reassert his leadership and avoid becoming a lame-duck president." How successful was President Reagan in meeting this challenge? Explain.

CHAPTER 34

A New Century Beckons: America and the World in the 1990s

Learning Objectives

After you have studied Chapter 34 in your textbook and worked through this study guide chapter, you should be able to:

1. Examine, evaluate, and discuss the consequences of the Bush administration's foreign-policy views, goals, and actions in relation to each of the following:
   a. global environmental issues
   b. international trade issues
   c. Japan
   d. China
   e. democracy movements in Eastern Europe
   f. disintegration of the Soviet Union
   g. the START talks
   h. German reunification
   i. Nicaragua
   j. El Salvador
   k. Haiti
   l. Latin-American debt crisis
   m. trade in illicit drugs
   n. Manuel Noriega (Panama)
   o. the Iraqi invasion of Kuwait
   p. the Arab-Israeli conflict
   q. war and famine in Somalia
2. Discuss George Bush's personal and political background; examine the domestic issues and political problems that faced the Bush administration; and explain and evaluate the administration's actions concerning those issues and problems.
3. Discuss the nomination of Clarence Thomas to the Supreme Court; explain the issues addressed by the Senate Judiciary Committee in its confirmation hearings; and discuss the reaction of the American people to those hearings.
4. Discuss both the immediate and underlying causes of the Los Angeles riots of April 1992.
5. Discuss the scandals that plagued Congress between 1988 and 1992, and explain the reaction of the American people to these scandals.
6. Examine the issues and personalities and explain the outcome of the 1992 presidential and congressional elections.

7. Discuss Bill Clinton's personal and political background; examine the domestic issues and political problems that faced the Clinton administration; and explain and evaluate the administration's actions concerning those issues and problems.
8. Examine, evaluate, and discuss the consequences of the defense and foreign policy views, goals, and actions of the Clinton administration.

Thematic Guide

In Chapter 34 the authors discuss the failed presidency of George Bush, the array of domestic and international problems facing the United States in the 1990s, and the 1992 election of William Jefferson "Bill" Clinton to the presidency. In 1988 George Bush rode into the presidency on the back of peace and prosperity. Although he presented himself as the heir of his conservative predecessor, Ronald Reagan, in deed and action he seemed indecisive and out of touch. Although he most certainly wanted to be president, he seldom seemed to know what he wanted to achieve as president. Therefore, rather than leading in a decisive and positive direction, he engaged in crisis management as he attempted to maintain the status quo. Wanting an unchanging world over which he could be the caretaker, President Bush instead inherited a world of rapid, even mind-boggling change—a world in which he often seemed out of place and out of step.

The world of the late 1980s and early 1990s was not the world that George Bush had come to understand through his many years of government and foreign service. As a dutiful soldier of the Cold War, Bush accepted the containment doctrine and the world it had shaped. Therefore, he was suddenly out of place and time when the Soviet empire collapsed, democracy movements swept over Eastern Europe, and the Soviet Union disintegrated into separate, competing ethnic entities. Although his lips pronounced the beginning of a "new world order," actions never matched the rhetoric. As fledgling democracies struggled and as former communist states attempted to claw their way out of the economic quagmire of managed economies, the aid extended by the United States was slow in coming and, when it did come, woefully inadequate. Active in the "containment" of communism for over four decades, the United States under George Bush's leadership largely stood as a bewildered and passive bystander to the cataclysmic changes caused by communism's collapse.

Inaction was also the order of the day with regard to global environmental issues, as can be seen in the administration's policies toward international family-planning agencies, and its opposition to the Law of the Sea Treaty and agreements reached at the Rio de Janeiro "Earth Summit." However, the United States did join 85 other nations in agreeing to end the use of ozone-destroying chemicals by the year 2000; and, along with 25 other nations, agreed to ban oil exploration and mining in Antarctica for 50 years.

After discussing the Bush administration's record on global environmental issues and briefly examining the North American Free Trade Agreement, the authors turn to a discussion of United States relations with Japan and China during the Bush administration. Relations with Japan were conditioned, in large measure, by economic competition between the two nations. This competition was characterized by a steady increase of Japan's economic power and the concomitant economic decline of the United States. Relations with China, on the other hand, were marred by the Chinese government's brutal assault against the prodemocracy movement at Tiananmen Square. Despite world outrage at the massacre of hundreds of unarmed students, the Bush administration believed friendly relations with the hard-line Chinese government were in the best interest of American security needs. As a result the American government's protest was mild and short-lived.

Despite the end of the Cold War, United States relations with the Third World remained turbulent, as can be seen in the discussion of Nicaragua and Haiti, the problems caused by the debt burdens of many Latin American states, the U.S. invasion of Panama, and the Persian Gulf War. A theme that runs through the discussion of the economic and political problems of the Third World is the contribution of the United States to problems that led to turmoil. From the U.S.-financed *contra* war in Nicaragua to military aid to Somalia's dictatorial regime; from the extension of U.S. aid to the drug-trafficking dictator of Panama, Manuel Noriega, to aid to Iraq's dictator Saddam Hussein, the story is much the same. Often in the name of "containment" of Communism and always in the name of national security, United States military aid often engendered the very instability the United States sought to prevent.

Nowhere was this clearer than in Panama and Iraq, two areas in which the United States ultimately used military force to deal with the excesses of dictators it had previously supported. Although Manuel Noriega was removed from power in Panama, the United States had few resources to help rebuild the devastated country. And although Iraq was decisively and humiliatingly defeated in the Persian Gulf War, its dictator Saddam Hussein remained in power and continued to repress the peoples of his war-ravaged nation. Although the Gulf War created an environment in which new Arab-Israeli peace talks began, those talks had produced no tangible results by early 1993.

Another theme runs through this story as well. Although the United States poured large sums of money into military solutions to problems in Third World regions, the military path usually left the nations in question in economic, political, and social chaos. Unfortunately, U.S. resources seemed to be more limited when it came to solving the problems of poverty, unemployment, famine, and disease. In one area, Somalia, the United States used its power and resources in the form of 20,000 American troops to ensure the delivery of relief aid to thousands of starving people; but little U.S. aid flowed to Nicaragua, El Salvador, and Panama to help rebuild economies devastated by years of internal strife.

After discussing foreign policy during the Bush years, we turn to a discussion of the domestic front and to the presidential and congressional elections of 1992. After Bush's election to the presidency in 1988, the economy slowly drifted into stagnation and recession. As businesses "downsized" in an effort to deal with overwhelming debt burdens, unemployment rose. Accepting the advice that the recession would quickly run its course and that federal action would only increase the already overwhelming federal debt, the Bush administration remained passive. Passivity was also the order of the day in dealing with the real problems that plagued the American system of public education and in dealing with the many social problems left over from the 1980s. In addition, Bush had pledged to be the "environmental" president, but allowed the Council on Competitiveness to gut the Clean Air Act; and, although he pledged in the 1988 presidential campaign that he would not raise taxes, he entered into a deal with the Democratic-controlled Congress in which the Democratic leaders agreed to cut spending and Bush endorsed a tax hike. As criticism of the administration mounted in these areas, the Clarence Thomas-Anita Hill confrontation galvanized many Americans, especially women, and increased opposition to the Republican party. Furthermore, the Los Angeles riots of 1992 were a shocking reminder that racial tensions continued to plague the nation, and the Bush administration's passivity in dealing with the plight of the urban poor and the problems associated with their plight led to still more criticism.

Although many Americans became increasingly critical of the Republican president, they were just as critical of the scandal-ridden Democratic-controlled Congress. As the 1992 election approached, the American people seemed genuinely dissatisfied with "Washington gridlock" and ready for change. They were also ready for the government to act in solving many long-standing problems. It was this desire for change and this readiness for action that fueled the campaigns of the independent presidential candidate H. Ross Perot and the Democratic candidate Bill Clinton. The chapter ends with a discussion of the presidential and congressional elections of 1992 and of President Clinton's agenda for the 1990s.

Building Vocabulary

Listed on pages 472–473 are important words and terms that you need to know to get the most out of Chapter 34. They are listed in the order in which they occur in the chapter. After carefully looking through the list, refer to a dictionary and jot down the definition of words that you do not know or of which you are unsure.

acrimonious

pander

prudence

reactive

unipolar

daunting

nettlesome

clique

chastise

fruition

mettle

chameleon

aversion

punster

plaudit

coalition

mercurial

disparage

impunity

portend

renege

volatile

taut

Identification and Significance

After studying Chapter 34 of *A People and a Nation,* you should be able to identify fully *and* explain the historical significance of each item listed below.

1. Identify each item in the space provided. Give an explanation or description of the item. Answer the questions *who, what, where,* and *when.*
2. Explain the historical significance of each item in the space provided. Establish the historical context in which the item exists. Establish the item as the result of or as the cause of other factors existing in the society under study. Answer this question: *what were the political, social, economic, and/or cultural consequences of this item?*

George Bush

    Identification

    Significance

James A. Baker III

    Identification

    Significance

© 1994 Houghton Mifflin Company. All rights reserved.

Chapter 34

the "declinists"

    Identification

    Significance

The Rise and Fall of the Great Powers

    Identification

    Significance

the "greenhouse effect"

    Identification

    Significance

Bush's environmental policies

    Identification

    Significance

the Rio de Janeiro "Earth Summit" of 1992

    Identification

    Significance

the North American Free Trade Agreement

    Identification

    Significance

© 1994 Houghton Mifflin Company. All rights reserved.

Japanese-American relations, 1988–1993

> Identification

> Significance

the Tiananmen Square Massacre

> Identification

> Significance

START I and START II

> Identification

> Significance

Boris Yeltsin

> Identification

> Significance

German reunification

> Identification

> Significance

the National Opposition Union of Nicaragua

> Identification

> Significance

Salvadoran leftists

    Identification

    Significance

Haitian refugees

    Identification

    Significance

Latin American debt crisis

    Identification

    Significance

the "drug war"

    Identification

    Significance

Manuel Antonio Noriega

    Identification

    Significance

Operation Just Cause

    Identification

    Significance

Saddam Hussein

    Identification

    Significance

the Persian Gulf War

    Identification

    Significance

Arab-Israeli peace talks, 1991–1993

    Identification

    Significance

Operation Restore Hope

    Identification

    Significance

economic recession, 1989–1992

    Identification

    Significance

John Sununu

    Identification

    Significance

© 1994 Houghton Mifflin Company. All rights reserved.

Chapter 34

Bush's "No-new-taxes" pledge

    Identification

    Significance

the Clean Air Act

    Identification

    Significance

the Council on Competitiveness

    Identification

    Significance

Clarence Thomas

    Identification

    Significance

Anita Hill

    Identification

    Significance

the Los Angeles riots of 1992

    Identification

    Significance

© 1994 Houghton Mifflin Company. All rights reserved.

the Americans with Disabilities Act of 1990

> Identification
>
> Significance

scandals in Congress, 1988–1992

> Identification
>
> Significance

the Twenty-seventh Amendment

> Identification
>
> Significance

Patrick Buchanan

> Identification
>
> Significance

the Republican coalition

> Identification
>
> Significance

Bill Clinton

> Identification
>
> Significance

480   Chapter 34

Albert Gore

    Identification

    Significance

H. Ross Perot

    Identification

    Significance

Dan Quayle

    Identification

    Significance

the presidential and congressional elections of 1992

    Identification

    Significance

the pardon of Iran-Contra figures

    Identification

    Significance

gays-in-the-military issue

    Identification

    Significance

© 1994 Houghton Mifflin Company. All rights reserved.

Clinton's 1993 economic plan

>Identification

>Significance

Warren Christopher

>Identification

>Significance

Evaluating and Using Information

Using the tables on pages 482–483 to help you look for and organize the information you will need, analyze the differences in the frames of reference of Presidents George Bush and Bill Clinton and the reflections of those frames of reference in the ways they have carried out their jobs as president. Use your analysis as the basis for a response to this question:

> Compare and contrast George Bush and Bill Clinton as presidents in terms of the conservatism that characterized the presidency since 1980.

In the tables, record reminders of the relevant information that you find in Chapter 34 and in your class notes. Then expand the reminders, first into full notes and then into the working draft of your essay.

Enter the working draft of your essay in your Reader's Notebook.

© 1994 Houghton Mifflin Company. All rights reserved.

Reflections of the Political Frame of Reference of George Bush

Role of Government	Promotion of Business, Trade, Commerce	Social, Economic Class Structure	"Traditional" Values	Foreign Aid (Military, Humanitarian)	Domestic Aid (Welfare, Social Programs, Subsidies, etc.)	Environmental Protection, Uses of Resources	Spending, Allocation of Revenues	Conclusion
Interventionism, Activism								
Appointments								
Trade Agreements, Arms Sales								
Taxation								
Other								
Conclusion								

Reflections of the Political Frame of Reference of Bill Clinton

Role of Government	Promotion of Business, Trade, Commerce	Social, Economic Class Structure	"Traditional" Values	Foreign Aid (Military, Humanitarian)	Domestic Aid (Welfare, Social Programs, Subsidies, etc.)	Environmental Protection, Uses of Resources	Spending, Allocation of Revenues	Conclusion
Interventionism, Activism								
Appointments								
Trade Agreements, Arms Sales								
Taxation								
Other								
Conclusion								

© 1994 Houghton Mifflin Company. All rights reserved.

Ideas and Details

Objective 1

_____ 1. In response to the global-warming problem, President Bush
   a. pledged to undertake an active worldwide campaign against the unproved theories of environmental extremists.
   b. pledged that the government would provide the research and development funds necessary for the American automobile industry to produce a marketable electric-powered automobile by the year 2000.
   c. warned against solutions that would interfere with the free marketplace.
   d. tried to persuade the 178 nations represented at the 1992 Earth Summit to accept binding limits on carbon emissions.

Objective 1

_____ 2. In response to American complaints about unfair trade practices, the Japanese contended that
   a. American goods were not competitive in the world market because they were manufactured with obsolete equipment.
   b. the American government spent too much money on job-retraining programs and not enough on marketing and advertising.
   c. Americans were more interested in quality public education than in the production of quality products.
   d. American-based multinational corporations controlled at least one-fourth of Japan's productive capacity.

Objective 1

_____ 3. In response to the rapid disintegration of the Soviet Union in 1991, the Bush administration
   a. offered to send military aid to Gorbachev to help him quell ethnic unrest and anti-Communist demonstrations.
   b. immediately offered direct financial support to the Russian republic.
   c. worked through both the United Nations and NATO to send a team of political and economic advisers to each newly independent republic.
   d. acted slowly, and initially seemed to be a passive bystander.

Objective 1

_____ 4. Which of the following posed a potential threat to the competitiveness of the United States in world markets?
   a. The economic resurgence of France
   b. Lithuanian and Latvian independence
   c. Poland's success in moving from a managed economy to a market economy
   d. German reunification

© 1994 Houghton Mifflin Company. All rights reserved.

Objective 1

_____ 5. The ongoing crisis in El Salvador between leftist forces and the U.S.-backed Salvadoran government eased as a result of which of the following?
   a. The leftists agreed to lay down their arms and seek change through the political process.
   b. The Salvadoran army decisively defeated the leftist forces.
   c. The Salvadoran president used his emergency powers to institute immediate land reform.
   d. The United States poured hundreds of millions of dollars into El Salvador to bring about meaningful social and economic reform.

Objective 1

_____ 6. In the drug war, the Bush administration
   a. proposed that most "recreational" drugs be legalized.
   b. concentrated on reducing the supply of drugs.
   c. relied solely on reducing the demand for drugs in the United States.
   d. mandated drug-testing for all American businesses with over 50 employees.

Objective 1

_____ 7. What did the United States want to accomplish by sending troops to the Persian Gulf and engaging in the Persian Gulf War?
   a. To defend Israel against attack by Syria and Labia
   b. To defend Saudi Arabia and force Iraq to abandon its takeover of Kuwait
   c. To enforce the cease-fire between Iraq and Iran
   d. To force the United Arab Emirates to stop preying on American tankers in the Persian Gulf

Objective 1

_____ 8. Which of the following is true with regard to American-Iraqi relations before the Persian Gulf War?
   a. Upon assuming power, the Bush administration cut off all foreign aid to Iraq to protest the human-rights abuses of Hussein's government.
   b. The United States demonstrated its hostility toward Iraq by supplying Iran with arms during the Iran-Iraq War.
   c. The United States supplied Iraq with nuclear-capable missiles during the Iran-Iraq War.
   d. American companies helped Iraq in its effort to develop nuclear weapons by shipping high-tech equipment to the country.

Objective 1

_____ 9. The objective of the United States military expedition to Somalia in late 1992 was to
   a. overthrow the dictatorial regime that held power.
   b. ensure the delivery of relief supplies to the Somali people.
   c. maintain the cease-fire between the warring ethnic groups in the beleaguered nation.
   d. arrest and bring to justice anti-American terrorists known to be hiding in the country.

Objective 2

_____ 10. Which of the following was a result of the 1990 budget negotiations between the White House and Congress?
   a. Congress agreed to pass legislation giving the President a line-item veto.
   b. Congress agreed to allow debate on a balanced-budget amendment to the Constitution while Bush agreed to release impounded funds.
   c. President Bush agreed to a tax hike while the Democrats agreed to budget cuts.
   d. President Bush and the Democrats agreed to increase the federal debt limit.

Objective 2

_____ 11. Which of the following is true of the Council on Competitiveness?
   a. It instituted a quality-control program in the automobile industry to make American cars more competitive in world markets.
   b. It gutted enforcement of the Clean Air Act of 1990 while arguing that environmental regulations slowed economic growth.
   c. It suggested government subsidies to American businesses that adopted Japanese management practices.
   d. It charged the Japanese with unfair trade practices and suggested protective tariffs against all Japanese imports.

Objective 4

_____ 12. The immediate cause of the Los Angeles riots of 1992 was the
   a. enactment of a city ordinance that forbade sleeping on park benches.
   b. shooting of three unarmed black teenagers by a white police officer.
   c. acquittal of four police officers charged with beating a black motorist.
   d. closing of a city-operated recreational center in Watts.

Objective 5

_____ 13. In the House banking scandal it was revealed that
   a. the manager of the House bank had secretly loaned money to non-congressional friends and colleagues.
   b. representatives were regularly allowed to overdraw on their accounts with no penalties.
   c. Vice-President Dan Quayle was allowed to write checks against the House bank even though he had no actual account there.
   d. money was secretly withdrawn from the bank to finance covert CIA operations.

Objective 6

_____ 14. For which of the following reasons was Dan Quayle a liability for Bush in the 1992 presidential campaign?
   a. He had a much better grasp of the issues than Bush seemed to have.
   b. He disagreed with Bush on the abortion issue by taking a pro-choice stance.
   c. The contrast with Al Gore made Quayle's shortcoming more obvious.
   d. The leaders of the Republican party openly ridiculed him.

Objective 7

_____ 15. The economic plan that President Clinton sent to Congress in February 1993 called for
   a. lower taxes on the middle class.
   b. tax breaks for the wealthy.
   c. an energy tax.
   d. lower corporate taxes.

Essay Questions

Objective 1

1. Discuss the foreign policy goals and objectives of the Bush administration, and examine the impact of those policies on the world community of nations and on the United States.

Objectives 1 and 2

2. Discuss the global and domestic environmental issues faced by the Bush administration, and explain Bush's actions concerning those issues.

Objective 1

3. Discuss and evaluate the Bush administration's policy toward the nations of Latin America.

Objective 1

4. Discuss the causes and consequences of the Persian Gulf War.

Objective 2

5. Examine the causes of the economic recession during the Bush administration, discuss the consequences of this recession, and explain President Bush's handling of the recession.

© 1994 Houghton Mifflin Company. All rights reserved.

Objective 6

6. Examine the issues and personalities in the 1992 presidential election, and explain the election's outcome.

Answers

Chapter 16

Ideas and Details

1a. No. The federal government changed its policy toward enlistment of black volunteers in the Union Army, but it did so out of necessity rather than out of a commitment to equal rights. Unfortunately, evidence from the 1860s indicates that there were as few victories over racial discrimination at the federal level as at the state level. See page 470.

1b. No. There was an element within the Republican party committed to equality, but the Democratic party consistently fought against equality. See page 470.

1c. No. A faction in the Republican party was devoted to fighting racism, but the evidence does not support the conclusion that the racist attitudes of white northerners changed because blacks participated in the war. For example, what stand did the voters in Connecticut, Minnesota, and Wisconsin take in 1865 concerning black suffrage? See page 470.

1d. Correct. There were signs that wartime idealism had caused some questioning of racism and some movement toward racial equality. However, there was also evidence of continued racial prejudice within northern society. This leads to the conclusion that securing equality for blacks would be difficult. See page 470.

2a. No. Although Johnson demonstrated a considerable amount of sympathy toward the South, he did not go so far as to promise federal aid to rebuild the region. See pages 471–473.

2b. Correct. At first it appeared that Johnson's Reconstruction plan would prevent the prewar southern elite from returning to power. But Johnson freely gave pardons to ex-Confederates whom southerners had defiantly elected to Congress. This caused Congress to question Johnson's plan. See pages 472–473.

2c. No. Congress supported the requirement in Johnson's plan that the Confederate war debt be repudiated. Congress was angered when two southern states defiantly refused to abide by this requirement. See pages 471–473.

2d. No. The Johnson plan stipulated that most white southern males, including yeoman farmers, could gain the right to vote by swearing an oath of loyalty to the United States government. See pages 471–473.

3a. No. Although some of the southern states were reluctant to admit that slavery was a thing of the past, the black codes did not require that freedmen pay "freedom dues" to their former masters. See pages 471–473.

3b. No. The black codes did not extend political rights to any freedmen. See page 473.

3c. Correct. The black codes, adopted by most southern state legislatures immediately after the war, were in large measure restatements of the old slave codes. Those responsible for enacting the codes intended permanently to relegate blacks to a subservient position in southern society. See page 473.

3d. No. The black codes did not indicate acceptance of the Thirteenth Amendment and did not protect the civil rights of the freedmen. See page 473.

4a. No. The Constitution stipulates that treaties must be ratified by the Senate, but Congress (the Senate and the House) did not base its claim that it had a right to have a voice in the Reconstruction process on this constitutional grant of power to the Senate. See page 473 and page A-16.

© 1994 Houghton Mifflin Company. All rights reserved.

4b. No. The Constitution does grant Congress the power to declare war, but this was not the basis for Congress's claim that it had a right to a voice in the Reconstruction process. See page 473 and page A-16.

4c. Correct. Article IV, Section 4, of the Constitution states: "The United States shall guarantee to every State in this Union a republican form of government." It was on the basis of this statement that Congress claimed its right to have a voice in Reconstruction. See page 473 and page A-16.

4d. No. The Preamble to the Constitution states that one of the purposes of the government is to "promote the general welfare," but this was not the section of the Constitution on which Congress based its claim to a voice in the Reconstruction process. See page 473 and page A-6.

5a. No. Most conservative and moderate Republicans believed that voting was a privilege, not a right. They did not ally with the Radical Republicans out of the belief that full political rights should be extended to blacks. See pages 474, 475.

5b. No. Most conservative and moderate Republicans viewed property rights as sacred. They rejected the contention by the Radical Republicans that a redistribution of southern land was necessary. See pages 474, 476.

5c. Correct. All those who questioned Johnson's program, even conservatives and moderates, were labeled as "radical" by Johnson and the Democrats. Therefore, to make changes they thought necessary, conservative and moderate Republicans were forced into an alliance with the Radicals. See page 474.

5d. No. The Radical Republicans held views that most northerners rejected. For example, some Radicals went beyond advocating equality under the law for freedmen by advocating political, social, and economic equality as well. See page 474.

6a. No. The Fourteenth Amendment allowed the southern states to decide whether or not to extend voting rights to freedmen. If a state denied voting privileges to its black citizens, the state's delegation to the House of Representatives would be reduced proportionately. This provision was never enforced. See pages 474–475.

6b. No. Johnson condemned the Fourteenth Amendment. He actively worked against the amendment by urging northerners to reject it and southern state legislatures to vote against ratification. See pages 474–475.

6c. No. The Fourteenth Amendment ignored women. See pages 474–475.

6d. Correct. Conservative and moderate Republicans disagreed with Radical Republicans over extension of voting rights to freedmen. The second section of the Fourteenth Amendment clearly indicates a compromise favoring the conservative/moderate view on this question. See pages 474–475.

7a. Correct. Only one southern state (Tennessee) had initially accepted and been reconstructed under the Fourteenth Amendment. However, under the Reconstruction Act of 1867 the southern states were required to ratify the amendment before returning to the Union. See page 476.

7b. No. Although most Radical Republicans called for redistribution of southern land, most people rejected the idea as being beyond the power of the federal government and as unwarranted interference in private property. See page 476.

7c. No. The act stipulated that the ten southern states to which it applied had to guarantee freedmen the right to vote in elections for state constitutional conventions and in subsequent state elections, but it did not guarantee freedmen the right to vote in federal elections. See page 476.

7d. No. The Reconstruction Act of 1867 did not stipulate a definite time period during which the Reconstruction process would take place. See page 476.

8a. No. Johnson's impeachment by the House and subsequent trial in the Senate rendered him almost totally powerless as president. See page 476.

8b. Correct. The Radical Republicans who led the prosecution of Johnson in his Senate trial advanced the belief that impeachment was political in nature. The Senate's acquittal of Johnson was a rejection of that idea. See page 477.

8c. No. The Senate fell only one vote shy of the two-thirds majority necessary to convict Johnson of the charges brought against him. This is not an indication that northern opinion toward Johnson and the South had softened. See page 477.

8d. No. The Senate's failure to convict Johnson did not cause a rift between the House and the Senate. See page 477.

© 1994 Houghton Mifflin Company. All rights reserved.

9a. Correct. By eliminating property qualifications for voting, the new state constitutions made the South more democratic and brought the South in line with the rest of the nation. See pages 479–480.

9b. No. Although these state constitutions extended more rights to women, women's suffrage, advocated by some black delegates, was considered radical and was not adopted. See pages 479–480.

9c. No. The new constitutions did provide for public schools, but attendance to these schools was not compulsory. See pages 479–480, 482.

9d. No. Yearly reapportionment of legislative districts was not made mandatory by the new state constitutions. See pages 479–480.

10a. Correct. Southern Republicans quickly restored the voting rights of former Confederates. This meant that the Republican party would face defeat if it could not gain white support. In courting the white vote, the Republican party abandoned its most loyal supporters—blacks. See pages 480–481.

10b. No. Although the southern Republicans appealed for support from a broad range of groups in the South, they were never able to build a broad popular base for the party. See pages 480–481.

10c. No. In the first place, southern Democrats were not more "liberal" than the southern Republicans. Furthermore, freedmen themselves supported restoration of the voting rights of former Confederates. See page 480–481.

10d. No. The evidence does not indicate that congressional Republicans were embarrassed by the decision of southern Republicans to restore the voting rights of former Confederates. See pages 480–481.

11a. No. The evidence indicates that freedmen throughout the South, and especially those participating in Reconstruction governments, were very interested in participating in the political process and did so with great dignity and distinction. See pages 482–483.

11b. Correct. Charges of "black domination" and "Negro rule" are examples of the racist propaganda used by white conservatives to discredit the Reconstruction governments. See page 482.

11c. No. Those blacks who participated in Reconstruction governments were practical and realistic in their approach to power. They extended the right to vote to former Confederates, did not insist on an integrated school system, and did not insist on social equality. See pages 479–481, 482.

11d. No. The evidence indicates that those blacks participating in Reconstruction governments were not vindictive toward their former masters. Their actions demonstrate their belief in "the Christian goal of reconciliation." See pages 479–481, 482.

12a. No. The evidence indicates that after 1867 the terrorist activities against blacks became more organized and purposeful, and the campaign of terror in Alamance and Caswell counties clearly fits this characterization. See pages 483–484.

12b. No. The campaign of terror in the North Carolina counties of Caswell and Alamance was organized by the wealthy and the powerful. See page 484.

12c. Correct. Terrorist campaigns by the Klan were organized and purposeful after 1867. This was clearly the case in these North Carolina counties where the wealthy and powerful organized the campaign of terror for the purpose of regaining political control. See page 484.

12d. No. Blacks and whites of the yeoman class were allies in Alamance and Caswell counties, and the Klan successfully used racism to destroy this coalition. See page 484.

13a. No. Although the Reconstruction governments were able to effect some reform in the South, they chose not to demand redistribution of land. This decision is one of the main reasons that these governments were not able to alter the social structure of the region. See page 484.

13b. No. The success of the Klan's terrorist campaign in Alamance and Caswell counties in North Carolina is evidence that there was not a lasting alliance between blacks and whites of the yeoman class. See page 484.

13c. No. Blacks were given the right to vote, but it was naive to believe that the ballot was an adequate weapon in the struggle by African-Americans for a better life. See page 484.

© 1994 Houghton Mifflin Company. All rights reserved.

13d. Correct. The Reconstruction governments did not demand and Congress did not bring about a redistribution of land in the South. As a result, blacks were denied economic independence and remained economically dependent on hostile whites. See page 484.

14a. Correct. John Campbell argued that the Fourteenth Amendment brought individual rights under federal protection by making the Bill of Rights applicable to the states. The Court disagreed and said that state citizenship and national citizenship were separate, with the former being more important. See page 493.

14b. No. The Court ruled that the Fourteenth Amendment protected only those rights that went along with national citizenship, and the Court narrowly defined those rights. See page 493.

14c. No. Although the Court later ruled that corporations were legal persons protected under the Fourteenth Amendment (the 1886 *Santa Clara* case), this was not its ruling in the *Slaughter-House* cases. See page 493.

14d. No. The Court ruled that, of the two, state citizenship was more important than national citizenship. See page 493.

15a. No. The monetary issue aroused a great deal of interest during the 1870s, especially among farmers, who tended to favor an inflationary policy. However, by the 1876 election a "sound money" policy had basically won out. See pages 494–495.

15b. No. William H. Seward was secretary of state from 1861 to 1869. His policies had no direct bearing on the outcome of the disputed presidential election of 1876. See pages 494–495.

15c. Correct. The fact that both candidates in this disputed election favored removal of federal troops from the South and an end to Reconstruction indicates that the electorate had lost interest in Reconstruction. This is especially important in relation to the northern electorate. See pages 494–495.

15d. No. Since the end of the Civil War, the government had been injecting money into the economy and extending indirect aid to business interests. Most people favored a continuation of this practice, which had spurred industrial growth, especially in the North. See pages 494–495.

Chapter 17

Finding the Main Idea

Exercise A

The first sentence is a transition sentence from a discussion of the mining frontier to a discussion of the lumbering frontier. Although it points out that the two industries were similar in that both were extractive, it implies a difference between the two industries by saying that lumbering required vast stretches of land.

1. *Paragraph topic:* Methods by which the lumber industry gained land.

2. *Main idea:* The main idea is developed in the first two sentences.
    a. Lumber production required vast stretches of land.
    b. Lumber companies exploited an act of Congress for their own purposes rather than adhering to the intent of the act. Lumber companies exploited the Timber and Stone Act to obtain the vast stretches of land required in lumber production.

3. *Supporting details:*
    a. The Timber and Stone Act was passed by Congress in 1878 to stimulate western settlement. Provisions of the act are noted to provide evidence that the intent of the act was to stimulate western settlement and to establish that the act was intended for "private citizens."

© 1994 Houghton Mifflin Company. All rights reserved.

    The point about Congress's intent in passing the Timber and Stone Act—to aid the settlement and development of the frontier—is an underlying theme in this chapter's discussions of natural resources, ranching, and farming.
  b. Lumber companies hired seamen to register claims to timberland; these claims were then turned over to the lumber companies. The point provides further evidence of exploitation.
  c. Most of the 3.5 million acres bought by 1900 under the Timber and Stone Act belonged to corporations.

Exercise B

Paragraph 1 The first paragraph is a functional paragraph. As such, it provides a transition from a discussion of the economic oppression and violence encountered by southern blacks to a discussion of their social and political oppression. The first paragraph also announces the theme for the entire paragraph series.

1. Paragraph topic: The social and political oppression of blacks.

2. *Main idea:*   Blacks experienced new forms of social and political oppression at the hands of white-supremacist southern leaders.

3. *Supporting details:*   As you recall from the introduction to this study guide, functional paragraphs "announce ideas and shifts of focus" and "offer no support." The main idea of this paragraph establishes the theme for four paragraphs. Although this paragraph also offers reasons for the political and social oppression of blacks, these reasons are logical inferences drawn from material presented in Chapter 16, pages 478–479, rather than additional supporting details. Therefore, we are told that blacks were socially and politically oppressed by white supremacists who
  a. sought ways to relegate blacks to a position of inferiority.
  b. were angry over northern interference in race relations in the South.
  c. wanted to reassert their power when federal troops withdrew.

Paragraph 2 The theme established in the functional paragraph is more fully developed in the second paragraph of the paragraph series.

1. *Paragraph topic*:   Black voting rights in the South after Reconstruction.

2. *Main idea:*   Although blacks continued to vote after Reconstruction, white politicians began actively to seek ways to reduce their political power.

3. *Supporting details:*
  a. Statistics concerning blacks elected to the North Carolina state house from 1877 to 1890.
  b. Poll taxes were instituted in the South, beginning with Georgia in 1877.
  c. In some cases voters were required to deposit ballots in the ballot box corresponding to the candidate for whom they voted. Because this required the ability to read, the votes of many blacks were invalidated.

Paragraph 3 The theme of the paragraph series is further developed in the third paragraph.

1. *Paragraph topic*:   Social discrimination against southern blacks.

2. *Main idea:*   The South's movement from an informal system of racial discrimination to a system codified in law was made possible by the Supreme Court's interpretation of the Fourteenth Amendment.

3. *Supporting details:*
  a. In the 1870s the Court ruled that the Fourteenth Amendment protected citizens' rights against infringement by state governments, but not by individuals or organizations.
  b. The Court further ruled that blacks wanting protection under the law would have to seek it from the states, not from the federal government.

Paragraph 4 In the fourth paragraph of the paragraph series, the discussion of the Supreme Court's role in the codification of racial discrimination in the South continues.

1. *Paragraph topic:*   The development of the separate-but-equal doctrine.

© 1994 Houghton Mifflin Company. All rights reserved.

2. *Main idea:* The federal courts took a hands-off approach concerning racially discriminatory legislation, an approach that led the Supreme Court to uphold the separate-but-equal doctrine.

3. *Supporting details:*
   a. In 1883 the Court declared the 1875 Civil Rights Act unconstitutional because, it said, the federal government could not regulate the behavior of individuals or organizations. As a result, public facilities like hotels, streetcars, railroads, and theaters could practice segregation legally.
   b. Lower-court cases in the 1880s established the separate-but-equal doctrine.
   c. In *Plessy* v. *Ferguson* and *Cummins* v. *County Board of Education*, the Supreme Court upheld *state legislation* that discriminated against blacks. The Court upheld this legislation on the basis of the separate-but-equal doctrine.

Paragraph 5 In the fifth paragraph of the paragraph series the discussion of the developing system of legal segregation in the South continues.

1. *Paragraph topic:* The spread of Jim Crow laws in the South.

2. *Main idea:* Because of the rulings by the Supreme Court (discussed in the two preceding paragraphs), a legally codified system of racial discrimination spread rapidly in the South.

3. *Supporting details:*
   a. A Birmingham, Alabama, law is cited as evidence that state laws and local ordinances were passed restricting blacks to the backs of streetcars, to separate drinking and toilet facilities, and to separate sections of hospitals, asylums, and cemeteries.
   b. Local laws were passed defining city districts or blocks as all-black or all-white.
   c. A Mobile, Alabama, law required blacks to abide by a curfew.
   d. An Atlanta, Georgia, law required separate Bibles for black witnesses swearing before the court.

Evaluating and Using Information

The two tables below lay out most of the key information needed to identify and explain similarities between the economic plight of the western Indians and the economic plight of southern backcountry yeoman farmers in the years following the Civil War.

The first table shows the kind of notes a student might have entered in the blocks in the Evaluating and Using Information table. Your own entries are not likely to be exactly the same because, of course, no two people take notes exactly the same way.

The second table represents a rearranging and refocusing of some of the information collected for the Organizing Information exercise. Don't worry if you used some other method of taking the relevant information from the Organizing Information exercise and putting it into a form that makes it easy for you to use. Your objective is to discover the nature of the relationship between the two groups' situations and to create an essay about that relationship.

As the information entered in these two sample tables suggests, your mock essay should identify and explain such areas of similarity between the two groups as these: (a) reduced self-sufficiency, (b) loss of control over land, (c) loss of resources previously available and important to survival, (d) victimization by those more successful in capitalistic society, and (e) increased competition and conflict with others in similar economic straits.

And your explanations of those areas of similarity would include details about subsistence agriculture, buffaloes, crop liens, the Dawes Severalty Act, railroad expansion, cash crops/cotton, ecological balance, the Homestead Act of 1862, tenant farming and sharecropping, Civil War destruction, and so forth.

Predicament of Southern Backcountry Yeoman Farmers, 1877–1892			
	Condition of Equipment and Stock	**Control of Farmland; Farm Size**	**Access To Markets**
Kind of Change and Features of Change	33% draft animals, 50% equipment lost;	dec. in farm size; large increase in proportion of farming done on rented land; large increase in sharecropping; reduction of amount of "communal" grazing land; shift from subsistence to commercial agric (cotton).	encouragement of heavy reliance on commercial crops, such as cotton
Cause(s) of Change	destruction during war; lack of upkeep during and after war	indebtedness incurred during war; laws closing southern range; indebtedness that made need for cash paramount	expansion of railroad system
Impact on the Farmer's Lifestyle, Economic Status	farmers had to rebuild with less equipment and stock than they had had before the war; purchases—at inflated prices—of stock and grain led to increased indebtedness and dependency on merchants, market economy	farmers began to buy necessities instead of supplying them via subsistence farming; farmers so poor they had to borrow for necessities (crop liens) and got deeper and deeper into debt and had to pay for privilege of buying on credit when crops did not bring in enough to pay off lien; fencing in of animals on land too poor to support them and lower spirit of community cooperation; increased strife between blacks and whites; exhausted soil	market accessibility encouraged use of larger percentage of land for cash crops by farmers which in turn meant that they had less land available on which to produce subsistence crops and stock and they found themselves at mercy of merchants

© 1994 Houghton Mifflin Company. All rights reserved.

	Predicament of Western Indians, 1877–1892		
Aspects of Indians' Environment and Economy Affected	**Features Seen Before Large-scale Settlement By Whites**	**Whites' Actions, Laws, Institutions Having an Impact**	**Features Seen After Large-scale Settlement By Whites**
Relationship to Land	communal ownership or nonownership of land; replenishing of resources by users	white encroachment; white hunting of buffalo; expansion of railroads; encouragement of imposition of capitalistic Christianity	loss of land or individual ownership of land; less conservation of resources; near extinction of some necessities, such as buffalo; increased strife between tribes
Land-holdings, Control of Land	Indian holdings at about 138 million acres in 1887	Dawes Severalty Act; exclusion of Indians from citizenship provisions of Fourteenth Amendment; 1906 law making mixed-blood adults "competent" to sell land allotments	Indian land holdings at about 52 million acres
Means of Satisfying Basic Economic Needs	economic independence due to reliance on hunting, fishing, gathering; subsistence agriculture	white encroachment on Indian lands; Homestead Act of 1862; enforced farming by Indians of sub-par parcels of land (Dawes Severalty Act); killing off of buffalo	Basics—food, etc.—supplied by government; dependency on government and white merchants
Products for Marketing, Trading	little need for trading because system of maintaining ecological balance assured Indians' ability to supply their own necessities; minor bartering for nonessentials	Buffalo hunts and legislation leading to reduction of Indian access to arable land and resources led to shift from production of own-use products, such as light, wool blankets, to such items as rugs that could be sold for cash to whites (or traded for necessities)	Dependence on white merchants and government subsidies for subsistence items; loss of land holdings to obtain cash

Ideas and Details

1a. No. Much of the life of Plains Indians centered on the buffalo, but they did not rely solely on the buffalo for subsistence. See pages 500–501.

1b. No. Although the western Indian tribes traded with whites and with other Indians, they did so mainly to obtain necessities and not for reasons of profit. Furthermore, they did not believe that they could depend only on trade and crop raising to achieve subsistence. See pages 500–501.

1c. No. The western Indians were not part of a market economy in which they sold items for the purpose of obtaining money to buy food and other necessities. See pages 500–501.

1d. Correct. Although western Indian tribes differed culturally, they all depended on a balance among four main economic activities to achieve subsistence—crop raising; livestock raising; hunting, fishing and gathering; and raiding. This system depended on an ecological balance that was destroyed as whites moved west. See pages 500–501.

© 1994 Houghton Mifflin Company. All rights reserved.

2a. Correct. The reservation policy was designed to "civilize" the Indian tribes. Three major problems characterized the policy (1) the Indians had no say over their own affairs; (2) it was impossible to keep reservations isolated; and (3) the government disregarded variations among tribes. See pages 503–504.

2b. No. Many Indians, in order to preserve their own culture, resisted involvement in a market economy. Furthermore, the trade relationships that emerged were generally imposed on the Indians, were beneficial to whites, and made Indians more dependent on whites. See pages 503–504.

2c. No. Under the reservation policy, the government, in an effort to engage the Indians more completely in the market economy, promised to provide natives with food, clothing, and necessities. As Indians concentrated on producing trade items demanded by whites, many were forced to give up crop production. See pages 503–504.

2d. No. Although the government, through the reservation policy, promised the Indians protection from white encroachment, in the long run it was impossible to keep the reservations isolated. Therefore, because whites continued to seek Indian land for their own purposes, they continued to encroach on that land. See pages 503–504.

3a. No. A boarding-school program was established by the Dawes Severalty Act in an attempt to "civilize" Indian children. However, most did not reject their culture and returned to their reservations. See pages 506–507.

3b. No. Under the Dawes Severalty Act, the Indian Bureau did establish religious schools for the Indians in an attempt to Christianize them. However, most Indians continued to practice their native religions. See pages 506–507.

3c. Correct. The Dawes Act attempted to "civilize" western Indians by dissolving tribal, or community-owned, lands and dividing this land among individual families. The policy was ineffective, was misused by whites, and was abandoned. See page 506.

3d. No. Indians had no voice in United States Indian policy as established under the Dawes Act and carried out by the Indian Bureau. The United States government assumed a paternalistic attitude and assumed that it knew what was best for Indians. See pages 506–507.

4a. No. In the earliest stages of development one sees the individual prospector in relation to the mining frontier, the individual rancher and cowboy in relation to open-range ranching, and, to some extent, the individual timberman. Such individuals did not need large outlays of capital. See pages 507–508, 522.

4b. No. Misuse of this act was important in the development of the lumber industry but not in the development of the mining and ranching industries. See pages 507–508, 522.

4c. Correct. Corporate interests had the capital necessary for profitable long-term development of these industries and replaced the individual lumberman, prospector, and cowboy. See pages 507–508, 522.

4d. No. Those involved in the development of these frontiers were usually more interested in profit than in conservation or planned use of natural resources. See pages 507–508, 522.

5a. No. California's imposition of a tax on foreign miners and the additional evidence noted on page 509 do not support the conclusion that ethnic minorities were welcomed into the frontier communities.

5b. Correct. Although there was an ethnic mixture in many of the frontier communities, ethnic minorities such as blacks, Chinese, Mexicans, and Indians experienced abuse as a result of white prejudice. See page 509.

5c. No. Undoubtedly some opportunities were available to ethnic minorities in the frontier communities, but the evidence does not support the conclusion that "opportunities abounded." See page 509.

5d. No. Blacks, Indians, Mexicans, and Chinese did not usually gain economic or political power in the frontier communities. See page 509.

6a. No. Although some individual railroad companies turned to central business offices to keep track of equipment, freight, rates, and schedules, the railroads did not collectively coordinate all their schedules through a "central clearing house." See page 512.

6b. No. The idea of daylight-saving time was first suggested by the resourceful and pragmatic Benjamin Franklin in the eighteenth century. The railroads did not request government establishment of this in 1883. See page 512.

© 1994 Houghton Mifflin Company. All rights reserved.

6c. No. Railroad companies generally accepted the philosophy of laissez-faire capitalism. Therefore, believing that property owners should be free to make their own economic decisions without government interference, the railroads did not ask for the creation of the ICC. See page 512.

6d. Correct. Because of the difficulties posed by the hodgepodge of times throughout the United States, the railroads established four standard time zones for the whole country in 1883. They did so without consulting anyone in government. See page 512.

7a. Correct. The railroads were given some 180 million acres of land by the federal government (pages 514–515). Much of this land was used as security for bonds or sold for cash. Ranchers often bought land bordering streams and allowed their cattle to graze on adjacent public domain (page 521).

7b. No. Although farmers became dependent on the railroad for transportation of goods, they bitterly complained about railroad abuses. Many farmers also complained about ranchers who denied them the use of fenced-in pastureland. See pages 514–515, 521.

7c. No. There is no indication from the evidence given that either the cattle industry or the railroad industry respected the rights and culture of Indians. See pages 514–515, 521.

7d. No. Both the railroad industry and the cattle industry objected to government regulation. See pages 514–515, 521.

8a. No. The Great Plains is characterized by climatic extremes. See page 516.

8b. No. Because of the absence of timber in the Great Plains, many farm families had to build their houses of sod and to use buffalo and cow chips for fuel. See page 516.

8c. Correct. One of the hardships of farm life on the Great Plains was the periodic grasshopper plagues of the 1870s and 1880s. See page 516.

8d. No. Although rainfall in the Plains was unpredictable and often inadequate during the fall and summer, the area was often plagued by flooding during March and April. These characteristics are not descriptive of a desert area. See page 516.

9a. No. Plains settlers were not so much in competition with each other as with their environment. A competitive frontier spirit was not the cause of social isolation on the Plains. See pages 517–518.

9b. No. A plain is by definition an area of flat, level land. Therefore, the Great Plains region of the United States is not an area in which travel is difficult because of "rugged terrain." See pages 517–518.

9c. No. The authors of the text state that increased use of farm machinery made conquering the Plains possible. Therefore, farm machinery was widely used in the Great Plains. See pages 517–518, 519.

9d. Correct. Settlers acquired 160-acre rectangular plots of land under the Homestead Act if they agreed to *live* on and improve the land. This restriction prevented European-style villages from emerging and led to social isolation. See pages 517–518.

10a. No. Railroad expansion in the late nineteenth century linked farmers of the Great Plains with an international marketplace, but the railroad did not relieve the loneliness of farm life. See page 519.

10b. No. Commercial radio broadcasts did not begin until 1920. In addition, most rural areas did not have electricity until the 1940s. See page 519.

10c. No. Because the majority of farm families did not have electricity until the 1940s, the telegraph did not lessen farm isolation in the late nineteenth century. See page 519.

10d. Correct. The availability of RFD after 1896 meant farmers could receive letters, newspapers, advertisements, and catalogues at home on a daily basis. See page 519.

11a. Correct. Machines, increasing productivity and reducing the time and cost of farming various crops, made the extension of the farming frontier possible. See page 519.

© 1994 Houghton Mifflin Company. All rights reserved.

11b. No. Truly effective and selective pesticides were not used on a wide scale until the mid-twentieth century. See page 519.

11c. No. Although scientists in the nineteenth century began to identify the nutrients necessary for plant growth, commercial fertilizers did not become widely available until the twentieth century. See page 519.

11d. No. Extensive use of migrant labor did not make the extension of the farming frontier possible. See page 519.

12a. No. Carver worked as a botanist and an instructor at Tuskegee Institute from 1896 until his death in 1943. His agricultural research was not subsidized by the federal government. See pages 519–520.

12b. Correct. The Hatch Act of 1887 provided for agricultural experiment stations in every state, thus encouraging the advancement of farming technology. See page 519.

12c. No. Luther Burbank, noted plant breeder and horticulturist, never headed the research division of the Department of Agriculture. See pages 519–520.

12d. No. The federal government did not fund a vast irrigation network in the Great Plains. See page 519.

13a. No. The crop-lien system did not make it possible for southern farmers to increase the prices of their agricultural products. See pages 522–523.

13b. Correct. The operation of the crop-lien system forced many farmers into perpetual debt and into a state of helpless peonage. See page 523.

13c. No. The crop-lien system was at the heart of sharecropping and tenant farming and did not create the opportunity for more southern farmers to become landowners. See pages 522–523.

13d. No. The growing of traditional cash crops, especially cotton, was emphasized rather than agricultural diversification. See pages 522–523.

14a. No. The Court upheld poll taxes in 1898 in *Williams v. Mississippi* (not mentioned in the text). Because southern blacks could not afford these taxes, this ruling limited the effectiveness of the Fifteenth Amendment in extending the vote to blacks. See page 525.

14b. No. The Court upheld literacy tests as a prerequisite for voting in 1898 in *Williams* v. *Mississippi* (not mentioned in the text). As a result, literacy tests became an effective means by which southern blacks were disfranchised. See page 525.

14c. Correct. The Court's ruling was based on the idea that the police powers of a state could be used to segregate the races as long as the separate facilities were "equal." This separate-but-equal doctrine was not overturned until the *Brown* decision in 1954. See page 525.

14d. No. The Court did not rule against separate-but-equal educational facilities until its 1954 Brown decision. See page 525.

15a. No. For the most part, the cotton textile industry in the South was not very innovative. See pages 525–526.

15b. Correct. Cigarette factories were located in southern cities, and textile mills were concentrated in small southern towns. See pages 525–526.

15c. No. Southern textile mills were usually financed by local investors, not by northern banking interests. See pages 525–526.

15d. No. Although whites often sought employment in the South's cotton mills to escape the crop-lien system, they usually found that their status changed very little. See pages 525–526.

© 1994 Houghton Mifflin Company. All rights reserved.

Chapter 18

Evaluating and Using Information

Because the value of collecting information and composing a mock essay based on it lies in the doing, what follows is not a complete "answer" to the hypothetical essay test question.

What you see first is the notes entered in the blanks for the third Evidence Set. The numbers in parentheses indicate the pages in the text on which the information was found.

Following the notes is the portion of a working draft of an essay in which the expanded notes have been incorporated. Notice that the student-writer's conclusion is expressed in the opening sentence. (Your conclusion for Evidence Set Three does not have to be exactly the same conclusion as the one presented here. As long as your conclusion is a logical derivative of the evidence you have offered in your essay, and if you have not ignored significant contradictory evidence, then your conclusion is acceptable.)

If your notes and entire working draft resemble what you see here, that's enough.

The "answers" for Chapters 16, 17, and 18, have been provided mainly to help you understand what is called for in most of the remaining Evaluating and Using Information exercises in this study guide. Many of those exercises will not include a series of questions directing you to specific bits of information as the exercise for Chapter 18 does. What you will be given instead are aids (usually tables) like those you see in the "answer" to the Evaluating and Using Information exercise for Chapter 17. You will have to ask yourself the questions that will direct you to the relevant, concrete, and specific information you will need in your essays. The "answer" to Chapter 17's exercise illustrates the use of notes in the abbreviated form you will need to use when you enter them in the tables. For more complex tables, your notes will have to be even more abbreviated, just topics really. Later on, you may also find that looking back at the "answer" to the Evaluating and Using Information Exercise for Chapter 16 is useful. It shows how the abbreviated notes (topics) you will be entering as reminders in tables can be translated into plans for essays.

Evidence Set 3 (Sample Notes)

Did the cost of living increase or decrease during the Machine Age? How much? Did incomes change in the same direction? As fast and as much as the cost of living?

> **Notes**   Cost of living rose faster than wages (34). Avg. yearly wage up from $486 to $630 between 1890 and 1910. Cost of living up 47% from 1889 to 1913 for typical working-class family of four.

How did economic conditions affect the number and ages of persons in a working class family who worked outside the home for pay?

> **Notes**   Women and childen in families took jobs to boost family income by somewhere between 33% and 50%.

How did the nature of working class families' expenditures change during the Machine Age? What items formerly considered luxuries, if any, were becoming necessities, and what items formerly considered necessities, if any, were becoming luxuries?

© 1994 Houghton Mifflin Company. All rights reserved.

Notes Working-class families still had to spend disproportionate amount of family income on necessities, such as food. About half of primary wage earner's pay bought food. Expenditures increased for life insurance, amusements, alcoholic beverages, and union dues. Bought more on credit when companies like International Harvester and Singer Sewing Machine introduced innovative financing schemes for customers. Bought more clothing ready-made rather than producing clothing themselves or doing without extra outfits. Bought more perishable fruits and vegetables because of advances in canning and refrigeration.

What important technological innovations and scientific discoveries affected the healthfulness of and variety in the diet of American factory workers from 1877–1920? Did the diet of American workers and their families improve or decline? Were perishable foods and foods produced in other parts of the country more or less readily available to working class families? Why?

Notes Working class families were not subjected to extreme malnutrition. Institution of big food chains like A&P meant food could be bought more cheaply than previously. Refrigeration, including home ice boxes, and canning technology, including an improved tin can, made perishable foods—including meat—available to just about everybody in greater variety (because what couldn't be produced locally could be brought in from great distances) than ever before. New nutritious foods, such as Kellogg's Corn Flakes and Post Grape-Nuts, peanut butter, and condensed milk (Borden) developed as knowledge about vitamins and nutritional principles spread.

How did death rates and life expectancy change during the Machine Age? How did disease-caused deaths change? How did suicide, homicide, and vehicular death rates change?

Notes From 1900 to 1920, life expectancy rose by six years and death rate fell 24% (40). Some dread diseases, such as typhoid, TB, intestinal ailments caused fewer deaths. Illnesses that would affect older people more than younger people—such as heart disease and cancer—resulted in more deaths.

What changes in technology affected sanitation in the American home and the privacy of individuals in the home during the Machine Age? Did sanitation and privacy increase or decrease?

Notes Indoor toilets and private bath tubs both increased both privacy and sanitation. Greater understanding of germ theory made people more concerned about sanitation. Advances in refrigeration and canning reduced food spoilage.

What innovations affected the amount and kinds of clothing working class families had and who produced it? What was the effect of these innovations?

Notes In 1850s Elias Howe and Isaac Singer perfected the sewing machine enough to make it widely used in manufacturing. Increasingly clothing was mass produced for retail sale in years after Civil War. Clothing for middle- and lower classes became more stylish and more comfortable partly because of department stores, which multiplied from end of Civil War and the turn of the century. Men's clothing—other than laborers' work clothes—became more lightweight and more seasonal. Work clothes for industrial workers did not change much.

© 1994 Houghton Mifflin Company. All rights reserved.

What, if any, opportunities opened up during the Machine Age that would make it reasonable for factory workers to think they or their children could move upward into the middle or upper economic classes? Were there any signs that people who might be seen as trapped on the lowest rungs of the economic ladder were taking advantage of whatever opportunities for their own or their children's advancement were available?

> **Notes** Two paths to upward mobility gave hope: public education through high school and compulsory attendance laws gave many working-class youngsters a head start their parents did not have and the opening up of new service-industry clerical jobs offered better working conditions and sometimes opportunities for advancement. The Women's Trade Union league pushed for apprenticeship programs and other educational programs to help women break into skilled trades.

Conclusion for Evidence Set 3

How did the overall quality of life change for the factory worker during the Machine Age (1877–1920)? Would it be reasonable for large numbers of such workers to look to the future with hope and optimism?

> **Notes** Improvements in the standard of living resulting primarily from technological and marketing advances made living conditions—not counting those associated with the job—better during the Machine Age than they had been earlier.

Sample Section of the Working Draft of an Essay (Based on Notes for Evidence Set Three)

Conditions off the job improved on the whole. Although wages did not keep pace with the cost of living, family income often did. The 47% rise in the cost of living experienced by a typical working-class family of four between 1890 and 1913 may not look good next to the improvement between 1890 and 1910 of only a little over 29% in the average yearly wage (from $486 to $630), but in many working-class families the pay of working women and children in the family boosted family income somewhere between 33 percent and 50 percent, and rent from boarders often helped, too. Working-class families still had to spend a disproportionate amount of the family income on necessities, about half the primary wage earner's pay going to food, for example, but they were also spending more for things that most people would not call necessities, such as amusements and alcoholic beverages. Instead of making their own clothing or making do with the same old clothes for both weekday and Sunday wear, they were buying ready-made clothes. Clothing became widely available because of the quickly multiplying department stores; and it was more likely to be within their means because of mass production—fostered by the spreading use in manufacturing of the Howe and Singer-improved sewing machine. And the food they bought was more varied and nutritious. Improvements in canning and refrigeration and the advent of innovations in marketing, such as chain grocery stores like the A&P, made more perishable fruits, vegetables, and meats both more available and more affordable. Advances in nutrition and sanitation meant that working-class families were likely to be healthier, too. Between 1900 and 1920, life expectancy rose by six years, and deaths caused by dread diseases such as TB and typhoid declined. More and more people understood the relationship between germs and disease, and the same sort of advances in technology that provided refrigeration and canning to reduce food spoilage also provided indoor toilets and bath tubs to advance both privacy and sanitation. Finally, working-class families began to enjoy the luxury of hope. The availability of public education through high school for their children and compulsory attendance laws and the opening up of opportunities to move into white-collar clerical positions gave parents and young people a vision of a better future.

Ideas and Details

1a. No. The use of precision machinery to make interchangeable parts was first seen as part of the "American system of manufacturing" during the first half of the nineteenth century. Therefore, the manufacture and use of interchangeable parts was well established long before the Ford Motor Company began operation in 1903. See pages 533–534.

1b. No. The machine-tool industry—the mass manufacture of specialized machines for various industries—was born in the 1820s, long before the Ford Motor Company opened for operation in 1903. See pages 533–534.

1c. Correct. When the Ford Motor Company began operation in 1903, it utilized mass production and, through use of the electric conveyor belt, introduced the moving assembly line at its Highland Park plant in 1913. This drastically reduced the time and cost of producing cars. See pages 533–534.

1d. No. Team production suggests that a team of workers is responsible for making and assembling the entire automobile. The Ford Motor Company was not organized in this way when it began operation in 1903. See pages 533–534.

2a. No. To increase efficiency in the work place, work was divided into specific tasks. A worker could then specialize in the repetitious performance of a given task in as little time as possible. Such a process does not increase the value of skilled labor. See page 535.

2b. No. Efficiency in the production of a product can lead to decreased production costs, higher profits, and higher wages. See page 535.

2c. No. In many cases efficiency in production leads to a reduction in the work force. For example, after studying the shoveling of ore, Frederick Taylor designed fifteen different shovels and outlined the proper motions for using each. As a result, a work force of 600 was reduced to 140. See page 535.

2d. Correct. Systems of efficiency, such as those espoused by Frederick Taylor, equated time with money. As a result, the time taken to perform specific tasks became as important as the quality of the end product. See page 535.

3a. No. Although employers argued that individual employees were free to negotiate with them for better wages, this was not the way the wage system operated in practice. See pages 539–540.

3b. No. The wages for most workers rose during the period from 1877 to 1914, but this increase was not necessarily due to job competition. Because few companies employed a full work force year-round, workers had little job security and often faced periods of unemployment. See pages 539–540.

3c. No. Most wage earners probably wanted better wages, but the number-one priority for many was getting and holding a job. Furthermore, advocating positive government action on their behalf, such as a Congressionally mandated minimum wage, was beyond the frame of reference of most workers. See pages 539–540.

3d. Correct. Although employers said that employees should be paid in accordance with the law of supply and demand, the wage system did not work that way in practice. Because most power was on the side of the employer, employees often felt exploited. See pages 539–540.

4a. No. This was not a distinction made by the Court in cases involving limitations on working hours. See pages 540–541.

4b. No. In striking down a maximum-hours law for bakers, the Court in *Lochner* v. *New York* held that the law violated the Fourteenth-Amendment guarantee that no state may deprive any person of property (wages) without due process of law. In this way, the Court applied the Fourteenth Amendment to state action. See pages 540–541.

4c. Correct. The Court's decisions in the *Holden, Lochner,* and *Muller* cases demonstrated a narrow interpretation of what constituted a dangerous job and, therefore, of which workers needed protection. See pages 540–541.

4d. No. The *Lochner* v. *New York* case is evidence that the Court did not always uphold the regulatory powers of the states. See pages 540–541.

5a. No. Neither the Knights of Labor nor the American Federation of Labor advocated the use of violence against corporate power. See pages 541–542.

© 1994 Houghton Mifflin Company. All rights reserved.

5b. No. Many of the goals of the Knights of Labor were long range, abstract, and vague. The objectives of the American Federation of Labor, in contrast, were much more specific and pragmatic. See pages 541–542, 543–544.

5c. No. The Knights of Labor generally opposed strikes. See pages 541–542, 543–544.

5d. Correct. The Knights of Labor welcomed all workers into its ranks, including women, blacks, and immigrants, and including both skilled and unskilled workers. In contrast, the AFL allowed only skilled workers, was openly hostile to women, and often excluded immigrants and blacks. See pages 541–542, 543–544.

6a. No. This answer suggests that Congress was receptive to organized labor and to its demands at the time of the Haymarket riot in 1886. Reread the section on the union movement on pages 542–543.

6b. No. Although the Haymarket riot was falsely identified in the newspapers and in the minds of many people as an "anarchist riot," the government did not respond by putting military forces on alert. See pages 542–543.

6c. Correct. As a result of strikes and labor unrest, a sense of crisis existed at the time of the Haymarket riot (May 1886) and increased as a result of the riot. This led to the consequences stated in the choice. See pages 542–543.

6d. No. As a result of its association with the Haymarket riot, the Knights of Labor was weakened rather than strengthened. See pages 542–543.

7a. Correct. Initially, the WTUL was dominated by middle-class as opposed to working-class women. However, this changed in the 1910s. See pages 545–546.

7b. No. The leadership of the WTUL accepted the idea that women needed protection from exploitation. On these grounds it supported protective legislation for women and argued against a constitutional amendment guaranteeing equal rights to women. See pages 545–546.

7c. No. The WTUL worked for women's suffrage. See pages 545–546.

7d. No. The WTUL did join with the Ladies Garment Workers Union in a strike against New York City sweatshops, but it did not advocate a war against capitalist society. Gradually, the union even backed away from active union organization. See pages 545–546.

8a. No. The data indicate that the wages of working-class wage earners increased between 1890 and 1920. See pages 547–548 and the table on page 549.

8b. No. The data indicate that wages increased for farm laborers, factory workers, and middle-class workers. See pages 547–548 and the table on page 549.

8c. Correct. Although the income of factory workers, farm laborers and middle-class workers rose in the period from 1890 to 1920, the cost of living rose as well and usually outpaced wage increases. See page 548 and the table on page 549.

8d. No. We are not given enough data on the income of professionals to determine the rate of increase from 1890 to 1920. We cannot logically infer from the data supplied that inflation caused professionals to suffer more than industrial workers. See pages 547–548 and the table on page 549.

9a. No. Most bathrooms have mirrors and mirrors make people conscious of personal appearance, but mirrors were available before indoor bathrooms. See page 550.

9b. Correct. Americans began to see bodily functions in a more unpleasant light as a result of two factors: (1) the germ theory of disease, which raised fears about the link between human pollution and water contamination, and (2) the indoor bathroom's association with cleanliness and privacy. See page 550.

9c. No. Although there is a certain amount of truth in this choice, it is important to remember two factors: (1) in the late nineteenth century few Americans could afford to stay in hotels; and (2) there is not sufficient evidence in the text to support this choice. See page 550.

9d. No. The fact that indoor bathrooms became more and more common in American society in the late nineteenth and early twentieth centuries indicates that Americans were concerned about human waste as a source of infection and water contamination. See page 550.

© 1994 Houghton Mifflin Company. All rights reserved.

10a. No. Although that was the task of the traditional salesperson, it is not the task of the advertiser in a society of abundance. See page 552.

10b. Correct. In a society of abundance, supply often outstrips demand. In such a society, it is the task of advertisers to *create* demand by convincing groups of consumers that they need a particular product. It is in this way that "consumption communities" are created. See page 552.

10c. No. The task of advertisers goes far beyond simply displaying products in an attractive way. See page 552.

10d. No. Advertisers are not necessarily concerned with the quality of the product with which they are dealing or with the price, except as those factors relate to their primary task. See page 552.

11a. Correct. Both centralized management, in the form of trusts, and centralized ownership, in the form of holding companies, were means by which business leaders of the late nineteenth century attempted to deal with the uncertainties of the business cycle. See pages 553–554.

11b. No. Trusts and holding companies were "devices of control" within a particular industry. Businesspeople did not turn to such devices out of a desire to be more responsive to the needs of consumers. See pages 553–554.

11c. No. Trusts and holding companies did not separate the management of production from the management of finances and were not used by businesspeople to achieve that end. See pages 553–554.

11d. No. Trusts, which brought several companies under centralized management, and holding companies, which brought several companies under centralized ownership, did not create a more open market. See pages 553–554.

12a. No. Social Darwinists believed that there would always be people within society who were less "fit" than others. Because of this belief, they argued that poverty would always be present. See page 555.

12b. Correct. Social Darwinists believed that human society should be allowed to operate in accordance with natural laws, with "survival of the fittest" being one of those laws. Therefore, they believed, wealth and power would flow into the hands of the "most capable." See page 555.

12c. No. Social Darwinists believed that if natural laws were allowed to operate freely, wealth would continue to be maldistributed. They did not desire, nor did they advocate, an equal distribution of wealth. See page 555.

12d. No. Social Darwinists believed that people are aggressive by nature. Therefore, if natural laws were allowed to operate freely, this aggressiveness would continue to be part of human society. See page 555.

13a. No. Because most businesspeople accepted the ideas of Social Darwinism and laissez-faire conservatism, they believed that extending help to the disadvantaged was beyond the proper sphere of government. See pages 555–556.

13b. No. In accepting the tenets of laissez-faire conservatism, most businesspeople believed that the use of government power to regulate prices would threaten the right of the producer to charge the highest price the market would bear. See pages 555–556.

13c. No. In accepting the tenets of laissez-faire conservatism, most businesspeople stood against organized labor as a threat to the rights of both factory owners and factory workers. See pages 555–556.

13d. Correct. Although business leaders argued against government aid to the disadvantaged, to labor unions, or to consumers, they advocated government aid to business interests in the form of protective tariffs, government loans, and the like. See pages 555–556.

14a. Correct. Ward challenged the determinism of Social Darwinism by arguing that human beings, unlike other animals, are not at the mercy of natural laws. On the contrary, they can, through cooperative activities, create a better society. See page 556.

14b. No. Lester Ward did not accept the theory, espoused by Social Darwinists, that human institutions and corporate structures are the product of an evolutionary process that follows the dictates of natural law. See page 556.

14c. No. Lester Ward did not accept the idea that a society's economy should be allowed to operate in accordance with natural economic laws, and he rejected the notion that tampering with such laws would have disastrous consequences. See page 556.

© 1994 Houghton Mifflin Company. All rights reserved.

14d. No. Lester Ward believed that government, as the agent of the people, could act as a positive force for good in human society. This, he believed, entailed more than merely providing for the national defense. See page 556.

15a. No. The Court did not declare all trusts to be illegal in this case involving the so-called Sugar Trust. See page 558.

15b. No. The case did not involve the Interstate Commerce Commission, which was established by Congress in 1887 to regulate the rail industry. See page 558.

15c. Correct. In this case the Court narrowly interpreted Congress's power to regulate interstate commerce by ruling that manufacturing (in this case the refining of sugar) took place within a state and did not fall under congressional control. See page 558.

15d. No. The *E. C. Knight Co.* case did not deal with organized labor. See page 558.

Chapter 19

Evaluating and Using Information

```
B        F O O T B A L L     S
A    C           I           P E E R S
S    G R A N D P A R E N T S     N
E    O           T     U         S
B    Q           H     C     N A A C P
A    U     B   W O R L D     T
L O W E R  O     F     E     I
L    T     S     A     A     O   D
           B O S T O N R     N   R
                       A     E A I
     J A N E H U N T E R     L   N
           E U         I     D I N K
M O D E L  L   B O A R D E R S   I
A          L   N           D M   N
C          I           M         G
H    R E F O R M M A Y O R S
R I I S    U           V
     N     S         W I L S O N
     E   B L U E L A W S
                       E
                       S
```

Across	Down
2. football	1. baseball
6. peers	3. Birth of a Nation
7. grandparents	4. sensationalism
9. NAACP	5. croquet
11. world	8. nuclear
12. lower	10. boss
15. Boston	13. extended
16. Jane Hunter	14. drinking
19. ink	17. Nellie
20. model	18. Hull House
21. boarders	20. machine
23. reform mayors	22. movies
24. Riis	
25. Wilson	
26. blue laws	

Ideas and Details

1a. No. Long-term mortgage financing did not become widely available until the early twentieth century; therefore, it was not the "primary agent" in making suburban life practical and possible. See pages 563–564.

© 1994 Houghton Mifflin Company. All rights reserved.

1b. No. The automobile revolutionized American life and was ultimately a factor in the success of suburban development, but the first suburbs were well established by the time the Model T began to come off the assembly line. Therefore, the automobile was not the "primary agent" in making suburban life practical and possible. See pages 563–564.

1c. No. Because shopping centers followed successful suburban development, the success of the suburbs did not depend on shopping centers. See pages 563–564.

1d. Correct. Development of an inexpensive and efficient mass-transit system, such as the electric trolley, made it possible for people of the late nineteenth and early twentieth centuries to commute from a suburban home to an inner-city job. See pages 563–564.

2a. No. In the late nineteenth and early twentieth centuries, urban death rates declined, but so did urban birthrates. Therefore, although some urban growth may be attributed to natural increase, it was not the most important factor in such growth. See pages 565–566.

2b. No. Although an urban area can grow by merging with surrounding areas (e.g., Manhattan's merger with four boroughs in 1898), such mergers were not the most important cause of urban population growth in the late nineteenth and early twentieth centuries. See pages 565–566.

2c. Correct. Of the three ways by which the population of a place may grow, migration and immigration contributed most to urban population growth in the late nineteenth and early twentieth centuries. See page 566.

2d. No. Annexation of outlying areas is one of the ways in which a place may grow, but it was not the most important source of urban population growth in the late nineteenth and early twentieth centuries. See pages 565–566.

3a. Correct. Because most of the new immigrants came from eastern and southern Europe, they were usually non-Protestants. See pages 570, 571.

3b. No. Family bonds were strong for both old and new immigrants. See pages 570, 571.

3c. No. Both old and new immigrants settled mainly in the cities. See pages 570, 571.

3d. No. The new immigrants were no more likely to be escaping from persecution than were the old immigrants, and most immigrants, old and new, sought opportunity in the United States. See pages 570, 571.

4a. No. The description of immigrant communities as "transplanted communities" does not support the idea that most immigrants quickly shed their Old World attitudes and beliefs. See pages 570–571.

4b. No. Although many immigrants wanted to retain their native language, the fact that English was taught in the schools and necessary on the job made this virtually impossible. See pages 570–571.

4c. No. The statement that immigrants "practiced religion as they always had" is later qualified by the statements that churches ultimately "had to appeal more broadly to the entire nationality in order to survive" and that groups accommodated their faiths to the new environment. This clearly implies change in the area of religion. See pages 570–571.

4d. Correct. Although immigrants kept many Old World customs, the evidence supports the conclusion that as they interacted with the diversity of peoples and ideas in American society, they were forced to change their traditional habits and attitudes. See pages 570–571.

5a. No. Most foreign immigrants were male, but most black migrants were women. Most jobs available to blacks in the cities were in domestic and personal service, and such jobs were traditionally held by women. See page 572.

5b. No. Blacks, like foreign immigrants, came from a peasant background. In other words, both had been small farmers or farm laborers in the areas from which they moved. See page 572.

5c. Correct. Blacks found it more difficult than foreign immigrants to find employment in northern factories. As a result, many went into the lower-paying service sector. See page 572.

5d. No. One characteristic that black migrants and foreign immigrants had in common was that both generally moved for economic reasons. See page 572.

© 1994 Houghton Mifflin Company. All rights reserved.

6a. No. Private investors, whether as individuals or collectively, were not willing to build housing for low-income residents because they would have to accept lower profits on such units. See pages 573–574.

6b. Correct. Traditional attitudes about the role of government often restricted what local government could do or was willing to do to solve urban problems, but some states did take action by legislating light, ventilation, and safety codes for new tenement buildings. See pages 573–574.

6c. No. Most Americans did not believe it was either the responsibility of the federal government or within the government's power to legislate a national housing code. See pages 573–574.

6d. No. People's beliefs and perceptions concerning the role of government placed restrictions on the response of local, state, and national governments to housing problems. It was believed that government subsidies would undermine private enterprise. See pages 573–574.

7a. No. Most Americans believed that factors other than luck were responsible for a person's socioeconomic position. See page 574.

7b. No. Although some reformers, most notably welfare workers, believed that poverty could be eliminated by changing the environment in which people lived, most Americans did not agree with this view of poverty. See page 574.

7c. Correct. Most Americans believed that the poor were unfit, weak, and lazy. By the same token, they believed that anyone could escape poverty through hard work, thrift, and clean living. See page 574.

7d. No. Most Americans of the late nineteenth and early twentieth centuries did not believe it to be the responsibility of the federal government to assist the poor. See page 574.

8a. No. Although boarding sometimes provided extra income to middle- and working-class families, it was not a means by which people *found* employment. See page 577.

8b. Correct. Although housing reformers complained that boarding caused overcrowding and lack of privacy, it provided many young people who had left home with the semblance of a family environment. Therefore, it was a transitional stage between dependence and total independence. See page 577.

8c. No. Boarding was not important as a provider of childcare for working mothers. See pages 577–578.

8d. No. Housing reformers charged that boarding caused overcrowding and a loss of privacy. This may have been true, but it does not indicate the importance of boarding, which was useful to many people. See pages 577–578.

9a. No. Because both sexes could participate in bicycling, it was instrumental in bringing men and women together. This was especially true of the bicycle-built-for-two. (The most popular song of 1892 was "Daisybelle.") See pages 579–580.

9b. No. There is no indication that bicycling groups demanded lighted suburban streets. See pages 579–580.

9c. Correct. Bicycling was an important sport for both men and women. In order to ride, women's garments had to be less restrictive than the traditional Victorian fashions. The freer styles necessary for cycling gradually influenced everyday fashions. See pages 579–580.

9d. No. Stop and go lights were a response to the advent of the automobile in the 1920s and were not installed because of the popularity of bicycling. See pages 579–580.

10a. Correct. Burt Williams mainly played stereotypical roles. *The Birth of a Nation* presents blacks in a stereotypical way. Therefore, information about both supports the inference that blacks were subjected to prejudicial stereotyping in popular entertainment in the United States. See pages 582–583.

10b. No. Ethnic humor was often gentle and sympathetic, allowing people to laugh at the human condition. However, such an inference about ethnic humor cannot be drawn from information about Burt Williams's career or from *The Birth of a Nation*. See pages 582–583.

10c. No. The statement that show business provided economic opportunities to immigrants is a true statement. However, it is not an inference that is logically derived from the information about Burt Williams's career or from *The Birth of a Nation*. See pages 582–583.

© 1994 Houghton Mifflin Company. All rights reserved.

10d. No. Although vaudeville was the most popular form of entertainment in early-twentieth-century America, this statement is not supported by the information about Burt Williams's career or by *The Birth of a Nation*. See pages 582–583.

11a. No. Statistics showing that the rate of upward mobility among manual laborers in Atlanta, Los Angeles, and Omaha was one in five do not support the conclusion that American society was static and offered little chance for occupational advancement. See pages 585–586.

11b. No. Although there were instances of people traveling the rags-to-riches path, this most certainly did not apply to 10 percent of the population of the United States. See pages 585–586.

11c. No. The evidence indicates that in general the rates of upward mobility were almost always double those of downward mobility. This would hold true in urban areas because that is where most opportunities for advancement existed. See pages 585–586.

11d. Correct. The evidence indicates that movement along the path from "rags to moderate success" was relatively common among white males. See pages 585–586.

12a. Correct. Rapid city growth created governmental chaos from which political machines emerged. Machine politicians gained and retained power by getting to know new urban voters and responding to their needs. See pages 588–589.

12b. No. Machine politicians often engaged in bribery, thievery, and extortion. They did not gain and retain their power because they brought honesty to city government. See pages 588–589.

12c. No. Urban political machines were not efficient or cost effective. Bosses solved many urban problems, but they often did so in a way that was costly to taxpayers. See pages 588–589.

12d. No. Urban political bosses granted "favors" to their supporters. Therefore, favors were not evenly distributed to all groups and classes. See pages 588–589.

13a. No. Civic reform leaders of the late nineteenth and early twentieth centuries saw political bosses as irresponsible leaders and a threat to American society. See pages 590–591.

13b. Correct. In an effort to remove politics from government, most civic reform leaders concentrated on structural changes. They focused only on the waste and corruption associated with political bosses and failed to recognize that bosses succeeded because they used government to meet people's needs. See pages 590–591.

13c. No. Most civic reform leaders wanted to make city government more businesslike and efficient. Only a few reformers, such as Thomas L. Johnson, attempted to make government responsive to the social ills of society. See pages 590–591.

13d. No. Most civic reform leaders supported citywide election of government officials and were opposed to the district representation associated with the ward system. See pages 590–591.

14a. No. Although settlement-house founders worked with immigrants, acting as an employment and housing agency for immigrants was not their primary focus. See page 591.

14b. No. Settlement-house founders were not primarily concerned with "street people." See page 591.

14c. No. It was not the aim of settlement-house founders to establish city-run, tax-supported social welfare agencies. See page 591.

14d. Correct. Settlement-house founders believed that they could improve the lives of working class people by providing education, job training, childcare, and other benefits to the residents of working-class neighborhoods. See page 591.

15a. Correct. Urbanization in the late nineteenth century created a culturally pluralistic society. In such a society, politics became important as the arena in which different interest groups were competing for power, wealth, and status. See page 594.

15b. No. The idea of a society in which ethnic groups had blended into one, unified people is an expression of the "melting pot" idea. Such a society was not created by the urbanization in America in the late nineteenth century. See page 594.

15c. No. The discussion of urban growth in Chapter 19 deals with overcrowding, inadequate housing, urban crime and violence, ethnic prejudice, and governmental confusion. These topics do not suggest the emergence of a "smoothly functioning society." See pages 593–594.

15d. No. Although some Americans attempted to use government as an agent for moral reform, the evidence does not support the conclusion that urbanization created a society in which most Americans accepted this as the proper role of government. See page 594.

Chapter 20

Ideas and Details

1a. Correct. Because voters were evenly divided between the two political parties, neither party was the "majority party" during the period from 1877-1897. As a result, there were frequent power shifts that prevented the passage of effective, lasting legislation. See page 600.

1b. No. Americans generally accepted a passive federal government that did not involve itself in economic and social matters. See page 600.

1c. No. This was an age in which party identification was important; voters were interested in politics, believed their votes were important, and voted in large numbers. See page 600.

1d. No. Politics was a popular form of mass entertainment and people formed strong loyalties to politicians and political parties. Consequently, political contests were often deeply personal. See page 600.

2a. No. Although the Supreme Court placed responsibility for the regulation of interstate commerce in the hands of Congress through the *Wabash* case, the Court did not broadly interpret those powers in cases arising under the Interstate Commerce Act. See page 602.

2b. No. The Interstate Commerce Act did not extend government aid to private industry; therefore, the Court did not rule on this issue in cases arising under the Interstate Commerce Act. See page 602.

2c. Correct. Through the *Wabash* case, the Court ruled that only Congress could limit railroad rates involving interstate commerce. But in cases arising under the Interstate Commerce Act, the Court reduced the regulatory powers of the Interstate Commerce Commission. See page 602.

2d. No. In the *Wabash* case the Court accepted the principle of government regulation of industry by holding that only Congress could limit railroad rates involving interstate commerce. This decision was not overturned by the Court in cases arising under the Interstate Commerce Act. See page 602.

3a. No. The Dingley Tariff was passed in 1897 and raised tariff rates to an average level of 57 percent. The passage of the tariff was not referred to as the "Crime of '73." See pages 603, 604.

3b. Correct. Congress passed legislation in 1873 that demonetized silver and stopped the coining of silver dollars. The United States thus went to the gold standard. This policy did not meet the demands of debtors who wanted to expand the money supply and was denounced as the "Crime of '73." See page 604.

3c. No. The Sherman Silver Purchase Act was passed by Congress in 1878 and required the U.S. Treasury to buy between $2 million and $4 million of silver per month. This law was an attempt by Congress to pacify groups calling for the "free coinage of silver" and was not referred to as the "Crime of '73." See page 604.

3d. No. The Pendleton Act was passed by Congress in 1882 and created the Civil Service Commission. It was not referred to as the "Crime of '73." See pages 601–602, 604.

© 1994 Houghton Mifflin Company. All rights reserved.

4a. No. The contention that women will demand national disarmament was not the most common argument against giving women the right to vote. See page 605.

4b. Correct. The most common argument in the Senate against the extension of the right to vote to women was the contention that it would interfere with their family responsibilities and ruin female virtue. See page 605.

4c. No. The contention that women were not well enough educated to vote was not the most common argument used by senators opposed to the extension of the vote to women. See page 605.

4d. No. The contention that women were too emotional was not the most common argument used by senators opposed to the extension of the vote to women. See page 605.

5a. No. The question of pensions to Civil War veterans and their widows concerned Union veterans only. Congress never considered pensions for Confederate veterans. See pages 600–601, 608–609.

5b. No. The events leading to congressional action on pensions for Civil War veterans and their widows make it obvious that the memories of the war were still alive and affected the decisions of Congress. See pages 600–601, 608–609.

5c. No. By providing generous pensions to Union veterans and their widows, Congress made one of the largest welfare commitments it has ever made. See pages 600–601, 608–609.

5d. Correct. Although angered by tactics of lobbyists for the Grand Army of the Republic, congressmen still voted in favor of providing generous pensions for Union veterans and their widows. They did so, in large measure, because of pressure from this politically powerful interest group. See pages 600–601, 608–609.

6a. No. The presidents during the Gilded Age were not "inspiring" figures to most of the electorate. See page 606.

6b. No. The presidents during the Gilded Age were hardworking men and may not accurately be described as lazy. See page 606.

6c. Correct. The presidents during the Gilded Age did not evoke much of an emotional response from the electorate, but they were honorable, proper, and honest. See page 606.

6d. No. Believing that it was their job to execute the laws passed by Congress, the presidents during the Gilded Age may not be described as forceful or active. See pages 606.

7a. Correct. Partly as a result of bribery and vote fraud, the Republicans carried Indiana by 2,300 votes and New York by 14,000 votes. See page 608.

7b. No. The British minister, to the delight of the Republicans, said that Democrat Grover Cleveland's election would be good for England. This offended Irish Democrats and weakened Cleveland's campaign. See page 608.

7c. No. Grover Cleveland is not known to have told ethnic jokes offensive to Irish Catholics. See page 608.

7d. No. Grover Cleveland was against high tariffs, and, even though he was convinced to temper his attacks against tariffs for political reasons, he never called for higher tariffs. See page 608.

8a. No. Through the formation of sales cooperatives, the Grange did attempt to eliminate the middleman. However, these cooperatives were failures. See pages 610–611.

8b. No. Although Grangers were involved in politics and successfully elected some sympathetic state legislators, their efforts to counter the political power of corporations by passing regulatory legislation failed in the end because the Supreme Court ruled against "Granger laws." See pages 610–611.

8c. No. Most farm families already accepted the values of thrift and hard work, and the promotion of these values was too simplistic to solve the problems experienced by farmers in the late nineteenth century. See pages 610–611.

8d. Correct. Although the Grange was not able to achieve its objectives, its economic and political activism served as a precedent for future action by farmers. For example, the Grange concept of cooperation was an important characteristic of the Farmers' Alliances, and its political activism was important to the People's party. See pages 610–611.

© 1994 Houghton Mifflin Company. All rights reserved.

9a. No. Although farmers complained about the cost of farm machinery, they did not see the subtreasury system as a way to lower those costs. See pages 611–612.

9b. No. The subtreasury system was not proposed as an agency that would make second mortgages available to farmers facing bankruptcy. See pages 611–612.

9c. Correct. The subtreasury system would give farmers a place to store their crops while waiting for higher prices, and it would allow them to borrow subtreasury notes amounting to 80 percent of the value of their crops. Through this system, farmers hoped to solve their cash and credit problems. See page 611.

9d. No. The subtreasury system was not a means by which transportation costs could be lowered. See pages 611–612.

10a. No. Although the Omaha platform called for increased government regulation of trusts, it did not call for the nationalization of the oil and steel industries. See page 613.

10b. No. Although Populists did call for a more active federal government in the Omaha platform, they did not advocate a welfare program for destitute farmers. They believed that an expansive money supply, brought about by the free coinage of silver, would solve the farmers' monetary problems. See page 613.

10c. No. The Populists clearly recognized the debt problems of farmers but did not call for a moratorium on debts in the Omaha platform. They believed that a graduated income tax, the creation of a postal savings bank, and the free coinage of silver would solve farmers' monetary problems. See page 613.

10d. Correct. Farmers believed that railroads had been built on public land with public funds, and it angered them that railroads were operated for the private enrichment of a few individuals. Therefore, the Omaha platform called for government ownership of the railroad lines. See page 613.

11a. Correct. The national economy had reached the point where business failures in one area had a ripple effect throughout the economic system, causing failures in other areas. See page 613.

11b. No. In some measure, the depression of the 1890s was due to overspeculation in certain industries, but it was not due to overspeculation in the stock market. See page 615.

11c. No. Although the Sherman Silver Purchase Act had a psychological impact that led to the dwindling of the nation's gold reserves, it was not the reason for the broad-based nature of the depression. In addition, repeal of the act did not halt the run on the Treasury. See page 615.

11d. No. The impact of the depression of the 1890s on other countries and the subsequent withdrawal of foreign investments from the United States are indications of the broad-based nature of the depression. However, this withdrawal did not cause the depression to be broad-based. See page 615.

12a. No. Jacob Riis (page 573) was a New York journalist and the author of *How the Other Half Lives*, published in 1890. The book exposed the horrors of life in the slums of New York. Although Riis was an active reformer, he was not a socialist. See page 616.

12b. Correct. Eugene Debs, president of the American Railway Union, was jailed in 1894 for defying a federal court injunction against the Pullman strike. While in jail, Debs became a socialist and, after his release, became the leading spokesperson for American socialism. See page 616.

12c. No. Ignatius Donnelly (page 000) was a leading Minnesota Populist during the 1890s and was not the leading spokesperson for American socialism. See page 616.

12d. No. Leonidas Polk (page 613) was president of the Southern Alliance in 1891 and a leading North Carolina Populist. See page 616.

13a. No. Although Jacob Coxey was a wealthy businessman from Ohio, his plan for dealing with the depression did not include government aid to business. See pages 616–617.

13b. No. The United States was already on the gold standard in 1894 when Coxey's "commonweal army" marched on the nation's capital. Coxey believed that the government's insistence on backing currency with gold was prolonging the depression. See pages 616–617.

© 1994 Houghton Mifflin Company. All rights reserved.

13c. No. The nation did not have a federal income tax in 1894, and Jacob Coxey did not advocate tax cuts as a way to end the depression. See pages 616–617.

13d. Correct. Jacob Coxey advocated that the government purposefully cause inflation by pumping $500 million of paper money into the economy through a federal jobs program. See pages 616–617.

14a. No. There is no indication that southern white Democrats believed their political power was jeopardized by a black-led, southern-based Socialist party. See page 618.

14b. No. Although blacks served in southern state legislatures for a brief period during the Reconstruction era, they had not served since the white southern Democrats had regained power. See page 618.

14c. Correct. Out of fear that a biracial Populist coalition would jeopardize their power in the South, southern white Democrats decided to disfranchise blacks completely. See page 618.

14d. No. Through the use of poll taxes and literacy tests, southern whites had already curtailed black voting to the point where blacks could not win elections at the state or local level. See page 618.

15a. Correct. Free silver was attractive to many farmers of the West and South, but its promise of inflation was not attractive to city dwellers and factory workers. As a result, Bryan was never able to build an urban-rural coalition. See page 621.

15b. No. McKinley conducted a "front-porch" campaign that can hardly be called "spirited." See page 621.

15c. No. When the Democrats nominated Bryan and endorsed many Populist ideas, the Populists decided to nominate Bryan for the presidency and Tom Watson of Georgia for the vice-presidency. See page 621.

15d. No. Bryan was not endorsed by the Socialist party. See page 621.

Chapter 21

Ideas and Details

1a. No. Voter loyalty to political parties began to decline during the Progressive era. See pages 627–628.

1b. No. These organizations were not responsible for introducing charismatic personalities to political campaigns. See pages 627–628.

1c. No. These organizations often served to stimulate debate on urban issues rather than stifle it. See pages 627–628.

1d. Correct. Organizations such as those mentioned lobbied for their own interests and, as a result, caused politics to become more fragmented. At the same time, however, their attempts to educate the public stimulated debate and made politics more issue-oriented. See pages 627–628.

2a. No. Progressives disliked professional politicians and the fact that they often selected candidates through the party caucus. It was for this reason that Progressives advocated the use of direct primaries to nominate candidates. See page 629.

2b. No. Although middle-class progressive reformers advocated direct primaries as a way of returning government to "the people," they often meant middle-class people like themselves, excluding the working classes, blacks, and women from their definition of "the people." See page 629.

2c. Correct. Most middle-class progressive reformers were opposed to party politics, which they believed had been corrupted by political machines and political bosses. Therefore, the reforms they advocated were intended to improve government by reducing the power of political parties. See page 629.

© 1994 Houghton Mifflin Company. All rights reserved.

2d. No. The direct primary was advocated as a way to nominate political candidates for office and does not demonstrate the belief that government should respect the rights of the individual. See page 629.

3a. No. Progressives were not necessarily against compromise, but they disliked the bargaining associated with "old style" politics. See pages 628–629.

3b. Correct. Professionals of the new middle class generally formed the progressive movement's leadership. They believed that practices important in their professions, such as systematic investigation and application of scientific techniques, could be used to solve society's problems. See pages 628–629.

3c. No. Although the evidence indicates that progressives wanted political reforms designed to make government more responsive to "the people" by correcting the ills of "boss-ridden" party politics, progressives did not advocate literacy tests as a requirement for voting. See pages 628–629.

3d. No. Although progressives advocated political reforms designed to make politicians more responsive to "the people," they did not suggest requiring full financial disclosure by all political candidates. See pages 628–629.

4a. No. Evidence indicates that most middle-class progressives were interested in political reform (the initiative, referendum, and recall), and most working-class progressives were interested in social reform (improvements in housing, safe factories, workers' compensation). See pages 629–630.

4b. No. By advocating reforms that would shorten working hours and ensure safe factories, working-class progressives demonstrated their belief that government should ensure the safety and welfare of the worker by regulating the work place. See pages 629–630.

4c. No. Working-class progressives usually rejected moral reforms such as prohibition and Sunday closing laws. See pages 629–630.

4d. Correct. In their belief that government should be responsible for alleviating many of the problems associated with urban-industrial growth, working-class progressives realized that political bosses could be useful and that they were not necessarily enemies of reform. See pages 629–630.

5a. No. Eugene Debs's personality is not the reason that most progressives rejected socialist ideology. See page 630.

5b. Correct. Most progressives of the middle and working classes accepted the capitalist system, had relatively comfortable economic and social positions within that system, and had too much of a stake in that system to advocate its overthrow. See page 630.

5c. No. A nationalist appeal is one that emphasizes devotion to country and nation. Progressives had a strong sense of devotion to the United States and often saw socialism as a radical attack against the nation's fundamental principles. See page 630.

5d. No. Progressives rejected the basic tenets of the laissez-faire philosophy as outdated and obsolete in an age of urban-industrial growth. See page 630.

6a. Correct. La Follette believed that corporate involvement in politics was a source of political corruption and that corporations had amassed power at the expense of the people. Therefore, he advocated that corporations be driven out of politics. See page 632.

6b. No. Although this was a belief held by Eugene Debs (the leader of the Socialist party), La Follette, a progressive, did not share this belief. See page 632.

6c. No. La Follette's program (known as the "Wisconsin Idea") involved the establishment of regulatory commissions staffed with experts. See page 632.

6d. No. Although La Follette advocated regulation of railroad rates, he did not advocate nationalization (government ownership) of the railroads. See page 632.

7a. No. Dewey did not believe that the teaching of moral principles should be the primary concern of public education. Furthermore, when such principles were dealt with, Dewey, who rejected the idea of moral absolutes, believed that they should be subjected to scientific inquiry. See page 635.

© 1994 Houghton Mifflin Company. All rights reserved.

7b. No. Dewey did not propose the accreditation of public school teachers by a national accreditation agency. See page 635.

7c. No. Dewey rejected the idea that there was a fixed body of knowledge to be conveyed to students. He favored the "student-centered" as opposed to the "subject-centered" school. See page 635.

7d. Correct. Dewey believed that education should be related to the interests of students and that the subjects taught should relate directly to their lives. See page 635.

8a. No. It is incorrect to say that Washington believed that black Americans should "passively" accept their position in American society. See page 640.

8b. Correct. Washington argued that while temporarily accepting their inferior position in American society, blacks should prove themselves worthy of equal rights by adopting a strategy of self-help. See page 640.

8c. No. Washington believed that actively demanding and fighting for their political and social rights would prove to be counterproductive for black Americans. See page 640.

8d. No. Although it is true that Washington secretly contributed money to support legal challenges to discriminatory legislation, he did not believe that black Americans should challenge such legislation in an open, direct, or active manner. See page 640.

9a. No. Although the suffrage crusade grew out of the 1830s abolitionist argument in favor of equal rights for all Americans, the idea was rejected by many Americans in the 1910s just as it had been rejected in the 1830s. See page 644.

9b. No. Because most Americans accepted traditional gender roles and the restrictions such roles placed on women, some suffragists used a traditionalist view (that women have "unique" qualities) to defend female suffrage. However, use of this argument was not "the most decisive factor" in the extension of the vote to women. See page 644.

9c. Correct. The efforts of women during the First World War were probably the most decisive factor in convincing legislators to extend the vote to women. See page 644.

9d. No. Although Carrie Chapman Catt organized women at the precinct level so that pressure could be put on male politicians who opposed the extension of the vote to women, she is considered a moderate and did not engage in militant tactics. See page 644.

10a. No. Roosevelt's policy toward the Northern Securities Company and his support of the Hepburn Act, the Pure Food and Drug Act, and the Meat Inspection Act demonstrate his rejection of the idea that business must be allowed to organize and operate without government interference. See page 646.

10b. Correct. Roosevelt preferred cooperation between government and business and preferred that business regulate itself. However, he was willing to prosecute trusts that unscrupulously exploited the public and refused to regulate themselves. See page 646.

10c. No. Roosevelt, recognizing that business consolidation could bring efficiency, did not see bigness as bad in and of itself. See page 646.

10d. No. Roosevelt's handling of the trusts does not indicate that he believed in using the tax power of the government (which was minimal because there was no income tax) to punish irresponsible corporations. See page 646.

11a. Correct. Roosevelt's handling of the trusts, his labor policy, and his actions on the issue of conservation indicate an assertion of presidential power. On the other hand, Taft's handling of the tariff issue and his inability to publicize issues he supported indicate caution and restraint. See page 648.

11b. No. Although Roosevelt preferred cooperation between business and government to confrontation, he often offended business leaders by speaking against their unscrupulous abuse of power. In contrast, although Taft supported federal regulation of business, he was quieter and his accomplishments were less publicized. See page 648.

11c. No. On the contrary, Roosevelt was far more willing to bend the law to his purposes than was Taft, who believed in the strict restraint of the law. See page 648.

11d. No. Both Roosevelt and Taft were sympathetic to reform. See page 648.

© 1994 Houghton Mifflin Company. All rights reserved.

12a. No. Neither Roosevelt nor Wilson called for the "destruction" of big business. See pages 649–650.

12b. No. Neither Roosevelt nor Wilson called for a restoration of the laissez-faire philosophy. See pages 649–650.

12c. Correct. Roosevelt called for federal regulatory commissions to establish cooperation between big business and big government, thereby protecting citizens' interests; but Wilson emphasized breaking up monopolies, returning to open competition, and using government to accomplish both. See page 649.

12d. No. Both Roosevelt and Wilson supported equality of economic opportunity. See pages 649–650.

13a. No. Wilson's support of the Clayton Antitrust Act and creation of the FTC demonstrates his acceptance of the fact that a return to free competition was impossible. See pages 650–651.

13b. No. Neither the Clayton Antitrust Act nor the bill creating the FTC was passed as a consequence of Supreme Court rulings. Therefore, they do not indicate a challenge by Wilson to the Court. See pages 650–651.

13c. No. The Democratic leadership in Congress favored passage of the Clayton Act and the bill creating the FTC. See pages 650–651.

13d. Correct. As president, Wilson realized that economic concentration had gone so far that a return to free competition was impossible. With this realization, Wilson supported expansion of the government's regulatory powers through support of the Clayton Act and creation of the FTC. See pages 650–651.

14a. Correct. By reducing tariffs and thus encouraging imports, the Underwood Tariff encouraged free competition and free trade. See page 651.

14b. No. President Wilson proposed and actively supported passage of the Underwood Tariff, including the income-tax provision. See page 651.

14c. No. The Underwood Tariff imposed a graduated income tax on residents of the United States; the maximum rate was 6 percent, and that rate was applied to incomes over $500,000. See page 651.

14d. No. Because the Underwood Tariff dramatically reduced tariff rates on imports, it did not lead to a trade war. See page 651.

15a. No. The strength of opposition to reform, court rulings against progressive legislation, and shortcomings of regulatory agencies are a few indications that, in many respects, progressives failed to bring about a redistribution of power. In 1920 government remained under the influence of business and industry. See page 652.

15b. No. Use of such devices as the initiative, the referendum, and the recall by special interests indicates that business and industrial interests still had influence and power at the state level, and the shortcomings of regulatory agencies indicate the same was true at the national level. See page 652.

15c. Correct. Although business and industrial interests still had influence in government, these interests had been forced to become more responsive to public opinion as a result of trustbusting. See page 652.

15d. No. Progressives stressed different themes and different causes and often worked at cross-purposes. See page 652.

Chapter 22

Ideas and Details

1a. No. The American public has not traditionally paid a great deal of attention to nor been well educated on foreign policy issues. As a result, foreign policy, unlike domestic policy, is not usually "shaped" by the people. See page 658.

1b. No. Although the business community has a hand in the shaping of foreign policy, it is a mistake to say that the business community alone was "largely" responsible for foreign policy decisions. See page 658.

1c. Correct. The foreign policy elite, made up of "opinion leaders" from many areas of American society (business, politics, the military, labor, agriculture), were instrumental in the late nineteenth century, as they are instrumental today, in shaping American foreign policy. See page 658.

1d. No. Although military leaders have a hand in the shaping of foreign policy, it is a mistake to say that such policy in the late nineteenth century was "shaped largely" by this one group. See page 658.

2a. No. Whether the United States has acted in a decisive or indecisive manner in foreign policy is not the issue in what William Appleman Williams calls the "tragedy of American diplomacy." See pages 659–660.

2b. Correct. The chauvinistic belief that American society is superior to other societies (American ethnocentrism), that only the American model of government will work, and a complete disregard for the rights to self-rule by other developing nations produced the "tragedy of American diplomacy." See pages 659–660.

2c. No. The willingness to use force in areas such as Latin America is more a consequence of the "tragedy" than an explanation of what produced this "tragedy." See pages 659–660.

2d. No. Although it is true that the American diplomatic corps was one of the worst in the world in the late nineteenth century, this is not the issue in what William Appleman Williams calls the "tragedy of American diplomacy." See pages 659–660.

3a. No. American farm leaders did not seek an expansionist foreign policy for the purpose of learning new agricultural techniques from foreign agricultural specialists. See pages 660–663.

3b. Correct. In the final third of the nineteenth century, depressions affected the economy about once a decade. Many business and farm leaders believed overproduction was a major cause of economic declines and advocated expansion into foreign markets as a preventive measure. See page 662.

3c. No. The expansionist sentiment of the late nineteenth century was not fueled by the belief that domestic labor problems could be solved by increasing the number of immigrants. See pages 660–663.

3d. No. Although United States economic and political influence increased in Latin America in the late nineteenth century, especially after the Spanish-American War, the states of Latin America did not want the United States to exert political control over them. See pages 660–663.

4a. No. Seward's vision of an American empire included Iceland, Greenland, Hawaii, and certain Pacific islands as well as expansion throughout the Americas. See pages 663–664.

4b. Correct. Seward advocated a canal through Central America as essential to the unity of the large American empire that he envisioned. See pages 663–664.

4c. No. Seward believed that other peoples would find the republican principles of American society attractive. Therefore, they would naturally gravitate toward the United States, making expansion by military means unnecessary. See pages 663–664.

4d. No. Although in 1867 Seward signed a treaty with Denmark to buy the Danish West Indies, the treaty was not ratified by the Senate. The Danish West Indies did not become part of the American empire until 1917. See pages 663–664.

5a. No. Andrew Carnegie was founder of the Carnegie Steel Company, which controlled most of the steel production in the United States by 1900. Although he supported the concept of the "New Navy" and signed a lucrative naval contract in 1883, he was not responsible for "popularizing" the New Navy. See page 665.

5b. No. Ulysses Grant was not responsible for popularizing the New Navy. See page 665.

5c. No. Hamilton Fish, secretary of state under President Grant, was not responsible for popularizing the New Navy. See page 665.

© 1994 Houghton Mifflin Company. All rights reserved.

5d. Correct. Alfred T. Mahan argued that a modern, efficient naval force was essential for any nation that aspired to great-power status. Through his lectures and published works, he had an enormous impact on the successful drive to modernize the United States Navy, popularly known as the "New Navy." See page 665.

6a. No. Grover Cleveland was an expansionist who recognized the economic advantages of annexing the Hawaiian islands. His opposition to annexation was not based on economic questions. See page 666.

6b. No. Cleveland's opposition to the annexation of Hawaii was not based on racial questions. See page 666.

6c. Correct. Cleveland supported economic expansion but did not believe it should lead to imperialism. (See pages 656–658 for the distinction between economic expansion and imperialism.) The facts of the Hawaiian revolution convinced Cleveland that because annexation was being forced on the Hawaiians it was imperialistic. See page 666.

6d. No. Cleveland's opposition to the annexation of Hawaii was not based on fear that it would lead to war. See page 666.

7a. Correct. The boundary dispute between Venezuela and Great Britain was settled by an Anglo-American arbitration board that barely consulted Venezuela in its deliberations. By disregarding Venezuela's rights and sensibilities in this manner, the United States displayed an imperialistic attitude. See page 666.

7b. No. The crisis did not center on the question of the type of government Venezuela had. See page 666.

7c. No. The United States sent a strong protest to the British concerning their actions in Venezuela. The British stalled at first but then, not wanting war, bowed to American pressure. As a result, the Monroe Doctrine was strengthened and the United States and Great Britain began to form closer ties. See page 666.

7d. No. The United States Navy did not become involved in the Venezuelan crisis of 1895. See page 666.

8a. No. The Teller Amendment did not announce American intentions to annex Cuba. See page 669.

8b. No. The Teller Amendment, passed by the U. S. Congress, was related to the Spanish-American-Cuban-Filipino War, but it was not a reason for the war. See page 669.

8c. No. The Teller Amendment did not have the effect of expanding the Spanish-American-Cuban-Filipino War to the South Pacific. See page 669.

8d. Correct. After passing resolutions declaring Cuba to be free, Congress adopted the Teller Amendment, which disclaimed any intention by the United States to annex Cuba. See page 669.

9a. No. Although there was a humanitarian aspect to United States entry into the Spanish-American War, it cannot be said that "in the final analysis" this was the reason Americans accepted the war. See pages 666–670.

9b. No. Although religious leaders supported the war and Protestant clergymen envisioned doing missionary work in Catholic Cuba, it is incorrect to say that "in the final analysis" Americans accepted the war because of a desire to carry the Christian message to other people. See pages 666–670.

9c. Correct. Because the spirit of expansionism had many sources, it may be labeled "multifaceted." Moreover, in dealing with the reasons for the war, each reason may be analyzed separately; but, "in the final analysis," we are left with multiple causation. See page 670.

9d. No. Although many imperialists supported the war because it offered an opportunity to fulfill the "large policy," most Americans had no idea of what that policy was. Therefore, it is a mistake to say that "in the final analysis" this was why Americans accepted the war. See pages 666–670.

10a. Correct. Of the over 5,400 Americans who died in the war, only 379 died in combat. All others died from malaria or yellow fever. See page 670.

10b. No. In the destruction of the Spanish fleet outside Santiago harbor, the Spanish suffered 474 killed and wounded, and the United States suffered one killed and one wounded. This does not constitute "most" of the 5,400 Americans who lost their lives in the Spanish-American War. See page 670.

© 1994 Houghton Mifflin Company. All rights reserved.

10c. No. In the Battle of Manila Bay (May 1, 1898) Spanish losses numbered 381 killed, and American casualties consisted of 8 wounded. See page 670.

10d. No. In the charge up San Juan Hill, the Rough Riders lost about 89 men. This does not constitute "most" of the 5,400 Americans who lost their lives in the Spanish-American War. See page 670.

11a. No. The anti-imperialists used a variety of arguments in their campaign against the Treaty of Paris. See pages 672–673.

11b. Correct. The anti-imperialists came from many different interest groups in American society. Each group looked at domestic issues differently and also found it impossible to speak with one voice on foreign policy issues. Therefore, they were hindered by the inconsistency of their arguments. See pages 672–673.

11c. No. Although Mark Twain and Andrew Carnegie spoke against the Treaty of Paris, the treaty passed by a 57-to-27 vote in the Senate. See pages 672–673.

11d. No. Believing it best to end the war and then push for Filipino independence, William Jennings Bryan supported the Treaty of Paris. However, his support for the treaty did not aid the anti-imperialist campaign. The treaty passed by a 57-to-27 vote. See pages 672–673.

12a. No. As an ideology rather than just a policy, the Open Door was not based on the preservation of the self-determination of other nations. See page 674.

12b. Correct. The ideology expressed in the Open Door was that the United States required exports; therefore, any area closed to American products, citizens, or ideas threatened the survival of the United States. See page 674.

12c. No. As an ideology rather than just a policy, the Open Door was not based on the idea that freedom of the seas would lead to the economic expansion of the world community of nations. See page 674.

12d. No. As an ideology rather than just a policy, the Open Door was not based on the belief that all nations of the world should be considered equals. See page 674.

13a. Correct. The Filipinos felt betrayed by the Treaty of Paris and, under the leadership of Emilio Aguinaldo, fought for their independence in the Philippine Insurrection. American forces finally suppressed the insurrection in 1901, leaving 5,000 Americans and 200,000 Filipinos dead. See pages 674–676.

13b. No. The Philippines were not granted independence until 1946. See pages 674–676.

13c. No. The United States assumed that it knew what was best for the Filipino people and held no referendum. See pages 674–676.

13d. No. The United States held sovereignty over the Philippines for forty-eight years. Although it attempted to establish democratic government over the years, the United States did not guarantee to the Filipino people the same rights enjoyed by American citizens. See pages 674–676.

14a. No. The United States did not extend aid to French colonies in Indochina in the early twentieth century. See pages 676–678.

14b. No. In its efforts to protect American interests in the Pacific (especially in the Philippines), the United States made concessions to Japan—the dominant power in Asia. Therefore, in the Taft-Katsura Agreement of 1905 the United States recognized Japanese hegemony in Korea and, in return, the Japanese pledged not to interfere with American interests in the Philippines. See pages 676–678.

14c. No. The United States did not want either Russia or Japan to become dominant in Asia but wanted each to balance the power of the other. Therefore, the U.S. remained neutral in the conflict and President Roosevelt, at the request of the Japanese, agreed to mediate the crisis. See pages 676–678.

14d. Correct. In an effort to increase American influence in Manchuria, President Taft was able to gain agreement on the inclusion of a group of American bankers in a four-power consortium to build a Chinese railway. In response (and in defiance of the Open Door policy), Japan signed a treaty with Russia by which the two staked out spheres of influence in China for themselves. This strengthened Japan's position in Manchuria and caused more friction between the U.S. and Japan. See page 677.

© 1994 Houghton Mifflin Company. All rights reserved.

15a. No. Both the Roosevelt Corollary and United States actions in Latin America support the "tragedy of American diplomacy" idea expressed on page 660—that America has persisted in the belief that only the American model of government will work. See pages 680–682.

15b. No. Although the United States has shared some of its wealth and resources with the people of Latin America, this clearly is not the rationale behind either the Roosevelt Corollary or the imperialistic behavior of the United States in its relations with Latin America. See pages 680–682.

15c. Correct. The United States deemed order essential to protect the Panama Canal and American commerce and investments and to prepare Latin Americans for American-style government. Both the Roosevelt Corollary and United States behavior in the region express this quest for order. See page 681.

15d. No. Although the United States did believe it had the right to exploit the resources of Latin America, this belief is not the best explanation for the rationale behind the Roosevelt Corollary and the imperialistic behavior of the United States in Latin America. See pages 680–682.

Chapter 23

Ideas and Details

1a. No. When Russia mobilized its armies to aid Serbia, Germany first declared war against Russia and then against France, Russia's ally. Through all of this, Austria-Hungary did not invade Russia and Britain did not declare war. See page 688.

1b. No. The act of terrorism that led to war was that of a Serbian nationalist against Archduke Franz Ferdinand, heir to the Austro-Hungarian throne. But Great Britain did not enter the war in response to this act of terrorism. See page 688.

1c. No. Serbia did not invade Austria-Hungary. See page 688.

1d. Correct. Whereas Austria-Hungary declared war against Serbia and Germany declared war against Russia and France, Great Britain hesitated. Only when Germany invaded Belgium, whose neutrality was guaranteed by Great Britain, did Britain enter the war. See page 688.

2a. No. Woodrow Wilson was sincere in his desire to keep the United States out of the war in Europe. See pages 688–690.

2b. No. The print media had not built broad-based sympathy for Serbian nationalism in the United States. Moreover, Serbian nationalism was not the major issue in the minds of most Americans. See pages 688–690.

2c. Correct. Wilson's appeal for neutrality clashed with three realities: (l) ethnic groups in the United States took sides; (2) economic links with the Allies made neutrality difficult; and (3) administration officials were sympathetic to the Allies. See pages 688–690.

2d. No. Secretary of State William Jennings Bryan insisted on a policy of strict neutrality. See pages 688–690, 691.

3a. No. Wilsonianism held that all diplomatic agreements among nations, including all alliance systems, should be openly negotiated. See pages 690, 712.

3b. No. Wilsonianism advocated decolonization (the breaking up of empires) and the principle of self-determination (the right of all people to determine their own future without outside interference). See pages 690, 712.

3c. No. Wilsonianism advocated reducing world armaments. See pages 690, 712.

3d. Correct. Wilsonianism advocated an open world in every respect and, in keeping with that concept, advocated a world community of nations with no barriers to commerce. See pages 690, 712.

© 1994 Houghton Mifflin Company. All rights reserved.

4a. Correct. Bryan believed that Germany had a right to prevent contraband from going to the Allies and faulted Great Britain for using passenger ships to carry such contraband. When Wilson rejected Bryan's advice that Americans not be allowed to travel on belligerent ships, Bryan resigned. See pages 691–692.

4b. No. Although Bryan protested Great Britain's blockade of Germany, no great public outcry led to his resignation. See pages 691–692.

4c. No. Bryan believed that the United States should remain strictly neutral in its relations with the European belligerents. See pages 691–692.

4d. No. Bryan did not advocate American entry into the war. See pages 691–692.

5a. No. Jay Gould was a railroad magnate of the late nineteenth century. Whereas he died in 1892, he did not help finance peace groups in the United States in the 1910s. See pages 692–693.

5b. Correct. Andrew Carnegie established the Carnegie Endowment for International Peace in 1910. This organization helped to finance peace groups during the prewar years. See pages 692–693.

5c. No. John Pershing, general in the United States Army and commander of the American Expeditionary Forces in Europe during the First World War, did not finance peace groups in the United States before the war. See pages 692–693, 698.

5d. No. Bernard Baruch was a financier who served as chairman of the War Industries Board during the First World War. He did not finance peace groups in the United States in the prewar years. See pages 692–693, 702.

6a. No. Wilson broke diplomatic relations with Germany on February 3, 1917, in response to Germany's resumption of unrestricted submarine warfare on February 1. Thus relations were severed before the Zimmermann note was given to the United States ambassador to Great Britain on February 24. See page 693.

6b. No. The Zimmermann telegram proposed an alliance between Germany and Mexico and did not cause Wilson to rethink his position on the application of international law to the submarine. See page 693.

6c. Correct. Mexican-American relations were strained in 1917, and Wilson saw this proposal of a Mexican-German alliance as proof of a German conspiracy against the United States. See page 693.

6d. No. American troops began to withdraw from Mexico in January 1917 and were fully withdrawn by February 5. Therefore, Wilson decided to change his policy toward Mexico before learning of the Zimmermann telegram on February 24. Furthermore, this change did not constitute "support" for the Mexican Revolution. See page 693.

7a. No. The training of recruits was not the responsibility of the Commission on Training Camp Activities. See page 697.

7b. Correct. The government created this commission to coordinate the efforts of private organizations in providing "wholesome" recreational activities to soldiers. In an added effort to preserve soldiers' morals, the commission declared five-mile "sin-free" zones around military bases. See page 697.

7c. No. The Commission on Training Camp Activities did not suggest the integration of military units. See page 697.

7d. No. No such spy network existed. See page 697.

8a. No. It was not Pershing's fear that he would lose control over American soldiers that led to his refusal to allow American soldiers to become part of Allied units. See page 698.

8b. No. Although General Pershing was concerned about the virtue of American soldiers, it was not for this reason that he refused to allow American soldiers to become part of Allied units. See page 698.

8c. Correct. Pershing refused to subject American soldiers to the horrors of trench warfare. For this reason the United States declared itself an Associated power and American soldiers did not become part of Allied units. See page 698.

8d. No. General Pershing had tremendous faith in the ability of American soldiers. See page 698.

9a. No. Antitrust laws were virtually suspended during the war. For example, the Webb-Pomerene Act granted immunity from antitrust legislation to companies that combined to operate in the export trade. See page 701.

© 1994 Houghton Mifflin Company. All rights reserved.

9b. No. Although the government did not institute a wage and price freeze during the war, it did fix prices on raw materials rather than on finished products. As a result, it lost control of inflation, and workers saw little improvement in their economic standing. See pages 701–703.

9c. Correct. Although government tax policies were designed to bring into the Treasury some of the profits reaped by business, the overall relationship between government and business was one of partnership. See page 701.

9d. No. The government did not demand cost-of-living increases for workers in war-related industries. See pages 701–703.

10a. No. Men protested that women were undermining the wage system by working for *lower* pay than that received by men. See pages 703–704.

10b. Correct. Men complained that the higher productivity rate of women destabilized the work environment. In other words, men felt that their jobs were threatened by women who worked at a faster pace. See pages 703–704.

10c. No. Although women moved into jobs formerly reserved for men, they were discriminated against when it came to promotions. See pages 703–704.

10d. No. Except for unions organized by women, organized labor was male dominated and openly hostile toward women. See pages 703–704.

11a. No. Blacks served in all-black units in the army. Some served in combat units, but most were relegated to menial jobs. Although racism was obvious in the military, military leaders did not suggest integration of units as a solution. See page 705.

11b. No. The northward migration of blacks created problems for southern white landowners and businessmen because it reduced their supply of cheap laborers. The problem was further complicated by the fact that white laborers were also moving away. See page 705.

11c. No. Blacks continued to experience racial discrimination at home during and after the First World War. See page 705.

11d. Correct. The massive influx of blacks into the North during the First World War caused anxiety among white northerners. This anxiety found expression in northern race riots in which whites terrorized blacks. See page 705.

12a. Correct. The CPI was organized to mobilize American opinion behind the war effort. Through its efforts it portrayed antiwar dissenters as being dangerous to national security and encouraged patriotic Americans to spy on their neighbors and report any "suspicious" behavior. See page 706.

12b. No. The CPI was established by Wilson in 1917 as a propaganda agency. As such, the CPI did not encourage Americans to debate openly the American war effort. See page 706.

12c. No. The CPI, established in 1917 by President Wilson, was interested in good propaganda. This goal did not always coincide with the dissemination of accurate war news. See page 706.

12d. No. President Wilson established the CPI in 1917 as a propaganda agency. The committee often found that exaggeration and rumor worked to its advantage. See page 706.

13a. No. There was no law requiring members of the Socialist party to register with the government. See pages 707–708.

13b. Correct. The Court, in a unanimous opinion, upheld the Espionage Act as constitutional. In doing so, the Court applied the "clear and present danger" test to free speech in time of war. See pages 707–708.

13c. No. The Court upheld the constitutionality of the Sedition Act by a 7 to 2 vote in *Abrams* v. *U.S.* (1919). See pages 707–708.

13d. No. The *Schenck* case did not involve the teaching of foreign languages in public schools. See pages 707–708.

14a. No. Although political and business leaders believed a conspiracy existed among American radicals, the evidence indicates that the American left was badly divided and not capable of a "well-organized conspiracy" against the United States government. See pages 709–710.

© 1994 Houghton Mifflin Company. All rights reserved.

14b. Correct. In the Palmer Raids, government agents were authorized by Attorney General Palmer to break into meeting halls, poolrooms, and homes without search warrants. Those arrested and jailed were denied legal counsel. These actions demonstrate a disregard for civil liberties. See page 710.

14c. No. Although the New York State legislature expelled five Socialist legislators, the expulsion was not done on instructions from President Wilson. See pages 709–710.

14d. No. Although some believed that the Boston police strike and the steel strike indicated radical infiltration of the union movement in the United States, labor organizations were not declared illegal. See pages 709–710.

15a. Correct. The argument at the core of the debate over the treaty concerned the question of collective security versus America's traditional unilateralism. Those who opposed the Paris Treaty rejected the idea of collective security contained in Article 10. See pages 712–714.

15b. No. Although some of the treaty's opponents charged that Wilson had compromised his stated principles of decolonization and self-determination by accepting the mandate system, opposition to the treaty did not rest on this issue. See pages 712–714.

15c. No. Those who opposed the Treaty of Paris had no problem with the "war guilt clause," which placed most of the blame for the war on Germany and its allies. See pages 712–714.

15d. No. The treaty contained a provision that a reparations commission would determine the amount Germany was to pay the Allies. This figure was later set at $33 billion. See pages 712–714.

Chapter 24

Ideas and Details

1a. Correct. The judicial branch of the government, along with the legislative and executive branches, took a probusiness, antireform, and antiregulatory stance in the 1920s. The *Bailey* case serves as an example of this stance. See page 721.

1b. No. The *Bailey* case did not deal with the issue of consumer protection, and the Court's stand did not indicate that its views were more liberal. See page 721.

1c. No. The *Bailey* case did not deal with the issue of government aid to industry. See page 721.

1d. No. The *Bailey* case did not deal with organized labor's right to strike. See page 721.

2a. No. Corporations, large and small, continued to see organized labor as a threat to property rights. See pages 721–722.

2b. No. The Court continued to demonstrate hostility toward organized labor. In cases such as *Coronado Coal Company* v. *United Mine Workers* (1922), the Court ruled that a striking union, like a trust, could be prosecuted for illegal restraint of trade. See pages 721–722.

2c. No. Union membership fell from 5.1 million in 1920 to 3.6 million in 1929. See page 722.

2d. Correct. Large corporations continued their hostility toward organized labor, but they attempted to neutralize the appeal of unions by offering pension plans and other amenities. This policy is known as welfare capitalism. See page 722.

3a. No. President Coolidge supported allocation of funds by Congress for construction of a national highway system. See page 723.

3b. Correct. Coolidge and Congress disagreed over how to respond to the plight of farmers. Coolidge, devoted to the concept of laissez faire, twice vetoed bills that would have established government-backed price supports for staple crops. See page 723.

3c. No. Coolidge and Congress agreed in the area of foreign policy. See page 723.

3d. No. Military spending was not a major issue during the Coolidge administration, and Coolidge and Congress did not disagree on this issue. See page 723.

4a. Correct. Marcus Garvey preached the idea that blacks have an African heritage of which they should be proud, and he asserted that blackness symbolizes strength and beauty. He taught racial pride in an era in which white racism found expression in race riots and lynchings. See pages 729–730.

4b. No. Marcus Garvey was opposed to the assimilation of blacks into white American society. See pages 729–730.

4c. No. Marcus Garvey encouraged blacks to take advantage of the free enterprise system by sharpening their management skills and opening businesses. See pages 729–730.

4d. No. Although Marcus Garvey preached that blacks could gain respect by lifting their native Africa to world-power status, he did not advocate the use of violence to obtain his objectives. See pages 729–730.

5a. No. The new technology did not cause a new sense of responsibility toward household management on the part of husbands and children. In fact, by decreasing the need for servants, the new technology placed the burden of household management more squarely on the shoulders of the wife herself. See pages 732–733.

5b. Correct. The urban housewife of the 1920s was no longer the producer of food and clothing that her female ancestors had been. However, it was still her responsibility to feed and clothe the family. Therefore, she became the family's chief consumer. See page 732.

5c. No. The new technology eliminated the need for servants in many cases. This placed more of the responsibility for childcare on the wife herself. See pages 732–733.

5d. No. The new technology did not relieve most housewives of a wide variety of responsibilities, and in many cases the "labor-saving" machines added new responsibilities. See pages 732–733.

6a. No. Newspaper circulation did not increase in the 1920s as a result of children being kept in school longer. See page 735.

6b. No. Consumption of consumer goods increased in the 1920s. See page 735.

6c. Correct. Children were kept in school longer as a result of child-labor laws and compulsory-school-attendance laws. As a consequence, the influence of the peer group in socializing children increased and the role of the family decreased. See page 735.

6d. No. Child-labor laws and compulsory-school-attendance laws did not cause a severe labor shortage. See page 735.

7a. No. The number of women working in factories showed very little increase during the decade of the 1920s. See pages 735–736.

7b. No. Sex segregation in the workplace showed no signs of decline during the 1920s. See pages 735–736.

7c. No. In 1920 there were some 10.4 million women in the work force, and by 1930 there were 10.8 million gainfully employed women. This meant that women constituted 22 percent of the total labor force in 1930, a 1.6 percent increase over 1920. See pages 735–736 and page A-25.

7d. Correct. Largely because of "need," as defined in the new consumer age, married women joined the work force in increasing numbers during the 1920s. The number of married women who were gainfully employed rose from 1.9 million in 1920 to 3.1 million in 1930. See pages 735–736, A-25.

8a. No. The failure of feminism to address what might be labeled "political issues" was not the reason feminism failed to appeal to most women. See page 736.

8b. Correct. In dealing with the economic exploitation and economic dependence of women, feminists in the 1920s stressed economic independence and sought greater economic opportunities for women. However, many women still valued cooperative as opposed to competitive goals. See page 736.

© 1994 Houghton Mifflin Company. All rights reserved.

8c. No. Economic feminists of the 1920s called for equal pay for women. See page 736.

8d. No. The issues raised by feminists of the 1920s were controversial to many people. In fact, this was one reason that the feminist message did not appeal to many women. See page 736.

9a. No. Although the "new" Klan of the 1920s was founded by William J. Simmons of Atlanta, its power spread into all regions of the country and by 1923 the organization claimed some 5 million members. See page 737.

9b. No. The new mood of nationalism and militancy among African Americans in the 1920s was more pronounced in the North than in the South. Furthermore, the "new" Klan of the 1920s gained power in the South. See page 737.

9c. Correct. The "new" Klan of the early 1920s was more broadly based than the first Klan, and it also directed its brand of hatred toward groups other than blacks. See page 737.

9d. No. Although the Klan operated through terrorism and fear, it was not outlawed by Congress as a terrorist organization. See page 737.

10a. No. The case demonstrates that the fear of radicalism, which was an important aspect of the Red Scare, was still very much alive. See page 737.

10b. No. The Sacco and Vanzetti case is an indication of anti-immigrant sentiment in the United States during the early 1920s. See page 737.

10c. No. The case did not involve blacks being tried in the South. See page 737.

10d. Correct. Modern ballistics studies suggest that Sacco was probably guilty, Vanzetti probably innocent. However, the evidence used in the 1920 trial was questionable, and the conviction and sentencing of the two men was based largely on their immigrant background and anarchist beliefs. See page 737.

11a. Correct. The age of mass consumerism robbed experiences and objects of their uniqueness, and as individuals became more anonymous and less significant in the fast-moving, materialistic world, they turned to "heroes" as a way of identifying with the unique. See pages 741–742.

11b. No. In the first place, how one defines a "great" actor is a matter of judgment. In addition, Rudolph Valentino is the only actor among the three people listed. See pages 741–742.

11c. No. Although "Babe" Ruth may be considered a "great" baseball player, this is not true of Jack Dempsey (boxer) or Rudolph Valentino (actor). See pages 741–742.

11d. No. The three people listed were not engaged in "lawless" acts. See pages 741–742.

12a. No. Prohibition was born out of the Puritan value system, which emphasized hard work and sobriety. Americans did not "completely" reject this value system. See pages 742–744.

12b. No. Rather than "foisting" illegal liquor on the public, organized crime provided it to a public that wanted to buy it. See pages 742–744.

12c. No. Although prohibition caused people in the legal liquor industry to lose their jobs, its negative economic impact was not the reason for its failure. See pages 742–744.

12d. Correct. Although most Americans continued to accept the Puritan value system on which prohibition was based, more and more Americans found the new diversions of "the age of play" attractive. Therefore, many willingly broke the law in favor of fun and personal freedom. See page 744.

13a. No. Many of the writers of the Harlem Renaissance spoke with pride of the African past of black Americans. See pages 744–745.

13b. No. Most of the writers associated with the Harlem Renaissance were not advocates of black nationalism and did not advocate the return of black Americans to Africa. See pages 744–745.

© 1994 Houghton Mifflin Company. All rights reserved.

13c. Correct. In addressing identity issues, black writers of the Harlem Renaissance rejected combining black and white cultures. Instead of advocating assimilation into white society, they urged blacks to find their identity in the richness and uniqueness of black culture. See page 744.

13d. No. The black writers of the Harlem Renaissance were concerned with issues relating to the reality of the black experience in white American society. They were not concerned primarily with economic issues. See pages 744–745.

14a. Correct. By carrying the nation's twelve largest cities, the Democratic party demonstrated that it was gaining power in the urban areas of the country. See page 746.

14b. No. Al Smith, the Democratic presidential nominee in 1928, carried eight states to Herbert Hoover's forty. Six of these were southern states from which he gained 69 of his 87 electoral votes. See page 746.

14c. No. The election indicated that Republicans had actually lost support in areas that were becoming more important in presidential elections. See page 746.

14d. No. The Republican party was still the majority party—that is, a majority of the people who were registered to vote were registered as Republicans. See page 746.

15a. No. The Hoover administration, like the Harding and Coolidge administrations, adhered to the laissez-faire philosophy and did not "impose" regulations on businesses. See pages 747–748.

15b. No. The government followed a policy of lowering income-tax rates, especially on the wealthy. Therefore, the tax policies of the government did not take large sums of money out of circulation. Furthermore, between 1920 and 1929, the after-tax income of the wealthiest 1 percent rose 75 percent as opposed to the average per-capita increase of 9 percent. This extra disposable income in the hands of the wealthy tended to fuel speculation in the stock market. See page 748.

15c. Correct. The Board's easy-credit policy before 1931 fueled speculation in the stock market, and its shift to a tight-money policy after 1931 denied the economy of funds needed for economic recovery. See page 748.

15d. No. The government did not give aid to organized labor. Furthermore, economic distress among farmers, factory layoffs, technological unemployment, and low wages caused production to outstrip demand. See pages 747–748.

Chapter 25

Ideas and Details

1a. No. Despite the hardships endured by Americans during the Great Depression, most people did not blame "the system" and they did not turn to radical movements as a solution to their despair. See page 754.

1b. No. Divorce rates declined from 206,000 in 1929 to 164,000 in 1932. See page 754.

1c. Correct. As a result of the Great Depression people postponed marriage. Furthermore, married couples postponed having children, causing the birthrate to fall from 21.3 live births per 1,000 in 1930 to 18.4 in 1933. See page 754.

1d. No. As amazing as it seems, although many Americans suffered from malnutrition and others died of starvation, a surplus of basic agricultural commodities piled up in the Farm Belt. Although overproduction caused low food prices, unemployed Americans lacked money to buy food. See page 754.

2a. No. Although government policies contributed to the crash and to the Great Depression, most people did not blame the government for the depression. See pages 754–755.

2b. No. In spite of the fact that the Great Depression may be seen as a major crisis within the capitalist system, Americans continued to accept capitalism and did not, as a general rule, lash out against that system in a violent way. See pages 754–755.

© 1994 Houghton Mifflin Company. All rights reserved.

2c. No. Although there was disillusionment, the failure of both the Communist and Socialist parties to make major gains indicates that most Americans did not turn to ideologies that might advocate revolution and that the masses did not seriously contemplate revolution. See pages 754–755.

2d. Correct. In spite of the fact that the capitalist system was "on its knees," most Americans continued to believe in that system, continued to demonstrate loyalty to their government, and blamed themselves for the Great Depression. See pages 754–755.

3a. Correct. Hoover saw the Bonus marchers as extremists, refused to meet with them after Congress defeated the Bonus Bill, and finally called out the army to attack and disperse the Bonus Expeditionary Force encamped in Washington. See page 755.

3b. No. Hoover remained steadfast in his belief in limited government, in individual initiative, and in self-help. He never suggested establishing a comprehensive pension plan for future veterans. See page 755.

3c. No. President Hoover urged Congress to defeat the Bonus Bill. See page 755.

3d. No. Hoover refused to meet with leaders of the Bonus Expeditionary Force. See page 755.

4a. No. The RFC was not based on the basic assumption of "supply-side" economics. See page 757.

4b. No. Hoover's reluctant support for the chartering of the RFC indicates that Hoover had gradually moved toward the idea of a more active federal role in dealing with the economic crisis and that by 1932 he was willing to accept limited federal "interference." See page 757.

4c. Correct. The RFC is an example of "trickle-down" economic theory: money in the hands of the wealthy will trickle down to the masses. See page 757.

4d. No. The RFC was not a tax measure and was not based on the theory that taxes are a disincentive to economic recovery. See page 757.

5a. No. When governor of New York Roosevelt did not believe in deficit spending, and his actions as governor do not indicate such a philosophy. See page 758.

5b. Correct. Some of Roosevelt's actions and suggestions as governor of New York indicated a willingness to experiment in finding solutions to the problems posed by the depression. See page 758.

5c. No. Roosevelt's actions as governor of New York do not indicate that Roosevelt wanted to embark on a trustbusting program. See page 758.

5d. No. Roosevelt believed that it was the responsibility of government to extend direct relief to the jobless. His support for New York's Temporary Emergency Relief Administration is an indication of that belief. See page 758.

6a. Correct. An assumption on which the AAA and the NIRA were based was that overproduction was the major factor preventing economic recovery. Therefore, through centralized national planning, farmers and industries would be encouraged to produce less. See pages 761, 763.

6b. No. The AAA sought to raise the prices of farm goods, and the NIRA attempted to do the same for manufactured goods. See pages 761, 763.

6c. No. Neither the AAA nor the NIRA called for deficit spending. See pages 761, 763.

6d. No. Both the AAA and the NIRA demonstrated Roosevelt's willingness to deal with problems from the national level. See pages 761, 763.

7a. No. Unemployment insurance was first provided to some workers through the Social Security Act of 1935. See page 763.

7b. No. Pension plans were not required under the NIRA. See page 763.

© 1994 Houghton Mifflin Company. All rights reserved.

7c. Correct. Because of concessions given to businesses under the NIRA, employers in turn had to accept the right of workers to unionize and bargain collectively. See page 763.

7d. No. Section 7(a) of the NIRA did not require workers to join company-sponsored unions. See page 763.

8a. No. Many conservative critics were business leaders. Rather than complaining about the close relationship between government and industry, they complained that there was too much government regulation of business. See pages 766–767.

8b. No. Conservatives were critical of relief programs such as the CCC and the FERA and claimed that such programs were based on socialist ideology. See pages 766–767.

8c. No. Conservatives, who believed that the economy should be allowed to operate in accordance with natural economic laws, criticized the Roosevelt administration for centralized economic planning. See pages 766–767.

8d. Correct. Conservatives believed that people should overcome personal hardships through self-reliance and individual initiative. Therefore, they charged that programs like the CCC and the FERA destroyed individual initiative. See pages 766–767.

9a. No. Although Long believed that the New Deal was too closely allied with business interests, he did not advocate nationalizing all major industry in the United States. See page 768.

9b. No. Long proposed a homestead *allowance* of $5,000, but did not propose actually giving land. Furthermore, families did not have to request the allowance. See page 768.

9c. Correct. Long proposed that the government provide a guaranteed annual income of $2,000 to every American family. See page 768.

9d. No. Although Long proposed a free college education for every American, he did not propose a national health insurance program. See page 768.

10a. No. The First Amendment deals with freedom of religion, speech, and the press and the right to assemble peacefully and petition the government for redress of grievances. The Court did not find that the NIRA abridged these rights. See pages 769–770.

10b. Correct. One of the grounds on which part of the NIRA was declared unconstitutional was that it delegated excessive legislative power to the executive branch of the government. See pages 769–770.

10c. No. The Court held part of the NIRA to be unconstitutional because it regulated businesses that were wholly involved in intrastate commerce, but it did not hold that the act discriminated against small businesses. See pages 769–770.

10d. No. The Court did not rule that the NIRA was in violation of the Fourteenth Amendment. See pages 769–770.

11a. Correct. Roosevelt believed that business leaders had placed their own interests above those of the nation. Therefore, during the Second New Deal, Roosevelt abandoned business-government cooperation and, to "cut the giants down to size," moved to enforce antitrust laws. See page 770.

11b. No. Both the First and the Second New Deals reflect Roosevelt's belief that the government could act as a positive force in American society. Therefore, he did not return to the idea of passive government embodied in the laissez-faire philosophy. See page 770.

11c. No. Although Roosevelt remained a fiscal conservative and was committed to a balanced budget, deficit spending characterized both the First and the Second New Deals. See page 770.

11d. No. Both the First and the Second New Deals strengthened the role of the federal government. However, state and local governments were given the task of implementing much of the legislation passed under both New Deals. See page 770.

12a. No. Although the Social Security Act established an old-age insurance program, the law did not apply to all workers. See pages 770–771.

12b. Correct. Although the law was a relatively conservative measure and did not apply to all workers, it established the idea of government responsibility toward the aged, dependent, and disabled. See pages 770–771.

© 1994 Houghton Mifflin Company. All rights reserved.

12c. No. The Social Security Act authorized money grants to the states for public health work, but it did not establish a national health insurance program. See pages 770–771.

12d. No. The measure is considered relatively conservative because benefits were to be paid by workers and employers, not by the government. See pages 770–771.

13a. No. Although Roosevelt's intention in cutting federal spending was to achieve a balanced budget, this was not the end result. See page 772.

13b. No. At the same time that Roosevelt cut spending, the Federal Reserve Board tightened credit, causing interest rates to rise. See page 772.

13c. No. At the same time that Roosevelt cut federal spending, the Federal Reserve Board tightened credit. This, in turn, caused business to cut back on spending for capital improvements. See page 772.

13d. Correct. The massive spending cuts ordered by Roosevelt in 1937, along with the tightening of credit by the Federal Reserve Board, caused a recession. As a result, Roosevelt returned to deficit spending, which brought some economic recovery by 1939. See page 772.

14a. No. Skilled workers were already heavily involved in the labor movement through the American Federation of Labor. See page 773.

14b. Correct. Workers in many major industries began to organize in industrial unions, such as the UMW and the UAW. See page 773.

14c. No. Organized labor did not consist of farm workers. See page 773.

14d. No. White-collar workers were not organizing in the 1930s. See page 773.

15a. No. These measures did not bring about a redistribution of wealth. See pages 777–778.

15b. No. Money spent on these programs tended to benefit middle- and lower-income groups, not the wealthy. See pages 777–778.

15c. No. The AAA and TVA helped people in rural areas more than people in urban areas, and the FHA and CCC benefited people in both areas. See pages 777–778.

15d. Correct. All of these acts indicate an antiblack bias and demonstrate that although blacks benefited from the New Deal, they did not get their fair share. See pages 777–778.

Chapter 26

Ideas and Details

1a. Correct. Secretary of State Hughes accepted the philosophy that economic expansion was necessary for world peace. As a result, he supported passage of legislation intended to foster international trade. See page 789.

1b. No. Secretary of State Hughes did not focus on the competition and rivalry that would accompany economic expansion. See page 789.

1c. No. Secretary of State Hughes did not encourage economic expansion abroad out of a desire to increase the power of the United States at the expense of "less virtuous" European nations. See page 789.

1d. No. Secretary of State Hughes did not encourage economic expansion abroad as a means by which the United States could promote economic nationalism. See page 789.

2a. No. None of the treaties negotiated at the Washington Conference placed limits on the construction of submarines, destroyers, or cruisers—the most destructive weapons of the age. See pages 790–791.

2b. Correct. As one of a total of nine treaties that came out of the Washington Conference, the Five-Power Treaty provided for a ten-year moratorium on the construction of capital ships and established a ratio of capital ships. Britain, the United States, and Japan had to dismantle some ships to meet the ratio. See pages 790–791.

2c. No. In the Nine-Power Treaty, all the nations represented at the Washington Conference agreed to respect Chinese sovereignty and to accept the Open Door principle. See pages 790–791.

2d. No. The Five-Power Treaty was drafted at the Washington Conference of 1921–1922. The Nazis were not in power in Germany at that time. See pages 790–791.

3a. No. No treaty signed during the 1920s placed limits on the number of submarines and destroyers to be built by the five major powers. See page 791.

3b. No. No limits were placed on international arms sales during the 1920s. See page 791.

3c. No. Although it is true that the United States began to send observers to League conferences, this was not accomplished by the Kellogg-Briand Pact. See page 791.

3d. Correct. The Kellogg-Briand Pact, signed by sixty-two nations in 1928, condemned war as a way of solving international problems and renounced war as an instrument of national policy. See page 791.

4a. No. Even though it worked a hardship on the debtor nations, the United States insisted that they pay their debts in full. This does not indicate a selfless handling of the war-debt issue. See pages 792–793.

4b. Correct. American loans to Germany, German reparations payments to the Allies, and Allied war-debt payments to the United States created a triangular arrangement that depended on German borrowing in the United States and was economically destabilizing. See pages 792–793.

4c. No. The Allies forced Germany to accept guilt for the First World War and insisted that Germany pay the $33 billion reparations bill levied by the Allies. See pages 792–793.

4d. No. The idea that the German government used the war-debt and reparations issue to create tensions between the United States and Great Britain is not a logical inference that can be drawn from the evidence presented. See pages 792–793.

5a. Correct. This tariff measure raised rates an average of 8 percent. As a result, many European nations were priced out of the United States market. In response, the European nations retaliated by raising tariff rates against American imports. See page 794.

5b. No. European imports to the United States declined as a result of the Hawley-Smoot Tariff. See page 794.

5c. No. The Hawley-Smoot Tariff was a general tariff measure and did not deal specifically with the Open Door policy, which applied to China. See page 794.

5d. No. Because most American imports came from Europe, the Hawley-Smoot Tariff primarily affected trade relations with that area. Therefore, this tariff did not give Japan a reason to impose an embargo against American products. See page 794.

6a. No. Although this act authorized the president to lower American tariffs by as much as 50 percent through special agreements with foreign countries, the United States did not adopt a free trade position. Such a position would have meant repealing all tariffs. See page 794.

6b. No. This act did not offer low-interest loans to countries agreeing to buy American goods. See page 794.

6c. Correct. Any nation entering into regular trade agreements with the United States would be given tariff rates matching those given to the "most-favored nation." This principle was important because it brought an overall lowering of tariff rates and fostered economic internationalism. See page 794.

6d. No. This act moved toward freer trade but did not establish a free trade zone within the Western Hemisphere. See page 794.

© 1994 Houghton Mifflin Company. All rights reserved.

7a. No. In spite of the Good Neighbor Policy, the United States saw order in Latin American as vital to its national interests. As a result, it was not willing to "strictly adhere" to the doctrine of nonintervention. See page 795.

7b. Correct. Some methods used by the United States to maintain its influence in Latin America had become counterproductive. Therefore, the Good Neighbor Policy was an attempt to use less controversial and less blatant means to accomplish the same end. See page 795.

7c. No. In spite of the Good Neighbor Policy, American businesses in Latin America continued to take their profits out of the region and invest them elsewhere (a process known as decapitalization). See page 795.

7d. No. The Good Neighbor Policy certainly did not mean that the United States would practice isolationism in Latin America. Rather, it included ways for the United States to stay involved in more subtle ways. See page 795.

8a. No. Trujillo and Somoza ruled as dictators in their respective nations. This does not indicate the acceptance and growth of American concepts of government. See pages 797–798.

8b. No. Trujillo and Somoza, who were supported by the United States government, ruled through the use of fraud and intimidation. They did not have the support of the masses of people in their respective countries. See pages 797–798.

8c. Correct. Trujillo and Somoza became leaders of a United States-trained national guard in their respective countries, and each used that position to gain dictatorial powers. See pages 797–798.

8d. No. The United States was interested in order, not in national liberation movements, in Latin America. See pages 797–798.

9a. Correct. Britain and France, after the policy of appeasement, accepted Hitler's seizure of the Sudetenland in September 1938. Hitler proceeded to take the rest of Czechoslovakia in March 1939. Then, in September 1939, when German forces attacked Poland, Britain and France declared war on Germany. See page 801.

9b. No. The British made no such pledge to France in the years leading up to the Second World War. See page 801.

9c. No. The Munich Conference did not result in a defensive alliance among Britain, France, and the Soviet Union against Nazi Germany. See page 801.

9d. No. At the time of the Munich Conference, Germany had seized the Rhineland (March 1936) and Austria (March 1938). Germany did not withdraw its troops from either area as a result of the conference. See page 801.

10a. No. Hearings by the Nye Committee indicate that some United States corporations lobbied against arms control and attempted to increase arms sales to foreign nations during the 1920s and 1930s. See pages 803–804.

10b. Correct. After Italy's invasion of Ethiopia, Roosevelt invoked an arms embargo against Italy as required by the Neutrality Act of 1935. The act did not require a ban on petroleum, copper, and iron and steel scrap exports; and, despite Roosevelt's call for a moral embargo on these products, exports of these items to Italy increased. See pages 803–804.

10c. No. Records indicate that twenty-six of the top one hundred United States firms still had contractual agreements with Germany in 1937, four years after Hitler and the Nazis came to power. See pages 803–804.

10d. No. Many United States firms continued to maintain lucrative economic ties with Germany after learning about the persecution of Jews. One exception was the Wall Street firm of Sullivan and Cromwell, which severed economic ties with Germany to protest Hitler's anti-Semitic practices. See pages 803–804.

11a. No. The intent of the Neutrality Acts was to prevent the United States from being drawn into war, not to provide aid to the Allies. See page 804.

11b. No. The Neutrality Acts contained no arms-control provisions. See page 804.

11c. No. In 1937, the United States declared itself neutral in the Spanish Civil War and Roosevelt embargoed arms shipments to both sides. See page 804.

© 1994 Houghton Mifflin Company. All rights reserved.

11d. Correct. Congress believed that bankers and munitions-makers had dragged the United States into the First World War. To prevent this from recurring, Congress passed the Neutrality Acts, which required a mandatory arms embargo against and forbade loans to all belligerents. See page 804.

12a. No. Although Roosevelt was sympathetic toward the British and saw Germany, Italy, and Japan as "bandit nations," he did not respond to the outbreak of war by promising American involvement if British defeat seemed imminent. See page 805.

12b. Correct. In spite of strong lobbying efforts by isolationists and the presence of strong opposition in Congress, the arms embargo, at Roosevelt's urging, was repealed in November 1939 and the sale of arms was placed on a cash-and-carry basis. See page 805.

12c. No. Although the United States condemned Russia's nonaggression pact with Hitler and the subsequent Russo-German conquest and partition of Poland, Washington did not break diplomatic relations with the Soviet Union. See page 805.

12d. No. In response to the outbreak of war in Europe, President Roosevelt declared the United States to be a neutral nation. See page 805.

13a. Correct. President Hoover, who was grappling with the problems of the Great Depression and who realized that the United States did not have the naval power to risk a Pacific war, refused to authorize anything stronger than the Stimson Doctrine, which was a moral condemnation of the Japanese. See page 806.

13b. No. The United States did not take definitive economic action against Japan in response to that nation's 1931 invasion of Manchuria, and Japanese assets were not frozen until after the Japanese occupation of southern Indochina in July 1941. See pages 806, 811.

13c. No. President Hoover refused to cooperate with the League in imposing economic sanctions on Japan. See page 806.

13d. No. The United States continued to follow a foreign policy characterized by nonalignment with foreign nations. See page 806.

14a. No. In September 1940, in the midst of the Battle of Britain, Roosevelt concluded the Destroyer-Bases Agreement with Great Britain. By this agreement, the United States traded fifty old destroyers to the British for ninety-nine-year leases to eight British bases in Newfoundland and the Caribbean. See pages 809–810.

14b. No. The Neutrality Acts of 1935, 1936, and 1937 were slightly modified in 1939; and, although the Lend-Lease Act may be considered a further modification, it did not "revoke" the provisions of the Neutrality Acts. See pages 804–805, 809–810.

14c. Correct. Designed primarily to aid the British, who were running out of money, the Lend-Lease Act (March 1941) authorized the president to transfer, sell, exchange, lend, or lease war material to any country whose defense was considered vital to the United States. See pages 809–810.

14d. No. In 1931-1932, President Hoover and Congress refused to cancel Allied debts incurred during the First World War. As a result, European nations were forced to default, but that happened some ten years before the Lend-Lease Act. See pages 792, 809–910.

15a. No. After the Japanese occupation of Indochina, Roosevelt's advisers, acting on the president's advice, tried to prolong talks with the Japanese so that the Philippines could be fortified and the fascists checked in Europe. See pages 812–813.

15b. No. The United States had broken the Japanese code and knew by December 1 that Japan had decided on war with the United States if the oil embargo was not lifted. See pages 812–813.

15c. Correct. The United States government knew of Japan's war plans but did not know where or when Japan would strike. When the location was learned, the telegram informing the base commanders at Pearl Harbor was delayed. See pages 812–813.

15d. No. The United States government and the base commanders at Pearl Harbor expected an attack at British Malaya, Thailand, or the Philippines. See pages 812–813.

© 1994 Houghton Mifflin Company. All rights reserved.

Chapter 27

Ideas and Details

1a. No. The Soviet Union, the United States, and Great Britain were allies against Nazi Germany in the Second World War. Although Roosevelt might have had some concern about future Russian expansion, that concern did not initially cause him to want to open a second front in 1942. See page 820.

1b. No. The North African campaign, which began in November 1942, was undertaken at Churchill's insistence and meant the postponement of a second front. See page 820.

1c. No. Churchill assertively argued against the opening of a second front in Europe in 1942. See page 820.

1d. Correct. In the European land war in 1942, Russia continued to suffer the brunt of the German onslaught. In light of this, Roosevelt was concerned that Russia might sue for a separate peace, leaving Germany free to invade England. See page 820.

2a. Correct. Meeting at Teheran in December 1943, the Allies agreed, at the insistence of Roosevelt and Stalin, to open the long-delayed second front. In return, Stalin agreed that Russia would enter the war in the Pacific once Germany was defeated. See page 822.

2b. No. The North Africa campaign began in November 1942 and ended in Allied victory in May 1943. The Teheran Conference was held in December 1943. See page 822.

2c. No. Although it is true that General Eisenhower recognized the pro-Nazi Vichy regime in French North Africa, he did so at the time of the Allied invasion of North Africa, which was some thirteen months before the Teheran Conference. See page 822.

2d. No. The battle for Stalingrad ended in Russian victory in January 1943, eleven months before the Teheran Conference. See page 822.

3a. No. The United States did not destroy Japan's merchant marine as a result of the Battle of Midway. See page 824.

3b. Correct. As a result of Operation Magic, American experts deciphered the secret Japanese code. With prior knowledge of Japanese plans, American forces sank four of Japan's aircraft carriers in the Battle of Midway and broke the enemy's momentum in the Pacific. See page 824.

3c. No. The Battle of Midway did not make Hawaii more vulnerable to attack. See page 824.

3d. No. The Battle of Midway did not cause Roosevelt to harbor fears of Japanese victory. See page 824.

4a. No. Truman knew that victory over Japan was virtually assured and did not totally depend on use of the atomic bomb. See page 827.

4b. No. Germany surrendered on May 8, 1945, three months before the first atomic bomb was dropped on Hiroshima on August 6. See pages 822–823, 827.

4c. No. The decision to use the atomic bomb was made unilaterally by the United States. Not only did the United States not consult the Allies, but at Potsdam Truman chose not to tell the Soviet Union of the successful atomic test in the New Mexico desert. See pages 827, 847.

4d. Correct. Truman decided to drop the bomb for several reasons: (1) it would save American lives by ending the war quickly; (2) it might deter future aggression; (3) it might prevent Soviet entry into the war in the Pacific, thus preventing the Soviet Union from having a role in the reconstruction of postwar Asia; and (4) in the face of United States power, it might cause the Soviet Union to make concessions in Eastern Europe. See page 827.

5a. No. Cooperation between government and business was essential for successful execution of the war effort. As a result, the government guaranteed that companies would be exempt from antitrust prosecution during the war. See page 827.

© 1994 Houghton Mifflin Company. All rights reserved.

5b. No. Because the government had to produce war material in the shortest time possible, competitive bidding was usually not possible. Although some attempts were made to award contracts to small businesses, most government contracts were awarded to big businesses. See page 827.

5c. Correct. Factories had to be converted from production of consumer goods to production of war material. This was the WPB's first task, a task at which it was very successful See page 827.

5d. No. The WPB was not responsible for analyzing the military situation. The efforts of the WPB were more concentrated on the home front. See page 827.

6a. No. Under the Smith-Connally Act, the NWLB's powers were broadened to include the legal authority to settle labor disputes until the end of the war. See pages 829–830.

6b. No. Although the act established a mandatory thirty-day cooling-off period before a strike could be called in a war-related industry, it did not prohibit strikes and made no reference to lockouts (the shutdown of a plant to bring workers to terms). See pages 829–830.

6c. No. The Smith-Connally Act did not guarantee cost-of-living increases in defense-related industries. See pages 829–830.

6d. Correct. This act, passed over President Roosevelt's veto, broadened the power of the president in handling labor disputes in war-related industries. See pages 829–830.

7a. No. The Second World War did not lead to a more vigorous enforcement of antitrust laws by the government and did not bring about the breakup of large economic units. See pages 829, 830–831.

7b. Correct. Because most government contracts were awarded to big corporations, the dominance of those corporations increased. Furthermore, the expense of farm machinery brought a decline in the number of family farms and led to agricultural consolidation. See pages 829, 830–831.

7c. No. During the Second World War the government poured massive sums of money into the economy. This may be seen by the increase of the national debt from $49 billion in 1941 to $259 billion in 1945. See pages 829–831.

7d. No. The banking industry remained in private hands. See pages 829, 830–831.

8a. Correct. Many soldiers who had never seen the world beyond their own cities, farms, and neighborhoods came into contact with other Americans and with peoples from other cultures. See page 833.

8b. No. In many instances, the technical training that soldiers received in the military served to foster their ambitions and to give them skills that made them more employable in the postwar years. See page 833.

8c. No. Soldiers went through basic training in which they learned skills basic to combat. In addition, many received advanced training in specialty areas through the military's technical schools. See page 833.

8d. No. Many soldiers were given orientation lectures and booklets that introduced them to the historical backgrounds and social customs of the foreign nations in which they served. See page 833.

9a. No. The evidence does not support the conclusion that Japanese-Americans were interned because of criminal behavior. As the authors point out: "Charges of criminal behavior were never brought against any Japanese-Americans; none was ever indicted or tried for espionage, treason, or sedition." See page 834.

9b. No. Japanese-Americans were not engaged in treasonable activities and did not display disloyalty toward the United States government. See page 834.

9c. Correct. Japanese-Americans, most of whom were native-born citizens, were interned in "relocation centers" because of their Japanese descent. See page 834.

9d. No. Although many of those who were engaged in economic competition with Japanese-Americans spoke in favor of internment, this competition was not the major reason for that action. See page 834.

10a. Correct. The movement of some 1.2 million blacks to industrial cities in the North and West, where they could exercise the right to vote, increased the political power of blacks in national, state, and local elections. See page 836.

© 1994 Houghton Mifflin Company. All rights reserved.

10b. No. Blacks continued to experience political, economic, and social discrimination during World War II. See pages 836–838.

10c. No. Overall, the economic position of African Americans improved during World War II. See pages 836–838.

10d. No. African Americans eagerly participated in and supported the American war effort. See pages 836–838.

11a. No. Roosevelt's victory in 1944 may be considered a landslide in terms of the electoral vote (432 to 99), but his margin of victory in the popular vote was his narrowest ever. See page 841.

11b. Correct. Victory was in sight in 1944, but many people were apprehensive about the postwar domestic economy. Remembering New Deal relief programs, they preferred Roosevelt over Dewey as a kind of insurance against hard times. See page 841.

11c. No. The South remained solidly Democratic in the 1944 election. See page 841.

11d. No. Roosevelt, not Truman, was the Democratic standard-bearer in the 1944 presidential election. See page 841.

12a. Correct. Both United States immigration policy and the voyage of the *St. Louis* indicate reluctance by the United States to deal decisively with the Jewish refugee problem. Decisive action was not taken until 1944, when Roosevelt created the War Refugee Board. See page 844.

12b. No. The United States refused to relax its immigration rules and restrictions. As a result many Jewish refugees were turned away because they did not have the legal documents required. See pages 843–844.

12c. No. The British refused to open Palestine to Jewish refugees. See pages 843–844.

12d. No. Although American officials knew the location of the Auschwitz death camp and bombed war industries located only five miles from the camp, they made no strikes against the camp itself. See pages 843–844.

13a. No. Although Roosevelt was physically ill while attending the Yalta Conference, the evidence indicates that he was mentally alert and that his health was not a factor in the decisions reached. See pages 844–847.

13b. No. Stalin, rather than Churchill, argued in favor of German reparations. The United States and Russia, without British acceptance, agreed to a rough figure of $20 billion "as a basis for discussion in the future." See pages 844–845.

13c. Correct. Because of the military positions of the Allied armies, the United States and Great Britain still needed the Soviet Union to win the war. This, and the fact that Russia occupied Eastern Europe, greatly affected decisions at Yalta. See page 845.

13d. No. Recognition of China as a major power was an American demand, not a Russian demand. See pages 844–847.

14a. No. About 357,000 Britons died as a result of the Second World War, but the British did not suffer the highest number of casualties in the war. See page 847.

14b. No. About 405,000 Americans died as a result of the Second World War, but this figure was far lower than the number of war dead in other countries. See page 847.

14c. No. Although the Japanese lost some 2 million people in the war, this loss was ten times less than the casualties experienced by the country with the highest number of war dead. See page 847.

14d. Correct. The Soviet Union lost some 20 million people in the Second World War. As a result, security was Russia's primary interest in the postwar era. See page 847.

15a. No. Great Britain came out of the Second World War with far less power than when it entered the war. As a result, the British empire was quite vulnerable. See pages 847–848.

15b. Correct. The United States was the only power to emerge from the Second World War more powerful than when it entered. See pages 847–848.

15c. No. Japan lay in ruins at the end of World War II. See pages 847–848.

© 1994 Houghton Mifflin Company. All rights reserved.

15d. No. The Soviet Union suffered enormously as a result of the war and emerged less powerful than when it entered. See pages 847–848.

Chapter 28

Ideas and Details

1a. Correct. Truman responded to a threatened railroad strike in 1946 by threatening to seize the rail industry and draft into military service all workers who refused to return to work. This threat and others alienated union members in general. See page 856.

1b. No. Beginning in 1945, Truman repeatedly proposed the creation of a nationwide health insurance program. Congress repeatedly refused to enact such a plan. See page 856.

1c. No. Truman initially directed the OPA to lift price controls, a decision which pleased manufacturers and farmers but displeased consumers. When the OPA reimposed price controls, angry producers withheld products from the market, causing shortages and angry consumers. See page 856.

1d. No. Truman won support from African Americans because of his strong stand in favor of civil rights. See pages 856, 859–861.

2a. No. Both the Progressive party candidate (Henry Wallace) and the Dixiecrat candidate (Strom Thurmond) continued their independent campaigns for the presidency through election day. See pages 857–859.

2b. No. The Democratic party, not the Republican party, was divided in 1948. See pages 857–859.

2c. Correct. The Eightieth Congress (1947–1949), dominated by Republicans, rejected most of Truman's proposals. Even when they were called into special session and told to enact the planks in the Republican party platform, they balked. As a result, they alienated many interest groups. See pages 857–859.

2d. No. The Republican party had taken a conservative stance on most issues and was perceived by the electorate as more conservative than the Democratic party. See pages 857–859.

3a. No. Congress did not pass effective voting rights legislation until 1965. See pages 859–862.

3b. Correct. The gap between American ideals and the realities of American society made it difficult to compete with the Soviet Union among the Third World nonaligned nations. To win the support of these nations, the United States had to begin to live up to its ideals. See pages 861–862.

3c. No. Although Truman sent a special message to Congress in February, 1948, calling for federal antilynching and anti-poll tax laws, southern congressmen were openly opposed to such legislation and Congress never formally responded to the message. See pages 859–862.

3d. No. Congress did not outlaw the Klan. See pages 859–862.

4a. Correct. Although McCarthy was probably the most successful redbaiter in the country, conservative and liberal politicians, labor leaders, religious leaders, and others used the public's fear of communism against their opponents. They all contributed to the anti-Communist hysteria known as McCarthyism. See page 864.

4b. No. There was no such treaty. See pages 864.

4c. No. Communist party membership declined from 83,000 in 1947 to 25,000 in 1954. See page 864.

4d. No. Henry Wallace was a liberal Democrat, not a Communist, and no such conspiracy existed. See page 864.

© 1994 Houghton Mifflin Company. All rights reserved.

5a. No. By freezing wages and prices in January 1951, the Truman administration brought inflation under control. See pages 866–867.

5b. No. There was displeasure among progressive Democrats because the military buildup took money away from Fair Deal programs. See pages 866–867.

5c. Correct. One of the issues that caused problems for the Democratic party in the 1952 election was the revelation of influence-peddling by some of Truman's presidential appointees. See pages 866–867.

5d. No. Eisenhower did not condemn McCarthyism. In fact, his running mate, Richard Nixon, used McCarthy-like tactics in public statements against Adlai Stevenson, the Democratic presidential nominee. See pages 866–867.

6a. No. During the 1950s, most Americans paid little attention to the "faults" of American society, shunned idealistic causes, and saw society's critics as maladjusted. See pages 868–870

6b. Correct. During the 1950s, most Americans unquestioningly accepted American society. Their belief that the country was engaged in a moral crusade against communism led most Americans to believe liberal reform was unnecessary. See page 869.

6c. No. During the 1950s, most Americans were convinced of their ability to stand against any foe. See pages 868–870.

6d. No. During the 1950s, most Americans trusted and respected those in positions of authority and seldom questioned their decisions. See pages 868–870.

7a. No. Although the Housing Act lowered down payments and lengthened amortization periods for some home buyers, it did not provide low-interest loans. See pages 870–871.

7b. No. There was not a provision in the Housing Act that established a national housing code. See pages 870–871.

7c. No. The Housing Act of 1954 did not provide federally funded rental housing for the elderly. See pages 870–871.

7d. Correct. The 1954 act authorized the construction of some 35,000 homes over a one-year period. People who had been displaced by slum clearance or urban renewal programs were allowed to purchase these homes. See pages 870–871.

8a. No. The intent of the termination policy was to dissolve Indian reservations, not expand them. See page 871.

8b. No. Although one in eight Indians left the reservations between 1954 and 1960, it cannot be said that they were either "successfully relocated" or "successfully assimilated." See page 871.

8c. Correct. In this attempt to dissolve reservations and end federal services to Native Americans, many Indians were displaced and many joined the ranks of the urban poor. See page 871.

8d. No. This was not a program designed to aid Indians in the extraction of natural resources from tribal lands. See page 871.

9a. No. The bill passed the Senate unanimously. See pages 871–872.

9b. No. No Republicans were expelled from the party for having opposed this act. See pages 871–872.

9c. Correct. This act, which made membership in the Communist party illegal, was passed with no dissenting votes by the Senate and with only two dissenting votes by the House. This indicates that both liberals and conservatives shared in the anti-Communist consensus of the age. See pages 871–872.

9d. No. There was little disagreement within either party over passage of this act. Furthermore, the Democrats retained control of both houses of Congress in the 1954 elections. See pages 871–872.

10a. Correct. When the American people were able to see McCarthy's behavior and hear his wild accusations, especially those leveled against army officers whose loyalty was not in doubt, they turned against him and his redbaiting tactics. See page 872.

10b. No. The Republican party never officially condemned McCarthy, nor did it oust him from its ranks. See page 872.

© 1994 Houghton Mifflin Company. All rights reserved.

10c. No. The senator's downfall was well under way when the Senate voted formally to condemn him for abuse of other senators. McCarthy was never expelled from the Senate. See page 872.

10d. No. Eisenhower avoided a direct confrontation with McCarthy. See pages 871–872.

11a. No. The *Brown* decision did not declare the poll tax to be unconstitutional. Use of the poll tax to abridge a citizen's right to vote was not made illegal nationally until ratification of the Twenty-fourth Amendment in 1964. See page 874.

11b. Correct. The NAACP's legal campaign against desegregation scored a major victory when the Court ruled separate educational facilities to be "inherently unequal." See page 874.

11c. No. In the *Brown* decision, the Supreme Court found that black Americans had suffered from segregated public educational institutions. See page 874.

11d. No. It was not until 1964 that the Civil Rights Act of that year made discrimination in public accommodations illegal. This was upheld by the Court in the same year. See page 974. See also page 993.

12a. Correct. Although the boycott began as a result of the arrest of Rosa Parks, Martin Luther King, Jr., organized and led the boycott of Montgomery's city bus system. The boycott was ultimately successful and led to repeal of the Jim Crow statute that required blacks to sit in the rear of city buses. See page 876.

12b. No. Medgar Evers was a desegregation leader in Mississippi and was assassinated in front of his home in Jackson, Mississippi, on June 12, 1963. See pages 876–877. See also page 992.

12c. No. Ms. Bethune was president of the National Council of Negro Women in the 1930s and was active in the New Deal's National Youth Administration. See pages 876–877. See also page 777.

12d. No. Rosa Parks was arrested in December 1955 for refusing to surrender her seat on a Montgomery city bus to a white passenger. The arrest led to the black boycott of Montgomery's bus system, but Ms. Parks did not lead and organize the boycott. See pages 876–877.

13a. No. The policy of accommodation is associated with Booker T. Washington, not with Martin Luther King, Jr. See page 876.

13b. No. Martin Luther King, Jr., did not urge his followers to accept a socialist philosophy. See page 876.

13c. Correct. King had studied and was impressed by the nonviolent philosophy of Mahatma Gandhi of India. See page 876.

13d. No. Black Power was a concept put forward by Stokely Carmichael in the late 1960s. See page 876.

14a. No. Dr. Martin Luther King, Jr., founded the SCLC in 1957, three years before the sit-ins began. See pages 876–877.

14b. No. White Citizens' Councils were organized throughout the South in opposition to the 1954 *Brown* decision. See pages 876–877.

14c. No. CORE was founded in 1942 by James Farmer. In 1961 the group sponsored "freedom rides" into the South to test the Court's decision banning segregation in bus, train, and air travel. See pages 876–877.

14d. Correct. SNCC was organized in the fall of 1960 in response to the sit-in movement that began in Greensboro, North Carolina, on February 1, 1960. See pages 876–877.

15a. No. Nixon's ineffective use of television in the 1960 campaign was a factor in his defeat. See page 878.

15b. Correct. Kennedy effectively played on the Cold War fears of the American people by contending that the United States had lost power and prestige during the Eisenhower-Nixon years. See page 878.

15c. No. Kennedy met the issue of his Catholicism head on and was able to nullify the anti-Catholic vote. See page 878.

15d. No. When asked what Nixon's major contributions were during his eight years as vice-president, Eisenhower responded that if given a week he might be able to think of one. This may not be considered a strong endorsement of Nixon by Eisenhower. See page 878.

© 1994 Houghton Mifflin Company. All rights reserved.

Chapter 29

Ideas and Details

1a. Correct. The data indicate that the economic well-being of the United States depended on maintaining the flow of United States goods into foreign markets. An activist foreign policy was a means by which to protect and expand foreign trade. See pages 886–887.

1b. No. The economic devastation of Europe seriously jeopardized America's export trade. See pages 886–887.

1c. No. The evidence supports the conclusion that the United States continued its policy of economic expansion. See pages 886–887.

1d. No. The automobile, steel, and machine-tool industries depended heavily on foreign trade. Furthermore, some 50 percent of American wheat was exported, and surplus tobacco and cotton were sold abroad. See pages 886–887.

2a. No. The Soviet Union emerged from World War II with a weakened military establishment and did not have the power to overrun Western Europe. See page 888.

2b. No. The Soviet Union emerged from the Second World War with its economy in ruins. Furthermore, in the twentieth century, Russia had twice been invaded by Germany. As a result, Russia was fearful of the West. See page 888.

2c. Correct. With its military establishment weakened, its economy hobbled, and its technology obsolete, Russia did not have the power to dominate the world in 1945. A logical inference that may be drawn from these facts is that Russia was a regional power, not a global menace in the years immediately after the war. See page 888.

2d. No. Taking into consideration certain facts about the Russian past and the Soviet Union's view of the world in 1945, it would not be logical to conclude that the Soviet Union had no territorial ambitions in the immediate aftermath of World War II. See pages 887–888.

3a. No. For all of his strong points, when it came to international affairs and relations between the United States and the Soviet Union, Truman sought simple answers. Therefore, Truman did not demand detailed information on Soviet society. See page 888.

3b. No. American officials realized that worldwide economic problems and poverty, as well as the unrest bred by such problems, would be detrimental to United States interests. See page 888.

3c. No. American officials fixed their attention on stated Soviet goals rather than on actual Soviet behavior. See page 888.

3d. Correct. On an annual basis, the military establishment had to persuade Congress that its budgetary requests were realistic. Military officers found that it was easier to convince Congress if they exaggerated the Soviet threat. See page 888.

4a. No. The containment policy did not include a commitment to extend aid to the impoverished. See pages 883–884, 890.

4b. No. The containment policy did not make American aid conditional on a country's demonstration of its determination to help itself. See pages 883–884, 890.

4c. Correct. The containment policy, as expressed by Truman and Kennan, pledged unconditional aid to peoples resisting Communist expansion. See pages 883–884, 890.

4d. No. The containment doctrine did not emphasize the use of diplomacy in international relations. See pages 883—884, 890.

5a. No. Many American officials became convinced that Mao was a Soviet puppet. Therefore, when Mao made secret overtures to the United States to begin diplomatic talks in 1945 and 1949, he was rebuffed by American officials. See page 894.

© 1994 Houghton Mifflin Company. All rights reserved.

5b. No. Most American officials saw the Chinese civil war as part of the East-West conflict and did not recognize the nationalist nature of Mao's struggle against Jiang. See page 894.

5c. No. The United States did take sides in the struggle between Jiang Jieshi and Mao Zedong. See page 894.

5d. Correct. Most American officials believed Mao was part of an international Communist conspiracy and failed to see him as an independent Communist fighting for a China free from outside interference, and, therefore, free to control its own future. See page 894.

6a. No. The Soviet Union did give aid to North Korea during the course of the Korean War. See page 896.

6b. Correct. It seems likely that if the Soviets had fomented the North Korean invasion, their delegate would have been present at the Security Council to veto United Nations aid to South Korea. See page 896.

6c. No. The Soviet Union was not sending military aid to South Korea. See page 896.

6d. No. North Korea saw itself as independent and probably undertook the invasion of the South for its own nationalistic reasons, but it had not broken its ties with the Soviet Union. See page 896.

7a. Correct. MacArthur began publicly to question President Truman's war policies. Therefore, Truman fired him for insubordination. See page 897.

7b. No. MacArthur demanded that Truman allow an attack on China, but Truman never agreed to the policy because he was sure it would widen the war. See page 897.

7c. No. MacArthur was not removed at the insistence of the U.N. Security Council. See page 897.

7d. No. The Inchon landing (September 1950) was successful for the United Nations forces under McArthur's command and led to the liberation of Seoul, the South Korean capital. See page 897.

8a. Correct. Eisenhower's desire to trim federal spending led to the New Look military. Based on the policies of "massive retaliation" and "deterrence," the New Look emphasized nuclear weaponry rather than conventional forces. See page 899.

8b. No. Eisenhower's New Look military did not involve a United Nations police force. See page 899.

8c. No. Eisenhower's New Look military de-emphasized conventional military force. See page 899.

8d. No. The New Look military did not involve Soviet-American cooperation in space. In 1957, the Soviets launched *Sputnik*, to the shock and surprise of many Americans. In response, the United States created the National Aeronautics and Space Agency in 1958. See pages 899–900.

9a. No. The Soviet Union responded to an uprising against its power in Hungary by sending troops and tanks to crush the rebellion. This was not done because of American weakness, but the United States could not aid the rebels without risking war. See page 900.

9b. Correct. The idea of a "missile gap" was a false notion. At the end of the 1950s, the United States continued to enjoy an overwhelming strategic advantage over the Soviet Union. See page 900.

9c. No. The United States did not "back down" in the 1958 Berlin crisis. Furthermore, the United States was testing its own ICBMs and had more nuclear warheads than the Soviets. See pages 900–901.

9d. No. The Eisenhower administration quickly responded to *Sputnik* by creating the National Aeronautics and Space Agency. The Russians never "dangerously surpassed" the United States in missile technology. See page 900.

10a. No. The islands were bombarded by the People's Republic of China, and this led to the signing of a mutual defense treaty between the United States and Nationalist China (Formosa) on December 2, 1954. The treaty was ratified by the Senate in February 1955. See page 901.

10b. No. The United States continued to refuse to recognize the People's Republic of China as the legitimate Chinese government. See page 901.

© 1994 Houghton Mifflin Company. All rights reserved.

10c. Correct. In reaction to the crisis, the United States signed a mutual defense treaty with Formosa (December 2, 1954), Congress passed the Formosa Resolution (January 1955), and the United States installed nuclear-capable missiles on Formosa (1957). See page 901.

10d. No. In response to Cold War pressures that increased the likelihood of a nuclear confrontation, Khrushchev called for "peaceful coexistence" between the United States and the Soviet Union. This was not in direct response to the Formosa crisis. See page 901.

11a. No. The policy of flexible response is not associated with the decision-making process in the executive branch of the government. See page 902.

11b. No. The Kennedy administration did not "track" the mood of the electorate with the frequency and sophistication of modern tracking (frequent scientific polling of the electorate's stand on particular issues), and "flexible response" was not an electioneering tool. See page 902.

11c. Correct. In rejecting Eisenhower's policy of massive retaliation, Kennedy oversaw a military build-up based on the policy of flexible response. This policy held that the United States should be able to meet the threat of guerrilla warfare and the threat of a nuclear confrontation. See page 902.

11d. No. Although Kennedy disagreed with the Eisenhower administration's emphasis on nuclear weapons, he did not envision and did not achieve a reduction of the nation's nuclear arsenal. In fact, from 1961 to mid-1964 there was a 150 percent increase in the nation's nuclear arsenal. See page 902.

12a. Correct. After the failure of the Bay of Pigs invasion, the Kennedy administration authorized Operation Mongoose. Through this project, as well as programs of diplomatic and economic isolation, the United States government worked to overthrow the government of Fidel Castro. See page 904.

12b. No. Kennedy recognized the Bay of Pigs invasion as a mistake because it was a defeat, not because it infringed on Cuban sovereignty. The president never apologized to the Cuban people. See page 904.

12c. No. The United States continued its attempt to isolate Cuba economically. See page 904.

12d. No. The United States continued its attempt to isolate Cuba diplomatically and did not restore diplomatic relations. See page 904.

13a. No. The Soviet Union made demands concerning Berlin in the summer of 1961. The Cuban missile crisis occurred in the fall of 1962. See pages 906, 907.

13b. No. Although Kennedy informally agreed to withdraw outdated missiles from Turkey at a future date, he did not agree to dismantle missiles in Western Europe. See pages 906, 907.

13c. Correct. The Soviets decided that they would never again allow themselves to be humiliated because of military and nuclear weakness. Therefore, they embarked on a military build-up program and by the late 1960s achieved nuclear parity with the United States. See pages 906, 907.

13d. No. Suggestions that the United States destroy the Cuban missiles through a surprise air attack were rejected. See pages 906, 907.

14a. No. Although the Soviets had more launchers (missiles), the United States had more deliverable nuclear warheads. See page 907.

14b. No. Limits were placed on the construction of ABM systems. Each side could build only two—one to protect the capital and one to protect an ICBM field. See page 907.

14c. Correct. Each launcher (missile) could be MIRVed; and, since no restriction was placed on MIRVs, the nuclear build-up continued. See page 907.

14d. No. The treaties placed only a five-year freeze on the number of offensive nuclear missiles that each side could have. See page 907.

© 1994 Houghton Mifflin Company. All rights reserved.

15a. No. Reagan never apologized for his statement that the Soviet Union was the source of evil in the world. See pages 911, 913–914.

15b. No. The Reagan administration did not agree to limit research on the Strategic Defense Initiative. See pages 913–914.

15c. No. There were no obvious signs of cooperation between the United States and the Soviet Union to combat international terrorism. See pages 913–914.

15d. Correct. When Gorbachev assumed power in the Soviet Union in 1985, he advanced policies intended to reduce international tensions. The new atmosphere led to the withdrawal of Soviet troops from Afghanistan and of Cuban troops from Angola. Largely because of such agreements, Soviet-American relations improved. See pages 913–914.

Chapter 30

Ideas and Details

1a. No. Because the number of births per thousand women increased (see the chart on page 925), average family size increased as well. See page 924.

1b. No. The urban middle class, consisting of professionals, white-collar workers, and college graduates, contributed disproportionately to the baby boom. See page 924.

1c. No. Many people having second, third, and fourth children had demonstrated in the past that they knew how to practice birth control, but during the 1950s they chose not to do so. See page 924.

1d. Correct. Because of their optimism about America's future, many Americans chose to have more children. See page 924.

2a. Correct. Two cornerstones of the economic boom were related to the baby boom: (l) the construction boom and (2) the upsurge in automobile sales and manufacturing. See pages 924–925.

2b. No. Although military spending was one of the three cornerstones of the postwar economic boom, it was not related to the baby boom. See pages 924–925.

2c. No. Fast-food restaurants did not become a growth industry in American society until the 1960s and 1970s. Therefore, they were not a cornerstone of the postwar economic boom. See pages 924–925.

2d. No. Although television sales surged in the 1950s, the production of televisions is not considered a cornerstone of the postwar economic boom. See pages 924–925.

3a. No. Vertical integration (the control by one firm of a complete operation from raw material to finished product) was not a major reason for the continued trend toward bigness in American industry. See pages 926–927.

3b. Correct. Because of the expense of computer technology, many small firms were forced out of competition or were swallowed up by large corporations. See pages 926–927.

3c. No. The postwar era was a time of economic expansion and stability. See pages 926–927.

3d. No. To increase competition in a quantitative sense, one would have to break big businesses into smaller economic entities. This, being the opposite of consolidation, would indicate a trend toward smaller businesses. See pages 926–927.

4a. No. Farming methods continued to be revolutionized by the introduction of new machines. See pages 928–929.

4b. No. The value of farm output increased by 120 percent from 1945 to 1970. See pages 928–929.

© 1994 Houghton Mifflin Company. All rights reserved.

4c. Correct. The increase in land values and in the cost of machinery and fertilizers meant that farming became more expensive. As a result, there was a movement toward agricultural consolidation and away from the family farm. See pages 928–929.

4d. No. Farm-labor productivity increased three-fold between 1945 and 1970. See pages 928–929.

5a. No. The Kinsey reports deal with sexual behavior among American men and women and do not emphasize "family togetherness." See page 930.

5b. Correct. Many parents of the 1950s had suffered economic deprivation during the 1930s and separation from their families during the 1940s. As a result, they emphasized family togetherness in the 1950s. See page 930.

5c. No. Television shows often reflected the emphasis that society placed on family togetherness, but they were not the primary cause of that emphasis. See page 930.

5d. No. Riesman, a sociologist, was a critic of suburban living and of the isolation that families experienced as a result of the emphasis on "family togetherness." See page 930.

6a. No. Keynesian economics advanced the belief that, through deficit spending, government can generate the spending necessary to end a recession. This economic philosophy did not directly contribute to the rise of the megalopolis. See page 932.

6b. No. Defense spending did not contribute to the rise of the megalopolis. See page 932.

6c. Correct. The highway construction boom and the growth of suburbs gave rise to megalopolises such as "Boswash," "Chipitts," and "San-San." See page 932.

6d. No. Government subsidies for low-income housing did not contribute to the rise of the megalopolis. See page 932.

7a. No. Although accused in the 1960s of encouraging permissiveness in child rearing, Dr. Spock never actually encouraged such an approach. See page 934.

7b. No. Because of Dr. Spock's advice, many working mothers felt even more guilty. See page 934.

7c. Correct. Dr. Spock advised mothers to consider their children's needs before their own. As a result, many mothers felt guilty if they were not all things to their children. See page 934.

7d. No. Although this is not true of Dr. Spock's advice in the 1990s, his advice in the 1950s and 1960s was directed to the mother, not to the father. See page 934.

8a. No. Although stocks and bonds rose in value, most Americans did not invest heavily in the stock market. Furthermore, rising stock values do not automatically translate into real money or increased purchasing power. See page 938.

8b. No. Although the nation's GNP rose from $286.5 billion in 1950 to $506.5 billion in 1960, this rise was a *consequence* of the consumer culture rather than the economic *basis* of that culture. See page 938.

8c. Correct. Americans were able to purchase consumer goods because of the availability of credit. See page 938.

8d. No. The computer, although an important technological achievement of the age, did not put money into the hands of consumers, allowing them to purchase consumer goods. Therefore, the computer was not the economic basis of the consumer culture. See page 938.

9a. No. Heavy industry (steel, rubber, automobile) continued to be concentrated in the Frostbelt (the Northeast). See pages 939–940.

9b. Correct. The population increase in the Sunbelt caused the region to become more important in national politics. The region's population increase meant that it gained more representatives in the House of Representatives and more electoral votes. See page 940.

9c. No. The Sunbelt is not a heavily unionized area. In fact some industries moved into the region because of the absence of organized labor. See pages 939–940.

© 1994 Houghton Mifflin Company. All rights reserved.

9d. No. A redistribution of wealth in the South and West was not a consequence of the migration of people into the region. See pages 939–940.

10a. No. Black Americans generally continued to suffer from economic discrimination and particularly from discrimination in housing practices. As a result, blacks continued to congregate in the inner-city ghettos. See page 940.

10b. Correct. Although the black population was 48.6 percent urban in 1940, by 1970 it was 81.3 percent urban. See page 940.

10c. No. Blacks continued to move from the South to the North. See page 940.

10d. No. Although economic expansion and anti-poverty programs caused an overall decline in the number of poor, black Americans continued to experience economic discrimination, and poverty among blacks did not decrease "dramatically." See page 940.

11a. No. Twenty-five percent of the poor were over sixty-five, but, from the choices given, a retired white man was not the most likely to be poor. See pages 940–942.

11b. No. Almost 50 percent of the African-American population lived in poverty in 1962. However, from the choices given, a black American was not the most likely to be poor. See pages 940–942.

11c. No. Twenty percent of America's poor were nonwhite in 1962; but, from the choices given, Mexican-Americans were not the most likely to be poor. See pages 940–942.

11d. Correct. More than 50 percent of Native Americans lived in poverty and constituted the nation's poorest group. See pages 940–941.

12a. Correct. Although urban redevelopment was supposed to include public housing for those living in slum clearance areas, poor coordination caused delays in building the housing units and resulted in displacement of the poor. See pages 941–942.

12b. No. There was no national debate on the subject of substandard housing. See pages 941–942.

12c. No. As a result of slum clearance, slums were often replaced by parking lots, shopping centers, luxury apartments, highways, and factories. See pages 941–942.

12d. No. The establishment of national standards for inner-city housing was not a part of the Housing Act of 1949. See pages 941–942.

13a. Correct. In 1960 the median annual earnings for full-time women workers were 60 percent of men's earnings. One reason for this disparity was occupational segregation of women into low-paying "women's jobs." See page 942.

13b. No. Many husbands failed to pay child support and were seldom prosecuted for nonpayment; nevertheless, the courts still awarded child-support payments in divorce proceedings. See page 942.

13c. No. Although more women were getting more education, "overeducation" was not the reason a woman was more likely than a man to be poor. See page 942.

13d. No. Women were not more likely to suffer from catastrophic illnesses than men. See page 942.

14a. No. Jazz and rock 'n' roll have some similarity in background because both evolved from African music. But it cannot accurately be said that rock 'n' roll is derived from jazz. See pages 944–945.

14b. No. Rock 'n' roll was not derived from bluegrass music, which is associated with Appalachia. See pages 994–945.

14c. Correct. Rock 'n' roll is derived from black rhythm-and-blues. Rhythm-and-blues was born of the black American experience and contains rhythmic elements of African music. See pages 944–945.

14d. No. Shape-note singing is associated with religious music of the eastern United States and is a method of teaching sight-singing. See pages 944–945.

© 1994 Houghton Mifflin Company. All rights reserved.

15a. No. The "bebop" style is associated with developments in jazz during the 1940s and 1950s, when musicians such as Dizzy Gillespie began to experiment with complicated chord patterns. See pages 945–946.

15b. No. The Beats are not associated with new advertising techniques. See pages 945–946.

15c. No. The Beats were not rock-'n'-roll performers. See pages 945–946.

15d. Correct. The Beats challenged the consensus of the 1950s by questioning the materialism of consumer culture. They openly flaunted their sexual freedom and consumption of drugs. Their writings and lifestyle inspired the counterculture of the 1960s. See pages 945–946.

Chapter 31

Ideas and Details

1a. Correct. The United States stood against Third World revolutions that threatened the interests of America's allies and threatened American investments and markets. As a major world power interested in its own security, the United States desired order and stability. See page 955.

1b. No. Racism in American society, rather than a negative reaction by diplomats to America's pluralistic society, made it difficult for the United States to make friends in the Third World. See pages 953–955.

1c. No. American business interests engaged in economic expansion and invested heavily in Third World countries. In 1959 over one-third of America's private foreign investments were in Third World countries. See pages 953–955.

1d. No. The Soviet Union enjoyed only a slight edge, if any, in the race to win friends in the Third World. See pages 953–955.

2a. No. Neither Arbenz of Guatemala nor Mossadegh of Iran agreed to the deployment of Russian missiles in their countries. See page 956.

2b. No. Both Arbenz of Guatemala and Mossadegh of Iran were strongly nationalist in their views. As nationalists, they tended to view American interests in the Third World as exploitative. See page 956.

2c. No. You may be thinking of the 1954 test that destroyed the island of Bikini and caused the death of a crew member aboard the *Lucky Dragon*. See page 956.

2d. Correct. Both Arbenz of Guatemala and Mossadegh of Iran threatened the interests of American-owned companies operating in their countries. As a result, the CIA, through covert actions, aided in the overthrow of these men. See page 956.

3a. No. The concept of nation building did not envision a collective effort by the industrialized nations of the world to aid the Third World. See page 958.

3b. Correct. Nation building was undertaken with the belief that American capitalism and democracy could be transferred to the Third World. As this was done, it was believed, Third World countries would be brought into the American orbit. Presidential adviser Arthur Schlesinger later called this notion "a ghastly illusion." See page 958.

3c. No. The concept of nation building did not insist on decolonization by European countries. See page 958.

3d. No. Nation building did not pay much attention to the unique historical experiences of other nations. See page 958.

4a. No. Although the United States was attempting to negotiate a cease-fire in the Chinese civil war in 1945, recognition of Vietnamese independence would not have jeopardized those negotiations. See page 960.

4b. No. During the Second World War, Ho Chi Minh, a Vietnamese nationalist, worked with the American Office of Strategic Services against Japanese domination of his country. See page 960.

4c. No. FDR never made such a pledge to France. See page 960.

4d. Correct. American leaders failed to see Ho Chi Minh as a nationalist seeking independence from foreign domination. They could see him only as a Communist. See page 960.

5a. No. Congress did not question Johnson's escalation of the Vietnam War through the Tonkin Gulf Resolution. See page 964.

5b. Correct. With only two dissenting votes, Congress authorized the president to "take all necessary measures" to defend American forces and "prevent further aggression." In accepting the resolution, Congress, in effect, surrendered its foreign policy powers. See page 964.

5c. No. The Gulf of Tonkin resolution was passed in 1964; the My Lai massacre occurred in March 1968 and was not made public until twenty months later. See pages 964, 967.

5d. No. The Tonkin Gulf Resolution was not an official declaration of war. See page 964.

6a. No. Although the People's Republic of China joined the nuclear club in 1964, it was generally understood that it did not have the launchers (missiles) necessary to wage nuclear war. Furthermore, China was preoccupied with the internal disorder caused by the Cultural Revolution in the late 1960s. See pages 966–967.

6b. No. The Republican party stood staunchly behind the government of South Vietnam. See pages 966–967.

6c. No. Ho Chi Minh's regime in North Vietnam was a totalitarian regime and was not democratic in nature. See pages 966–967.

6d. Correct. As many Americans watched the horrors of the Vietnam War each evening on the nightly news, they began to question the United States involvement in the conflict. See pages 966–967.

7a. No. Although many American soldiers smoked marijuana and about one-third became addicted to opium and heroin, those who participated in atrocities such as the My Lai massacre were not necessarily addicts. See pages 967, 968.

7b. Correct. The enemy was everywhere in Vietnam. Every Vietnamese—women, children, old men, and impoverished peasants—was a potential Vietcong terrorist. The enemy was elusive in Vietnam, often hiding in underground bunkers. The nature of the conflict sometimes drove frustrated and frightened soldiers to commit atrocities. See page 967.

7c. No. Although saturation-bombing of the North was ordered by such officials, they did not order American soldiers to commit atrocities such as that at My Lai. See page 967.

7d. No. Atrocities such as that at My Lai were committed by American soldiers, not by CIA operatives. See page 967.

8a. No. The Soviet Union did not send troops to Vietnam as a result of the Tet offensive. See pages 969–970.

8b. No. The chairman of the Joint Chiefs of Staff, General Earle Wheeler, persuaded General Westmoreland to request an additional 206,000 soldiers. Furthermore, he favored calling the army and marine reserves to active duty. See pages 969–970.

8c. No. Although the Vietcong and North Vietnamese suffered heavy losses in the Tet offensive, they still had not been defeated and did not retreat to North Vietnam. See pages 969–970.

8d. Correct. The Tet offensive demonstrated that three years of search-and-destroy tactics had not destroyed the power of the Vietcong and North Vietnamese. As a result, Johnson announced an end to the bombing of most of the North and requested that Hanoi open peace negotiations. See pages 969–970.

9a. No. Nixon's policy of Vietnamization was accompanied by other policies that further destabilized Indochina. See pages 970–971.

9b. Correct. The policy of Vietnamization brought, among other things, a widening of the war into Cambodia, increased bombing of North Vietnam, and the mining of Haiphong harbor. See pages 970–971.

9c. No. The South Vietnamese army proved itself a rather ineffective fighting force, incapable of defending the South. See pages 970–971.

9d. No. Vietnamization did not bring about a coalition government, and the war did not quickly draw to a close. See pages 970–971.

10a. Correct. Some Americans pointed to the war as an example of the softening of American resolve against communism; others questioned, among other things, the containment doctrine. See pages 972–973.

10b. No. The United States did not withdraw from the United Nations in the aftermath of the Vietnam War. See pages 972–973.

10c. No. In fact, many leaders talked of a Vietnam syndrome—a mood that would prevent the United States from becoming involved in any foreign entanglements. See pages 972–973.

10d. No. Some Americans blamed the Vietnam experience on the "imperial presidency" and insisted that Congress retake the foreign policy power it had relinquished to the executive branch. See pages 972–973.

11a. No. Kissinger's "shuttle diplomacy" did not lead to the creation of a Palestinian state. See pages 975–976.

11b. No. In spite of Kissinger's "shuttle diplomacy," the PLO continued to refuse to recognize Israel's right to exist. See pages 975–976.

11c. No. Although Kissinger's diplomatic missions brought an end to the OPEC oil embargo, they did not lead to an OPEC agreement to reduce oil prices. See pages 975–976.

11d. Correct. Kissinger, acting as mediator by shuttling back and forth between Egyptian and Israeli officials, obtained an agreement between the two nations establishing a United Nations peacekeeping force in the Sinai. See pages 975–976.

12a. Correct. The United States economy was dependent on exports of finished products, imports of strategic raw materials, and foreign investments. Threats to these interests threatened the American standard of living and partially explain why America became an interventionist power. See page 976.

12b. No. The economic instability of the 1970s had a more severe impact on Third World nations than on the United States. See page 976.

12c. No. Extensive American investments abroad did not cause improved relations with developing nations. See page 976.

12d. No. The United States did not increase its commitment to the United Nations because of extensive American investments abroad. See page 976.

13a. No. Although the extent and nature of the aid from industrialized nations was a divisive issue, division did not occur because of the refusal of industrialized nations to send any aid. See page 976.

13b. Correct. Many Third World nations complained that the multinationals robbed them of natural resources and infringed on their political and economic sovereignty. See page 976.

13c. No. Many developing nations had no surplus food and had to rely on food aid and purchases to feed their own people. See page 976.

13d. No. Industrialized nations usually supported the excavation and extraction of seabed resources by private enterprise. See page 976.

14a. No. Although the Reagan administration warned that Nicaragua was supplying the El Salvadoran rebels with Soviet-made weapons, it did not warn that the Soviets were installing nuclear missiles in El Salvador. See page 980.

14b. No. Although the Reagan administration at times demonstrated some concern for the impoverished conditions in El Salvador, its policies in the region relied on military solutions. Therefore, it did not defend its policies by emphasizing the relationship between the insurgency and impoverished conditions. See page 980.

14c. Correct. By and large, the Reagan administration relied on military solutions to the problems in El Salvador. Therefore, to defend those policies, it relied on the old and discredited domino theory. See page 980.

© 1994 Houghton Mifflin Company. All rights reserved.

14d. No. The Reagan administration, in keeping with the policies of previous administrations, viewed right-wing governments in Latin America as better than governments with leftist leanings. Therefore, the administration supported right-wing governments even if they did not have mass popular support. See page 980.

15a. No. Although the administration criticized the Sandinistas for not holding elections, when elections were held in November 1984, the administration called them a "sham." See pages 980–982.

15b. Correct. The economic embargo against Nicaragua, covert activities by the CIA, and United States aid to the contras all indicate that the administration wanted to topple the Nicaraguan government. See pages 980–982.

15c. No. Although the Reagan administration criticized the presence of Cuban advisers and Soviet arms in Nicaragua, it wanted more than simply a reduction of foreign military bases and advisers. In fact, it rejected the Contadora peace plan which would have reduced foreign bases and advisers in Nicaragua. See pages 980–982.

15d. No. The Reagan administration's actions toward Nicaragua do not indicate a desire for a negotiated settlement. In fact, two peace plans were put forward during the 1980s by representatives of Latin American countries. The administration's out-of-hand rejection of both the Contadora peace plan and the Arias peace plan is further indication that a negotiated settlement was not the Reagan's goal in Nicaragua. See pages 980–982.

© 1994 Houghton Mifflin Company. All rights reserved.

Chapter 32

Evaluating and Using Information

Across

2. Baker
6. Hoover
7. Carmichael
12. Ray
13. Friedan
14. Evers
15. Malcolm X
17. NOW
19. ERA
20. Pentagon
22. Miranda
25. One
26. Dream
28. New Left
30. Stonewall Inn
31. Kent State

Down

1. Humphrey
2. Black Panthers
3. CORE
4. Kerner
5. Escobeda
8. Warren
9. Sex
10. FSM
11. SCLC
16. Meredith
18. Savio
21. Mitchell
23. SDS
24. Wallace
27. Watts
29. SNCC

Ideas and Details

1a. No. Although the work of the "Freedom Riders" in 1961 raised the national consciousness concerning civil rights, their work did not lead directly to passage of the Civil Rights Act of 1964. See pages 990–991, 992.

1b. No. Kennedy had to deal with a Congress controlled by conservative Republicans and southern Democrats. As a result, he was not very successful in getting Congress to act on his programs. See pages 990, 992.

1c. Correct. Although black activism and television news programs raised the national consciousness concerning civil rights, it took these two tragedies to convince reluctant politicians that action on civil rights was necessary. See page 992.

1d. No. Although SNCC's involvement in the sit-ins, the Freedom Rides, and voter registration drives in the South did raise the national consciousness concerning civil rights, it did not lead directly to passage of the Civil Rights Act of 1964. See pages 991, 992.

2a. No. These were not provisions of the 1965 Elementary and Secondary Education Act. See page 995.

2b. Correct. This act, which granted $1.3 billion to school districts on the basis of the number of needy children, was the first general program of federal aid to education. See page 995.

2c. No. This was not a provision of the 1965 education bill, and such certification is still left in the hands of the states. See page 995.

2d. No. The establishment of a federal job-placement service for teachers was not a provision of the 1965 education bill. See page 995.

3a. No. The right to vote was extended to eighteen-year-olds by the Twenty-sixth Amendment, ratified in 1971. See page 995.

3b. Correct. Whereas only 29 percent of the South's black population was registered to vote in 1960, around 66 percent was registered by 1969. See page 995.

3c. No. Literacy and other voter tests were suspended by the Voting Rights Act of 1965 in those states where such tests had been used to bar qualified people from the voting rolls and where less than half of the voting-age residents were registered. See page 995.

3d. No. The act authorized federal supervision of voter registration in areas where less than half of the voting-age minority residents were registered, but it did not require all eligible voters to register through federal registrars. See page 995.

4a. No. The Court did not sanction required nondenominational prayers in public schools. See page 998.

4b. No. The Court did not rule that God has no place in the public schools. See page 998.

4c. Correct. The Court held that the state could not require the reciting of an official prayer in public schools. See page 998.

4d. No. The Court did not ban all prayers in public schools. See page 998.

5a. No. These cases did not deal with religious issues and did not broaden the definition of religion. See page 998.

5b. No. Freedom of expression was not at issue in these cases. See page 998.

5c. Correct. These criminal cases extended coverage of the Fourteenth Amendment to include the right of a poor person charged with a felony to a state-appointed lawyer and the right of a suspect to be informed of his or her rights. See page 998.

5d. No. These cases did not deal with sexual issues. See page 998.

6a. Correct. The civil rights movement had been largely southern in focus and did not deal with the deteriorating conditions of blacks in inner-city ghettos. Black frustration was expressed through urban riots and in the voices of black nationalism. See pages 999–1002.

6b. No. There is no evidence to support the contention that there was "communist infiltration" of civil rights groups and that such infiltration caused the urban race riots of the 1960s and the emergence of black nationalism. See pages 999–1002.

6c. No. Northern blacks had long had and exercised the right to vote. See pages 999–1002.

© 1994 Houghton Mifflin Company. All rights reserved.

6d. No. The SCLC, under the direction of Martin Luther King, Jr., continued to use the nonviolent tactic of passive resistance. See pages 999–1002.

7a. No. The drug culture of the 1960s is associated more with the counterculture than with the New Left. See pages 1003–1004.

7b. No. The counterculture's desire to build a "Woodstock nation" based on love, drugs, and rock music was not very realistic. Furthermore, the New Left was not a single movement with a single set of goals. See pages 1003–1004.

7c. Correct. Although the New Left tended to be political in its orientation and used direct-action tactics, the counterculture used music to attack the status quo. See pages 1003–1004.

7d. No. Student activists, the New Left, and the counterculture were united in their opposition to the Vietnam War. See pages 1003–1004.

8a. Correct. The riot that erupted between police and the gay patrons of the Stonewall Inn is considered to be the beginning of the gay rights movement. See pages 1005–1006.

8b. No. The Stonewall riot did not occur in Atlantic City and was not undertaken by radical feminists. See pages 1005–1006.

8c. No. The Stonewall riot occurred in New York City and was not associated with the 1968 Democratic Convention in Chicago. See pages 1005–1006.

8d. No. The Stonewall riot was not related to King's assassination. See pages 1005–1006.

9a. No. George Wallace ran for president under the banner of the American Independent Party in 1968. In 1972 he was a candidate for the Democratic presidential nomination and was seriously wounded by a would-be assassin. See pages 1007, 1008–1009.

9b. Correct. With polls showing him as the leading presidential candidate among Democrats and having just won the California primary, Robert Kennedy was assassinated on June 5, 1968. See page 1007.

9c. No. McCarthy challenged President Johnson's war policies in 1968, and his victory in the New Hampshire primary was a factor in Johnson's decision to withdraw as a candidate. But McCarthy was not assassinated. See pages 1006–1007.

9d. No. Edmund Muskie was not a Democratic candidate for the presidency in 1968. See pages 1006–1007.

10a. No. In the late 1960s radical feminists were more likely to support the gay rights movement than were members of NOW. See pages 1010–1011.

10b. No. Radical feminists were concerned with the political, social, and economic inequality of women. They also challenged women's legal inequality and sex-role stereotyping. See pages 1010–1011.

10c. No. Although Friedan inspired the founding of NOW, she was not repudiated by the radical feminists. See pages 1010–1011.

10d. Correct. While NOW concentrated on lobbying for legislation and testing laws through the courts, radical feminists became involved in direct action to achieve their goals. See page 1010.

11a. No. Nixon did not advocate national health insurance and even strongly opposed expansion of Medicare, which applied only to the elderly. See pages 1012–1013.

11b. No. Nixon had instituted his Vietnamization policy; but, while American ground troops were being withdrawn, the air war widened. See pages 1012–1013.

11c. No. Nixon imposed wage and price controls in August 1971, nine months after the November 1970 congressional elections. See pages 1012–1013.

11d. Correct. The speeches of Vice President Agnew provide evidence that the Nixon administration deliberately tried to associate the Democratic party with radicalism and violence before the 1970 congressional elections. See pages 1012–1013.

© 1994 Houghton Mifflin Company. All rights reserved.

12a. Correct. Middle-class Americans were frightened by McGovern's proposals and demonstrated their fear at the polls. See page 1016.

12b. No. Nixon's attorney general, John Mitchell, worked to prevent the extension of the Voting Rights Act of 1965 and, in the process, pleased many southerners. See pages 1015–1016.

12c. No. Although Nixon had run as a fiscal conservative in 1968, he had authorized large budget deficits. See pages 1015–1016.

12d. No. Much of the environmental-protection legislation that passed in the early 1970s was due to the support of Congress, not necessarily that of Nixon. See pages 1015–1016.

13a. No. James McCord, one of the defendants in the Watergate break-in and a former security coordinator of CREEP, revealed in a letter to Judge Sirica that the defendants had been pressured to plead guilty and that perjury was committed at the trial. See page 1017.

13b. No. John Mitchell, who resigned as Nixon's attorney general to head the President's re-election campaign, knew of the payments but did not authorize them. See page 1017.

13c. Correct. President Nixon authorized CREEP to pay over $460,000 to keep Hunt and others from implicating the White House in the Watergate burglary. See page 1017.

13d. No. John Ehrlichman, Nixon's adviser on domestic affairs, had knowledge of the payments but did not authorize them. See page 1017.

14a. Correct. The committee voted for impeachment on three counts: obstruction of justice, defiance of a congressional subpoena, and abuse of power through the improper use of the CIA, FBI, and IRS. See page 1018.

14b. No. The article of impeachment accusing Nixon of demeaning the office of the presidency by misconduct of his personal financial affairs was voted down by a vote of 26 to 12. Furthermore, one cannot be declared guilty as the result of impeachment hearings. See page 1018.

14c. No. The committee voted on the articles of impeachment brought against Nixon and made a recommendation to the full House. See page 1018

14d. No. The committee held hearings to determine if there was just cause to refer articles of impeachment to the full House, not to determine Nixon's guilt or innocence. See page 1018.

15a. Correct. The act, in an attempt to put some restrictions on the president's war-making powers, required the president to consult with Congress "in every possible instance" before sending troops into foreign wars. See page 1018.

15b. No. In an effort to put restrictions on the president's war-making powers, the act required the chief executive to withdraw troops after sixty days (as opposed to 10 days) unless Congress authorized otherwise. See page 1018.

15c. No. The president, as commander-in-chief of the armed forces, still had the authority to respond to threats to national security and send troops to foreign territory. See page 1018.

15d. No. The president, as commander-in-chief of the armed forces, still had the authority to respond to threats to national security and send troops into a foreign war without getting a declaration of war from Congress. See page 1018.

© 1994 Houghton Mifflin Company. All rights reserved.

Chapter 33

Evaluating and Using Information

S	U	P	P	L	Y	S	I	D	E		S	C	H	L	A	F	L	Y
		A									L					
		C	O	M	P	A	R	A	B	L	E	W	O	R	T	H
T		S			I				A						O	
H			H	Y	D	E			Z		P	A	T	C	O	
R					S		B		E	J					O	
E		G				S	T	A	G	F	L	A	T	I	O	N
E	L	D	E	R	L	Y		K	A	C					N	
M		A				K		C	K						E	
I	A	I	M		S	U	N	B	E	L	T		S		R		R
L		M						O		S	O		H		
E	W	O	R	K	I	N	G	P	O	O	R		N		E	
I		U												N	
S		D		M		P						Q		F	
L	S	I	M	P	S	O	N	R	O	D	I	N	O		U		E
A	C	A		R		O						I		R	
N	A	N		A		L						S		R	
D	L			L		I	R	A	N	C	O	N	T	R	A	
	I					F								R	
C	H	A	V	E	Z		D	E	F	I	C	I	T		K	O	O	P

Across

1. Supplyside
3. Schlafly
4. comparable worth
8. Hyde
9. PATCO
13. Stagflation
14. Elderly
15. AIM
16. Sunbelt
18. Working poor
22. Simpson-Rodino
23. Iran-Contra
24. Chavez
25. Deficit
26. Koop

Down

2. PACs
3. Sleaze Factor
5. AIDS
6. Three-Mile Island
7. O'Conner
10. Bakke
11. Jackson
12. Gramm-Rudman
17. Rhenquist
19. Moral
20. Pro-Life
21. Ferraro
22. Scalia

Ideas and Details

1a. No. The increase in oil prices caused double-digit inflation in 1974, but this is not the best answer. See pages 1025–1026.

1b. No. The 350 percent increase in oil prices in 1973 slowed overall economic growth, but this is not the best answer. See pages 1025–1026.

© 1994 Houghton Mifflin Company. All rights reserved.

1c. No. The high cost of oil caused a lingering recession in the automobile and related industries, but this is not the best answer. See pages 1025–1026.

1d. Correct. The 350 percent increase in oil prices from January 1973 to January 1974 brought double-digit inflation, slowed overall economic growth, and led to a recession in the automobile and related industries. See pages 1025–1026.

2a. No. Despite the slow growth in productivity, many workers continued to expect wage increases that would give them more purchasing power each year. See pages 1026–1027.

2b. No. The slow growth in productivity did not lead to a decline in interest rates. See pages 1026–1028.

2c. Correct. The slow growth in productivity was one reason that American goods cost more than comparable foreign goods. High prices made American goods less competitive in foreign markets. See page 1026.

2d. No. The slow growth in productivity did not cause an increase in business investments. See page 1026.

3a. Correct. Most liberal Democrats believed that regulation of such industries as the airline industry was to the advantage of the consumer. Carter's stand in favor of deregulation angered these Democrats and made it more difficult for Carter to work with Congress. See page 1030.

3b. No. The number of PACs quadrupled between 1974 and 1980. See page 1030.

3c. No. From 1961 to 1981, no president was elected to two terms. During this same period the nation experienced the traumas of Vietnam and Watergate. The combination of these factors caused power to flow into the hands of Congress and presidential authority to decline. See page 1030.

3d. No. President Carter supported imposing a windfall-profits tax on oil companies; Republicans were generally opposed to it. Furthermore, Democrats controlled both houses of Congress during the Carter administration. See pages 1029–1030.

4a. Correct. Both Proposition 13 and the alliance between evangelical Christians and members of the Hoover Institute (a conservative think-tank) are associated with the swing toward conservatism in the late 1970s. See page 1032.

4b. No. As people continued to move from the Frostbelt to the more politically and socially conservative Sunbelt, the latter became more important politically. See page 1032.

4c. No. Although it is true that economic issues were very important in the late 1970s, the three pieces of evidence offered do not support the inference that economic issues were dominant. See page 1032.

4d. No. The passage of Proposition 13 and the emergence of evangelical Christians and the Hoover Institute as political forces do not indicate that Americans were unconcerned about Communist expansion. See page 1032.

5a. No. Although Reagan denounced welfare, after he became governor of California he presided over reform of the welfare bureaucracy in the state. Therefore, he did not dismantle the state's welfare system. See page 1033.

5b. Correct. Before the prochoice and prolife arguments became major political issues, Governor Ronald Reagan had signed one of the nation's most liberal abortion laws. See page 1033.

5c. No. Ronald Reagan did not propose the legalization of marijuana when he was governor of California. See page 1033.

5d. No. Ronald Reagan did not institute a statewide healthcare program for California during his two four-year terms as governor of that state. See page 1033.

6a. No. Those in the poorest fifth received essentially no tax cut, and by 1984 the after-tax income of those in the second-poorest fifth increased by only 1.4 percent. See pages 1034–1035.

6b. Correct. Wealthy people gained the most from the 1981 tax reductions. See pages 1034–1035.

6c. No. Although the after-tax income of those Americans in the middle fifth increased by 2.8 percent by 1984, another group's after-tax income increased by a higher percentage. See pages 1034–1035.

© 1994 Houghton Mifflin Company. All rights reserved.

6d. No. Among the groups listed, married couples did not save the most as a result of the 1981 income-tax reductions. See pages 1034–1035.

7a. No. During 1981 and 1982 there was less than a 1 percent increase in the rate of productivity. See page 1035.

7b. Correct. The recession brought soaring unemployment, severe economic hardship to many farmers, and an overall increase in the poverty rate. As a result, the inflation rate and, in some cases, prices declined. See page 1035.

7c. No. An increase in spending by Americans did not cause prices to decline. See page 1035.

7d. No. Both the GNP and investment spending fell during this period. See page 1035.

8a. No. Although this practice was used by companies and was declared constitutional by the Supreme Court, Reagan's appointees to the NLRB did not *actively* encourage companies to declare bankruptcy as a way of canceling union contracts. See page 1037.

8b. No. The right of union members to strike was not questioned by Reagan's appointees to the NLRB. See page 1037.

8c. Correct. Reagan's appointees on the NLRB demonstrated their hostility toward organized labor by consistently voting in favor of management. See page 1037.

8d. No. A closed shop or union shop is a business whose employees are required to be union members. Reagan's appointees to the NLRB did not favor the closed shop. See page 1037.

9a. No. President Reagan oversaw a multi-trillion-dollar defense-spending program that favored building the B-1 bomber, enlarging the navy, increasing the production of poison gas, deploying the MX missile, and deploying an antimissile defense system in space. See pages 1039–1040.

9b. No. Although Reagan's opposition to abortion did concern some people, this was not of major concern to most people and did not generally cause "growing public concern." See pages 1039–1040.

9c. Correct. Although candidate Reagan promised to balance the federal budget, President Reagan oversaw the accumulation of more new debt than the combined deficits of all previous presidents. See pages 1039–1040.

9d. No. Although the United States certainly did not dictate to Israel, there was not a "lack of influence" either. See pages 1039–1040.

10a. No. Occupational segregation continued as the shift from an industrialized to a service-oriented economy took place. See pages 1040–1041.

10b. No. The shifting occupational structure meant the loss of many blue-collar jobs and an increase in skilled, white-collar, high-technology jobs. See pages 1040–1041.

10c. Correct. As the economy shifted from an industrial to a service orientation, jobs that had traditionally been available to the unskilled and impoverished disappeared. The labor demand was in the area of skilled, white-collar, high-technology jobs. See pages 1040–1041.

10d. No. The shift from an industrialized to a service-oriented economy, and the resulting shift in labor demand, caused unions to devote more energy to organizing white-collar workers. See pages 1040–1041.

11a. No. The number of blacks attending college increased dramatically during the 1970s and 1980s. See page 1041

11b. Correct. Because the plight of poor blacks worsened and the black middle class expanded, it is logical to conclude that the gap between poor blacks and middle-class blacks widened during the 1970s and 1980s. In fact, because of this widening gap, the sociologist William Julius Wilson spoke of the emergence of two black Americas. See page 1041.

11c. No. In the period from 1960 to 1975 the number of fatherless black families rose 130 percent. See page 1041.

11d. No. The black middle class expanded during the 1970s and 1980s. See page 1041.

© 1994 Houghton Mifflin Company. All rights reserved.

12a. No. Although the Reagan administration did express opposition to court-ordered busing, it did not openly encourage local school districts to defy court orders under which they operated. See pages 1041–1042.

12b. Correct. Although the Voting Rights Act was in large measure responsible for the increased political power of African Americans, especially in the South, and was extended by Congress in 1971 and 1975, the Reagan administration stood against renewing the act intact. See pages 1040–1042.

12c. No. Although the Reagan administration was criticized for lax enforcement of fair-housing laws, it did not seek repeal of those laws. See pages 1041–1042.

12d. No. Although the Reagan administration was opposed to affirmative action, it did not gain passage of legislation outlawing it. See pages 1041–1042.

13a. No. A nationwide strike by working women was not a tactic employed by the antifeminist forces in their efforts to prevent ratification of the Equal Rights Amendment. See page 1046.

13b. No. The Senate did not rescind its approval of this amendment. See page 1046.

13c. No. Antifeminist leaders such as Phyllis Schlafly refused to acknowledge the existence of gender-based discrimination, but no such study was ever conducted and the facts do not support such a conclusion. See page 1046.

13d. Correct. Antifeminist forces used scare tactics, for the most part, as part of an emotional campaign against ratification of the Equal Rights Amendment. This had the desired effect, and the ERA fell three states short of ratification. See page 1046.

14a. No. Older Americans were not heavily involved in the crack epidemic. See pages 1049–1050.

14b. No. Although there are doubtless crack addicts among the transportation workers in the United States, the epidemic's impact on another group is more alarming. See pages 1049–1050.

14c. Correct. In poor neighborhoods, young single mothers became addicted to crack. The epidemic's impact on this group is more alarming than its impact on the other groups because of the impact of addiction on both mother and child. See pages 1049–1050.

14d. No. Although there are doubtless crack addicts among Mexican immigrants, the epidemic's impact on another group is more alarming. See pages 1049–1050.

15a. No. The evidence indicated that President Reagan was aware of the sale of arms to Iran and that he did not instruct Robert McFarlane not to engage in such a sale. See pages 1051–1052.

15b. No. The evidence is inconclusive on this point, but it is likely that Reagan did not know about the diversion of funds from the Iranian arms sales to the Nicaraguan contras. See pages 1051–1052.

15c. No. The evidence indicated an attempt on the part of the Reagan administration to subvert the will of Congress on certain foreign policy issues. See pages 1051–1052.

15d. Correct. Evidence presented in the Iran-contra hearings revealed a "hands-off" management style and indicated that the president was an unengaged and uninformed leader. See pages 1051–1052.

Chapter 34

Ideas and Details

1a. No. Although President Bush and the members of his administration expressed doubts about theories relating to global warming, Bush did not go so far as to pledge a worldwide campaign against those theories. See page 1062.

© 1994 Houghton Mifflin Company. All rights reserved.

1b. No. Carbon emissions from gas-powered automobiles are a major contributor to the greenhouse gases that produce global warming. However, President Bush did not pledge government funding for production of a marketable electric-powered automobile. See page 1062.

1c. Correct. In response to a proposal at the Earth Summit that all participating nations agree to a plan to stabilize carbon emissions at their 1990 levels by the year 2000, President Bush complained that such an agreement would interfere with the free marketplace. See page 1062.

1d. No. Japan and the European nations proposed that the 178 nations represented at the Earth Summit accept an agreement imposing binding limits on carbon dioxide emissions. President Bush opposed this proposal and binding limits were not included in the final agreement. See page 1062.

2a. Correct. Japan argued that United States products were of poorer quality than Japanese products because they were manufactured with obsolete equipment, American workers were poorly educated, and the United States did not adequately fund research and development. See pages 1063-1064.

2b. No. Japan argued that the United States government did not adequately fund research and development. It did not contend that the United States spent too much on job-training programs. See pages 1063-1064.

2c. No. The Japanese government did not believe that the United States was overly concerned about the quality of public education in America. In fact, it argued that poorly educated American workers was one reason that American products were not as competitive as Japan's in the world marketplace. See pages 1063-1064.

2d. No. American-based multinational corporations did not control twenty-five percent of Japan's productive capacity, and the Japanese never used such an argument against American complaints about unfair trade practices. See pages 1063-1064.

3a. No. The Bush administration never offered to send military aid to Gorbachev for any reason. See page 1065.

3b. No. The United States was generally slow in offering aid to the states that were part of the former Soviet Union and offered no direct financial support to any of those states in 1991. See page 1065.

3c. No. Although business and economic advisers from the United States have gone to Russia and to Eastern European countries such as Poland and Czechoslovakia, the United States did not work through the U.N. and NATO to send a "team" of advisers to each newly independent republic of the former Soviet Union. See page 1065.

3d. Correct. At first, the Bush administration did not seem to know how to respond to the breakup of the Soviet Union. See page 1065.

4a. No. France experienced high unemployment rates during the late 1980s and early 1990s and did not undergo an economic resurgence. See page 1066.

4b. No. Independence for these former republics of the Soviet Union did not pose an economic threat to the United States. See page 1066.

4c. No. Although there were signs by 1992 that the Polish economy was moving in a positive direction, the move toward a market economy and toward privatization had been difficult for the country and its people. Poland is not seen as a potential economic threat to the United States. See page 1066.

4d. Correct. A unified Germany could potentially have a great deal of economic clout in Europe and in the world. See page 1066.

5a. Correct. The twelve-year-old civil war ended in El Salvador in early 1992 when the government and the leftist rebel forces reached an agreement that brought about a cease fire. As part of the cease-fire agreement, the leftist forces agreed to disarm and participate in the political process to bring about change. See page 1066.

5b. No. The easing of the crisis in El Salvador did not come about because the Salvadoran army decisively defeated the rebel forces. In fact, in the easing of the crisis the Salvadoran government had to give a number of concessions to the rebels. See page 1066.

5c. No. The president of El Salvador did not use his emergency powers to institute land reform. See page 1066.

© 1994 Houghton Mifflin Company. All rights reserved.

5d.   No. After having poured large sums of money into a military solution in El Salvador, the United States did not seem to have the funds available to bring about meaningful social and economic reform. Therefore, such funds did not cause the easing of the crisis in El Salvador. See page 1066.

6a.   No. The Bush administration was always adamantly opposed to the legalization of illicit drugs. See page 1066.

6b.   Correct. Although critics contended that the United States should concentrate on trying to reduce the demand for drugs within the country, the Bush administration continued to concentrate on reducing the supply. See page 1066.

6c.   No. Critics contended that the Bush administration should emphasize reducing the demand for drugs in the country, but this was not the course taken by the administration. See page 1066.

6d.   No. Although many businesses in the United States engage in drug-testing, the Bush administration never suggested drug-testing by all American businesses with over 50 employees. See page 1066.

7a.   No. Although there was concern that Israel's enemies might use the Persian Gulf War to attack Israel, worry over such an attack was not the reason that troops were sent to the Persian Gulf region. See page 1067.

7b.   Correct. After Iraq's invasion and takeover of Kuwait, the United States was afraid that Iraq would attack Saudi Arabia. Therefore, American troops were sent to the Persian Gulf region to defend Saudi Arabia and were ultimately used to force Hussein out of Kuwait. See page 1067.

7c.   No. The cease-fire between Iraq and Iran had been in effect since 1988, and the United States did not send troops to enforce this cease-fire. See page 1067.

7d.   No. The United Arab Emirates (UAE) was not preying on American tankers in the Persian Gulf. See page 1067.

8a.   No. Foreign aid continued to go to Iraq after Bush assumed the presidency. See pages 1068-1069.

8b.   No. Although the United States did secretly sell arms to Iran during the Reagan administration—an act that was part of the Iran-*contra* scandal—those arms were sold for the purpose of gaining the release of American hostages. Therefore, the sale of arms to Iran was not a demonstration of hostility toward Iraq. See pages 1068-1069.

8c.   No. Foreign aid from the United States was used by Hussein to purchase arms during his war with Iran, but the United States did not supply Iraq with nuclear-capable missiles. See pages 1068-1069.

8d.   Correct. During the years and months before the Persian Gulf War, American companies aided Hussein's attempts to develop nuclear weapons by shipping high-tech equipment to Iraq. See pages 1068-1069.

9a.   No. When U.S. troops were sent to Somalia in 1992 there was really no regime in power in Somalia. The nation had been reduced to civil war among rival war lords and did not have an effective central government. See page 1069.

9b.   Correct. The action was a humanitarian gesture on the part of the United States. See page 1069.

9c.   No. There was no cease-fire in effect among the rival warlords in Somalia. See page 1069.

9d.   No. There were no terrorists known to be hiding in Somalia. See page 1069.

10a.   No. Although President Bush had consistently asked Congress to pass legislation allowing a line-item veto, Congress never agreed to such legislation. See page 1072.

10b.   No. Bush was not impounding funds appropriated by Congress and the budget negotiations did not produce an agreement by Congress that there would be a debate on a balanced-budget amendment. See page 1072.

10c.   Correct. Although candidate Bush had pledged that he would not raise taxes, President Bush agreed to a tax hike when the Democrats who controlled Congress agreed to budget cuts. See page 1072.

10d.   No. Although the federal debt limit was increased during the Bush administration, the agreement to do this did not come out of the 1990 budget negotiations. See page 1072.

11a.   No. The Council on Competitiveness did not show concern over the quality of American automobiles. See page 1072.

© 1994 Houghton Mifflin Company. All rights reserved.

11b. Correct. Headed by Vice President Dan Quayle, the Council on Competitiveness used the argument that environmental regulations slowed economic growth to justify gutting enforcement of the Clean Air Act of 1990. See page 1072.

11c. No. The Council on Competitiveness did not attempt to persuade American businesses to adopt Japanese management practices. See page 1072.

11d. No. The Council on Competitiveness did not suggest protective tariffs against Japanese imports. See page 1072.

12a. No. Although ordinances of this type did cause protest in some American cities, such an ordinance was not the cause of the Los Angeles riots of 1992. See page 1073.

12b. No. Such an incident did not cause the Los Angeles riots of 1992. See page 1073.

12c. Correct. The incident that was the immediate cause of the Los Angeles riots of 1992 was the acquittal by an all-white jury of four Los Angeles police officers in the beating of Rodney King. See page 1073.

12d. No. The city of Los Angeles did not close a recreational center in Watts and such a closing was not the cause of the Los Angeles riots of 1992. See page 1073.

13a. No. The House banking scandal did not involve the misuse of funds on the part of the manager of the House bank. See page 1074.

13b. Correct. It seemed to most Americans that members of the House of Representatives had unwarranted privileges when it was revealed that many representatives overdrew their accounts and were not penalized. See page 1074.

13c. No. Vice-President Quayle did not write checks against the House bank. See page 1074.

13d. No. Money in the House bank was not used to finance CIA operations. See page 1074.

14a. No. Quayle was not especially articulate and did not appear to have a better grasp of the issues than President Bush. See page 1075.

14b. No. Vice-President Quayle was adamant in his antiabortion stance. See page 1075.

14c. Correct. Senator Al Gore was articulate and well versed on the issues in the 1992 campaign. Vice-President Quayle was not as articulate as his political rival, had made many misstatements as Vice-President, and was the subject of many jokes. See page 1075.

14d. No. Although some Republicans had suggested to George Bush that Quayle should be dropped from the ticket in 1992, Quayle was not openly ridiculed by leaders of the Republican party. See page 1075.

15a. No. While campaigning in the primaries against his rivals for the Democratic nomination, Bill Clinton indicated that he would reduce the tax burden on the middle class. However, Clinton was not making that pledge by the time of the Democratic Convention, did not make that pledge during the general campaign, and did not make that part of the economic plan he sent to Congress in 1993. See page 1077.

15b. No. Clinton was very consistent in the primaries and the general campaign in calling for higher taxes on the wealthiest Americans. His 1993 economic plan did not call for tax breaks for the wealthy. See page 1077.

15c. Correct. Clinton's 1993 economic plan called for an energy tax. See page 1077.

15d. No. Clinton's 1993 economic plan called for higher corporate taxes. See page 1077.

© 1994 Houghton Mifflin Company. All rights reserved.

Duplicate Outline Maps

The maps on the following pages contain duplicates of the outline maps that appear in this study guide. They may be removed for class use.

Outline Map for Chapter 22—U.S. and Latin America

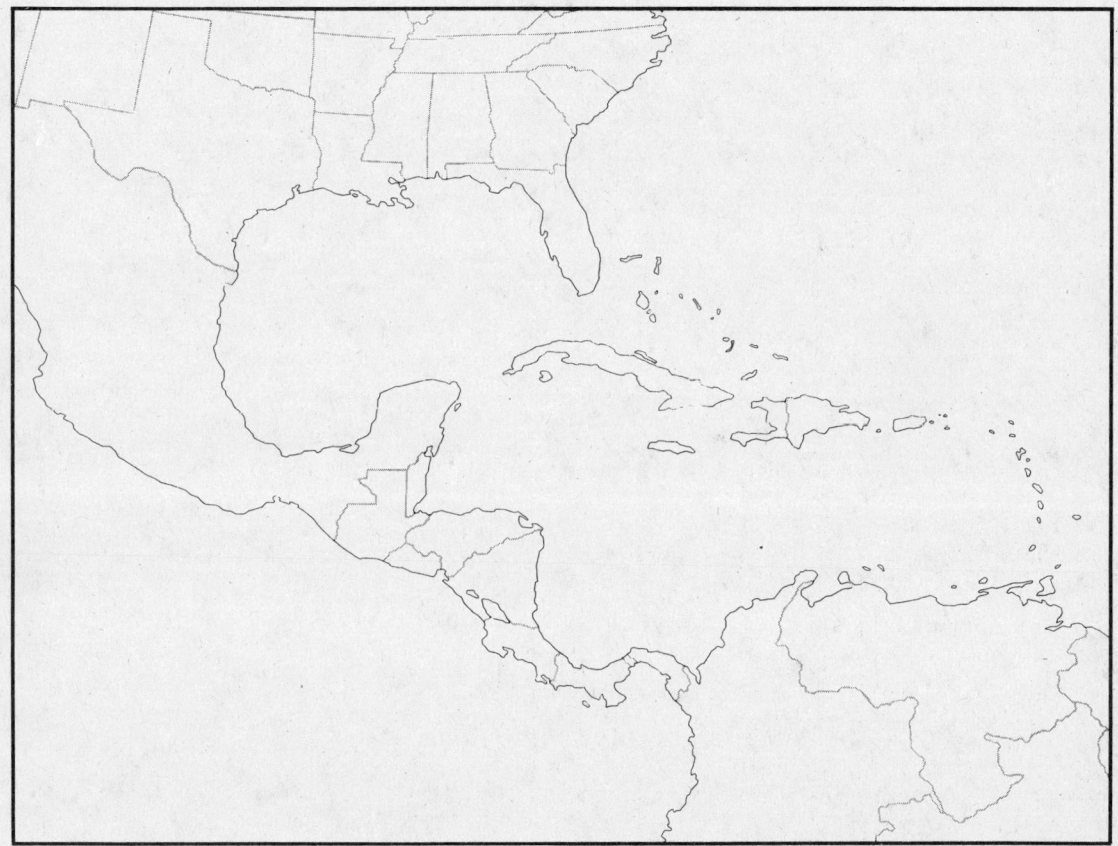

© 1994 Houghton Mifflin Company. All rights reserved.

Outline Map for Chapter 29—World (left side)

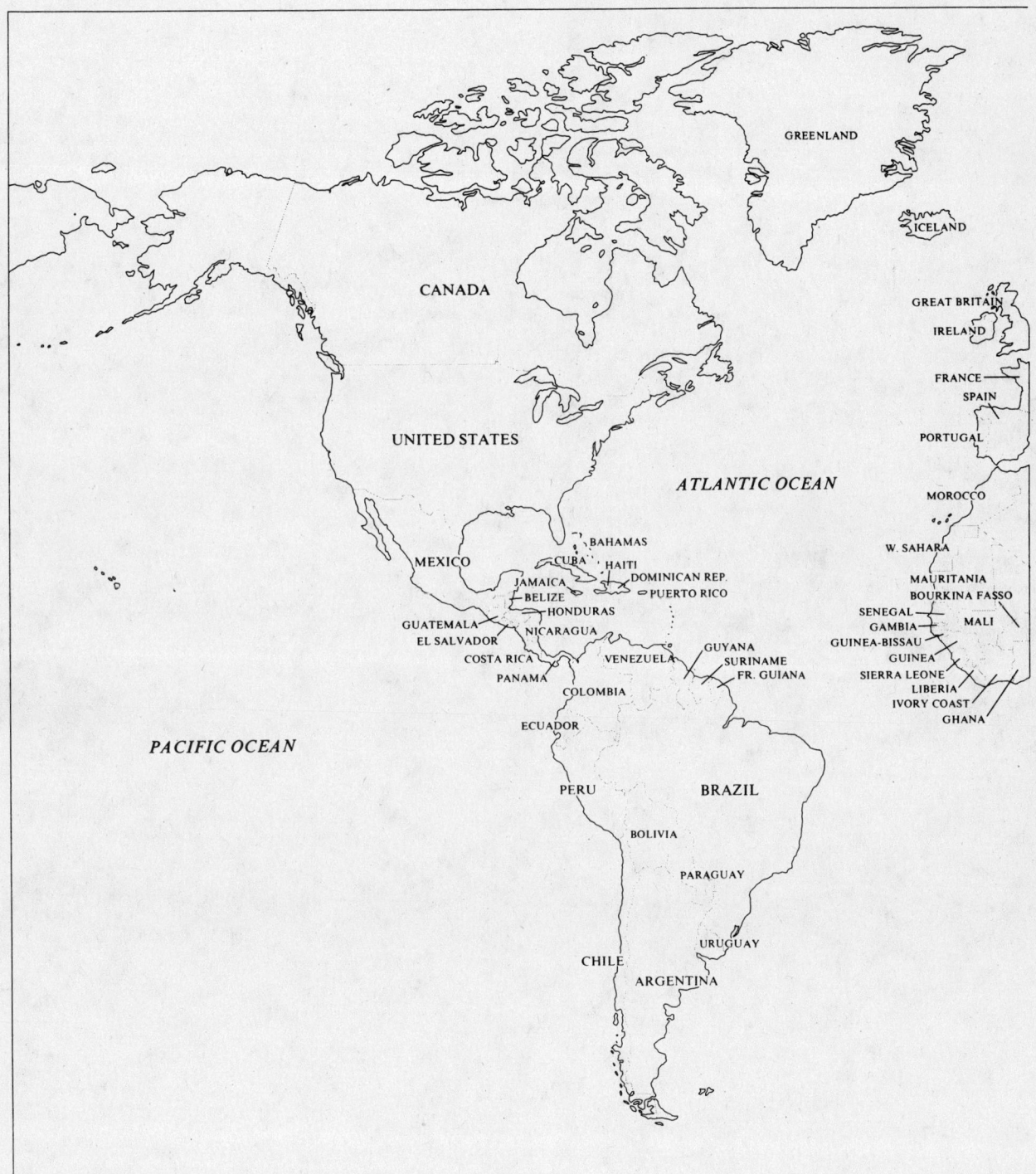

Outline Map for Chapter 29—World (right side)

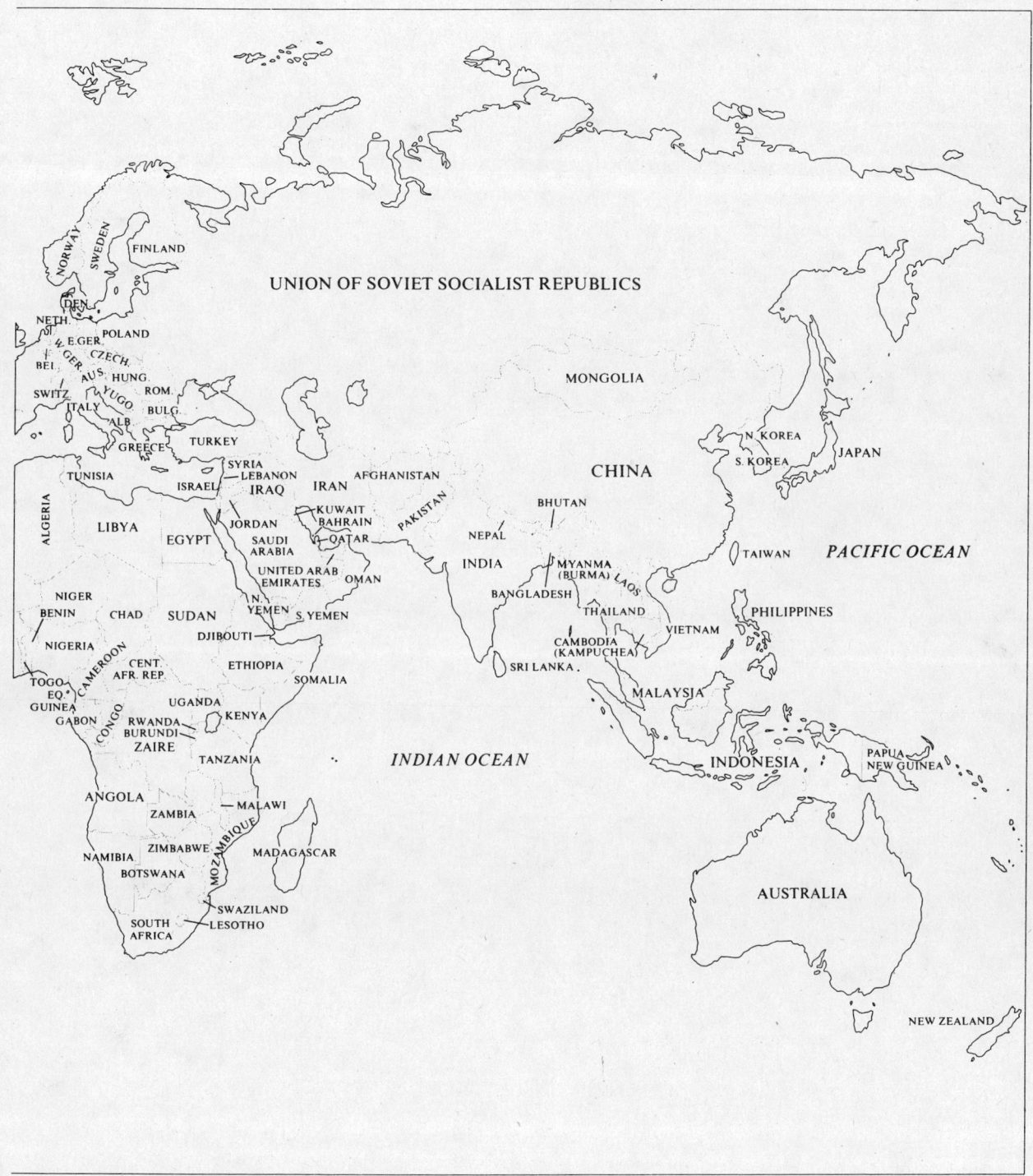

Outline Map for Chapter 29—Former Soviet Union

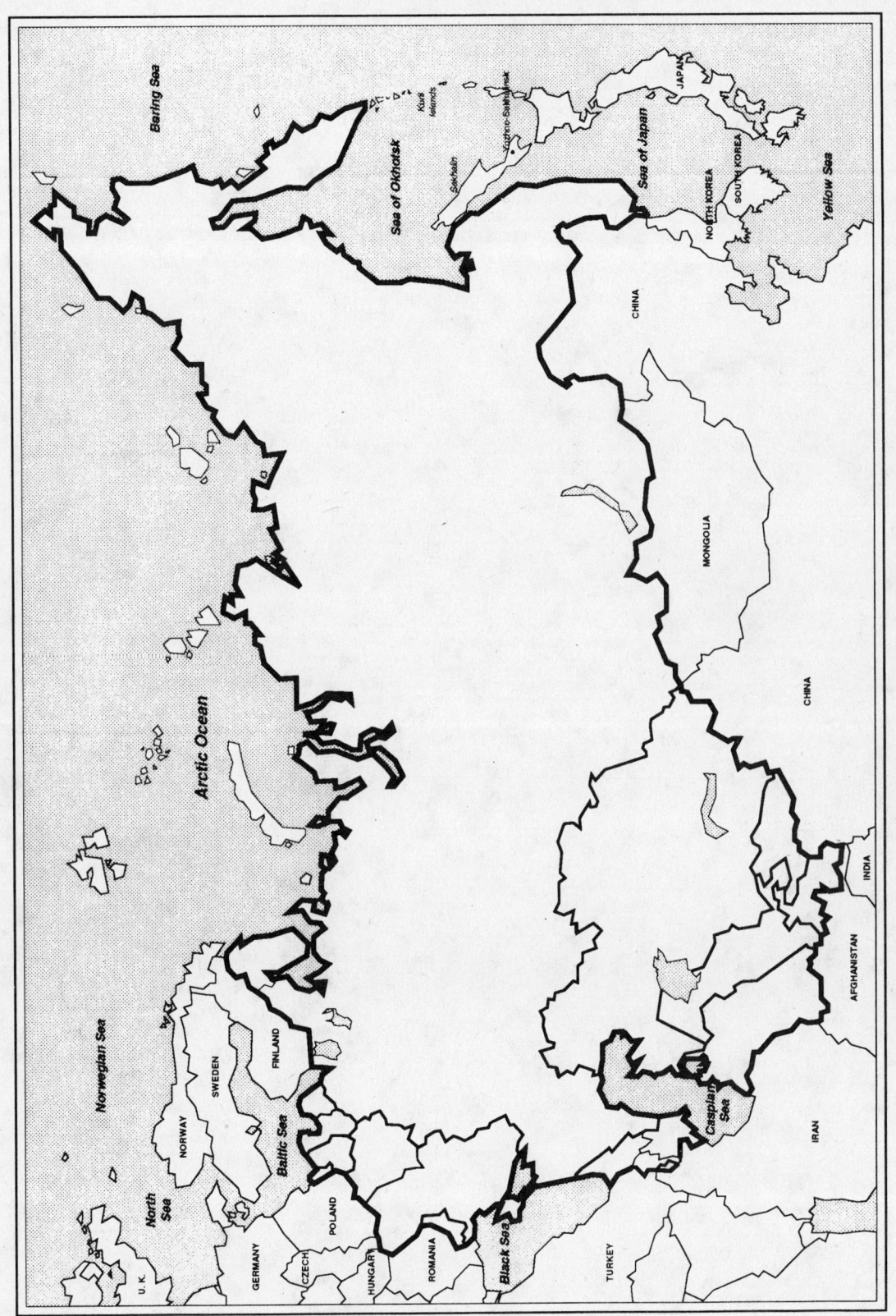

Outline Map for Chapter 31—Middle East

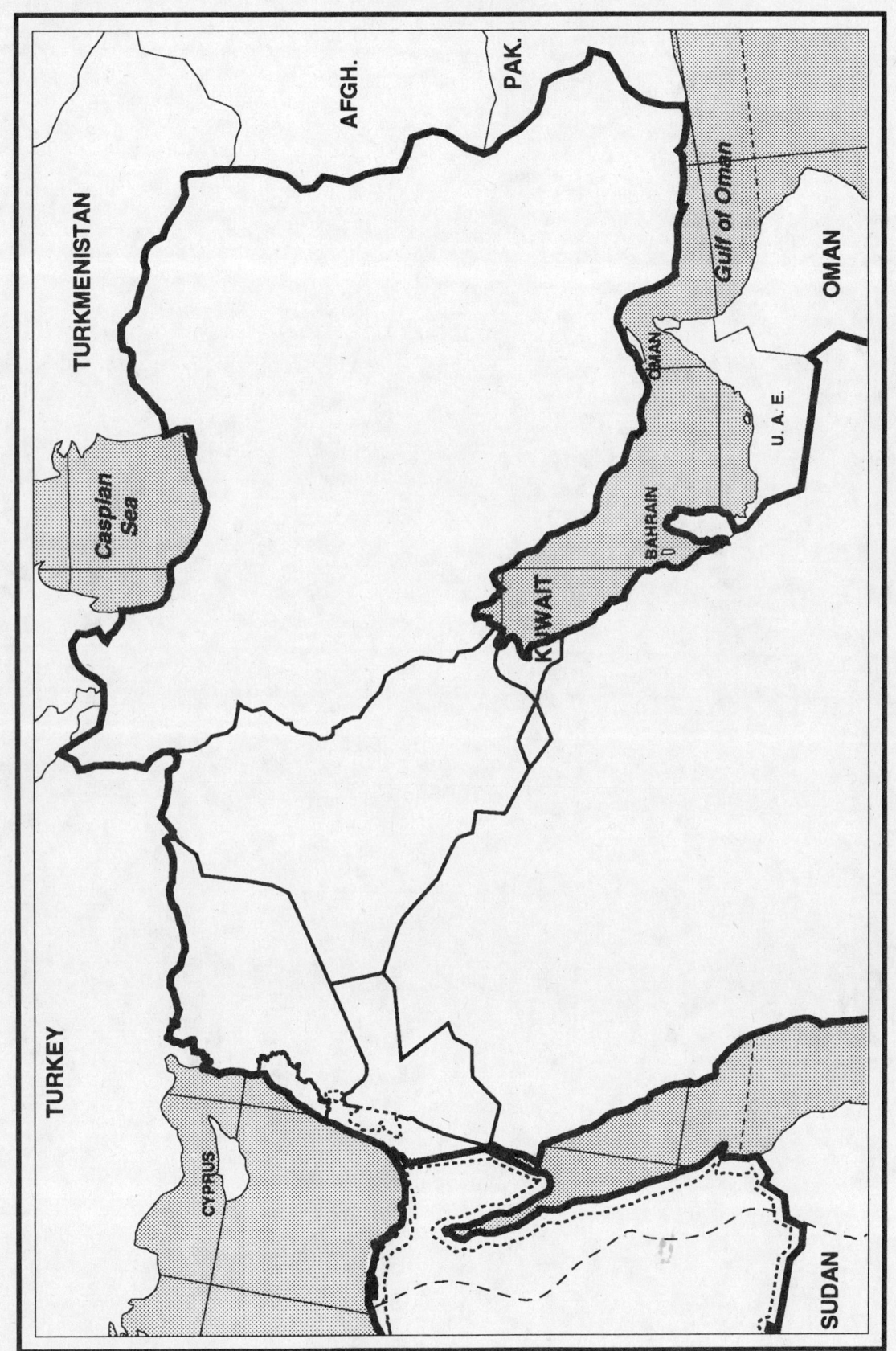